Frommer's®

W9-DBC-937

Caribbean Ports of Call

5th Edition

by Heidi Sarna & Matt Hannafin

Here's what the critics say about Frommer's:

"Amazingly easy to use. Very portable, very complete."
—*Booklist*

"Detailed, accurate, and easy-to-read information for all price ranges."
—*Glamour Magazine*

"Hotel information is close to encyclopedic."
—*Des Moines Sunday Register*

"Frommer's Guides have a way of giving you a real feel for a place."
—*Knight Ridder Newspapers*

WILEY

Wiley Publishing, Inc.

Published by:

Wiley Publishing, Inc.

111 River St.
Hoboken, NJ 07030-5774

ISBN 0-7645-6899-X

Editor: Liz Albertson
Production Editor: Ian Skinnari
Cartographer: Elizabeth Puhl
Photo Editor: Richard Fox
Production by Wiley Indianapolis Composition Services

For information on our other products and services or to obtain technical support, please contact our Customer Care Department within the U.S. at 800/762-2974, outside the U.S. at 317/572-3993 or fax 317/572-4002.

Wiley also publishes its books in a variety of electronic formats. Some content that appears in print may not be available in electronic formats.

Manufactured in the United States of America

5   4   3   2   1

Contents

List of Maps

An Invitation to the Reader

In researching this book, we discovered many wonderful places—hotels, restaurants, shops, and more. We're sure you'll find others. Please tell us about them, so we can share the information with your fellow travelers in upcoming editions. If you were disappointed with a recommendation, we'd love to know that, too. Please write to:

Frommer's Caribbean Ports of Call, 5th Edition
Wiley Publishing, Inc. • 111 River St. • Hoboken, NJ 07030-5774

An Additional Note

Please be advised that travel information is subject to change at any time—and this is especially true of prices. We therefore suggest that you write or call ahead for confirmation when making your travel plans. The authors, editors, and publisher cannot be held responsible for the experiences of readers while traveling. Your safety is important to us, however, so we encourage you to stay alert and be aware of your surroundings. Keep a close eye on cameras, purses, and wallets, all favorite targets of thieves and pickpockets.

About the Authors

Heidi Sarna has cruised on more than 75 ships of all shapes and sizes, and she loves them all (well, OK, some more than others). Her work appears regularly in *Condé Nast Traveler,* Frommers.com, and numerous other magazines, major guidebooks, websites, and newspapers, including the *New York Times, Star Ledger,* and *Boston Herald.* When she's not off cruising somewhere, she lives in the Big Apple with her husband, Arun, and their young sons.

Matt Hannafin is freelance writer, editor, and musician based in New York City. A former Frommer's senior editor and senior online writer at *Expedia Travels* magazine, he currently writes a biweekly cruise newsletter for Frommers.com and a monthly column for the *Boston Herald,* contributes to various magazines and newspapers, edits for several UN agencies and most of the major New York publishing houses, and was co-editor and contributor to the *New York Times* bestseller *1,000 Places You Must See Before You Die* (Workman, 2003).

Frommer's Star Ratings, Icons & Abbreviations

Every hotel, restaurant, and attraction listing in this guide has been ranked for quality, value, service, amenities, and special features using a **star-rating system.** In country, state, and regional guides, we also rate towns and regions to help you narrow down your choices and budget your time accordingly. Hotels and restaurants are rated on a scale of zero (recommended) to three stars (exceptional). Attractions, shopping, nightlife, towns, and regions are rated according to the following scale: zero stars (recommended), one star (highly recommended), two stars (very highly recommended), and three stars (must-see).

In addition to the star-rating system, we also use **seven feature icons** that point you to the great deals, in-the-know advice, and unique experiences that separate travelers from tourists. Throughout the book, look for:

Finds	Special finds—those places only insiders know about
Fun Fact	Fun facts—details that make travelers more informed and their trips more fun
Kids	Best bets for kids and advice for the whole family
Moments	Special moments—those experiences that memories are made of
Overrated	Places or experiences not worth your time or money
Tips	Insider tips—great ways to save time and money
Value	Great values—where to get the best deals

The following **abbreviations** are used for credit cards:

AE American Express	DISC Discover	V Visa
DC Diners Club	MC MasterCard	

Frommers.com

Now that you have the guidebook to a great trip, visit our website at **www.frommers.com** for travel information on more than 3,000 destinations. With features updated regularly, we give you instant access to the most current trip-planning information available. At Frommers.com, you'll also find the best prices on airfares, accommodations, and car rentals—and you can even book travel online through our travel booking partners. At Frommers.com, you'll also find the following:

- Online updates to our most popular guidebooks
- Vacation sweepstakes and contest giveaways
- Newsletter highlighting the hottest travel trends
- Online travel message boards with featured travel discussions

Introduction: Cruising
to the Ports of Call

Though today's cruise ships are sailing to more and more places, the Caribbean is still number one, the reigning heavyweight champ among destinations. You're guaranteed nearly constant sunshine, white sand and palm trees, plenty of beaches, and relaxation, but you're also likely to find rich culture, Mayan ruins, European colonial architecture, lush rainforests, winding mountain roads, beautiful tropical flowers and marine life, and opportunities to be as active or laid-back as you want to be. And it's all so easy: Between the major Florida home ports (Miami, Ft. Lauderdale, Cape Canaveral, Tampa, and Jacksonville) and the newer "alternative" home ports (New York; New Orleans; Charlotte, South Carolina; and Galveston, Texas), anyone in the eastern part of the U.S. could easily drive to their ship if they wanted to. And once there, of course, it's all smooth sailing.

1 Choosing the Itinerary & Shore Excursions That Are Best for You

If you count every rocky little outcropping and sandbar, there are hundreds of islands in the Caribbean, but of the 40 or 50 that make it onto the map, cruise ships regularly visit only about 25 of them. Most Caribbean cruises are 7 nights long and visit anywhere from three to six different ports, with the 2,000-passenger-plus megaships tending toward the lower number, spending the rest of their time on leisurely (and more profitable) days at sea. There are also 3- and 4-night cruises out of Florida visiting the Bahamas or Mexico's Yucatán Peninsula; 4- and 5-night cruises out of Tampa, Miami, New Orleans, and Galveston, Texas, doing western Caribbean itineraries; and 10- to 14-night Caribbean cruises that transit the Panama Canal, either sailing round-trip from Florida or one-way between Florida and Acapulco, visiting three to seven ports.

While they're all appealing in some way, the Caribbean islands were not all created equal. Some are better for shopping, others for beaches or scenic drives. Some are quite built up, while others are not developed at all. Some have piers that can accommodate large ships, and others require that ships anchor up to a mile offshore and shuttle passengers back and forth in small, motorized launches called "tenders." Big ships tend to visit the more commercialized, developed islands, while small ships are able to access the less-developed, off-the-beaten-path islands. Typically, the big lines divide Caribbean itineraries into eastern, western, and southern routings, but smaller ship lines rarely adhere to such rigid labels.

The Gulf of Mexico & the Caribbean

Bermuda

ATLANTIC OCEAN

BAHAMAS
Freeport/
Lucaya
Nassau

Andros Is.

Turks & Caicos
Islands

Great
Inagua

CUBA
Camagüey

San Juan

VIRGIN
ISLANDS

St. Martin/
Sint Maarten
Barbuda
Antigua
Montserrat
Guadeloupe

DOMINICAN
REPUBLIC

HAITI

Puerto
Rico

St. Kitts
& Nevis

Dominica

Port-au-Prince

Santo
Domingo

Martinique

S.

GREATER ANTILLES

See *Eastern Caribbean* map
on following page

St. Lucia

Barbados

Kingston

JAMAICA

St. Vincent

Grenada

Tobago

Caribbean Sea

LESSER ANTILLES

Trinidad

Aruba

Curaçao

Bonaire

Caracas

Maracaibo

Barranquilla

Orinoco

Caroni

PANAMA

Colon

Panama
City

Apure

San Cristóbal

VENEZUELA

Cauca

Gulf of
Panama

Medellín

COLOMBIA

Magdalena

Bogotá

Meta

Uraricuera

BRAZIL

Guaviare

Branco

How Many Ports for You?

These days, many of the largest ships in the Carnival, Royal Caribbean, Princess, and Norwegian fleets are visiting only three ports during a typical weeklong cruise, and spending the rest of the days at sea. What's the story? Are the ports too crowded? Are the ships too big to dock at other ports? Do cruise lines want to keep passengers on board to spend more money in the shops, bars, and casinos? Do passengers just *want* to stay on board? All of the above, if you ask us. If what you're looking for is pure, unadulterated relaxation—sitting by the pool reading a good book, with a steward to bring you fresh drinks— a cruise including three ports may suit you perfectly. If you want to maximize the number of islands you visit, there are still plenty of ships that visit five ports on their 7-night itineraries, and the small-ship adventure and luxury lines really pack in the ports, visiting a different island nearly every single day and sometimes even making two stops, one in the morning and another after lunch. Check the cruise lines' websites or talk to your travel agent to find out the number of port days and the number of sea days for each ship.

MEGASHIP ITINERARIES

WESTERN CARIBBEAN   Western Caribbean itineraries depart from Miami, Fort Lauderdale, Tampa, New Orleans, and Galveston, Texas, and usually visit Grand Cayman, Jamaica, and Cozumel or one of the other ports on Mexico's Yucatán Peninsula. This is a popular itinerary for many lines, so you'll see throngs of other cruise passengers in each port—often three or four (or more) ships will be visiting at a time. Belize City and the Bay Islands of Honduras are also popping up more frequently on western Caribbean itineraries.

EASTERN CARIBBEAN   Eastern Caribbean itineraries typically sail out of Florida and from the alternative home ports up the Eastern seaboard, and may include visits to San Juan (Puerto Rico), the U.S. Virgin Islands (particularly St. Thomas), St. Martin, and Nassau or Freeport in the Bahamas—all very popular and busy ports of call, especially St. Thomas, Nassau, and San Juan.

SOUTHERN CARIBBEAN   Southern itineraries typically sail round-trip out of San Juan or sometimes out of Aruba or Barbados. They often overlap with eastern Caribbean itineraries, and may visit St. Thomas, St. Martin, St. Lucia, Martinique, Antigua, and maybe Dominica, Guadeloupe, Aruba, and Grenada or one of the other islands in the Grenadines.

SMALL-SHIP ITINERARIES

Most small ships cruise in the eastern and southern Caribbean, where distances between islands are shorter. Instead of Florida, they may sail out of Barbados, Grenada, St. Kitts, or San Juan and visit more remote islands.

EASTERN CARIBBEAN   These itineraries may include visits to St. Barts, the British Virgin Islands, and the U.S. Virgin Islands (lush St. John as well as more touristy St. Thomas).

SOUTHERN CARIBBEAN   Southern Caribbean cruises may visit Guadeloupe, Dominica, Les Saintes, St. Kitts, Nevis, Martinique, St. Lucia, St. Vincent,

The Eastern Caribbean

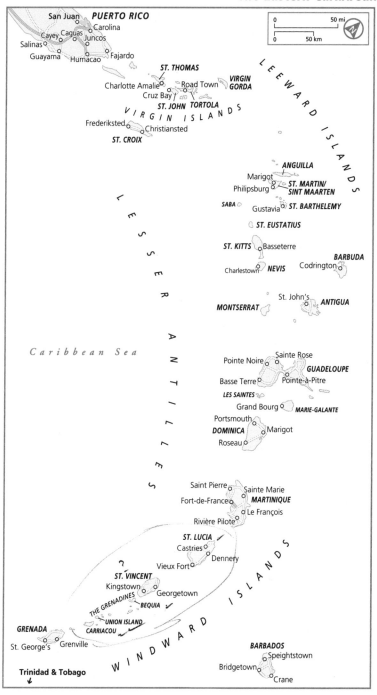

0 50 mi
0 50 km

San Juan **PUERTO RICO**
Carolina
Cayey Caguas Juncos
Salinas
Guayama Humacao Fajardo

ST. THOMAS
Charlotte Amalie   Road Town   **VIRGIN GORDA**
Cruz Bay
ST. JOHN TORTOLA
V I R G I N   I S L A N D S
Frederiksted   Christiansted
ST. CROIX

L E E W A R D   I S L A N D S

ANGUILLA
Marigot
Philipsburg   **ST. MARTIN/ SINT MAARTEN**
SABA   Gustavia   **ST. BARTHELEMY**
ST. EUSTATIUS
ST. KITTS   Basseterre   **BARBUDA**
Charlestown **NEVIS**   Codrington
St. John's   **ANTIGUA**
MONTSERRAT

L E S S E R   A N T I L L E S

Caribbean Sea

Pointe Noire   Sainte Rose
GUADELOUPE
Basse Terre   Pointe-à-Pitre
LES SAINTES
Grand Bourg   **MARIE-GALANTE**
Portsmouth
DOMINICA   Marigot
Roseau

Saint Pierre   Sainte Marie
Fort-de-France   **MARTINIQUE**
Le François
Rivière Pilote

ST. LUCIA
Castries
Dennery
Vieux Fort
ST. VINCENT
Kingstown
Georgetown
THE GRENADINES   **BEQUIA**
UNION ISLAND
GRENADA   **CARRIACOU**
St. George's   Grenville

W I N D W A R D   I S L A N D S

BARBADOS
Speightstown
Bridgetown
Crane

Trinidad & Tobago

Grenada, and Bequia, and maybe the truly unspoiled and remote Palm, Canouan, Mayreau, and Carriacou islands.

SHORTER ITINERARIES

Today, there are more 3-, 4-, and 5-night cruise itineraries than ever before (plus a small handful of 2-nighters), as cruise lines continually look for new ways to fill all of their big ships. Short and affordable, **2- and 3-night cruises** offer a more action-packed, nonstop party ambience than longer 7-night Caribbean itineraries. It's obvious why: These are weekend cruises, departing Thursday or Friday afternoons, so people are ready to squeeze in as much fun, relaxation, drinking, gambling, dancing, and eating as possible before going back to work on Monday. Though you'll definitely find more 20- and 30-somethings on these shorties than on any other type of cruise, you'll still see a wide range of ages. Aside from the fun factor, short cruises are a great way for first-time cruisers to test the waters (so to speak) before committing to a full week. They're also a good idea if you're short on time or moola.

The ships that offer these minicruises tend to be the oldest in their fleets and are a bit beat-up compared to the newest megaships. We've also noticed that service tends to not be as good on the short party cruises, probably owing to crew exhaustion. Then again, most passengers don't notice the difference—they're too busy having fun.

Because they typically depart on Sunday or Monday afternoon and sail through the workweek, **4- and 5-night cruises** represent the opposite end of the liveliness spectrum, tending to attract an older and less party-oriented crowd.

Many cruise lines offer weeklong **land-sea packages** that pair a cruise with a land vacation either before or after your cruise. For instance, Disney, Carnival, and Royal Caribbean will combine a 3- or 4-night cruise out of Port Canaveral with a 3- or 4-night visit to one of central Florida's theme parks, like Walt Disney World, Universal Studios, SeaWorld, or Busch Gardens.

MATCHING YOUR HABITS TO YOUR ITINERARY

Some ports are better for certain things than others. Here's a short rundown; see p. 84 for a comparison chart that rates shore excursions, activities, beaches, shopping, and dining for all the Caribbean ports. The island reviews in chapter 5, "The Ports of Call," provide detailed information.

PORTS FOR SHOPPERS

Eastern Caribbean: St. Thomas, San Juan, Nassau, St. Martin. **Western Caribbean:** Grand Cayman, Cozumel. **Southern Caribbean:** Aruba, Barbados.

PORTS FOR BEACH LOVERS

Eastern Caribbean: Antigua, British Virgin Islands, St. John, St. Martin, St. Barts. **Western Caribbean:** Grand Cayman, Jamaica. **Southern Caribbean:** Aruba, Grenada, Bequia, Barbados, Nevis, Martinique.

PORTS FOR SCUBA DIVERS & SNORKELERS

Eastern Caribbean: St. Croix, St. John, St. Thomas, Dominica. **Western Caribbean:** Grand Cayman, Belize, Cozumel. **Southern Caribbean:** Bonaire, Curaçao.

PORTS FOR HISTORY & ARCHAEOLOGY ENTHUSIASTS

Eastern Caribbean: San Juan. **Western Caribbean:** Cozumel and the other Yucatan ports. **Southern Caribbean:** Barbados, Curaçao.

PORTS FOR NATURE BUFFS

Eastern Caribbean: St. John, San Juan. **Southern Caribbean:** Aruba, Dominica, St. Kitts, Grenada, Trinidad.

PORTS FOR FRANCOPHILES

Eastern Caribbean: Guadeloupe, Les Saintes, St. Martin, St. Barts, Martinique.

SHORE EXCURSIONS: THE WHAT, WHY & HOW

No matter what size ship you're on or what its itinerary is, you'll be able to choose from among three to several dozen shore excursions in any given port, from walking and bus tours to more active excursions like biking, hiking, snorkeling, scuba diving, horseback riding, golfing, kayaking, and river tubing. Prices range from about $25 to $200 per person, and most excursions are run by concessionaires on the islands rather than by the cruise lines themselves. You book the excursions through the cruise lines (either before you sail, via an online or phone reservation system, or once you're onboard) and payments are charged to your onboard account. Some ports are best explored through these tours (which depart directly from the pier), and some ports are best seen on your own. In chapter 5, "The Ports of Call," we discuss shore excursions in more depth, providing information on the best excursions and noting where you may want to skip the excursions entirely and set out on your own.

2 When to Go

With temperatures in the balmy 80s (upper 20s Celsius) almost year-round, dozens of ships stay in the Caribbean full-time, and a bunch more spend the winters there after summering in Alaska or Europe. The only trouble in paradise is **hurricane season,** which officially runs June 1 to November 30, but rarely causes cruisers any problems bigger than a few days of rain and a bit of rocking and rolling. We've taken many cruises in the Caribbean during this period and have only occasionally run into stormy weather; it's rare, but it's a risk you take. The chance of actually getting caught in the perfect storm is next to nil, as modern communications (and generally speedy vessels) allow captains to change course and pilot their ships out of danger as soon as they get word of a storm.

Defining seasons as "low" and "high" is hardly a science, since most lines seem to come up with their own unique pricing schemes, and some don't bother dividing rates by season at all. For those that do, it's generally accepted that **high season** in the Caribbean is mid-December through mid-April. During this time, weather will most likely be perfect, the islands and ships will be packed, and the prices will be higher. The **holiday weeks** of Christmas, New Year's, Presidents' Day, and Easter are the absolute busiest and most expensive periods, especially on the family-oriented megaships—these are often the few times in the year when the cruise lines' brochure rates are not discounted.

Despite it being hurricane season, the **summer months** of June, July, and August are the next busiest times; in fact, many lines consider these months high season along with December through April, because families traditionally vacation during the summer and because many ships migrate to Alaska and Europe for the season, leaving fewer vessels in the Caribbean. Temperatures may be a bit hotter in summer, but the islands' colorful flowering trees are at their most lush.

September, October, and early November are considered **low season** (often referred to as "value season") and are the times when you'll encounter the fewest crowds onshore and on board, and some of the lowest rates. Sometimes there will be a lull during the first 2 weeks of January, just after the rush of the holi-days, and sometimes in late April and May, so look for good prices then as well.

The **Panama Canal cruise season** generally parallels the Caribbean high sea-son, with most cruises generally departing between about November and April. Some ships offer only two Panama Canal cruises annually, when repositioning between their summer season in Alaska and their fall/winter season in the Caribbean. These days, many cruise lines are including partial Canal crossings as part of extended western Caribbean itineraries from Florida, sailing through the Canal's locks westbound to Gatun Lake, docking for a day of excursions, and then sailing back out in the evening.

2

The Cruise Lines in Brief

People feel very strongly about ships. For centuries, mariners have imbued their vessels with human attributes, and even though cruise passengers are typically aboard for only a week at a time, they really do bond with their vessels. They find themselves in the gift shop, buying T-shirts with the ship's name emblazoned on the front. They get to port and the first question they ask other cruisers they meet is, "Which ship are you sailing on?"—and after engaging in a friendly comparison, they walk away knowing in their hearts that their ship is the best. We know people who have sailed the same ship a dozen times or more, and feel as warmly about it as though it were their own summer cottage.

Following is a quick primer on the cruise lines operating in the Caribbean. If you're an experienced cruiser you may already have a favorite, but if not, these will give you a little background to help you make your choice. The important thing is to find a cruise line and a ship that says "you." To make your selection easier (and to make sure you're not comparing apples and oranges), we've divided the cruise lines into three distinct categories based on the type of experiences they offer: mainstream, ultraluxury, and "adventure" (which includes small-ship cruises of all kinds). If you want more info, with in-depth discussions of the different aspects of each line's onboard experience, detailed reviews of the different ships, and all scheduled Caribbean itineraries, pick up a copy of *Frommer's Cruises & Ports of Call 2005*, which covers all cruises sailing from U.S. and Canadian home ports to the Caribbean, Alaska, Hawaii, the Mexican Riviera, New England/Eastern Canada, and more.

1 The Mainstream Lines

The term "mainstream" covers a lot of ground, and that's the point. These ships are generalists, attempting to offer a little something for almost everyone—all ages, backgrounds, and interests. These ships are big and bustling and exciting, and they attract a cross section of mostly American guests, from country club moms to Nascar dads and everything in between. There's lots to eat, lots to buy on board, and lots of other people sharing the experience with you. If you tire of the crowds, you can always hide out on your cabin balcony—these ships have hundreds of them—or stake out a secluded patch of deck far away from the pool, where you can commune quietly with the sea. The theme on these ships is choice, and lots of it.

Since the mainstream cruise category is the most popular, it's the one that's seen the most growth, innovation, and investment in recent years, meaning that the ships are, as a general rule, remarkably new—and also remarkably big. This is the category where the **megaships** reside, those hulking 1,200- to 3,200-passenger floating resorts that offer the widest variety of activities and entertainment on the ocean. Most of the lines in this category (but particularly the "Big

Four"—Carnival, Royal Caribbean, Princess, and Norwegian) have been pumping billions into building newer, bigger, and fancier ships that offer a wide variety of different cabins—inside (no windows), outside (with windows), suites, and cabins with private balconies and without. These ships have both formal and several informal dining options, a wide array of entertainment (heavy on the Vegas-style stuff), Internet centers with e-mail access, and more activities than you can possibly squeeze into a day. The lines are on a constant quest to outdo each other with cool stuff you'd never expect to find on a cruise ship, from rock-climbing walls to pottery studios, water slides to multi-million-dollar art collections (we're talking Warhols and van Goghs). You'll be able to choose from a dizzying number of activities, from line-dancing lessons to bingo games, game show–style contests, singles mixers, lectures, galley tours, spa demos (a ploy, of course, to get you to sign up for one of the expensive spa treatments), art auctions (some passengers actually like these things), and nutty doings by the pool that pit passengers against each other in contests to see who can stuff the most Ping-Pong balls down his or her bathing suit, or who can swim across the pool fastest with a bagel in their mouth (no kidding). Overall, the atmosphere is very casual and very social, with passengers sunning, strutting, and sipping their favorite drinks out on the deck.

Within this category, the more elegant and refined cruise lines are commonly referred to as **premium,** a notch up in the sophistication department from others that are described as **mass market.** Quality-wise, all of the mainstream ships are generally on equal footing, and are more alike than they are different, especially in areas such as dining and entertainment. We've lumped a few lines that don't fit well with the megaships into this category: Oceania Cruises, whose mid-size ships don't have tons in common with the Carnivals and Royal Caribbeans of the world, and Imperial Majesty, with its one midsize antique ocean liner.

CARNIVAL CRUISE LINES

3655 NW 87th Ave., Miami, FL 33178-2428. Ⓒ **800/227-6482** or 305/599-2200. Fax 305/405-4855. www.carnival.com.

THE LINE IN A NUTSHELL   The Wal-Mart of cruising, Carnival specializes in colorful, jumbo-size resort ships that deliver plenty of bang for your buck. If you like the flash of Vegas and the party-hearty feel of New Orleans, you'll love Carnival's brand of flamboyant fun.

THE EXPERIENCE   Nobody does it better in the party department. The line with the most recognized name in the biz serves up a very casual, down-to-earth Caribbean vacation. While the food and service are pretty average, there sure are a lot of choices to keep most people satisfied, including round-the-clock entertainment, sushi bars, upscale supper clubs on the Spirit-class ships, and huge kid and teen centers on the Conquest-class ships.

The line's decor, like its clientele, has mellowed a bit since its riotous, partying beginnings, but each ship is still an exciting collage of textures, shapes, and images. Where else but on these floating playlands would you find life-size mannequins of Hollywood stars such as Marilyn Monroe and Humphrey Bogart, a San Francisco trolley car, and real oyster-shell wallpaper? The outrageousness of the decor is part of the fun: Carnival ships provide a fantasyland you can't get at home. Call it whatever you want, but don't call it dull. **Pros:** Fun, theme-park ambience; large cabins (among the roomiest in the mainstream category); wide range of passengers; and big-time nightlife. **Cons:** Things are always busy, all the time, and if you're looking for enriching lectures or anything highbrow, you'll have to look elsewhere.

PASSENGER PROFILE   Carnival's passengers run the gamut from couples to singles to families, and from young to older, with lots of ages in between. Carnival estimates that about 30% of its passengers are under age 35, another 40% are between 35 and 55, and 30% are over age 55. Regardless of their age, passengers tend to be young at heart and keyed up for nonstop, round-the-clock activities. Many have visited Vegas, Atlantic City, and the resorts of Cancún and Jamaica, and at least half are first-time cruisers. Passengers like to dress casually, with jeans and T-shirts just as prevalent as Dockers and Hush Puppies on all but formal nights—and even then, it's not uncommon for some to change back into casual after dinner, before heading out to the bars.

While Carnival is one of the best lines to choose if you're single, families and couples are definitely in the majority. The line's 3-, 4-, and 5-night cruises tend to attract the most families with kids and the highest number of 20- and 30-something single friends traveling together in groups.

CELEBRITY CRUISES

1050 Caribbean Way, Miami, FL 33132. © **800/437-3111** or 305/539-6000. Fax 800/722-5329. www.celebritycruises.com.

THE LINE IN A NUTSHELL   Celebrity offers the best of both worlds: elegance without stuffiness, fun without bad taste, and pampering without a high price. If this appeals, Celebrity might be the line for you.

THE EXPERIENCE   With the most elegant big ships in the industry, Celebrity offers a refined cruise experience that's also fun and active. Each ship is spacious, glamorous, and comfortable, mixing sleekly modern and Art Deco styles, and throwing in cutting-edge art collections to boot. An exceedingly polite and professional staff contributes greatly to the elegant atmosphere. Dining-wise, Celebrity's Millennium-class ships shine, offering stylish alternative restaurants. Featuring the signature nouveau French cuisine of celebrity chef Michel Roux, they're the best at sea both for the quality of their food and for their gorgeous decor.

Like all the big-ship lines, Celebrity offers a lot for its passengers to do, but a focus on mellower pursuits and innovative programming sets it apart from competitors. Niceties such as roving a cappella groups lend a warmly personal touch, while expert-led seminars on topics like astronomy, photography, personal investing, and history offer a little more cerebral meat than the usual. Celebrity pampers suite guests with butler service, and treats all guests to in-cabin pizza delivery. **Pros:** Celebrity gets the "best of" nod in a lot of categories: The AquaSpas on its megaships are the most attractive at sea, the art collections are the most compelling fleetwide, the decor is the most original, the dining is fabulous, and the onboard activities are among the most varied. **Cons:** They may all be optional, but between the boutiques, the pricey spa treatments, the wine tastings, and the $25 cover charge in the alternative restaurants, there are lots of potential extra costs if you don't exercise some self control.

PASSENGER PROFILE   Celebrity tries to focus on middle- to upper-middle-income cruisers and wealthy patrons who want the best megaship experience out there, but since the rates are comparable to those of Carnival and Royal Caribbean, you'll find a very wide range of folks aboard, from those who appreciate the elegance of the ships to those who could care less. Clients who choose their cruise based on more than just price like Celebrity because it's not Carnival and because it offers a well-balanced cruise, with lots of activities and a glamorous, exciting atmosphere that's both refined (think champagne and cozy lounges) and fun (think "dress your husband up in women's clothes" contests). Most passengers are couples in their mid-30s and up (the average age in 2003 was 45), with decent numbers of honeymooners and couples celebrating anniversaries, as well as families with children in summer and during the holidays.

COSTA CRUISES
200 South Park Rd., Ste. 200, Hollywood, FL 33021–8541. ℂ **800/462-6782** or 954/266-5600. Fax 954/266-2100. www.costacruises.com.

THE LINE IN A NUTSHELL   Imagine a Carnival megaship run by an Italian circus troupe: That's Costa. The words of the day are "fun," "festive," and "international," with two Italian-American megaships providing the venue. Expect a really good time, but don't set your sights too high for food and service.

THE EXPERIENCE   For years, Costa has played up its Italian heritage as the main factor that distinguishes it from Carnival, Royal Caribbean, and the rest, and that's still true, though the line employs far fewer Italian crew members today than in years past. You'll find more pasta dishes on the menu than you'll find on other lines, more opera singers among the entertainment offerings, a *"Bon giorno"* from every other crew member you pass, and Italian-flavored activities facilitated by the young, mostly Italian, and ridiculously attractive "animation staff." The line's strength in the Italian-American market also helps distinguish it from the other mainstream lines, and the number of Europeans sailing aboard (fewer in the Caribbean than on the line's Mediterranean sailings, but still significant at about 15%) means you get a more international passenger mix. Physically, the line's new ships are a hybrid: modern mainstream megaships built on the same chassis and layout as Carnival's Spirit-class ships, with interiors designed by Carnival's designer-in-chief Joe Farcus, who took inspiration from Italy's traditions of painting and architecture but still stuck close to his signature "more is more" style—think Venice à la Vegas. **Pros:** All that Italian flavor, and all those fun activities. **Cons:** Surprisingly, despite Italy's worldwide rep for great food, Costa's cuisine is generally disappointing. Dining and bar service can also be chaotic and unpolished.

PASSENGER PROFILE   Costa's winter Caribbean sailings attract retirees and young couples alike, although there are more passengers over 50 than under. In general, Costa passengers want lots of fun and action, and are big on participation—the goofier the better. Italian-Americans are heavily represented. Typically you won't see more than 40 or 50 kids on any one cruise except during holidays such as Christmas and spring break. While about 80% to 90% of passengers are from North America, there's usually a healthy percent from Europe and South America as well. Because of the international mix, public announcements, lifeboat drills, and some entertainment are translated into five languages: English, Italian, German, French, and Spanish. While these announcements can seem to go on *forever,* the line does go out of its way to keep the number of broadcasts to a minimum. The cruise director is usually American or British during Caribbean sailings, but much of the activities staff is comprised of multilingual Italians.

DISNEY CRUISE LINE
P.O. Box 10210, Lake Buena Vista, FL 32830. ℂ **800/951-3532** or 888/325-2500. Fax 407/566-3541. www.disneycruise.com.

THE LINE IN A NUTSHELL Though Royal Caribbean, Carnival, Celebrity, and Princess all devote significant attention to kids, it took Disney to create vessels where kids and adults are really catered to equally, and with style. If you love Disney, you'll love these two floating theme parks.

THE EXPERIENCE Both classic and ultramodern, the line's two ships are like no others in the industry, designed to evoke the grand transatlantic liners but also boasting a handful of truly innovative features, including extra-large cabins for families, several restaurants through which passengers rotate on every cruise, separate adult pools and lounges, and the biggest kids' facilities at sea. In many ways, the experience is more Disney than it is cruise (for instance, there's no casino); but on the other hand, the ships are surprisingly elegant and well laid out, with the Disneyisms sprinkled around subtly, like fairy dust, amid the Art Deco and Art Nouveau design motifs. Head to toe, inside and out, these ships are a class act. Disney is nothing if not organized, and its 3- and 4-night cruises aboard *Disney Wonder* are designed to be combined with a Disney theme park and hotel package to create a weeklong land/sea vacation. You can also book these shorter cruises (as well as *Disney Magic*'s weeklong cruises) separately. **Pros:** Amazing kids' program, great shows (the line's family-oriented musicals are some of the best onboard entertainment in the industry), a spacious onboard feel, and innovative dining. **Cons:** Limited adult entertainment, small gyms, and the fact that cruises usually cost a few hundred dollars more than the competition.

PASSENGER PROFILE Disney's ships attract a wide mix of passengers, from honeymooners to seniors, with a handful of international passengers, though naturally a large percentage is made up of young American families with children. Because of this, the overall age demographic tends to be younger than that aboard many of the other mainstream ships, with many passengers in their 30s and early to mid-40s. The bulk of the line's passengers are first-time cruisers, and since the line attracts so many families (sometimes large ones), more than 50% of bookings are for multiple cabins.

HOLLAND AMERICA LINE

300 Elliott Ave. W., Seattle, WA 98119. © 877/724-5425 or 206/281-3535. Fax 800/628-4855. www.hollandamerica.com.

THE LINE IN A NUTSHELL Holland America has been in business since 1873, and has managed to hang on to more of its seafaring history and tradition than any line today except Cunard. It offers a moderately priced, classic, and casual-yet-refined cruise experience.

THE EXPERIENCE Holland America consistently delivers a solid product with old-world elegance. Though the line has been retooling itself to attract younger passengers and families, it still caters mostly to older folks, and generally offers a more sedate and stately experience than other mainstream lines, plus excellent service and cuisine. Its fleet, which until a few years ago consisted of midsize, classically styled ships, is in the process of being supersized, and the new Vista-class megaships are downright bold in their color palate. New or old, the vessels are all well-maintained and have excellent (and remarkably similar) layouts that facilitate easy passenger movement. Throughout the public areas, you'll find flowers that testify to Holland's importance in the floral trade, Indonesian fabrics and woodcarvings that evoke the country's relationship with its former colony, and seafaring memorabilia that often harks back to Holland America's own history. **Pros:** Great service (the line's primarily Indonesian and Filipino staff is exceptionally gracious and friendly); classic, traditional ambience; and great gyms. **Cons:** Sleepy nightlife and a fairly homogenous passenger profile.

PASSENGER PROFILE   For years, HAL was known for catering to an almost exclusively older crowd, with most passengers in their 70s on up. Today, following intense efforts to attract younger passengers, about 40% of the line's guests are under age 55, with a few young families peppering the mix, especially in summers and during holiday weeks. While the average age skews a bit lower on the newer Vista-class ships, HAL isn't Carnival or Disney, and their older ships especially were designed with older folks in mind—a few even have fold-down seats in the elevators. Passengers tend to be amiable, low-key, and better educated than their equivalents aboard sister line Carnival, and much more amenable to dressing up—you'll see lots of tuxedos and evening gowns on formal nights.

IMPERIAL MAJESTY CRUISES

2950 Gateway Dr., Pompano Beach, FL 33069. ✆ **954/956-9505.** Fax 954/971-6678. www.imperialmajesty.com.

THE LINE IN A NUTSHELL   Imperial Majesty operates nothing but two-night round-trips between Ft. Lauderdale and Nassau, year-round. The one big reason to sail? The line's ship, the 1953-vintage *Regal Empress,* is probably the last chance you'll ever get to sail on a real, old-fashioned ocean liner. They don't make 'em like this anymore.

THE EXPERIENCE   If you want to get a glimpse of what ocean travel was like in the 1950s, plunk down a couple hundred bucks and take a quick ride aboard *Regal Empress.* Today, the 52-year-old vessel is more over-the-hill vaudeville trouper than glamorous star, but she's one of the very few ships left on which you can see the kind of woody interiors and chunky steelwork that characterized the great old liners. She's a real ship-ship, totally unlike today's hotel-like megaships. Former owners Regal Cruises kept her in good shape, initiating several well-planned refurbishments that ripped out the overly glitzy '80s additions and reemphasized the classic elements of her decor. Let's not be dishonest, though: The *Empress* shows her age, and for every classic element there's a worn one to balance it, like scuffed cabin walls, stained or sagging ceiling tiles, and a "been at sea too long" smell in some areas. Quirks and all, though, the *Regal Empress* is an absolute classic—and with safety regulations mandating the scrap yard for vessels like this by 2010, time is running out. **Pros:** Time-machine vibe, classic nautical lines, and bargain-basement prices. **Cons:** Wear and tear and a crowded feel when the ship is sailing full.

PASSENGER PROFILE   At any given time, about 50 percent of the passengers book the ship as part of land-sea package deals, often sold via telemarketers. The other 50 percent are generally south Florida locals and vacationers looking to add a quick Bermuda hop to their Florida vacation. A fair number are first-timers sampling the cruise experience before committing to a longer voyage.

MSC ITALIAN CRUISES

420 Fifth Ave., New York, NY 10018. ✆ **800/666-9333** or 212/764-4800. Fax 212/764-1486. www.msccruises.com.

THE LINE IN A NUTSHELL   The cruise wing of Mediterranean Shipping Company, one of the world's largest container ship operations, MSC is an Italian line that operates several older cruise ships in Europe and one new midsize vessel in the Caribbean, sailing low-priced, port-packed, 11-night itineraries catering to both Europeans and North Americans.

THE EXPERIENCE   In 2003, after several years of operating one of the old Premier "Big Red Boats" in the Caribbean, MSC launched its first purpose-built ship, MS *Lirica,* a modern, midsize, 58,600-gross-ton, 1,590-passenger vessel with 130 balcony suites among its 795 cabins. A thoroughly modern Millie, *Lirica* was obviously designed with American passengers in mind, offering a Broadway-style theater called "The Broadway Theatre" and a Las Vegas–style casino called "The Las Vegas Casino." Decor throughout avoids flash in favor of a pleasantly traditional style, like an Italian version of a Princess ship. Bar/lounges range from the English-style Lord Nelson Pub to the more brassy Beverly Hills Bar, while workout facilities include a gym, spa, jogging track, and Turkish bath and sauna. Daytime activities on sea days include aerobics and step classes, enrichment classes on topics like Italian cooking and language, card tournaments, and goofy pool games. At night, two dining rooms serve dinners in traditional fixed seatings, offering mostly Italian cuisine; the ship boasts one of the few daily midnight buffets left in the industry. Cabins are pleasantly bright and B&B comfortable, with homey fabrics and modern Italianesque art. Balcony cabins also have small seating areas. Other cabins have large picture windows.

PASSENGER PROFILE   The typical passenger age range is currently mid-40s and up, with a mix of roughly 75% to 80% American and 20% to 25% European passengers. Announcements are made in four or five languages, though the main language onboard in the Caribbean is English. There's a children's center and program aboard *Lirica,* but to date the line's Caribbean itineraries have been too long to draw families. This situation may change when the line begins offering weeklong trips in winter 2005.

NORWEGIAN CRUISE LINE

7665 Corporate Center Dr., Miami, FL 33126. ℂ **800/327-7030** or 305/436-4000. Fax 305/436-4126. www.ncl.com.

THE LINE IN A NUTSHELL   NCL makes its mark with its always casual, open-seating dining. Overall, its new ships are standouts, giving the newest Royal Caribbean and Princess ships a run for their money.

THE EXPERIENCE   After a major multiyear retooling that transformed it from near-budget brand to one of the industry's innovation leaders, NCL continues to roll out exciting innovations, especially in the dining department. The 2,000-passenger *Norwegian Sky,* 1,960-passenger *Norwegian Sun,* and 2,224-passenger *Norwegian Dawn* represent the new, higher-quality NCL, while the line's four other midsize vintage-1980s vessels, carrying about 1,500 passengers each, represent its more budget-conscious, catch-as-catch-can past. In May 2000, the company launched its "Freestyle Cruising" concept, a revolutionary ultraflexible dining program that appeals to people who don't like the regimentation and formality of traditional cruise dining. Now offered fleetwide, "freestyle" means that all restaurants on the ships operate with a casual dress code and have open seating between about 5:30 and 10pm every evening. **Pros:** Total, amazing flexibility; restaurants galore (9 or 10 on *Sun* and *Dawn* and about 5 each on the other Caribbean ships); and above-average entertainment. **Cons:** Small cabin fleetwide (standard inside and outside cabins are generally smaller than aboard competing ships), and a few older ships that aren't quite up to the standards of the newer models.

PASSENGER PROFILE   NCL attracts a diverse lot, and passengers in general are younger, more price-conscious (the *Sea* and *Majesty* are often advertised at incredibly low rates, like $250 for a 7-night cruise), and more active than those aboard lines such as HAL, Celebrity, and Princess. Typical NCL passengers are couples ages 25 to 60, plus a fair number of honeymooners and families with kids during summers and holidays. Kids under age 2 sail free. The atmosphere aboard all NCL vessels is informal and well suited to the party-maker taking a first or second cruise, since the line isn't steeped in traditions like fixed dining times, formal nights, and cash tipping.

OCEANIA CRUISES

8120 NW 53rd St., Miami, FL 33166. © **800/531-5658** or 305/514-2300. www.oceaniacruises.com.

THE LINE IN A NUTSHELL   Oceania is the phoenix that rose from the ashes of Renaissance Cruises, which went belly up in September 2001. Headed by former Renaissance and Crystal Cruises executives, the new line operates three of Renaissance's ships and mimics some attributes of much pricier lines, with excellent service and cuisine, and a quiet and refined onboard feel.

THE EXPERIENCE   Oceania is positioned as an "upper premium" line intended to fill the gap between big-ship premium lines like Celebrity, and luxe lines like Radisson, both in terms of ship size and level of luxury. It's going for a kind of floating-country-club feel, with a relaxed ambience, few organized activities, low-key entertainment, a casual and sporty dress code, an emphasis on cabin comfort, and 12- to 14-night itineraries that favor smaller, less visited ports like Dominica, Nevis, Tortola, and St. Barts. Despite the line's luxe-travel touches, prices are competitive with—and often even lower than—those of the other premium lines. **Pros:** Excellent cuisine (some of the best in the mainstream category), terrific personal service, intimate ship size, and a strict no-smoking policy—it's only allowed in two small areas of the pool deck and nightclub (of course, this is a "con" for smokers). **Cons:** Few outside decks (just a pool deck, a sun deck, and the deserted promenade/boat deck), few activities (by design, but still . . .), and so-so entertainment.

PASSENGER PROFILE   Due partially to the length of these cruises (mostly 12 and 14 days) and partially to the low-key onboard atmosphere, Oceania tends to attract older passengers who prefer to entertain themselves, reading in the library and enjoying the destination-heavy itineraries. Most are Americans, with many from the West Coast and many "returning," having sailed previously with Renaissance. A sprinkling of younger couples usually find themselves onboard as well, though children are rare enough to be surprising. Whatever their age, passengers tend to be drawn by the line's all-casual, all-the-time dress code and ambience.

PRINCESS CRUISES

24305 Town Center Dr., Santa Clarita, CA 91355. © **800/PRINCESS** or 661/753-0000. Fax 661/259-3108. www.princess.com.

THE LINE IN A NUTSHELL   With a fleet of mostly large and extra-large megaships, including some of the biggest vessels at sea, L.A.-based Princess offers a quality mainstream cruise experience with a nice balance of tradition and innovation, relaxation and excitement, casualness and glamour. Its newest ships—*Coral, Island, Diamond, Sapphire,* and *Caribbean*—are some of the most beautiful megaships in the biz.

THE EXPERIENCE   If you were to put Royal Caribbean, NCL, and Holland America in a big bowl and mix them together, then add a pinch each of British maritime tradition and California style, you'd come up with Princess. Dining, entertainment, and activities are geared to a wide cross-section of cruisers: The more tradition-minded can spend some time in the library, join a bridge tournament, enjoy a traditional dinner in a grand dining room, and then take in a show. Those seeking something different can learn the basics of Photoshop or Web design, work toward their PADI scuba certification, dine in an intimate Italian or New Orleans–style restaurant, and then take in a set of small-group jazz. The line's largest vessels are large indeed, exceeded in size only by Royal Caribbean's Voyager-class ships and Cunard's *Queen Mary 2.* They offer a plethora of bars, lounges, and theaters, yet you'll also find the kind of quiet, intimate nooks and calm spaces that are more typical aboard smaller vessels. **Pros:** Lots of dining choices and flexibility (the line's "Personal Choice" program allows you to dine at a fixed time and place, or wing it as you go along), and excellent lounge entertainment. **Cons:** Surprisingly small gyms for ships this large.

PASSENGER PROFILE   The majority of Princess's passengers are in their 50s, 60s, and older, though more and more 30- and 40-somethings (and their families) are sailing these days, particularly during the summer. Overall, Princess passengers are less rowdy and boisterous than those aboard Carnival and not quite as staid as those aboard Holland America. Princess's ships all have extensive kids' facilities and activities, making them suitable for families, while their balance of formal and informal makes them a good bet for a romantic vacation, with opportunities for doing your own thing mixed in among more traditional cruise offerings.

ROYAL CARIBBEAN INTERNATIONAL

1050 Caribbean Way, Miami, FL 33132. © **800/327-6700** or 305/539-6000. Fax 800/722-5329. www.royalcaribbean.com.

THE LINE IN A NUTSHELL   Royal Caribbean offers some of the best-looking, best-designed, most activity-packed, and most fun megaships in the biz. Along with NCL, they're out in the forefront of innovation, always challenging the status quo regarding what can and can't be done aboard ships.

THE EXPERIENCE   Though still trailing industry-leader Carnival in terms of size and profit, Royal Caribbean has definitely taken the lead in the excitement and cool-appeal department. You've seen the ads: fit 30- and 40-somethings hiking across a glacier, kayaking through crystalline water, and climbing up a sheer rock face as Iggy Pop's "Lust for Life" plays, then sipping wine on deck as the sun goes down. That's obviously the Madison Avenue take, but the weird thing is, it isn't all just hype: Somehow, Royal Caribbean has managed to turn the "overfed, newly wed, almost dead" cruise stereotype on its ear, and created a more youthful product that delivers fun, humor, a touch of class, and a bit of "feel the burn" active excitement, all without charging an arm and a leg. Cruises on these fun, active, and glamorous megaships offer a wide range of experience for a wide range of people, whether your idea of a good time is getting superactive or relaxing in the Solarium pool. There are huge children's centers for the kids, and entertainment for adults is varied and sometimes even novel: The Voyager-class ships have a resident troupe of clowns that teach juggling, clown history, and makeup application when they're not doing their act. **Pros:** Activity central (with rock-climbing walls, miniature golf, basketball courts, and even ice skating, these ships are tops in the adrenaline department); beautiful public areas; and great indoor/outdoor pool "Solariums" on the Vision-, Voyager- and Radiance-class ships. **Cons:** Small cabins on the older ships (at just about 120–160 sq. ft., most cabins aboard the Vision- and Sovereign-class ships are downright teeny, ranking with NCL's as the smallest cabins in the mainstream category).

PASSENGER PROFILE   You'll find all walks of life on a Royal Caribbean cruise: passengers in their 20s through 60s, many couples (including a good number of honeymooners), some singles traveling with friends, and lots of families—more than 300,000 kids sailed with Royal Caribbean in 2001. Overall, passengers are active, social, and looking for a good time, no matter what their age. While the majority of passengers come from somewhere in North America, the huge Voyager-class ships in particular attract a lot of international travelers, including many Asians and Latin Americans. There are books in the library in French, Spanish, and Dutch, and in-cabin documents (such as room-service menus) are in five languages, including Italian and Portuguese. As we mentioned before, the line has recently made a big push for younger, hipper, more active passengers who want a less glitzy, less theme-parkish, and less party-on experience than they'd get from RCI's main competitor, Carnival. RCI's shorter 3- and 4-night cruises tend to attract more of the partying crowd, as is the case with most short cruises.

2 The Ultraluxury Lines

On these top-shelf cruises, guests don't line up for a look at an ice sculpture or a slice of pepperoni pizza en route to St. Thomas or Nassau. Instead, they sip a '98 Bordeaux with their filet *de boeuf* in truffle sauce while sailing to Les Saintes or St. Barts. They order jumbo shrimp from the room-service menu, and take luxurious baths in ritzy marble-covered bathrooms. There's doting service, the best food and wine you'll find at sea, and a calm, elegant retreat to call home for a week or two.

These cruise lines' ships are the closest thing you'll find to five-star on the ocean. Mostly small and intimate, these are the sports cars of cruise ships, and they cater to discerning travelers who don't blink at paying top dollar to be pampered. Aboard all the lines, delicious French, Italian, and Asian cuisine often rivals that of respected shoreside restaurants and is served in high style by large staffs of doting, gracious waiters who know how to please. A full dinner can even be served to you in your cabin if you like. Aboard most of the lines (aside from casual Windstar and SeaDream), formal nights see the vast majority of guests dressed in tuxedos and sparkling dresses and gowns, dining in elegant rooms with the finest linens, stemware, and china. In the evening, guests tend to amuse themselves with cocktails and conversation in a piano bar, or with small-scale Broadway-inspired song-and-dance medley shows.

Most people attracted to these types of cruises are sophisticated, wealthy, relatively social, and used to the finer things in life. Most are well traveled, though not necessarily adventurous, and tend to stick to five-star experiences. These ships are not geared to children, although some may show up on holiday sailings and summertime cruises. Babysitting can often be arranged privately with an off-duty crew member. The larger Crystal ships have playrooms, and as many as 100 children are not uncommon during holiday cruises.

CRYSTAL CRUISES

2049 Century Park E., Suite 1400, Los Angeles, CA 90067. ✆ **800/446-6620** or 310/785-9300. Fax 310/785-0011. www.crystalcruises.com.

THE LINE IN A NUTSHELL Fine-tuned and fashionable, Crystal's three dream ships (two newly refurbished and one brand new) offer top-shelf service and cuisine, lots of outdoor deck space, generous fitness facilities, tons of activities, multiple restaurants, and more than half a dozen bars and entertainment venues.

THE EXPERIENCE Crystal has the three largest truly upscale ships in the industry. Carrying 940 to 1,080 passengers, they aren't huge, but they're big enough to offer much more than their high-end peers. You won't feel hemmed in and you likely won't be twiddling your thumbs from lack of stimulation. Service is excellent and the line's Asian cuisine is tops. Unlike Seabourn's small ships, which tend to be more calm and staid, Crystal's sociable California atmosphere and large passenger capacity tend to keep things mingly, chatty, and more active. **Pros:** Multiple restaurants (in addition to the formal dining room, there are two or three alternative restaurants on each ship, plus an indoor cafe and a casual restaurant that puts on great theme luncheon buffets), great fitness choices (with nice-size gyms, paddle-tennis courts, shuffleboard, Ping-Pong, a jogging circuit, golf-driving nets, and a putting green), and great enrichment programs, with complimentary computer-training classes on every cruise, plus dozens of theme sailings focused on food and wine, art, film, jazz music, wellness, and other subjects. **Cons:** Compared to the other luxe lines, they're the least all-inclusive (only nonalcoholic drinks are included in the rates, not tips, booze, and so on), and their accommodations and cabin bathrooms are smaller than those aboard Silversea, Seabourn, and Radisson (especially on *Harmony* and *Symphony*).

PASSENGER PROFILE Like other high-end lines, Crystal draws a lot of repeat passengers. On many cruises, more than 50% of the passengers hail from affluent regions of California, and most step aboard for their second, third, or fourth Crystal cruise with a definite sense of how they want to spend their time on board. There's commonly a small contingent of passengers (about 15% of the mix) from the United Kingdom, Australia, Japan, Mexico, Europe, and South America. Most passengers are well-heeled couples over 55, and most enjoy dressing up at dinner. A good number of passengers step up to Crystal from lines such as Princess and Holland America. Though not kid-centric in the way the mainstream lines are, Crystal is the most accommodating of the high-end lines for families with kids. Each ship has a dedicated playroom, and supervised activities are offered when demand warrants it. During the holidays, the summer months of July and August, and on Alaska cruises, 100 or so kids on board is not that unusual.

Specialty Dining: Who's Got What

Cruise Line & Ships	Type of Specialty Restaurants	Extra Charge
Carnival		
Spirit and Conquest classes	Steakhouse/Seafood	$25 per person
Celebrity		
Millennium class	Continental	$25 per person
Costa		
CostaAtlantica, CostaMediterranea	Italian	$23 per person

Cruise Line & Ships	Type of Specialty Restaurants	Extra Charge
Crystal		
Crystal Harmony	Asian, Italian	"suggested" $6 tip
Crystal Serenity	Asian, Sushi, Italian	"suggested" $6 tip
Cunard		
Queen Mary 2	Mediterranean	$30 per person
	Chef's Galley	$30 per person
	Italian, Asian, Carvery	No extra charge
Disney		
Disney Magic, Disney Wonder	Italian	$10 per person
Holland America		
Fleetwide	Pacific Northwest	$20
Norwegian		
Dawn, Star	Steakhouse	$17.50 per person
	French/Continental	$12.50
	Pan-Asian	$10
	Sushi	a la carte pricing, $10–$12
	Teppanyaki	a la carte pricing, $10–$12
	Tapas, Italian	no extra charge
Majesty, Sea Dream, Wind, Crown	French/Continental	$10 per person
Pride of Aloha	French/Continental, Pan-Asian, Italian	$10 per person
Sun	French/Continental, Pan-Asian, Italian	$10 per person
	Sushi, Teppanyaki	a la carte pricing, $10–$12
	Tapas	no extra charge
Oceania		
Regatta, Insignia	Italian, Steakhouse	no extra charge
Princess		
Caribbean Princess	Italian trattoria	$20
	Steakhouse	$15
	Caribbean	no extra charge
Diamond, Sapphire	Italian, Steakhouse, Southwestern, Asian	no extra charge
	Italian trattoria	$20 per person
Golden, Grand, Star	Italian trattoria	$20 per person
	Tex-Mex	$8 per person
Coral, Island Princess	Italian	$20 per person
	New Orleans	$10 per person
Sun class	Steakhouse	$15 per person
	Sit-down pizzeria	no extra charge
Radisson		
Seven Seas Mariner	French, International	no extra charge
Seven Seas Voyager	French, American	no extra charge
Diamond, Navigator	Italian	no extra charge

Cruise Line & Ships	Type of Specialty Restaurants	Extra Charge
Royal Caribbean		
Radiance class	Italian, Steakhouse	$20 per person
Voyager class, *Empress of the Seas*	Italian	$20 per person
Seabourn		
Legend, Pride	Asian, Mediterranean, Steakhouse*	no extra charge
Silversea		
Wind, Cloud, Shadow, Whisper	French, Italian, Asian, and others*	no extra charge

* Seabourn and Silversea host varying theme nights in one restaurant aboard each ship.

CUNARD

6100 Blue Lagoon Dr., Miami, FL 33126. © **800/5-CUNARD** or 305/463-3000. Fax 305/463-3010. www.cunard.com.

THE LINE IN A NUTSHELL   Can you say "history"? Can you say "God Save the Queen"? Cunard, almost 165 years old at this writing, is a bona fide cultural icon, a tangible reminder of the days when Britannia really did rule the waves, and that's what sets it apart—that and the fact that its newest vessel, *Queen Mary 2,* is not only the biggest passenger ship ever built, but also maybe the most famous currently sailing, having made a huge media splash on her launch in January 2004.

THE EXPERIENCE   Catering to a generally wealthy, well-traveled, soft-spoken, and heavily British clientele in their 50s and up, plus some families, Cunard offers an onboard experience that's high-brow genteel British all the way, from the formal service to the decor, which through artwork and historical displays pays tribute to England and to Cunard's long history. *QM2* is the first true transatlantic liner built since Cunard's famous *QE2* entered service in May 1969, and in addition to taking over her older sister's historic transatlantic route, she also offers Caribbean cruises at various times during the year. **Pros:** Remarkable ship, built to a standard of strength and endurance that hardly exists anymore; touches of classic liner elegance (several of the ship's public rooms were designed as modern versions of liners past); multiple dining options, including the gorgeous main dining rooms (which, as on *QE2,* are assigned based on the level of cabin you book), the specialty Todd English restaurant, and several other options; a great enrichment program; and total cool cachet—people will sit up and take notice when you say you've sailed on the *Queen.* **Cons:** Cost—there's so much hype associated with this ship that her prices are remaining high. Also, if you're a dedicated small-d democrat, you might bridle at the class distinctions inherent in the way dining rooms are segregated.

PASSENGER PROFILE   In general, Cunard attracts a well-traveled crowd of passengers in their fifties and up, many of them repeaters who appreciate Cunard's old-timey virtues and are more the 4 o'clock tea crowd than the hot-tub-and-umbrella-drink set. That said, the hoopla surrounding the launch of *QM2* is attracting a much wider demographic, to the point where even Cunard is, at press time, unable to say exactly who's booking the ship. What they are sure of is nationality: In its first season, *QM2* drew approximately 70% of its passengers from the

U.S., with the remaining 30% being heavily British, sprinkled with other guests from around the world. Going forward, the line expects to draw between 60 and 65% of its guests from the U.S.

RADISSON SEVEN SEAS CRUISES
600 Corporate Dr., Suite 410, Fort Lauderdale, FL 33334. ⓒ **800/285-1835.** Fax 402/501-5599. www.rssc.com.

THE LINE IN A NUTSHELL   Operating a fleet of stylish and extremely comfortable midsize vessels, Radisson offers a casually elegant and subtly luxurious cruise experience. Its service is as good as it gets, and its cuisine is near the top.

THE EXPERIENCE   If you insist on luxury but like to keep it subtle, Radisson might be your cruise line of choice. Its ships are spacious and understated, with a relaxed onboard vibe that tend to be less stuffy than Seabourn and Silversea. As aboard most of the luxury ships, entertainment and activities are low-key, with passengers left to enjoy their vacations at their own pace. Dress tends toward casual, though tuxedos and gowns aren't uncommon on formal evenings. **Pros:** Absolutely spot-on and friendly service; some of the best cuisine at sea in both the formal dining rooms and the alternative restaurants (even if what tickles your fancy isn't on the menu, the galley will make an effort to prepare it for you); lots of veranda cabins (*Radisson Diamond* has private balconies in almost 70% of her cabins, the all-suite *Seven Seas Navigator* has them in 90% of hers, and the all-suite *Mariner* and *Voyager* have them in every single stateroom); and amazing bathrooms on *Navigator* and *Voyager* (with separate shower stalls and full-size bathtubs long enough for normal-size humans). **Cons:** Less all-inclusive than Silversea, Seabourn, and SeaDream (gratuities, wine with dinner, and unlimited soda and bottled water are included, but there are no complimentary shore excursions, and the only free liquor is a one-time loading up of your cabin minibar).

PASSENGER PROFILE   This line appeals primarily to well-traveled and well-heeled passengers in their 50s and 60s, but younger passengers and honeymooners pepper the mix. Many passengers are frequent cruisers who have also sailed on Silversea, Seabourn, and Crystal, or are taking a step up from Holland America, Celebrity, or one of the other mainstream lines. Though they have sophisticated tastes (and can do without inane activities like napkin-folding classes), they appreciate the line's less formal ambience. On recent *Navigator* and *Diamond* cruises, our social circle included an Atlantic City nightclub owner, a retired recycling executive, a graphic artist, a theatrical casting director, and a woman who owned a string of Taco Bell franchises. The limited number of third berths on all the ships tends to limit the numbers of families that choose this line.

SEABOURN CRUISE LINE
6100 Blue Lagoon Dr., Suite 400, Miami FL 33126. ⓒ **800/929-9391** or 305/463-3070. www.seabourn.com.

THE LINE IN A NUTSHELL   Small and intimate, these quiet, comfortable megayachts lavish all guests with personal attention and very fine cuisine, and their small size encourages mingling.

THE EXPERIENCE   Strictly upper-crust Seabourn caters to guests who are well mannered and prefer their fellow vacationers to be the same. No pool games and deck parties here; instead, guests prefer a good book, cocktail chatter, trivia games, and presentations by guest lecturers. They'll probably also go for recent enhancements such as free minimassages on deck and soothing eucalyptus-oil baths drawn in suites upon request. **Pros:** Top-shelf service (the crew-member-to-guest ratio is higher than on almost any other line and service is very personal, with staff members greeting you by name from the moment you check in—your wish is their command); totally all-inclusive rates (unlimited wines and spirits, plus gratuities); excellent dining (even the breakfast buffets are exceptional); and interesting itineraries that visit less-touristed ports of call. **Cons:** Limited activities and nightlife (but then, many guests like it that way); no cabin balconies; and a bit of an aging feel, since these vessels were built about a decade and a half ago. Due to their size, they're also susceptible to motion in rough seas, though you shouldn't encounter too many of those in the Caribbean.

PASSENGER PROFILE   Seabourn's guests are well-traveled, mature adults mostly in their 50, 60s, and 70s (a company spokesman claims the average age is 53), who are used to the five-star treatment. Many have net worths in the millions. You are likely to encounter former CEOs, lawyers, investment bankers, real-estate tycoons, and entrepreneurs. The majority of passengers are couples, and there are always a handful of singles as well, usually widows or widowers. A few European and Australian guests usually spice up the mix, but no matter what their nationality, these are experienced globetrotting travelers. While you'll occasionally see families with children during the holidays and summers, it's the exception rather than the rule. These ships do not cater to kids in any way, and many passengers prefer it that way.

SEADREAM YACHT CLUB

2601 S. Bayshore Dr., Penthouse 1B, Coconut Grove, FL 33133. ℂ **800/707-4911** or 305/856-5622. Fax 305/856-7599. www.seadreamyachtclub.com.

THE LINE IN A NUTSHELL   SeaDream's two intimate small ships deliver an upscale yet casual experience without the regimentation of traditional cruise itineraries and activities.

THE EXPERIENCE   SeaDream—a line created a few years ago by Seabourn founder Atle Brynestad with that line's two *Sea Goddess* ships—will entice those who value impeccable service, a mellow atmosphere, and a good batch of sevruga Malossol caviar. But the line is seeking another kind of traveler as well: one who straddles a WaveRunner, barhops in Monte Carlo, and enjoys a spontaneous mountain-bike trek as well as extreme pampering. How fancy is the cruise? Tickets for SeaDream cruises were included in the decadent gift baskets given to presenters and performers at the Oscars in 2004, that's how fancy. **Pros:** Flexible itineraries (captains have the authority to duck inclement weather by visiting a different port or to extend a stay off an island because of perfect snorkeling conditions); truly all-inclusive rates, covering unlimited wines and spirits as well as tips; cool tech stuff (flat-screen TVs, Internet access, MP3 players, and even Segway Human Transporters available for passenger use); and late-night departures from key ports, which allow you to sample the local nightlife. **Cons:** Limited entertainment (a piano player is about it), and the small size of the ships—which is a selling point, yes, but also means the ships can bob around a lot in rough seas.

PASSENGER PROFILE   Most passengers are in their 40s to 60s and are not veteran cruisers. Seventy percent are American (with Brits and other Europeans making up most of the remainder). In theory, passengers have refined tastes but balk at the rigid structure of cruise itineraries. They're happy to strike up a game of backgammon beside the pool, or to venture into town with the chef in search of the evening's fish. They want top-notch service and gourmet food, but are secure enough to dispense with a stuffy atmosphere. At least that's the plan. So far, more than 50% of business comes from full charters of the ships, often by large (and rich) families. Smaller groups can take advantage of a deal that gives one free cabin for every four booked, up to a maximum of 25 cabins.

SILVERSEA CRUISES

110 E. Broward Blvd., Fort Lauderdale, FL 33301. ✆ **800/722-9955.** Fax 954/522-4499. www.silversea.com.

THE LINE IN A NUTSHELL   It doesn't get better than free-flowing Philipponnat Royale Reserve champagne and marble bathrooms stocked with wonderful Bulgari bath products. These gorgeous ships offer the best of everything.

THE EXPERIENCE   Fine-tuned and genteel, a Silversea cruise caters to guests who won't settle for anything but the best. The food and service are the finest at sea, and nothing seems to have been forgotten in the creation of the plush fleet, which features warm and inviting Italian-style decor and tables set with Christofle silver and Schott-Zwiesel crystal. These are dignified vessels for a dignified crowd that likes to dress for dinner. If you want the VIP treatment 24-7, this is your cruise line. **Pros:** Doting, gracious, and ultraprofessional service; truly all-inclusive rates (covering gratuities and unlimited wines and spirits); excellent cuisine that rivals the best restaurants ashore; large staterooms; and great bathrooms. **Cons:** Stuffy crowd. Of course, not every guest fits that bill, but expect a good portion of the crowd on any cruise to be, shall we say, reserved.

PASSENGER PROFILE   While Silversea's typical passenger mix is 55-plus, shorter cruises and Caribbean sailings often skew the mix a tad younger, adding at least a handful of 30- and 40-something couples. Typically, about 85% are well-traveled, well-heeled, well-dressed Americans who are not afraid to flaunt five-carat diamonds and gold Rolexes the size of Texas. Most guests are couples, though singles and small groups of friends traveling together are usually part of the scene too. Many have cruised with Silversea before, and they expect the best of everything. 'Hup hup!

WINDSTAR CRUISES

300 Elliott Ave. W., Seattle, WA 98119. ✆ **800/258-7245** or 206/281-3535. Fax 206/281-0627. www.windstarcruises.com.

THE LINE IN A NUTSHELL   The no-jackets-required policy defines this line's casually elegant attitude. These sleek, small ships really do feel like private yachts—they're down-to-earth, yet service and cuisine are first-class.

THE EXPERIENCE   Windstar offers a truly unique cruise experience, giving passengers the delicious fantasy of adventure aboard its fleet of four- and five-masted sailing ships, along with the ever-pleasant reality of first-class cuisine, service, and itineraries. This is no barefoot, rigging-pulling, paper-plates-in-lap, sleep-on-the-deck kind of cruise, but a refined yet down-to-earth, yachtlike experience for a sophisticated, well-traveled crowd who wouldn't be comfortable on a big ship with throngs of tourists. On board, stained teak, brass details, and lots of navy-blue fabrics and carpeting lend a traditional nautical ambience. While the ships' proud masts and white sails cut a traditional profile, they're also state-of-the-art, controlled by a computer so that they can be furled or unfurled at the touch of a button. When at all possible, the captain shuts off the engines and moves by sail only to give passengers a real taste of the sea. Under full sail, the calm tranquillity is blissful. **Pros:** Excellent dining, with ambience, service, and cuisine created by renowned Los Angeles chef Joachim Splichal; informal and unregimented onboard feel; and interesting itineraries, typically visiting a port every day. **Cons:** Limited activities and entertainment (which is the way most passengers want it, but not good if you need lots of organized hoopla) and no cabin verandas.

PASSENGER PROFILE   Overall, passengers are sophisticated and well-traveled, and want a somewhat adventurous, port-intensive Caribbean cruise. They're people who expect high-caliber service and very high-quality cuisine but dislike both the formality of the other high-end ships and the mass mentality of the megaships. Most are couples in their 30s to early 60s (with the average around 50), with a smattering of parents with adult children and some single friends traveling together. The line is not a good choice for singles or for families with children under 15 or 16. About a third of the passengers on most cruises have sailed with the line before, while about 20% are first-time cruisers. There are usually a handful of honeymoon couples on board any given sailing.

3 Soft-Adventure Lines & Sailing Ships

Often more adventure-tour than Love Boat, the vessels in this section are about as far as you can get from a typical cruise and still be on a ship. All of them are small and intimate, carrying about 100 to 150 passengers, and are designed to take you close to nature, island culture, and the sea. Of the lines reviewed here, American Canadian Caribbean Line and Clipper operate motorized coastal cruisers that are like hostels and B&Bs at sea, respectively, while Star Clippers and Windjammer both operate sailing ships, the former with a yachtlike vibe, the latter more like summer camp for adults. There may not be TVs in the cabins, and you won't find a casino or glitzy dance revue; instead, you'll find people who have booked this type of ship because they want to meet their fellow passengers, develop friendships, and—aboard ACCL, Clipper, and Star Clippers—actually learn something about the places they're visiting. (Passengers on Windjammer Barefoot Cruises are . . . well, they're looking for a good time.) Food will be relatively basic, and you won't find room service, midnight buffets, or overly doting stewards, but you will get very personal attention, as crew and passengers get friendly fast. These ships generally visit a port every day, concentrating on small, out-of-the-way islands that the big cruise ships would run aground trying to approach, and shore excursions often include hiking, snorkeling, bird-watching, and history-oriented tours . . . plus beach parties for the Windjammer folks, naturally. The downside? Small-ship cruises are usually more expensive than mainstream cruises, though Windjammer keeps its fares pretty low. Also, people who are very susceptible to seasickness should note that smaller ships rock more in rough seas.

AMERICAN CANADIAN CARIBBEAN LINE

461 Water St., Warren, RI 02885. ✆ **800/556-7450** or 401/247-0955. Fax 401/ 247-2350. www.accl-smallships.com.

THE LINE IN A NUTSHELL   A family-owned New England line, ACCL operates tiny, no-frills ships that travel to offbeat places and attract a well-traveled, extremely casual, and down-to-earth older crowd.

THE EXPERIENCE   ACCL began in 1966 when Rhode Island shipbuilder Luther Blount realized that there was a demand for small-ship sailing on the rivers, canals, and coast of New England and Canada. Over the years, his vessels have gone well beyond their regional home, and now offer cruises down the Intracoastal Waterway and in the Caribbean and Central America. With an innovative, exploratory design, Blount's extremely informal small ships won't win any awards for decor, amenities, meals, or service (they are, in fact, about the most bare-bones vessels you'll find), but that's not what they're about. Instead, this is a line that gets passengers close to the real life of the regions it visits. **Pros:** Casual and unpretentious vibe; innovative itineraries; and a BYOB policy (the bus or van that transports passengers from the airport or hotel to the ship stops at a reasonably priced liquor store en route so you can stock up, providing a big savings on onboard bar bills). **Cons:** No frills—cabins are tiny, decor is bland, bathrooms are minuscule, and meals are served family-style. Also, the ships can feel crowded when they're full or near full. Your cabin is your only sanctuary, and thin cabin walls will make you feel closer to your neighbors than you may prefer.

PASSENGER PROFILE   This ultracasual line appeals to a sensible, early-to-bed crowd of mostly senior couples in their 60s through 80s, with the average age being 72. While some are physically fit, there are usually a few walking with canes and using hearing aids. Besides senior couples, there may be a few mother-daughter teams. All are attracted by the line's casual atmosphere (windbreakers and wash-and-wear sportswear is about as fancy as these folks get on vacation) and want to visit some unusual, interesting ports. Many have sailed with the line before, and appreciate its lack of glitz and gimmicks, as well as its "just us folks" features like a BYOB policy.

CLIPPER CRUISE LINE

11969 Westline Industrial Dr., St. Louis, Missouri 63146-3220. © **800/325-0010** or 314/655-6700. Fax 314/655-6670. www.clippercruise.com.

THE LINE IN A NUTSHELL   Clipper's comfortable small ships focus on offbeat ports of call, learning, and mingling with your fellow passengers. It's the ideal small-ship cruise for people who've tried Holland America or one of the other mainstream lines and want a more intimate cruise experience.

THE EXPERIENCE   Clipper caters to mature, seasoned, easygoing, relatively affluent, and well-traveled older passengers seeking a casual and educational vacation experience heavy on the nature, history, and culture of the ports visited. Naturalists and historians sail on all itineraries to provide context, and they also accompany excursions. A cruise director helps organize the days, answers questions, and assists passengers. The line falls mostly on the "port-to-port" side of small-ship cruising, stressing island culture and nature rather than active adventure. **Pros:** Casual, informal atmosphere; interesting itineraries; young, enthusiastic crews; and great opportunities for learning. **Cons:** Very few—just engines that are a bit noisy on *Yorktown* and *Nantucket Clipper.*

PASSENGER PROFILE   The majority of Clipper passengers are well-traveled 45- to 75-year-old couples (and occasionally singles) who are attracted by the casual intimacy of small ships and by the opportunity to learn something about the places they visit. As a company spokesman noted a few years back, "Our aim is to offer an experience that adds something special to one's understanding of the world while providing a sense of enjoyment." Most passengers are well educated though not academic, casual, and adventurous in the sense that they're up for a day of snorkeling and hiking but are happy to get back to their comfortable ship afterward. Many passengers are repeaters, or have sailed with other small-ship lines.

STAR CLIPPERS

4101 Salzedo Ave., Coral Gables, FL 33146. ℂ **800/442-0551** or 305/442-0550. Fax 305/442-1611. www.starclippers.com.

THE LINE IN A NUTSHELL   With the sails and rigging of classic clipper ships and some of the cushy amenities of modern megas, a cruise on this line's 170- to 228-passenger ships offers adventure with comfort.

THE EXPERIENCE   On Star Clippers, you'll have the best of two worlds: On one hand, the ships offer comfortable, almost cushy public rooms and cabins. On the other, they espouse an unstructured, let-your-hair-down, hands-on ethic—you can climb the masts (with a harness, of course), help raise the sails, crawl into the bow netting, or chat with the captain on the open-air bridge. Furthermore, listening to the captain's daily talk about the next port of call, the history of sailing, or some other nautical subject, you'll feel like you're exploring some of the Caribbean's more remote stretches in a ship that really belongs there—an exotic ship for an exotic locale. In a sea of look-alike megaships, *Star Clipper* and the newer *Royal Clipper* stand out, recalling a more romantic and exploratory age of ship travel. **Pros:** Rich, hands-on ambience (ducking under booms, stepping over coils of rope, leaning against railings just feet above the sea, and watching sailors work the winches are constant reminders that you're on a real working ship); comfortable amenities including pools, piano bars, and clubby, wood-paneled libraries; and offbeat itineraries visiting the Grenadines and the French West Indies. **Cons:** None we can think of.

PASSENGER PROFILE   With no more than 227 passengers aboard the largest ship in the fleet, each Star Clippers cruise feels like a triumph of individuality and intimacy. While you're likely to find a handful of late-20-something honeymoon-type couples and an extended-family group or two, the majority of passengers are well-traveled couples in their 40s to 60s, all active and intellectually curious professionals (executives, lawyers, and doctors are common) who appreciate a casual yet sophisticated ambience, and enjoy mixing with fellow passengers. During the day, polo shirts, shorts, and topsiders are standard issue; for dinner, many passengers simply change into cleaner and better-pressed versions of the same, with perhaps a switch from shorts to slacks for most men. However, men in jackets and women in snazzy dresses aren't uncommon on the night of the captain's cocktail party. With a nearly even mix of Europeans and North Americans on a typical Caribbean cruise, the international onboard flavor is as intriguing as the ship itself.

WINDJAMMER BAREFOOT CRUISES

1759 Bay Rd., Miami Beach, FL 33139 (P.O. Box 190–120, Miami Beach, FL 33119). ℂ **800/327-2601** or 305/672-6453. Fax 305/674-1219. www.windjammer.com.

THE LINE IN A NUTSHELL   Ultracasual and delightfully carefree, this eclectic fleet of cozy, rebuilt sailing ships (powered by both sails and engines) lures passengers into a fantasy world of pirates-and-rum-punch adventure.

THE EXPERIENCE   When you see that the captain is wearing shorts and shades and is barefoot like the rest of the laid-back crew, you'll realize that Windjammer's vessels aren't your typical cruise ships. Their yards of sails, pointy bowsprits, chunky portholes, and generous use of wood create a swashbuckling, storybook look; and while passengers don't have to fish for dinner or swab the decks, they are invited to help haul the sails, take a turn at the wheel, sleep out on deck whenever they please, and (with the captain's permission) crawl into the bow net. With few rules and lots of freedom, this is the closest thing you'll get to a real old-fashioned Caribbean adventure, visiting off-the-beaten-track Caribbean ports of call. The ships are ultrainformal, and hokey yet endearing rituals make the trip feel like summer camp for adults. Add in the line's tremendous number of repeat passengers (and a few of its signature rum swizzle drinks) and you have an experience that's ultracasual, ultrafun, and downright chummy. **Pros:** Extreme informality; fun, down-to-earth passengers; adventurous feeling; and cheap rates. **Cons:** Aging ships (all these vessels have been sailing the seas for many years, and show it) and small cabins, some of them very small indeed.

PASSENGER PROFILE   Can we say nutty, quirky, nonconformist? That's why Windjammer is so appealing. Unlike some "all things to all people" lines, Windjammer is for a particular kind of informal, fun-loving, down-to-earth passenger. Age doesn't seem to play any role: From honeymooning couples in their 20s to grandparents in their 70s, the line attracts a broad range of adventurers who like to have fun and don't want anything resembling a highly regimented vacation. Passengers are pretty evenly divided between men and women, 15% to 20% overall are single, and a huge proportion are repeaters back for their 3rd, 10th, or 20th Windjammer cruise. Passengers aboard the commissary ship *Amazing Grace,* which has a less romantic cargo-ship appearance, tend to be older than those aboard the sailing ships (mostly 60-plus), due to the ship's longer itineraries.

3

Things to Know Before You Go

You've bought your ticket and you're getting ready to cruise. But what about passports, money, packing, and other practicalities? There are a few details you need to consider before you go.

1 Passports & Visas

Good news in the convenience category: None of the countries and ports covered in this book require U.S. and Canadian citizens to have anything more than a passport to enter. However, if you're flying to a non-U.S. port to start your cruise, you may have to obtain a tourist card and pay a minimal fee at the cruise terminal or airport or on the plane.

Many of the ports in this book don't even require U.S. and Canadian citizens to have a passport, simply insisting on **proof of citizenship** (such as an expired passport, a certified copy of your birth certificate, a Certificate of Naturalization, a Certificate of Citizenship, or a Report of Birth Abroad) plus a **photo ID** such as a driver's license. (Note that a driver's license is not acceptable as the sole form of identification.) Your travel agent can advise you as to whether you need a passport for the islands you'll be visiting on your itinerary, and the documents that your cruise line sends with your tickets will also provide this information. All that said, though, our advice is to carry a passport anyway. In these days of heightened security, it can't hurt.

If you don't currently have a passport or need to replace an expired one, the **U.S. State Department website** (www.travel.state.gov/passport_services.html) provides information. You can also call the **National Passport Information Center** (© 877/ 487-2778) for information. Fees for new passports are $85 adults, $70 children under 16. Renewals cost $55. If you're leaving within a few weeks, you can pay the additional $60 fee to have your passport expedited for delivery within 2 weeks.

As you would before any trip abroad, make two photocopies of your documents and ID before leaving home. Take one set with you as a backup (keeping it in a different piece of luggage from your originals) and keep one at home.

Vaccinations Required?

Travel to the Caribbean does not generally warrant inoculations against tropical diseases. Ditto for the Mexican ports you might be visiting. The Centers for Disease Control (CDC) recommends prescription antimalarial drugs for travelers in certain parts of Central America, including Panama's San Blas Islands and Honduras's Roatan Island—both of them cruise destinations. CDC recommendations and warnings can be viewed at www.cdc.gov/travel/destinat.htm.

Safety at Sea in the New World (Dis)Order

Traditionally, safety-at-sea issues have included the occasional hurricane, fire, gastrointestinal bug, petty theft, and rogue iceberg. But in the wake of the September 11, 2001, terrorist attacks, the threat of terrorism immediately assumed a high place on that list, prompting the cruise lines, port authorities, and the U.S. Coast Guard to implement a number of new security measures.

Logistically, ships are more difficult to protect than planes because of their larger passenger loads and multicountry itineraries, their numerous labyrinthine public and "crew only" areas, their regular presence at public port facilities, and the access they offer to the numerous contractors who come aboard on turnaround days to refresh flowers, service machinery, and perform other needed functions. For these reasons, all the major cruise lines have their own dedicated onboard security forces, though events over the years—such as the 1985 hijacking of the *Achille Lauro*—have periodically forced enhancements to security procedures. These latter have included the hiring of ex–Navy SEALs as top-level security consultants, the drilling of deck officers in how to react to takeover attempts, and a mandate that ships have alternative onboard command sites, making it difficult for a small number of terrorists to take and maintain control of a ship. Following September 11, all cruise ships went to Security Level III, the highest dictated by the Coast Guard, but because stringent security measures were already in place, onboard changes have been relatively few. At press time, there were no cruise ports or regions at Level III (changes in levels are typically in conjunction with recommendations of the U.S. Department of Homeland Security). The cruise lines already had used metal detectors at the gangways,

After using your passport or proof of citizenship to board ship at the beginning of your cruise, the cruise line might hang on to your documents for the duration of your cruise, thus allowing them to facilitate clearance procedures quickly at each port. Your documents are returned to you after you depart the last foreign port of call, en route back to your home port.

Non-U.S./Canadian citizens departing from and/or returning to the U.S./Canada should check with their travel agent or cruise line to determine required paperwork. Generally, you'll need a valid passport, alien-registration card as applicable, and any visas required by the ports of call.

2 Money Matters

Cruise ships operate on a cashless basis. Basically, this means that you have a running tab and simply sign for what you buy on board during your cruise—bar drinks, meals at specialty restaurants, spa treatments, shore excursions, gift-shop purchases, and so on—then pay up at the end. Very convenient, yes—and also very, very easy to forget your limits and spend more than you intended to.

Shortly before or after embarkation, a purser or check-in clerk in the terminal or on board will take an imprint of your credit card and issue you an required that anyone boarding be on a preapproved list, and employed computerized systems that could tell instantly who is aboard at any given time. New regulations dictate a no-visitors policy; a 300-foot (or more) security zone around all cruise ships; the use of sniffer dogs, concrete barriers, patrol boats, and other security measures at some ports; and the screening of all luggage, ship's stores, mail, and cargo. Many cruise lines are photographing passengers digitally at embarkation and matching face to picture every time travelers get back aboard in port, and many lines have hired dedicated security personnel—in some cases Gurkhas, the famed Nepalese fighters—to assist officers at the gangway and be on hand as needed.

Starting July 1, 2004, new international regulations will go into effect. Called the International Ship and Port Facility Security Code, created by the International Maritime Organization (IMO), the intent is for all ports around the world to operate in a consistent framework to address security issues. A port will identify itself as being under either Marine Security Level I, II, or III.

Because Level III guidelines apply only to U.S. ports, the cruise lines have been working diligently with foreign port officials to beef up security around the ships (through tightening access to ports), and to protect passengers on shore excursions that the cruise lines sell. On July 1, 2004, the IMO began enforcing its new International Ship and Port Facility Security (ISPS) code, a series of standardized security regulations that's intended to provide a standardized, consistent framework for evaluating risk, enabling governments to offset changes in threat by reducing vulnerabilities to ships and port facilities.

onboard charge card, which on most ships also serves as your room key and as your cruise ID, which you swipe through a scanner when leaving and returning to the ship from port. Some ships issue separate cards for these functions, or a card and an old-fashioned room key. Some adventure lines that carry 100 or fewer passengers just ask for your cabin number for onboard purchases.

On the last night of your cruise, an **itemized account** of everything you've charged will be slipped beneath your cabin door. If you agree with the charges, they'll automatically be billed to your credit card. If you'd rather pay in cash or if you dispute any charge, you'll need to stop by the office of the ship's cashier or purser. There may be a long line, so don't go if you don't have to.

BRINGING CASH ASHORE

The cashless system works just fine on board, but remember: You'll need cash in port. Many people get so used to not carrying their wallets aboard ship that they get off in port and find themselves without any money in their pockets—an annoyance if your ship is docked and it just means trudging back aboard for cash, but a major annoyance if it's anchored offshore and ferrying passengers back and forth by tender.

You can put any shore excursions you sign up for on your room tab, and credit cards are accepted at most port shops, but we recommend having some real cash, ideally in small denominations, to cover the cost of taxi rides, tips for tour leaders, and purchases you make from craft markets and street vendors. We've included information on local currency in each of the port reviews, but for the most part you don't have to worry about exchanging money at all if you've got U.S. dollars. In the Caribbean, the U.S. dollar is the legal currency of the U.S. Virgin Islands, Puerto Rico, and (oddly enough) the British Virgin Islands, but even on islands that have their own currency, most vendors will accept U.S. dollars—for example, on Guadeloupe and Les Saintes, where vendors may prefer euros (both islands are legally part of France), neither of us had our U.S. dough turned away. Mexican and Central American ports are similarly dollar friendly.

If you're running low on cash, **ATMs** are easy to find in nearly every cruise port covered in this guide, often right at the cruise terminal. Remember that you'll get local currency from machines where the U.S. dollar isn't in use, so don't withdraw more than you need. Many megaships also have ATMs (surprise, surprise: usually near the casino), but you can expect a hefty fee for using them—up to $5 in addition to what your bank charges you.

Many lines, such as Carnival and Royal Caribbean, will cash **traveler's checks** at the purser's desk, and some lines will cash **personal checks** of up to about $200 or $250.

Except aboard some of the ultraluxury lines, **gratuities for the crew** are not normally included in the cruise rates, though many lines these days are either automatically adding a suggested gratuity to your end-of-cruise bill or offering passengers the option of charging gratuities. Where this is not the case, you should reserve some cash so that you won't feel like a schmuck at the end of your cruise. See "Tipping, Customs & Other End-of-Cruise Concerns," later in this chapter, for more on this subject.

3 Keeping in Touch While at Sea

Some people take a cruise to get away from it all, but others are communication addicts. For them, today's megaships offer a spectrum of ways to keep in touch, though they're anything but cheap.

PHONING HOME

Aside from most of the adventure lines, almost all ships today have **direct-dial telephones** in their cabins. From most, you can call anywhere in the world via satellite, but it'll cost you between $4 and $15 a minute, with $8 or $9 being about average. It's cheaper by far to call home from a public telephone in port—or from your cellphone in ports where you have coverage (check with your service provider).

In addition to your cabin phone, each ship has a central phone number, fax number, and e-mail address, which you'll sometimes find in the cruise line's brochure and usually in the documents you'll get with your tickets. Distribute these to family members and friends in case they have to contact you in an emergency. It also can't hurt to leave behind the phone numbers of the cruise line's headquarters and/or reservations department, both of which will be able to put people in touch with you.

INTERNET & E-MAIL AT SEA

The thought of being out of touch has become objectionable to many people over the past half-dozen years, leading most cruise lines to add computer rooms and Internet cafes to their ships. Decked out with state-of-the-art flat-screen monitors, these centers offer e-mail and Internet access, have webcams so that users can send their vacation pictures to family and friends, and are often open 24 hours. Many offer classes to help computer novices get up and running.

E-mail access is usually available in two ways: either through your AOL, Earthlink, Hotmail, Yahoo!, or other personal account, which you can access through the Web at a per-minute charge that averages about 50¢ to $1, or through a temporary account that you set up once aboard ship (with rates averaging roughly $1–$4 per message). Neither is what you'd call inexpensive, but they're still loads cheaper than the per-minute charge of a phone call from ship to shore. Some lines offer a kind of all-you-can-eat Web package, charging a flat fee for unlimited Web use during the course of your cruise—say, $40 for a 3- or 4-night cruises or $90 for a 7-night cruise.

Many ships built over the past several years (including the newest Celebrity, Crystal, Costa, HAL, NCL, Royal Caribbean, Cunard, Radisson, and Silversea ships) have been wired with **dataports** in all, most, or some cabins and suites, allowing passengers who travel with laptops to log on in privacy. The fees for in-room Internet access tend to be higher than the fees for access in the Internet centers. **Wireless Internet** is another new trend, offered aboard the Carnival, Holland America, and Princess fleets, usually in designated areas such as the pool deck and some public rooms. To take advantage of this service you must either have a wireless card for your laptop, rent a wireless card for your laptop, or rent a laptop. You then purchase minutes either on an as-used basis or in packages of 33 to 500 minutes. The SeaDream and Oceania ships (and some of the Silversea ships) offer Internet connectivity through cabin TVs.

Family Cruising Tips

Here are some suggestions for better sailing and smoother seas on your family cruise.

- **Cribs.** If you'd like one, reserve one when booking your cruise. The same advice holds for mini-fridges; if your cabin doesn't have one, you can sometimes request one be brought in (we have done this on Celebrity's *Zenith* and *Horizon*).
- **Pack some basic first-aid supplies, and even a thermometer.** Cruise lines have limited supplies of these items, and charge for them, too. If an accident should happen on board, virtually every ship (except the smallest ones) has its own infirmary staffed by doctors or nurses. Keep in mind that first aid can usually be summoned more readily aboard ship than in port.
- **Warn younger children about the danger of falling overboard,** and make sure they know not to play on the railings.
- **Make sure your kids know their cabin number** and what deck it's on. The endless corridors and doors on the megaships often look exactly alike, though some are color-coded.
- **Prepare kids for TV letdown.** Though many ships today receive satellite TV programming, you won't get the range of options you have at home.

KEEPING ON TOP OF THE NEWS

CNN junkies take note: Most ships have the station as part of their regular TV lineup. Some ships also have other news stations. Many ships also maintain the tradition of reprinting headline news stories pulled off the wire and slipping them under passengers' doors each morning.

4 Packing

One of the great things about cruising is that even though you'll be visiting several countries on a typical weeklong itinerary, you need to unpack only once: You check into your cabin on day one, unpack, and settle in. The destinations come to you.

Just what do you need to pack? To some extent, that depends on the kind of cruise you're taking. Overall, though, cruise ship life mirrors life on land—and these days, for Americans especially, that mostly means casual. Here are some pointers.

DAYTIME CLOTHES

In the **Caribbean,** the temperature stays within a fairly narrow range year-round, averaging between 75°F and 85°F (24°C–29°C), though in summer the combination of sun and humidity can get very intense, especially at midafternoon. Trade winds and/or rain help cool things off on many of the islands. Rainfall differs from island to island—Aruba, for instance, is very dry, while it seems to rain briefly every other time we're in Nassau. Temperatures on Mexico's Yucatán Peninsula and in **Central America** can feel much hotter, especially on shore excursions to the humid interior.

Across the board, casual daytime wear means shorts, T-shirts, bathing suits, and sundresses. Remember to bring a coverup and sandals if you want to go right from your deck chair to one of the restaurants or to some activity in a public room. When in port, the same dress code works, but err toward modesty if you're straying from the beach area (that is, something more than a skimpy bikini top). Bring good walking shoes or sandals so that you can explore the islands as comfortably as possible, and buy or rent aqua socks if you plan to snorkel or participate in watersports or shore excursions that require them, such as Jamaica's Dunn's River Falls trip. (Aqua socks are cheap to buy, but many cruise lines rent them for about $5 a pair.)

If you plan on hitting the gym, don't forget sneakers and your workout clothes. And it can't hurt to bring along one pair of long casual pants and a long-sleeved sweatshirt (mostly to deal with air-conditioning), as well as an umbrella or lightweight raincoat in case the weather turns dicey.

EVENING CLOTHES

As America as a whole gets more casual—witness "business casual" law offices and the baseball-cap-and-furs-wearing Park Avenue set—some cruise lines are responding by toning down or turning off their dress codes.

Norwegian Cruise Line has pretty much ditched the concept of formal nights completely (though an "optional formal" captain's cocktail night allows many people to choose to dress up, so you have sequins and suits next to chinos and polo shirts). Other lines (Disney, for instance) have toned formality down to the point where a sports jacket is considered formal. However, most mainstream and luxury ships still have two traditional formal nights during any 7-night itinerary—usually the second and second-to-last nights of the cruise. Imagine what you'd wear to a nice wedding: Men are encouraged to wear tuxedos or dark suits; women show up in cocktail dresses, sequined jackets, gowns, or other fancy attire. If you're a woman who just hates dressing up, you can get away with a blouse and skirt or pants. And of course, jewelry, scarves, and other accessories can dress up an otherwise ordinary outfit.

The other nights are much more casual, and are designated either semiformal (which is the same as "informal") or casual, though lately many lines have done away with semiformal nights and have just gone with a combination of formal and casual. Semiformal calls for suits or sports jackets for men and stylish dresses or pantsuits for women; casual nights call for chinos or dress pants and collared shirts for men, and dresses, skirts, or pantsuits for women.

The suggested dress codes are usually described in the back of the cruise line's brochure, but you'll still witness a wide variety of outfits. Naturally, one person's "formal" is quite different from another's. Almost anything goes, but passengers are asked not to wear baseball caps, shorts, and T-shirts for dinner in the formal dining rooms—though some inevitably do and are rarely turned away. And pretty much every major line—Carnival, Celebrity, Costa, Holland America, NCL, Princess, and Royal Caribbean—offers a nightly casual dining option where full dress-down is the norm.

Despite the casual trend, there's usually a contingent of folks on board who like to get all decked out for dinner—including us. It's part of the fun; after all, how many chances do you get these days to dress like you're in a Fred Astaire/Ginger Rogers movie? Put on the tux and opera shoes, plunk yourself down in some heavily trafficked lounge an hour or two before dinner, and do some old-fashioned people-watching. It's a veritable fashion show! If you bring your good jewelry, it's wise to keep it under lock and key when you're not wearing it. Most cabins have personal safes operated by a digital code, a credit card, or, once in awhile, a key lock. If your cabin doesn't have one (usually it's the older ships that don't), the ship's purser can hold on to your valuables.

The dress rules outlined above don't apply to ultracasual small-ship lines such as Windjammer and American Canadian Caribbean, where shorts, T-shirts, and sandals can take you through the day and into the evening (although most people tend to dress up a tad more for dinner). Windstar and Star Clippers encourage a "smart casual" look, and have a no-jackets-required rule the entire week, though some men don sport jackets and some women put on dresses for dinner. Similarly, passengers aboard Clipper Cruise Line go casual during the day and usually dress up a little at dinnertime.

SUNDRIES

Like hotel rooms, most cabins (especially those aboard the newest and most high-end ships) come with toiletries such as soap, shampoo, conditioner, and lotion, although you still may want to bring your own products—the ones provided often seem watered down. If you forget something, note that all but the very smallest adventure ships have at least a small shop on board selling various toiletries at inflated prices.

Most cabins also have hair dryers, but they tend to be weak, so don't expect miracles—if you have a lot of hair, bring your own. Almost all ships in the American market run on 110 AC current, and some offer both 110 and 220, so you won't need an adapter if you have an American or Canadian appliance.

You don't need to pack a beach towel, as they're almost always supplied on board (exceptions: Windjammer and ACCL), but sometimes they're kinda small

---

(*Tips* **Tuxedo Rentals**

If you don't own a tux or don't want to bother lugging one along, you can often arrange a rental through the cruise line or your travel agent for about $75 to $120 (the higher prices for packages with shirts and shoes). In some cases, a rental offer arrives with your cruise tickets; if not, a call to your travel agent or the cruise line can facilitate a rental. If you choose this option, your suit will be waiting in your cabin when you arrive.

---

and thin, so bring your own if you like large and fluffy. Bird-watchers will want their binoculars and manuals, golfers their clubs unless they intend to rent, and snorkelers their gear (which can also be rented, usually through the cruise lines).

Aside from the small ships, most vessels have a laundry service on board and some have dry cleaning, too, with generally about a 24-hour turnaround time; a price list will be in your cabin. Cleaning services tend not to be cheap—$1 or $1.50 per pair of socks, $2.50 to $3 for a T-shirt, and $9 to dry-clean a suit—so if you plan to pack light and wear the same outfit several times, you many want to use the self-service laundry rooms on board some ships (Carnival, Crystal, Princess, and Holland America, among others).

If you like to read but don't want to lug hefty novels on board, know that most ships of all sizes have libraries stocked with books and magazines. Most ships also carry paperback bestsellers in their shops.

Lastly, remember to pack sunglasses, a hat, and **sunscreen.** All are available aboard ship and in the ports, but sunscreen in particular will be a lot cheaper at your local market than in a gift shop. You might also consider bringing a **plastic water bottle** that you can refill aboard ship, rather than buying overpriced bottled water in port.

5 Tipping, Customs & Other End-of-Cruise Concerns

We know you don't want to hear about the end of your cruise before you've even gone, but it's best to be prepared. Here's a discussion of a few matters you'll have to take care of before heading home.

TIPPING

Most cruise lines pay their service staff low base wages with the understanding that the bulk of their income will come from tips. Each line has clear guidelines for gratuities, which are usually printed in their brochures and on their website, on your cruise documents, and in the daily schedule toward the end of your trip. (They may also be announced toward the end of the cruise.) The traditional way of tipping was to simply hand your waiter, assistant waiter, and cabin steward cash in a little envelope, but these days more and more lines are automatically adding tips to passengers' onboard accounts. Norwegian, Princess, Cunard, and Carnival do it this way, with the amount adjustable if you request it at the purser's desk before the end of the cruise. Some lines, such as Royal Caribbean, Crystal, Star Clippers, Disney, and Windjammer, give you the option of paying cash directly to staff or adding the gratuities onto your account. Some small-ship lines pool the tips and divide them equitably among all crew. Ultraluxury lines Silversea, Seabourn, SeaDream, and Radisson include tips in the cruise rates. Holland America and Windstar promote their "tipping not required" policies, but "required" is the operative word: Tipping really is expected.

Suggested tipping amounts vary slightly with the line and its degree of luxury, from a total of about $9 to $13 per person per day (half that for children). As a rule of thumb, each passenger (not each couple) should expect to tip at least $3.50 per day for their cabin steward, $3.50 per day for their dining room waiter, and about $2 per day for their assistant waiter, and sometimes 75 cents per day for their headwaiter. Some lines suggest you that tip the maitre d' about $5 per person for the week and slip another couple bucks to the chief housekeeper, but it's your choice; if you've never even met these people, don't bother. Guests staying in suites with butler service should also send $3.50 per day his way. A 15% gratuity is usually included on every bar bill to cover gratuities to bartenders and wine stewards. The captain and other professional officers definitely do not get tips. It'd be like tipping your doctor.

On lines that follow traditional person-to-person gratuity policies, tip your waiter and assistant waiter during the cruise's final dinner, and leave your cabin steward his or her tip on the final night or morning, just before you disembark. Tip spa personnel immediately after they work on you, but note that on some lines (especially those with Steiner spa personnel), the staff will automatically add a tip to your account unless you indicate otherwise, so inquire first before adding one yourself.

DISEMBARKING

It's a good idea to begin packing before dinner on your final night aboard. Be sure to fill out the luggage tags given to you and attach them securely to each piece of baggage. You'll be asked to leave your luggage outside your cabin door by midnight or so, after which service staff will pick it up and spirit it away. Two points here: (1) First-time cruisers always worry about leaving their bags out in public, but we've never heard of anything being stolen; (2) Since the ship's personnel have to get thousands of pieces of luggage into bins and off the ship, don't expect your luggage to be treated gently. Rather than packing bottles of duty-free liquor and other breakables, carry them off the ship yourself.

Once you debark, you'll find your bags waiting for you in the terminal, organized by the colored or numbered tags you attached. Attendants are standing by to help you should your bag not be where it's supposed to be.

Ships normally arrive in port on the final day between 6 and 8am, and need at least 90 minutes to unload baggage and complete docking formalities. So no one disembarks much before 9am, and sometimes it may be 10am before you're allowed to leave the ship, usually according to debarkation numbers assigned based on flight times. (Not surprisingly, suite passengers get expedited debarkation.) Have breakfast. Have coffee. Have patience.

In the cruise ship terminal, claim your luggage and then pass through Customs before exiting. This normally entails handing the officer your filled-out declaration form as you breeze past, without even coming to a full stop. There are generally porters available in the terminals (to whom most people pay at least $1 per bag carried), but you may have to haul your luggage through Customs before you can get to them.

U.S. CUSTOMS

Since you'll be visiting foreign ports on your cruise, you are subject to duty-free purchase allowances and you will have to go through Customs when you return. We've found clearing Customs at U.S. cruise ports painless and speedy for the most part, with officials rarely asking for anything more than your filled-out declaration form as they nod you through. Of course, better safe than sorry: Keep

Getting Married on Board or in Port

If you'd like to have your marriage and honeymoon all in one, you can legally get hitched on many cruises, either aboard ship or at one of your ports of call.

Practically all the mainstream lines offer wedding packages, with Carnival, Princess, and Royal Caribbean being the romance leaders, followed by NCL, Celebrity, Disney, Holland America, and Costa. In almost all cases a local justice of the peace, notary, or minister must officiate, so even if you choose to hold your ceremony aboard ship, it will have to take place while the ship is in port, not at sea. Eight of Princess's ships (the Diamond-, Coral-, and Grand-class ships) have wedding chapels on board, as do Royal Caribbean's Voyager-class ships, Carnival's Spirit-class ships, and NCL's *Norwegian Sun, Star, Dawn,* and *Pride of America.* Other ships hold ceremonies in lounges that are decorated for the occasion.

If you want non-sailing family and friends to attend, you can hold the ceremony and reception at your port of embarkation, before the ship leaves. Guests will be on a special list with port security, though they'll have to bring the requisite ID to board. Ceremonies can also be arranged at various ports of call, including Aruba, Barbados, Grand Cayman, St. Thomas, Sint Maarten, San Juan (Puerto Rico), Ocho Rios and Montego Bay (Jamaica), and Cozumel (Mexico) in the Caribbean; Nassau in The Bahamas; Key West, Florida; and Bermuda. If contemplating marriage in a port of call, remember that your cruise itinerary limits how far afield you can go, since ships generally stay in port for only 3 to 10 hours.

Wedding packages generally start around $750 for shipboard ceremonies, that price usually includes the services of an officiant (though you can bring your own if you prefer), a bouquet and boutonniere, champagne and keepsake glasses, wedding cake with the little bride and groom on top, and the services of a photographer but not the photos themselves—those will cost extra, should you choose to buy them. The $750 package offered by Carnival—one of the big leaders in shipboard weddings—accommodates eight people including the bride and groom. Prices go up from there based on the complexity and size of any reception you want to have (from a simple open bar and hors d'oeuvres to a formal meal in the ship's restaurant). Prices are also higher for off-ship weddings in port. The top base price for a Carnival package is $2,145 for an onboard wedding and 90-minute reception in New York

receipts for all purchases you make abroad. And if you're carrying a particularly new-looking camera or expensive jewelry and are the worrying sort, you may want to consider carrying proof that you purchased these items before your trip. It's unlikely that you'll need it, but it is possible. If you use any medication containing controlled substances or requiring injection, carry an original prescription or a note from your doctor.

Depending on which countries you visited, your **personal exemption** will be $600, $800, or $1,200 worth of items. There are also limits on the amount of or Baltimore, covering bride, groom, and 18 guests. Additional guests can be accommodated at a rate of $24 per person.

THE LEGAL DETAILS   No matter where you choose to wed, you must arrange for a marriage license from the U.S. or foreign port far in advance of the cruise itself. Policies vary from country to country, so you'll save a lot of headaches by having the cruise line help you with the details. When you're arranging your cruise, the line or your travel agent can fill you in on the rules and regulations of your marriage port and assist you with the application form and any other paperwork. Carnival and Princess have actual wedding departments to help you with these matters; other lines handle wedding planning through their guest-relations office or refer you to a wedding consultant with whom they work. Be sure to check with these departments before booking your cruise to be sure wedding space is available on the date you have in mind.

HAVING THE CAPTAIN OFFICIATE   Have your heart set on the big boss performing your marriage rites at sea? If so, you've got only one choice: Princess Cruises' Diamond-, Coral-, and Grand-class are currently the only ships where the captain himself performs about six or seven bona fide, 100% legal civil ceremonies a week. Adorned with fresh flower arrangements as well as ribbons strung along the aisle, the ships' charming wedding chapels are tastefully designed in warm caramel-colored wood tones and stained glass, and there is seating for a few dozen friends and family members. Assistant pursers, decked out in their handsome dress blues, are available to escort a bride down the mini-aisle. Three different ceremony packages are offered, starting at $1,400 per couple. Depending on which you choose, they include photography, video, music, and salon treatments for the bride. And if you've got friends and family on board, reception packages start at $28 per person (for 1 hr.), and include hors d'oeuvres, champagne, and wedding cake. Friends and relatives who aren't sailing can even monitor the wedding courtesy of the ships' chapel web-cams, which broadcast an updated photo every minute or so. (From the Princess website, click on "Ships," then on the misleading "Live Bridge Cams," and then choose one of the wedding chapels.) Don't wait till the last minute if you're considering Princess for your wedding, since there's often a waiting list.

alcoholic beverages (usually 1 liter), cigarettes (1 carton), cigars (100 total, and no Cubans!), and other tobacco products that you may include in your personal duty-free exemption.

The standard personal duty-free allowance for U.S. citizens is $800, an amount that applies to **Mexico** and everywhere else except most Caribbean Basin countries and U.S. insular possessions (the U.S. Virgin Islands, American Samoa, and Guam). In the **Caribbean,** the Customs Service allows U.S. citizens a $600 allowance when returning from Antigua and Barbuda, Aruba, the

Bahamas, Barbados, Belize, Bonaire, the British Virgin Islands, Costa Rica, Curaçao, Dominica, the Dominican Republic, Grenada, the Grenadines, Haiti, Jamaica, Nevis, Panama, Saba, St. Eustatius, St. Kitts, St. Lucia, St. Martin, and Trinidad and Tobago. If you're returning directly from the **U.S. Virgin Islands,** you may bring in $1,200 worth of merchandise duty-free, including 5 liters of alcohol, of which at least 1 liter should be a product of those islands. If you visit only Puerto Rico, you don't have to go through Customs at all, since it's an American commonwealth. Other Caribbean islands (such as the French islands of Guadeloupe and Martinique) fall under the $800 limit.

Since you may be visiting both foreign and U.S.-territory ports, things get more complicated: If, for instance, your cruise stops in the U.S. Virgin Islands and the Bahamas, your total limit is $1,200, of which no more than $600 can be from the Bahamas. Note that you must declare on your Customs form all gifts received during your cruise.

Joint Customs declarations are possible for family members traveling together. For instance, for a husband and wife with two children, total duty-free exemption on goods from the U.S. Virgin Islands is $4,800.

Note that most meat or meat products, fruit, plants, vegetables, or plant-derived products will be seized by U.S. Customs agents unless they're accompanied by an import license from a U.S. government agency.

For more specifics, visit the **U.S. Customs Service** website at www.customs. gov. Canadian citizens should look at the **Canada Border Services Agency** site (www.cbsa-asfc.gc.ca), citizens of the U.K. should visit the **U.K. Customs and Excise** site (www.hmce.gov.uk), Australian citizens should check out the **Australian Customs Service** (www.customs.gov.au), and New Zealand residents should surf to **New Zealand Customs** (www.customs.govt.nz).

The Ports of Embarkation

4

Hands down, the busiest of the ports of embarkation is **Miami,** followed by **Port Everglades** in Fort Lauderdale; **Port Canaveral** at Cape Canaveral, directly east of Orlando; **Tampa,** on Florida's west coast; and **New Orleans,** which is popular for ships sailing to Mexico and the western Caribbean. We profile all of these ports in detail in this chapter. **San Juan, Puerto Rico,** is both a major port of embarkation in the eastern Caribbean and a major port of call, so we include its review in chapter 5. These ports of embarkation are tourist destinations themselves, so most cruise lines now offer special deals so that passengers can extend their vacations with a stay in the port of embarkation either before or after their cruise. These packages, for 2, 3, or 4 days, often offer hotel and car-rental discounts, as well as sightseeing discounts. Have your travel agent or cruise specialist check for the best deals. In this chapter, we describe the major ports of embarkation, tell you how to get to them, and suggest things to see and do there, including shopping and hitting the beach. We also recommend a sampling of restaurants and places to stay.

The big news this year is alternative ports of embarkation, U.S. population centers where the lines are positioning ships to allow passengers to drive rather than fly to their cruise (or, at the least, to allow a wider range of flight options). For the Caribbean, the most significant of these alternative ports are **Galveston, Texas; New York City;** and **Charleston, South Carolina.**

We've included brief descriptions of each of the cities at the end of this chapter.

Note that the hotel prices listed here are winter rates for standard double rooms unless stated otherwise. Prices in the off season will be lower. In addition to the hotels listed in this chapter, the following motel chains have branches in all the mainland port cities unless noted otherwise:

- **Best Western,** (C) 800/780-7234; www.bestwestern.com
- **Clarion,** (C) 877/424-6423; www.clarioninn.com (no Galveston branch; Houston only)
- **Comfort Inn,** (C) 800/424-6423; www.comfortinn.com (no New Orleans branch)
- **Comfort Suites,** (C) 800/424-6423; www.comfortsuites.com
- **Courtyard by Marriott,** (C) 800/321-2211; www.courtyard.com (no Galveston branch; Houston only)
- **Days Inn,** (C) 800/329-7466; www.daysinn.com
- **Doubletree,** (C) 800/222-8733; www.doubletree.com
- **Econo Lodge,** (C) 800/424-6423; www.econolodge.com
- **Holiday Inn,** (C) 800/465-4329; www.holiday-inn.com
- **Howard Johnson,** (C) 800/466-4656; www.hojo.com (no Galveston branch; Houston only)
- **Motel 6,** (C) 800/466-8356; www.motel6.com (no Miami or New York City branch)
- **Quality,** (C) 800/424-6423; www.qualityinn.com (no Galveston branch; Houston only)

- **Red Roof Inns,** © 800/733-7663; www.redroof.com (no Galveston branch; Houston only)

All the ports in this chapter can be reached by train as well as by air and car. Amtrak (© **800/872-7245;** www.amtrak.com) has a New York–Miami route that stops at Miami, Fort Lauderdale, and Orlando (for Cape Canaveral); a New York–Tampa route that stops at Tampa; a Los Angeles–Orlando route that stops at Orlando,

New Orleans, and Houston (for Galveston); and a route from Chicago to New Orleans.

For more information about each destination, check out *Frommer's Florida, Frommer's South Florida, Frommer's New Orleans, Frommer's Puerto Rico, Frommer's New York City, Frommer's Philadelphia & the Amish Country,* and *Frommer's The Carolinas & Georgia.*

1 Miami

The most Latin city in the U.S. offers a hot-hot-hot club scene, sparkling beaches, crystal-clear waters, and more palm fronds, glittering hotels, and red sports cars than you'd find just about anywhere else, save Monte Carlo and Rio de Janeiro maybe. On top of all that, Miami is also the undisputed cruise capital of the world. More cruise ships, especially supersize ones, berth here than anywhere else on earth, and more than three million cruise passengers pass through yearly. Not surprisingly, the city's port facilities are extensive and state of the art, and Miami International Airport is only 8 miles away from the port, about a 15-minute drive.

Industry giants Carnival and Royal Caribbean both have long-term agreements with the port, and to accommodate the influx of new ships over the past few years, Miami has spent $76 million on major improvements to Terminals 3, 4, and 5, and added a 750-space parking facility.

GETTING TO MIAMI & THE PORT

The **Port of Miami** is at 1015 N. America Way, in central Miami. It's on Dodge Island, accessible via a four-lane bridge from the downtown district. For information, call © **305/371-7678** or head online to www.miamidade.gov/port ofmiami.

BY PLANE   Miami International Airport is about 8 miles west of downtown Miami and the port. If you've arranged air transportation and/or transfers through the cruise line, a cruise line rep will meet you at the airport and direct you to shuttle buses to the port. Taxis are also available; the fare is about $21. Some leading taxi companies include **Central Taxicab Service** (© **305/532-5555**), **Diamond Cab Company** (© **305/545-5555**), and **Metro Taxicab Company** (© **305/888-8888**).

SuperShuttle (© **305/871-2000**) charges about $10 per person with two pieces of luggage ($5 each additional piece), for a ride within Dade County, which includes the Port of Miami. Their vans operate 24 hours a day. Call to make a reservation.

BY CAR   The Florida Turnpike (a toll road) and Interstate 95 are the main arteries for those arriving from the north. Continue south on I-95 to I-395 and head east on I-395, exiting at Biscayne Boulevard. Make a right and go south to Port Boulevard. Make a left and go over the Port Bridge. Coming in from the northwest, take Interstate 75 to State Road 826 (Palmetto Expwy.) south to State Road 836 east. Exit at Biscayne Boulevard. Make a right and go south to

ATTRACTIONS & SHOPPING
Art Deco district **5**
Bal Harbour Shops **1**
Bass Museum of Art **4**
Bayside Marketplace **10**
CocoWalk and the
  Streets of Mayfair **12**
Coral Gables Merrick
  House & Gardens **11**
Crandon Park Beach **15**
Lincoln Road shopping **5**
Miami Seaquarium **14**
Miracle Mile **11**
Monkey Jungle **18**
Parrot Jungle Island **17**
Vizcaya Museum & Gardens **13**

ACCOMMODATIONS
The Beach House Bal Harbour **2**
Best Western South Beach **5**
Biltmore Hotel **11**
Biscayne Bay Marriott **10**
The Delano **5**
The Eden Roc Renaissance Resort **3**

Fontainebleau Hilton **3**
The Hotel **6**
Hotel Astor **5**
Hotel Ocean **5**
Hotel Place St. Michel **11**
Indian Creek Hotel **4**
The Kent **5**
Miami Hotel Inter-Continental **10**
Park Washington Hotels **5**
Ritz-Carlton Coconut Grove **12**
Ritz-Carlton Key Biscayne **16**
Shore Club **4**
Sonesta Beach Resort
  Key Biscayne **15**
The Tides **5**
The Townhouse **5**
Wyndham Grand Bay Hotel **12**

DINING & NIGHTLIFE
Aria **16**
Café Nostalgia **8**
Café Tu Tu Tango **12**
Casa Panza Restaurant **8**
ClubSpace **10**

crobar **6**
Forge **3**
Joe's Stone Crab **6**
Joia **6**
Larios on the Beach **6**
Level **6**
Mark's South Beach **6**
Nemo **6**
Nikki Beach Club **6**
Nobu **4**
Norman's **11**
Opium Gardens **6**
Pacific Time **6**
Rose Bar **6**
Rumi **5**
Rusty Pelican **15**
Skybar **4**
Soyka **7**
Spris **6**
Sushi Samba **5**
Tobacco Road **9**
Van Dyke Cafe **6**
Versailles **8**

Port Boulevard. Make a left and go over the Port Bridge. Parking lots right at street level face the cruise terminals. Parking runs $10 per day. Porters can carry your luggage to the terminals.

EXPLORING MIAMI

A sizzling, multicultural mecca, Miami offers cutting-edge restaurants, unusual attractions, entertainment, shopping, beaches, and a whole range of hotels, from luxury to boutique, kitschy to charming. South Beach is a people-watching paradise.

VISITOR INFORMATION   Contact or visit the **Greater Miami Convention and Visitors Bureau,** 701 Brickell Ave., Suite 2700, Miami, FL 33131 (© **888/76-MIAMI** for a free vacation planner and 305/539-3000 for questions), or visit their website at www.gmcvb.com.

GETTING AROUND   See "Getting to Miami & the Port," above, for taxi contact information. The meter starts at $1.50, and ticks up another $2 each mile and 30¢ for each additional minute, with standard flat-rate charges for frequently traveled routes. **Metromover** (© **305/770-3131**), a 4⅓-mile elevated line, circles downtown, stopping near important downtown attractions and shopping and business districts. It runs daily from about 5am to midnight, and is a fun way to see the sights if you've got time to kill. The fare is 25¢.

HITTING THE BEACH

A 300-foot-wide (and that's really wide for a beach) sand beach runs for about 10 miles from the south of Miami Beach to Haulover Beach Park in the north. (For those of you who like to get an all-around tan, Haulover is a known nude beach.) Although most of this stretch is lined with a solid wall of hotels, beach access is plentiful, and you are free to frolic along the entire strip. A wooden boardwalk runs along the hotel side from 21st to 46th streets—about 1½ miles.

You'll find lots of public beach areas along the stretch of beach, wide and well maintained, with lifeguards, toilet facilities, concession stands, and metered parking (bring lots of quarters). There are also public parking garages on 7th and 13th streets. Prices range from $7 to $24. Lifeguard-protected public beaches include 21st Street, at the beginning of the boardwalk; 35th Street, popular with an older crowd; 46th Street, next to the Fontainebleau Hilton; 53rd Street, a narrower, more sedate beach; 64th Street, one of the quietest strips around; and 72nd Street, a local old-timers' spot. At the southern tip of the beach is family-favorite South Pointe Park, where you can watch the cruise ships. Lummus Park, in the center of the Art Deco district, is the best place for people-watching and model spotting. The beach between 11th and 13th streets is popular with the gay crowd. The beach from 1st to 15th streets is popular with seniors.

In Key Biscayne, **Crandon Park,** 4000 Crandon Blvd. (© **305/361-5421**), is one of metropolitan Miami's finest white-sand beaches, stretching for some 3½ miles. There are lifeguards, and you can rent a cabana with a shower and chairs for $20 per day. The beach can be extremely crowded on Saturday and Sunday. Parking nearby is $4 per car and $10 for campers, minivans, SUVs, and buses.

ATTRACTIONS

Miami's finest attraction is a part of the city itself. Located at the southern end of Miami Beach below 20th Street, **South Beach's Art Deco district** is filled with outrageous and fanciful 1920s and 1930s architecture that shouldn't be missed (oh, and the characters strolling about in teeny-tiny beachwear are pretty interesting, too). This treasure-trove, called "the Beach" or "SoBe," features more than 900 pastel, Pez-colored buildings in the Art Deco, Streamline Moderne, and Spanish Mediterranean Revival styles. The district stretches from 6th to 23rd streets, and from the Atlantic Ocean to Lennox Court. Ocean Drive boasts many of the premier Art Deco hotels.

Also in South Beach is the **Bass Museum of Art,** 2121 Park Ave. (© **305/ 673-7530;** www.bassmuseum.org), which has a permanent collection of old masters, along with textiles, period furnishings, objets d'art, ecclesiastical artifacts, and sculpture. Rotating exhibits cover subjects such as pop art, fashion, and photography. The museum is open from 10am to 5pm Tuesday, Wednesday, Friday, and Saturday; 10am to 9pm on Thursday; and 11am to 5pm on Sunday. Admission is $6 for adults, $4 seniors and students.

The adjoining **Coral Gables** and **Coconut Grove** neighborhoods are also fun to visit for their architecture and ambience. In Coral Gables, the Old World meets the new as curving boulevards, sidewalks, plazas, fountains, and arched entrances evoke Seville. Today, the area is an Epicurean's Eden, boasting some of Miami's most renowned eateries as well as the University of Miami and the ½-mile-long Miracle Mile, a 5-block retail mecca (see "Shopping," below). You can even visit the boyhood home of George Merrick, the man who developed Coral Gables. The **Coral Gables Merrick House & Gardens,** 907 Coral Way (© **305/460-5361**), has been restored to its 1920s look and is filled with Merrick memorabilia. At press time, the property was closed for renovation but was expected to reopen in fall 2004. For updates, call the Coral Gables Historical Resources Department at © 305/460-5090.

Coconut Grove, south Florida's oldest settlement, remains a village surrounded by the urban sprawl of Miami. It dates back to the early 1800s, when Bahamian seamen first came to salvage treasure from the wrecked vessels stranded along the Great Florida Reef. Mostly people come here to shop, drink, dine, or simply walk around and explore. Don't miss the **Vizcaya Museum & Gardens,** 3251 S. Miami Ave. (© **305/250-9133;** www.vizcayamuseum.com), a spectacular 70-room Italian Renaissance–style villa. It is open every day except Christmas from 9:30am to 5pm. The $12 admission fee ($5 for children 6–12, children 5 and under are free) includes a guided tour.

THE ANIMAL PARKS Just minutes from the Port of Miami in Key Biscayne, the **Miami Seaquarium,** 4400 Rickenbacker Causeway (© **305/361-5705;** http://miamiseaquarium.com), is a delight. Performing dolphins such as Flipper, TV's greatest sea mammal, perform along with Lolita the Killer Whale. You'll also discover sea lions, a tropical-fish aquarium, and the gruesome shark feeding. The park is open daily from 9:30am to 6pm. Admission is $25 for adults and $20 for children 3 to 9 (free for children under 3).

At **Monkey Jungle,** 14805 SW 216th St., Miami (© **305/235-1611;** www.monkeyjungle.com), the trick is that the visitors are caged and nearly 500 monkeys frolic in freedom and make fun of them. The most talented of these free-roaming primates perform shows daily for the amusement of their guests. Monkey Jungle's site contains one of the richest fossil deposits in south Florida, with some 5,000 specimens. The park is open daily from 9:30am to 5pm. Admission is $16 for adults, $10 for children 3 to 9, and free for children under 3.

Parrot Jungle Island, 1111 Parrot Jungle Trail (© **305/2-JUNGLE;** www.parrotjungle.com), is a botanical garden, wildlife habitat, and bird sanctuary all rolled into one. Children can enjoy a petting zoo and a playground. It's open daily from 10:00am to 6pm. Admission is $24 for adults, $19 for children 3 to 10, and free for children under 3.

ORGANIZED TOURS

BY BOAT   September through May, **Heritage Schooner Cruises** (© 305/442-9697; www.heritageschooner.com) offers daily 2-hour jaunts at 1:30, 4, and 6:30pm aboard the 85-foot schooner *Heritage of Miami II,* departing from the Bayside Marketplace. Tickets cost $20 for adults and $10 for children under 12. On Friday, Saturday, and Sunday evenings, 1-hour tours at 8, 9, 10, and 11pm show off the lights of the city ($15 adults, $10 children).

ON FOOT   An **Art Deco District Walking Tour,** sponsored by the Miami Design Preservation League (© **305/672-2014;** www.mdpl.org), leaves every Thursday at 6:30pm and every Wednesday and Saturday at 10:30am from the Art Deco Welcome Center at 1001 Ocean Dr., Miami Beach. The 90-minute tour costs $15.

SHOPPING

Most cruise ship passengers shop right near the Port of Miami at **Bayside Marketplace,** 401 Biscayne Blvd. (© **305/577-3344;** www.baysidemarketplace. com), a mall with 150 specialty shops, street performers, live music, and some 30 eateries, including a Hard Rock Cafe and restaurants serving everything from Nicaraguan to Italian food. Many restaurants have outdoor seating right along the bay for picturesque views of the yachts harbored there. Bayside Marketplace can be reached via regular shuttle service from the port or by walking over the Port Bridge.

You can find a Miami version of Rodeo Drive at **Bal Harbour Shops,** 9700 Collins Ave. (© **305/866-0311;** www.balharbourshops.com). This complex features big-name stores, from Chanel and Prada to Lacoste and Neiman Marcus (and Florida's largest Saks Fifth Avenue).

In South Beach, **Lincoln Road,** an 8-block pedestrian mall, runs between Washington Avenue and Alton Road, near the northern tier of the Art Deco district. It's filled with popular shops such as Gap and Banana Republic, interior-design stores, art galleries, and even vintage-clothing outlets, as well as coffeehouses, restaurants, and cafes. Despite the recent influx of commercial anchor stores, Lincoln Road still manages to maintain its funky, arty flair, attracting an eclectic, colorful crowd.

Coconut Grove, centered on Main Highway and Grand Avenue, is the heart of the city's boutique district and features two open-air shopping and entertainment complexes, **CocoWalk** (www.cocowalk.com) and the **Streets of Mayfair.**

In Coral Gables, **Miracle Mile,** actually a ½-mile stretch of SW 22nd Street between Douglas and Le Jeune roads (aka 37th and 42nd aves.), features more than 150 shops.

For a change from the fast-paced glitz of South Beach or the serene luxury of Coral Gables, head for Little Havana, where pre-Castro Cubans commingle with the young artists who have begun to set up performance spaces in the area. Little Havana is located just west of downtown Miami on SW 8th Street. In addition to authentic Cuban cuisine, you'll find a lively Cubano cafe culture.

WHERE TO STAY

Thanks to its network of highways, you can stay virtually anywhere in greater Miami and still be within 10 to 20 minutes of your ship.

DOWNTOWN   Two hotels—the 34-story **Hotel Inter-Continental Miami,** 100 Chopin Plaza (© **800/327-3005** or 305/577-1000; www.miami.interconti. com; rates: $199–$269), and the **Biscayne Bay Marriott,** 1633 North Bayshore

(© **800/228-9290** or 305/374-3900; www.marriott.com; rates: $149–$400)—
are right across the bay from the cruise ship piers, near Bayside Marketplace
(p. 46), a mecca of shops and restaurants.

SOUTH BEACH   The Art Deco, comfy-chic **Hotel Astor,** 956 Washington
Ave. (© **800/270-4981** or 305/531-8081; www.hotelastor.com), originally
built in 1936, reopened in 1995 after a massive renovation. In December 2002,
the hotel launched a new restaurant, Metro Kitchen and Bar (which replaced
Astor Place), and also made significant renovations to its guest rooms and public areas. Rates: $145 to $900. The Astor is only 2 blocks from the beach, but if
that's still too far for you, the upscale **Hotel Ocean,** 1230–1238 Ocean Dr.
(© **800/783-1725** or 305/672-2579; www.hotelocean.com) may be the one for
you. Rates: $149 to $280. If you're on a budget but want a cozy Deco feel, try
the **Best Western South Beach,** which comprises four buildings—the Ken-
more, Taft, Belaire, and Davis—right next door to the Astor at 1020–1050
Washington Ave. (© **305/532-1930;** www.bestwestern.com/southbeach).
Rates: $85 to $145. **The Delano,** 1685 Collins Ave. (© **800/555-5001** or 305/
672-2000; www.ianschragerhotels.com), is a sleek, postmodern, self-consciously
hip celebrity hot spot; it's worth at least a peek. Rates: $475 to $675. **The Hotel,**
801 Collins Ave., at the corner of Collins and 8th Street (© **305/531-5796;**
www.thehotelofsouthbeach.com), formerly known as The Tiffany Hotel (until
the folks behind the little blue box threatened to sue) is a Deco gem, and is the
most fashionable hotel on South Beach, thanks to the whimsical interior
designed by haute couturier Todd Oldham. Rates: $275 to $425. **The Townhouse,** 150 20th St. (© **877/534-3800** or 305/534-3800; www.townhousehotel.
com), a funky newcomer with exercise bikes in the hallways and CD players and
dataports in all rooms, caters to young, trendy movers and shakers. Rates: $135
to $195. **The Kent,** 1131 Collins Ave. (© **866/826-5368** or 305/604-5068)
attracts a less upwardly mobile yet no less chic crowd of young, hip travelers.
Rates: $145 to $350 suite. The trendy **Shore Club,** 1901 Collins Ave. (© **877/
640-9500** or 305/695-3100; www.shoreclub.com), is where you'll find Miami's
very first Nobu, a branch of the Japanese restaurant that took Manhattan by
storm some years ago. Rates: $295 to $775.

MIAMI BEACH   At the **Indian Creek Hotel,** 2727 Indian Creek Dr., at 28th
Street (© **800/491-2772** or 305/531-2727; www.indiancreekhotelmb.com),
each room is an homage to the 1930s Art Deco age. Rates: $150 to $170. The
Eden Roc Renaissance Resort, 4525 Collins Ave. (© **800/327-8337** or 305/
531-0000; www.edenrocresort.com; rates: $259–$400), and the **Fontainebleau
Hilton,** next door at 4441 Collins Ave. (© **800/548-8886** or 305/538-2000;
www.fontainebleau.hilton.com; rates: $209–$309), are both popular, updated
1950s resorts that evoke the bygone Rat Pack era, with health clubs, outdoor
swimming pools, and beach access. The **Beach House Bal Harbour,** 9449
Collins Ave., in Surfside (© **877/782-3557** or 305/535-8600; www.rubellhotels.
com/beach.html), brings a taste of Nantucket to Miami with soothing hues,
comfortable furniture, oceanfront views, and a Ralph Lauren–decorated interi-
or. Rates: $155 to $379.

COCONUT GROVE   Near Miami's City Hall and the Coconut Grove
Marina, the **Wyndham Grand Bay Hotel,** 2669 S. Bayshore Dr. (© **305/858-
9600;** www.wyndham.com), overlooks Biscayne Bay. Rates: $179 to $319 suite.
The **Ritz-Carlton Coconut Grove,** 3300 SW 27th Ave. (© **800/241-3333** or
305/644-4680; www.ritzcarlton.com), the third and smallest of Miami's

Ritz-Carlton hotels, is surrounded by 2 acres of tropical gardens and overlooks Biscayne Bay and the Miami skyline. Decorated in an Italian Renaissance style, the hotel's understated luxury is a welcome addition to an area known for its gaudiness. Biscaya Grill is the hotel's extremely elegant restaurant—we're talking footstools for women to put their purses on! Rates: $369 to $479.

CORAL GABLES   The famous **Biltmore Hotel,** 1200 Anastasia Ave. (✆ **800/448-8355** or 305/445-1926; www.biltmorehotel.com), was restored a few years ago, but despite renovations, it still exudes an old-world, stately glamour and is rumored to be haunted by ghosts of travel days past. Rates: $339 to $509. The **Hotel Place St. Michel,** 162 Alcazar Ave. (✆ **800/848-HOTEL** or 305/444-1666; www.hotelplacestmichel.com), is a three-story establishment reminiscent of an inn in provincial France. Rates: $165.

KEY BISCAYNE   The **Sonesta Beach Resort Key Biscayne,** 350 Ocean Dr. (✆ **800/SONESTA** or 305/361-2021; www.sonesta.com/keybiscayne), offers relative isolation from the rest of congested Miami. Rates: $319 to $359. The **Ritz-Carlton, Key Biscayne,** 455 Grand Bay Dr. (✆ **800/241-3333** or 305/365-4500; www.ritzcarlton.com), offers a to-die-for spa, not to mention stunning ocean views. Rates: $359 to $709 suite.

WHERE TO DINE
DOWNTOWN   Up Biscayne Boulevard near the burgeoning Miami Design District is **Soyka,** 5556 NE 4th Court (✆ **305/759-3117**), the hip downtown sibling of South Beach's News and Van Dyke cafes, serving American food. Dinner main courses: $11 to $30.

SOUTH BEACH   Join the celebs and models for pan-Asian cuisine at **Nemo,** 100 Collins Ave. (✆ **305/532-4550**). Dinner main courses: $24 to $36. Take time to stroll down the pedestrian mall on Lincoln Road, which offers art galleries, specialty shops, and several excellent outdoor cafes such as **Spris,** a pizzeria at 731 Lincoln Rd. (✆ **305/673-2020**), and the **Van Dyke Cafe,** 846 Lincoln Rd. (✆ **305/534-3600**). Prices at Spris range from $5 to $14, main courses at the Van Dyke from $10 to $20. The standout culinary trendsetter on Lincoln Road is **Pacific Time,** 915 Lincoln Rd. (✆ **305/534-5979**), where you can enjoy a taste of the Pacific Rim with a deliciously modern South Beach twist. Dinner main courses: $24 to $32. The newest haute eateries-cum-lounges imported from New York (or at least inspired by the city's hot spots) include **Rumi,** 330 Lincoln Rd. (✆ **305/672-4353;** www.rumimiami.com), which was inspired by Lotus—Manhattan's restaurant of the moment—and overflows with mirrors, mushy couches, and even a queen-size Murphy bed (dinner main courses $18–$30); **Sushi Samba,** 600 Lincoln Rd. (✆ **305/673-5337**), which features a delectable fusion of South American and Japanese cuisine (dinner main courses $14–$39; sushi priced by the piece); and **Nobu,** 1901 Collins Ave. (✆ **305/695-3232**), the revered name in nouvelle Japanese cuisine. Dinner main courses: $28 to $80.

At the legendary **Joe's Stone Crab,** 11 Washington Ave., between South Point Drive and 1st Street (✆ **305/673-0365**), about a ton of stone-crab claws are served daily during stone-crab season from October to May (the joint is usually closed May 15–Oct 15), and people are kept waiting for up to 2 hours for a table. Crab prices vary depending on the market rate, but start around $23 per order. If the sky's the limit in the budget department, try **Mark's South Beach** in the Hotel Nash, 1120 Collins Ave. (✆ **305/604-9050**), for fine dishes such as slow-roasted salmon with horseradish. Dinner main courses: $28 to $46.

Even if Gloria Estefan weren't co-owner of **Larios on the Beach,** 820 Ocean Dr. (© **305/532-9577**), the crowds would still flock to this bistro, which serves old-fashioned Cuban dishes such as *masitas de puerco* (fried pork chunks). Dinner main courses: $11 to $25.

COCONUT GROVE   If you want to people-watch while you eat, head for **Café Tu Tu Tango,** 3015 Grand Ave., Suite 250 (© **305/529-2222**), on the second floor of CocoWalk. Designed to look like a disheveled artist's loft, it has original paintings (some half-finished) on easels or hanging from the walls. The tapas courses range from $6 to $10.

CORAL GABLES   **Norman's,** 21 Almeria Ave. (© **305/446-6767**), possibly the best restaurant in the entire city of Miami, is run by its namesake, Norman Van Aken, a James Beard–award winning chef and pioneer of New World and Floribbean cuisine. Dinner main courses: $29 to $40.

KEY BISCAYNE   The surf and turf is routine at the **Rusty Pelican,** 3201 Rickenbacker Causeway (© **305/361-3818**), but it's worth a visit for a drink and to catch the spectacular sunset view. Dinner main courses: $17 to $38. **Aria,** 455 Grand Bay Dr., at the Ritz-Carlton (© **800/241-3333** or 305/365-4500), serves gorgeous (not to mention delicious) Mediterranean fare. Dinner main courses: $20 to $40.

LITTLE HAVANA   Little Havana offers excellent Spanish and Cuban cuisine. **Casa Panza Restaurant,** 1620 SW 8th St. (© **305/643-5343**), a taste of old Seville in Little Havana, is a feast for the senses with flamenco dancers, tempting tapas, and a lively atmosphere that reels in crowds nightly. At 11pm, everyone, no matter what their religion, is given a candle to pray to La Virgen del Rocio, one of Seville's most revered saints—it's a party with piety! Dinner main courses: $10 to $16. Another place to check out is **Versailles,** 3555 SW 8th St. (© **305/444-0240**), a late-night (open till 2am Sun–Fri, 4am Sat), palatial, mirrored diner serving all the Cuban mainstays in large and reasonably priced portions. Dinner main courses: $9 to $22.

MIAMI AFTER DARK

Miami's nightlife is as varied as its population, and the sizzling scene is no stranger to A-list celebrities from Leonardo DiCaprio and Gwyneth Paltrow to Al Pacino, Sylvester Stallone, and Madonna. Look for the klieg lights to direct you to the hot spots of South Beach. While the blocks of Washington Avenue, Collins Avenue, and Ocean Drive are the main nightlife thoroughfares, you're more likely to spot a celebrity in a off-the-beaten-path eatery such as **Joia,** 150 Ocean Dr. (© **305/674-8871**), a popular, chic Italian restaurant with a new upstairs lounge called Pure Lounge, where you can sip martinis among the beautiful people; or **The Forge,** 432 41st St. (© **305/538-8533**), an ornately decorated rococo-style steakhouse boasting one of the finest wine selections around. Dinner main courses: $22 to $65.

Restaurants and bars are open late—usually until 5am. Hotel bars are very popular, particularly Delano's **Rose Bar** (see p. 47 for Delano information) and the Shore Club's hot, hauter-than-thou celeb magnet **Skybar,** 1901 Collins Ave. (© **877/640-9500** or 305/695-3100; www.shoreclub.com). Command central for the chic elite at all hours of the night include the restaurants-cum-lounges Rumi, Sushi Samba, and Nobu, listed in the "Where to Dine" section.

As trends come and go, so do clubs, so before you head out for a decadent night of disco, make sure the place is still in business! At press time, some of the clubs at which to see, be seen, and, of course, dance, include **Crobar,** 1445 Washington Ave. (© **305/531-5027**); **Level,** 1235 Washington Ave. (© **305/ 532-1525**); and **Opium Gardens,** 136 Collins Ave. (© **305/531-5535**), an open-air nightclub that's a magnet for the trendoid brass (be sure to check out the hot new V-VIP lounge, called Privé). For a Playboy Mansion–type scene by day, check out the **Nikki Beach Club,** 1 Ocean Dr. (© **305/538-1111**), complete with tiki huts and teepees.

But South Beach isn't the only place for nightlife in Miami. Not too far from the Miami River is the city's oldest bar, **Tobacco Road,** 626 S. Miami Ave. (© **305/374-1198**), a gritty place that still attracts some of the city's storied, pre–Miami Vice natives. **ClubSpace,** 142 NE 11th St. (© **305/372-9378**), occupies a very large warehouse in downtown Miami and is vaguely reminiscent of a funky, SoHo-style dance palace. Down in Little Havana is **Café Nostalgia,** 2212 SW 8th St. (© **305/541-2631**), where salsa is not a condiment but a way of life.

Other nocturnal options abound in Coconut Grove and Coral Gables and, slowly but surely, the Downtown/Design District areas. Check the *Miami Herald, Miami New Times,* and www.miami.citysearch.com for specific events.

2 Fort Lauderdale

Broward County's Port Everglades is the second-busiest cruise port in the world, drawing more than three million cruise passengers a year. It boasts the deepest harbor on the eastern seaboard south of Norfolk, 12 ultramodern cruise ship terminals, and an easy access route to the Fort Lauderdale–Hollywood International Airport, less than a 10-minute drive away.

The port itself is fairly free of congestion, offering covered loading zones, drop-off and pickup staging, and curbside baggage handlers. Terminals are comfortable and safe, with seating areas, snack bars, lots of taxis, clean restrooms, and plenty of pay phones. Parking lots have recently been expanded to offer a total of 4,500 spaces.

GETTING TO FORT LAUDERDALE & THE PORT

Port Everglades is located about 23 miles north of Miami within the city boundaries of Fort Lauderdale, Hollywood, and Dania Beach. I-595 will take you right onto the grounds. For information, contact **Port Everglades** (© **954/523-3404;** www.broward.org/port).

BY AIR Small and extremely user friendly, the **Fort Lauderdale–Hollywood International Airport** (© **954/359-6100**) is less than 2 miles from Port Everglades (5 min. by bus or taxi), making this the easiest airport-to-cruiseport trip in Florida. (Port Canaveral, by contrast, is about a 45-min. drive from the Orlando airport.) If you've booked air or transfers through the cruise line, a representative will show you to your shuttle bus after you land at the airport. If you haven't, taking a taxi to the port costs less than $10.

BY CAR The port has three passenger entrances: Spangler Boulevard, an extension of State Road 84 East; Eisenhower Boulevard, running south from the 17th Street Causeway/A1A; and Eller Drive, connecting directly with Interstate 595. Interstate 595 runs east-west, with connections to the Fort Lauderdale–Hollywood Airport, Interstate 95, State Road 7 (441), Florida's Turnpike, Sawgrass Expressway, and Interstate 75. Parking is available at the port in two large garages. The 2,500-space Northport Parking Garage, next to the Greater Fort Lauderdale/Broward County Convention Center, serves

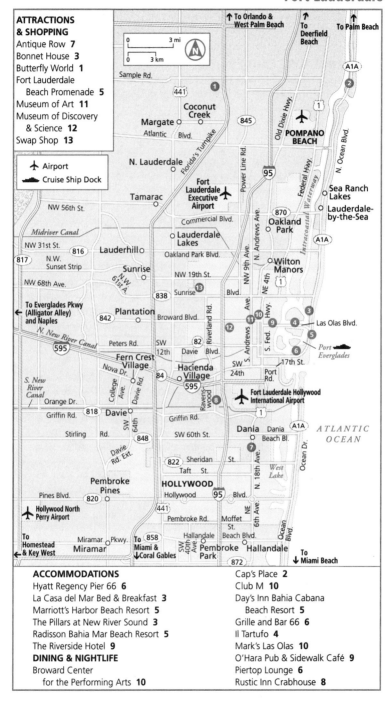

ATTRACTIONS & SHOPPING

Antique Row **7**
Bonnet House **3**
Butterfly World **1**
Fort Lauderdale
Beach Promenade **5**
Museum of Art **11**
Museum of Discovery
& Science **12**
Swap Shop **13**

✈ Airport
🚢 Cruise Ship Dock

ACCOMMODATIONS

Hyatt Regency Pier 66 **6**
La Casa del Mar Bed & Breakfast **3**
Marriott's Harbor Beach Resort **5**
The Pillars at New River Sound **3**
Radisson Bahia Mar Beach Resort **5**
The Riverside Hotel **9**

DINING & NIGHTLIFE

Broward Center
for the Performing Arts **10**

Cap's Place **2**
Club M **10**
Day's Inn Bahia Cabana
Beach Resort **5**
Grille and Bar 66 **6**
Il Tartufo **4**
Mark's Las Olas **10**
O'Hara Pub & Sidewalk Café **9**
Piertop Lounge **6**
Rustic Inn Crabhouse **8**

Terminals 1, 2, and 4. The 2,000-space Midport Parking Garage serves Terminals 18, 19, 21, 22, 24, 25, and 26. Garages are well lit, security patrolled, and designed to accommodate RVs and buses. The 24-hour parking fee is $12 daily.

EXPLORING FORT LAUDERDALE

Fort Lauderdale Beach, a 5-mile strip along Florida A1A, gained fame in the 1950s as a spring-break playground, popularized by the movie *Where the Boys Are.* But in the 1980s, partying college kids (who brought the city more mayhem than money) began to be less welcome, as Fort Lauderdale sought to attract a more mainstream, affluent crowd, a task at which it has largely been successful.

In addition to miles of beautiful wide beaches, Fort Lauderdale has more than 300 miles of navigable natural waterways, as well as innumerable artificial canals that permit thousands of residents to anchor boats in their backyards (and which has led the city's nickname: "Venice of the Americas"). You can easily get onto the water by renting a boat or hiring a private, moderately priced water taxi.

VISITOR INFORMATION   The **Greater Fort Lauderdale Convention & Visitors Bureau,** 1850 Eller Dr., Suite 303, Fort Lauderdale, FL 33316 (✆ **954/765-4466;** www.sunny.org), is an excellent resource, distributing a comprehensive guide on accommodations, events, and sightseeing in Broward County.

GETTING AROUND   For a taxi, call **Yellow Cab** (✆ **954/565-5400**). Rates start at $2.75 for the first mile and $2 for each additional mile. **Broward County Mass Transit** (✆ **954/357-8400**) runs bus service throughout the county. One-day passes are $2.50. **Water Taxi** (✆ **954/467-6677;** www.water taxi.com) offers all-day passes for $5.

HITTING THE BEACH

Backed by an endless row of hotels, and popular with visitors and locals alike, the **Fort Lauderdale Beach Promenade** underwent a $30 million renovation not long ago, and it looks marvelous. The beach is located along A1A, also known as the Fort Lauderdale Beach Boulevard, between SE 17th Street and Sunrise Boulevard. The fabled strip from *Where the Boys Are* is **Ocean Boulevard,** between Las Olas and Sunrise boulevards. On weekends, parking at the oceanside meters is difficult to find.

Fort Lauderdale Beach at the Howard Johnson is a perennial local favorite. A jetty bounds the beach on the south side, making it rather private, although the water gets a little choppy. High-school and college students share this area with an older crowd. One of the main beach entrances is at 4660 N. Ocean Dr. in Lauderdale-by-the-Sea.

ATTRACTIONS

The **Museum of Discovery & Science,** 401 SW Second St. (✆ **954/467-6637;** www.mods.org), is an excellent interactive science museum with an IMAX theater. Check out the 52-foot-tall "Great Gravity Clock" in the museum's atrium. Admission is $14 for adults, $12 for children, and $13 for seniors and students. It's open from 10am to 5pm Monday through Saturday, Sunday noon to 6pm.

The **Museum of Art,** 1 E. Las Olas Blvd. (✆ **954/763-6464;** www.moafl. org), is a truly terrific small museum whose permanent collection of 20th-century European and American art includes works by Picasso, Calder, Warhol, Mapplethorpe, Dalí, Stella, and William Glackens. African, South Pacific, pre-Columbian, Native American, and Cuban art are also on display. Admission is $7 for adults, $6 for seniors, and $5 for students. Kids under 6 are free. The museum is open 10am to 5pm Tuesday through Saturday and noon to 5pm on Sunday.

Bonnet House, 900 N. Birch Rd. (© **954/563-5393;** www.bonnethouse. org), a plantation-style home and 35-acre estate, survives in the middle of an otherwise highly developed beachfront condominium area, offering a glimpse into the lives of Fort Lauderdale's pioneers. Guided tours are offered Wednesday through Sunday. From December through April, hours are 10am to 4pm. From May to November, hours are 10am to 3pm. Bonnet House is closed for tours on Monday and Tuesday. Cost is $10 adults, $9 seniors, $8 students, and free for children under 6.

Butterfly World, Tradewinds Park South, 3600 W. Sample Rd., Coconut Creek, west of the Florida Turnpike (© **954/977-4400;** www.butterflyworld. com), is home to more than 150 species of butterfly. In the park's walk-through, screened-in aviary, visitors can watch newly hatched butterflies emerge from their cocoons and flutter around as they learn to fly. It's open from 9am to 5pm Monday through Saturday and 1 to 5pm Sunday. Admission is $16 adults, $11 kids 4 to 12, and free for kids under 4.

ORGANIZED TOURS

BY BOAT   The Mississippi-style riverboat **Jungle Queen,** Bahia Mar Yacht Center, Florida A1A (© **954/462-5596;** www.junglequeen.com), is one of Fort Lauderdale's best-known attractions. Dinner cruises and 3-hour sightseeing tours take visitors up the New River past Millionaires' Row, Old Fort Lauderdale, the new downtown, and the Port Everglades cruise ship port. Call for prices and departure times.

Water Taxis of Fort Lauderdale, 651 Seabreeze Blvd. (© **954/467-6677;** www.watertaxi.com), operates a fleet of old port boats that offer taxi service on demand around this city of canals, carrying up to 72 passengers each. You can be picked up at your hotel and shuttled to the dozens of restaurants and bars on the route for the rest of the night. The service operates daily from 6:30am to midnight. The cost is $4 per person per trip, $5 for a full day. Opt for the all-day pass—it's worth it.

SHOPPING

Not counting the discount "fashion" stores on Hallandale Beach Boulevard, there are a few places visitors should know about, including **Antique Row,** a strip of U.S. 1 around North Dania Beach Boulevard (in Dania, about 1 mile south of Fort Lauderdale–Hollywood International Airport) that holds about 200 antiques shops. Most shops are closed Sunday.

The Swap Shop, 3291 W. Sunrise Blvd. (© **954/791-SWAP;** www.florida swapshop.com), is one of the world's largest flea markets. In addition to endless acres of vendors, there's a miniamusement park, a 13-screen drive-in movie theater, and even a free circus, complete with elephants, horse shows, high-wire acts, and clowns. It's open daily.

WHERE TO STAY

Fort Lauderdale Beach has a hotel or motel on nearly every block, and the selection ranges from run-down to luxurious.

Located very close to the port, the **Hyatt Regency Pier 66,** 2301 SE 17th St. (© **800/233-1234** or 954/525-6666; www.pier66.hyatt.com), is a circular landmark with larger rooms than some equivalently priced hotels in town. Its famous Piertop Lounge, a revolving bar on the roof, is often filled with cruise ship patrons. Rates: $219 to $259.

Located just south of Fort Lauderdale's strip, **Marriott's Harbor Beach Resort,** 3030 Holiday Dr. ((C) **800/222-6543** or 954/525-4000; www.marriott harborbeach.com), is set on 16 acres of beachfront property. Most rooms have private balconies overlooking either the ocean or the Intracoastal Waterway. Rates: $349 to $429.

Radisson Bahia Mar Beach Resort, 801 Seabreeze Blvd. ((C) **800/327-8154** or 954/764-2233; www.radisson.com/ftlauderdalefl), is scattered over 42 acres of sea coast. The 4-story and 16-story row of units is adjacent to Florida's largest marina. Rates: $199 to $410. **The Riverside Hotel,** 620 E. Las Olas Blvd. ((C) **800/325-3280** or 954/467-0671; www.riversidehotel.com), which opened in 1936, is a local favorite. Try for one of the ground-floor rooms, which have higher ceilings and more space. Rates: $129.

The Spanish Mediterranean–style **La Casa del Mar Bed & Breakfast,** 3003 Granada St. ((C) **954/467-2037;** www.lacasadelmar.com), has 10 individually furnished rooms and is only a block away from Fort Lauderdale Beach. Rates: $110 to $145. The **Pillars at New River Sound,** 111 N. Birch Rd. ((C) **800/ 800-7666** or 954/467-9639; www.pillarshotel.com), is a small 23-room hotel, the best of its size in the region. Rates: $169 to $199. Several **Best Western** hotels (www.bestwestern.com) in the area are reasonably priced and within 5 miles of the airport and port: Best Western Inn, 1221 W S.R. 84 ((C) 800/528-1234 or 954/462-7005; rates: $99–$199); Best Western Marina Inn & Yacht Harbor, 2150 SE 17th St. ((C) **800/327-1390** or 954/525-3484; rates: $89–$129); and Best Western Oceanside Inn, 1180 Seabreeze Blvd. ((C) **800/ 367-1007** or 954/525-8115; rates: $109–$119). Call the **Greater Fort Lauderdale** Convention & Visitors Bureau ((C) **954/765-4466;** www.sunny.org) for a copy of *Superior Small Lodgings,* a guide to small accommodations in the area.

WHERE TO DINE

Cap's Place, 2765 NE 28th Court ((C) **954/941-0418;** www.capsplace.com), is a famous old-time seafood joint, offering good food at reasonable prices. The restaurant is on a peninsula, so you get a ferry ride over (see their website for directions). Dolphin (not the mammal but a local saltwater fish also known as mahimahi) and snapper are popular and, like the other meat and pasta dishes here, can be prepared any way you want. Dinner main courses: $14 to $33.

Il Tartufo, 2400 E. Las Olas Blvd. ((C) **954/767-9190**), serves oven-roasted specialties and Italian standards, plus a selection of fish baked in rock salt. Dinner main courses: $15 to $22. **Grille and Bar 66,** 2301 SE 17th St. ((C) **954/ 728-3500**), serves steak, seafood, and pasta dishes at affordable prices. Dinner main courses: $14 to $48.

Mark's Las Olas, 1032 E. Las Olas Blvd. ((C) **954/463-1000**), is the showcase of Miami restaurant mogul Mark Militello. The continental gourmet menu changes daily and may include white duck with sweet-potato-and-vanilla-bean purée and a superb sushi-quality tuna. Dinner main courses: $14 to $46.

Garlic crabs are the specialty at the **Rustic Inn Crabhouse,** 4331 Anglers Ave. ((C) **954/584-1637**), located west of the airport. This riverside dining choice has an open deck over the water. Dinner main courses: $12 to $29.

The restaurant and patio bar at the **Day's Inn Bahia Cabana Beach Resort,** 3001 Harbor Dr./A1A ((C) **954/524-1555;** www.bahiacabanaresort.com), are charming and laid-back, serving inexpensive American-style dishes on a covered open-air deck overlooking Fort Lauderdale's largest marina. The Fort Lauderdale water taxi makes a stop here. Dinner main courses: $10 to $17.

FORT LAUDERDALE AFTER DARK

From the area's most famous bar, the revolving **Piertop Lounge,** in the Hyatt Regency at Pier 66 (© **954/525-6666**), you'll get a 360-degree panoramic view of Fort Lauderdale. The bar completes a revolution every 66 minutes, and has a dance floor and live music, including blues and jazz.

On weekends, pack yourself into **Club M,** 2037 Hollywood Blvd. (© **954/ 925-8396**), one of the area's busiest music bars, featuring live bands playing blues, rock, and jazz.

O'Hara Pub & Sidewalk Café, 722 E. Las Olas Blvd. (© **954/524-1764**), is often crammed with a trendy crowd that comes to listen to live R & B, pop, blues, and jazz. Call their jazz hot line (© **954/524-2801**) to hear the lineup.

The **Broward Center for the Performing Arts,** 201 SW Fifth Ave. (© **954/ 462-0222;** www.browardcenter.org), hosts top opera, symphony, dance, and Broadway productions. Call the 24-hour **Arts Entertainment Hotline** (© **954/ 357-5700**) for schedules and performers, or look for listings in the *Sun-Sentinel* or the *Miami Herald.*

3 Cape Canaveral & Cocoa Beach

Known as the "Space Coast" because of nearby Kennedy Space Center, the Cape Canaveral/Cocoa Beach area boasts 72 miles of beaches, plus fishing, golfing, surfing, and close proximity to Orlando's theme parks, which are only about an hour west—this is exactly why long-underutilized Port Canaveral is now busier than ever before, offering many 3- and 4-night cruise options (often sold as packages with pre- or postcruise visits to the Orlando resorts) as well as weeklong itineraries. This year, Port Canaveral has even become a port of call, with NCL's *Norwegian Dawn* visiting on round-trip Florida/Caribbean itineraries from New York.

Outside the port area, Cape Canaveral is . . . well, it's no Miami. Highways, strip malls, chain stores, and tracts of suburban homes predominate from the port area south into Cocoa Beach, where most of the hotels, restaurants, and beaches discussed here are located. The central areas of Cocoa Beach are mildly more interesting, with some great '50s and '60s condo and hotel architecture, but stylish they're not.

GETTING TO CAPE CANAVERAL & THE PORT

Port Canaveral is located at the eastern end of the Bennett Causeway, just off State Road 528 (the Bee Line Expwy.), the direct route from Orlando. From the port, the 528 turns sharply south and becomes State Road A1A, portions of which are known as Astronaut Boulevard and North Atlantic Avenue. For information about the port, contact the **Canaveral Port Authority** (© **888/767-8226** or 321/783-7831; www.portcanaveral.org).

BY AIR The nearest airport is the **Orlando International Airport** (© **407/ 825-2001;** www.orlandoairports.net), a 45-mile drive from Port Canaveral via the State Road 528 Bee Line Expressway. Cruise line representatives will meet you at the airport if you've booked air and/or transfers through the line. **Cocoa Beach Shuttle** (© **800/633-0427** or 321/784-3831) offers shuttle service between Orlando's airport and Port Canaveral; the trip costs $22 per person each way.

BY CAR Port Canaveral and Cocoa Beach are about 45 miles east of Orlando and 186 miles north of Miami. They're accessible from virtually every interstate highway along the East Coast. Most visitors arrive via Route 1, Interstate 95, or State Road 528. At the port, park in the North Lots for north terminals nos. 5 and 10 and the South Lots for nos. 2, 3, or 4. Parking costs $10 a day for vehicles up to 20 feet, $20 a day for vehicles 20 feet and over.

EXPLORING CAPE CANAVERAL & COCOA BEACH

Port Canaveral probably wouldn't be on the cruise industry's radar if it weren't so close to Orlando; most passengers shuttle directly from theme park to pier rather than spending any significant time here. Nevertheless, anyone interested in the space program and its history should plan to arrive a day early (or stay a day after) to check out Kennedy Space Center and the Astronaut Hall of Fame.

VISITOR INFORMATION   Contact the **Florida Space Coast Office of Tourism,** 8810 Astronaut Blvd./A1A, Suite 102, Cape Canaveral, FL 32920 (© **800/872-1969** or 321/868-1126; fax 321/868-1139; www.space-coast.com). Their office is in the Sheldon Cove building, right on the corner of Central Boulevard and the A1A, and is open Monday to Friday from 8am to 5pm.

GETTING AROUND   For taxis, call **Brevard Yellow Cab** (© **321/723-1234**).

THE ORLANDO THEME PARKS

All it took was a sprinkle of pixie dust in the 1970s to begin the almost-magical transformation of Orlando from a large swath of swampland into the most visited tourist destination in the world. Today, the city is home to three giants— Walt Disney World, Universal Orlando, and SeaWorld, and to seven of the eight most popular theme parks in the United States.

Many cruises from Port Canaveral are sold as land-sea packages that include park stays; if you decide to visit Orlando before or after your cruise, it's essential to plan ahead. Otherwise, the number of attractions begging for your time and the hypercommercial atmosphere can put a serious dent in your psyche as well as your wallet and stamina. Even if you had 2 weeks, it wouldn't be long enough to hit everything, so don't even try. Stay selective, stay sane. That's our motto.

It would take a significant portion of this book to detail everything to do in Orlando, but we list some basic information on the major theme parks below. If you plan to spend a considerable amount of time here, we suggest picking up a copy of *Frommer's Walt Disney World & Orlando.*

WALT DISNEY WORLD

Walt Disney World is the umbrella above four theme parks: the Magic Kingdom, Epcot, Disney–MGM Studios, and Animal Kingdom, which combined drew over 37 million guests in 2002 despite a decline in international visitors, according to *Amusement Business* magazine. Besides its theme parks, Disney has an assortment of other attractions, including three water parks, several entertainment venues, and a number of shopping spots.

VISITOR INFORMATION   Walt Disney World is located southwest of Orlando off Interstate 4, west of the Florida Turnpike. For information, vacation brochures, and videos, call © 407/934-7639; for general information, call © 407/824-2222 or visit **www.disneyworld.com.**

TICKET PRICES   At press time, **1-day/1-park tickets,** for admission to the Magic Kingdom, Epcot, Animal Kingdom, or Disney-MGM, were $54 for adults, $45 for children 3 to 9, and free for children under 3. Discounted multiday, multipark passes are available, and many land-sea cruise packages include these passes.

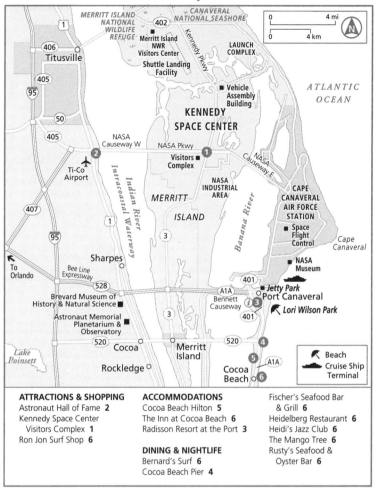

ATTRACTIONS & SHOPPING
Astronaut Hall of Fame **2**
Kennedy Space Center
   Visitors Complex **1**
Ron Jon Surf Shop **6**

ACCOMMODATIONS
Cocoa Beach Hilton **5**
The Inn at Cocoa Beach **6**
Radisson Resort at the Port **3**

DINING & NIGHTLIFE
Bernard's Surf **6**
Cocoa Beach Pier **4**

Fischer's Seafood Bar
   & Grill **6**
Heidelberg Restaurant **6**
Heidi's Jazz Club **6**
The Mango Tree **6**
Rusty's Seafood &
   Oyster Bar **6**

OPERATING HOURS   Park hours vary and are influenced by special events and the economy, so call ahead or go to www.disneyworld.com to check. Generally, expect Animal Kingdom to be open from 8 or 9am to 5 or 6pm; Epcot to be open 10am to 9pm; and Magic Kingdom and Disney-MGM to be open 9am to 5 or 7pm. All may open or close earlier or later.

The Parks
MAGIC KINGDOM   The most popular theme park on the planet offers some 40 attractions, plus restaurants and shops, in a 107-acre package. Its symbol, Cinderella Castle, forms the hub of a wheel whose spokes reach to seven "lands" simulating everything from an Amazonian jungle to colonial America. If you're traveling with little kids, this is the place to go.

EPCOT   This 260-acre park (the acronym stands for Experimental Prototype Community of Tomorrow) has two sections. **Future World** is centered on Epcot's icon, a giant geosphere that looks like a big golf ball. Major corporations sponsor the park's 10 themed areas, and the focus is on discovery, scientific achievements, and tomorrow's technologies in areas ranging from energy to undersea exploration. The **World Showcase** is a community of 11 miniaturized nations surrounding a 40-acre lagoon. All of these "countries" have indigenous architecture, landscaping, restaurants, and shops; and cultural facets are explored in art exhibits, dance or other live performances, and innovative films. This park definitely appeals more to adults than children. It has few thrill rides, so if that's a requirement, go elsewhere. *Note:* Hiking through this park will often exhaust even the fittest person—some folks say Epcot really stands for "Every Person Comes Out Tired"—so we recommend splitting your visit over 2 days if possible.

DISNEY–MGM STUDIOS   You'll probably spy the Earful Tower—a water tower outfitted with gigantic mouse ears—before you enter this 110-acre park, which Disney bills as "the Hollywood that never was and always will be." You'll find pulse-quickening rides such as the Aerosmith-themed **Rock 'n' Roller Coaster** and the **Twilight Zone of Terror,** and movie- and TV-themed shows such as **Jim Henson's Muppet*Vision 3D,** as well as some wonderful street performers. Adults and kids both love it, and, best of all, it can be done comfortably in 1 day.

ANIMAL KINGDOM   This 500-acre park opened in 1998, combining animals, elaborate landscapes, and a handful of rides. It's a conservation venue as much as an attraction, so it's easy for most of the animals to escape your eyes here (unlike at Tampa's Busch Gardens, the state's other major animal park). The thrill rides are better at Busch, but Animal Kingdom has much better shows, such as **Tarzan Rocks!** and **Festival of the Lion King.** The park is good for both adults and children and can be done in a single outing, but if you come on a hot summer day, come early or it's unlikely you'll see many of the primo animals, who are smart enough to seek shade.

UNIVERSAL ORLANDO

Universal Orlando is Disney World's number-one competitor in the ongoing Orlando-area "anything you can do we can do better" theme brawl. Although it's a distant second in terms of attendance, it's unquestionably the champion at entertaining teenagers and the older members of the thrill-ride crowd, with two major parks—the original Universal Studios Florida and the newer Islands of Adventure—plus an entertainment district and several resorts.

VISITOR INFORMATION   Located at Universal Boulevard, Orlando, off Interstate 4. For information, call © **800/837-2273** or 407/363-8000, or visit www.universalorlando.com.

TICKET PRICES   A **1-day/1-park** ticket costs $54 (plus 6% sales tax!) for adults, $45 for children 3 to 9; a **Universal Orlando Bonus Pass** gets you 5 consecutive days at Universal Studios and Islands of Adventure for $90 for adults, $77 for children 3 to 9 (available online only).

OPERATING HOURS   The parks are open 365 days a year, generally from 9am to 6pm, though often later, especially in summer and around holidays, when they're sometimes open until 9pm. Call before you go for hours on the days you're visiting.

The Parks

UNIVERSAL STUDIOS FLORIDA   Even with fast-paced, grown-up rides such as **Back to the Future, Terminator,** and **Men in Black Alien Attack,** Universal Studios Florida is fun for kids. It's also a working motion-picture and TV studio, so filming is often going on at Nickelodeon's sound stages or elsewhere in the park. A talented group of actors portraying a range of characters from Universal films usually roam the park. You can do the park in a day, although you'll be a bit breathless when you get to the finish line.

ISLANDS OF ADVENTURE   This 110-acre theme park opened in 1999 and is, bar none, *the* Orlando theme park for thrill-ride junkies. With areas themed on Dr. Seuss, Jurassic Park, and Marvel comics, the park successfully combines nostalgia with state-of-the-art technology. Roller coasters roar above pedestrian walkways and water rides slice through the park. The **Amazing Adventures of Spider-Man** is a 3-D track ride that is arguably the best all-around attraction in Orlando; the **Jurassic Park River Adventure**'s 70-foot drop scared creator Steven Spielberg into jumping ship before going over; and **Dueling Dragons** draws more raves from coaster crazies than any other in Orlando. Unless it's the height of high season, the park can be done in a day. It is not, however, a park for families with young kids: Nine of the park's 14 major rides have height restrictions. If, however, you have teens or are an adrenaline junkie, this is definitely the place for you.

SEAWORLD

A 200-acre marine-life park, SeaWorld explores the deep in a format that combines conservation awareness with entertainment—pretty much what Disney is attempting at Animal Kingdom, but SeaWorld got here first, and its message is subtler and a more integrated part of the experience. The park is fun for everyone from small children to adults (who doesn't like dolphins and whales?) and is easily toured in a single day. The pace is much more laid-back than at Universal or Disney, so it makes for a nice break if you're in the area for several days. SeaWorld has a handful of high-tech roller coasters such as **Journey to Atlantis** and **Kraken,** but all in all, the park can't compete in this category with Disney and Universal. On the other hand, those parks don't let you discover the crushed-velvet texture of a stingray or the song of a sea lion, not to mention the killer whale **Shamu,** the park's star attraction, and the six other resident orcas.

VISITOR INFORMATION   The park entrance is at the intersection of Interstate 4 and State Road 528 (the Bee Line Expwy.), 10 minutes south of downtown Orlando and 15 minutes from Orlando International Airport. For information, call © **800/423-8368** or 407/351-3600; www.seaworld.com.

TICKET PRICES   A **1-day ticket** costs $52 for ages 10 and over, $43 for children 3 to 9, plus 6% sales tax; age 2 and under, free.

OPERATING HOURS   The park is usually open 9am to at least 6pm, and later during summer and holidays when there are additional shows at night.

KENNEDY SPACE CENTER & THE ASTRONAUT HALL OF FAME

Set amid 150,000 acres of marshy wetlands favored by birds, reptiles, and amphibians, the **Kennedy Space Center** (© **321/449-4444;** www.kennedy spacecenter.com) is where astronauts left for the moon in 1969, where the shuttles have lifted off since 1981, and where America's components of the International Space Station are sent into orbit. Even if you've never really considered yourself a science or space buff, you can't help but be impressed by the achievements this place represents.

Security restrictions mean that most of the center is off-limits, but the **Visitors Complex** is designed to offer a glimpse of the works, with real NASA spacecraft; exhibits; hands-on activities for kids; a daily Q & A with a real astronaut; IMAX movies; a space shuttle mock-up; a Launch Status Center where presentations are given on current shuttle missions; an outdoor rocket garden displaying now-obsolete Redstone, Atlas, Saturn, and Titan rockets; and more. There's also the obligatory gift shop and several ridiculously pricey stops where you can grab a bite. Plan to eat before or after your visit.

Some visitors stick to the visitor center, but for a more complete insight into the space age, take the **bus tour** of the larger complex. Buses depart at 15-minute intervals, but the wait to get aboard can easily take an hour or more, so figure this into your planning. In the past, buses have stopped at three sites around the complex, with visitors allowed to spend as much time at each as they liked before catching the next bus back; but at press time, security restrictions had put Launch Complex 39 and the International Space Station Center off-limits, leaving only one stop still open to the public—the Apollo/Saturn V Center. Here, visitors experience a narrated simulation of the Apollo 8 launch while looking into an actual Mission Control room that was used for the mission. Following the show, visitors enter an enormous hall where an entire Saturn V rocket is on display, held up horizontally by huge metal supports. Numerous exhibits cover various aspects of the Apollo program, and a lunar module hangs from the ceiling above the snack bar.

A privately owned operation until 2002, the **Astronaut Hall of Fame,** located 6 miles west of the Space Center visitors complex on State Road 405, near the intersection with U.S. 1, focuses on the heroic human element of the space program, and holds the world's largest collection of astronaut memorabilia. Film presentations introduce visitors to the origins of rocketry and to the sheer power of the rockets themselves; displays of personal memorabilia offer insight into the astronauts' lives; and displays of NASA memorabilia are just plain awesome: actual Mission Control terminals at which you can sit to access interactive information; Jim Lovell's logbook from Gemini VII; and, most mind-blowing of all, the actual Apollo 14 command module Kitty Hawk, whose plaque bears the inscription "This spacecraft flew to the moon and back January 31–February 9, 1971." 'Nuff said.

But let's get down to brass tacks. The Astronaut Hall of Fame offers one main thing the rest of the KSC Visitors Complex doesn't: the chance to pretend you're an astronaut through various simulations. In the G-force simulator, two wannabe spacemen at a time are strapped tightly into pods at opposite ends of what looks like a giant barbell, which then whirls around on its axis so fast that your cheeks start to flap, just like in the movies. A film projected in the pod simulates a high-speed test flight. Just across the room, the 3D 360 simulator takes a group of passengers on a simulated shuttle flight from Earth to the new International Space Station, pitching you backward, forward, sideways, and upside down along the way. At the Walk on the Moon simulator, visitors are strapped into a harness, which is then counterbalanced to their weight so that they can bounce around as if weightless, doing their "one small step for man" imitation. Next door, the Mission to Mars simulator bumps you over the surface of the red planet in a rover. Not bad, but of the group, it's the simulator to skip if you've got limited time. Now, the warnings: Simulators are off-limits to folks under 48 inches, which is okay because smaller kids would probably freak out anyway. Also, if you tend to suffer from motion sickness, you'll probably want to avoid everything except the weightlessness simulation. Lastly, on the off-chance you're there on a slow day, be sure to allow at least a few minutes between simulations, even if you've got a cast-iron constitution. Trust us on this one.

Kennedy Space Center is accessible via State Road 405, just off U.S. 1. The Visitors Complex, including the Astronaut Hall of Fame, is open daily, except Christmas and certain launch days, from 9am to 5:30pm. The last bus tour departs at 2:15pm at the Visitors Complex. Admission to the Visitors Complex is $28 adults, $18 children 3 to 11; admission to the Hall of Fame is $14 adults, $10 children. Combined tickets are available for $33 adults, $23 children. Parking at the Visitors Complex and Hall of Fame is free, and there is no shuttle between the two. Be sure to pick up maps as you enter each branch, and expect to spend most of the day here to get a full experience.

HITTING THE BEACH

Though the Cape Canaveral/Cocoa Beach area doesn't have the spectacular beach culture of Miami, it doesn't lack for pleasant coastline. The following beaches (or "parks," in the local lingo) are located within an easy drive of the port area.

Closest to the cruise ship port and actually part of the larger port complex, the clean, nicely landscaped **Jetty Park,** 400 E. Jetty Rd. (© **321/783-7111**), is the most elaborate and possibly the nicest of the local beaches, perched at a point from which the whole expanse of the Cape Canaveral/Cocoa Beach coastline stretches away to the south. It's some view. A massive stone jetty juts seaward as protection for the mouth of Port Canaveral, and alongside is an elevated platform from which fishermen dangle their lines right into the surf. A snack bar, bathrooms, showers, picnic facilities, a children's playground, and fishing are among the perks here. Parking costs $5 per car. Follow the signs after entering the port area, near where State Road 528 and the A1A intersect.

A series of beaches are accessible (and generally signposted) off the A1A heading south from the port. The **Cocoa Beach Pier** area, off the A1A at Meade Avenue, is a great surfing spot with volleyball, an open-air bar, and a party atmosphere. **Lori Wilson Park,** farther south at 1500 N. Atlantic Ave., is another nicely landscaped area on the order of Jetty Park, with bathrooms and showers; a rustic boardwalk with some shaded picnic areas and benches; a nature center; and The Hammock, a ¼-mile boardwalk nature trail that winds through ferns, twisted trees, and other Jurassic Park–looking foliage, while butterflies flutter by and spiders eye them from their webs. Parking is free.

SHOPPING

Let's be unkind: You could shop here, but why bother? The offerings in Cape Canaveral and Cocoa Beach are mostly the kind of national mall shops that you've probably got at home, so save your energy and dollars for the Caribbean. An exception—as much for the experience as for the goods—is the **Ron Jon Surf Shop,** 4151 N. Atlantic Ave./A1A (© **321/799-8888;** www.ronjons.com). Inside the blue-and-yellow South Beach–looking Art Deco building is enough au courant beachwear to transform you and a good-size army into surfer dudes. The store also rents beach bikes, body boards, surfboards, kayaks, beach chairs, and other equipment by the hour, day, or week. It's open 24 hours a day, 365 days a year.

WHERE TO STAY

Only a 5-minute drive from the port, **Radisson Resort at the Port,** 8701 Astronaut Blvd./A1A (© **800/333-3333** or 321/784-0000; www.radisson.com/cape canaveralfl), offers comfortable standard rooms, and very comfortable two-room suites that are a great option for families, featuring a kitchenette with microwave, fridge, and place settings; a living room with sofa bed and giant TV; and a bedroom with a Jacuzzi and second giant TV. The great jungle-motif front courtyard has a large amoeba-shaped pool, and a second courtyard has tennis courts. Cruise passengers who are arriving by car can leave their vehicles in the hotel's lot for free during their cruise and can take the complimentary Radisson shuttle to and from the port. Rates: $159 standard rooms; $189 suites.

At the other end of the spectrum, **The Inn at Cocoa Beach,** 4300 Ocean Beach Blvd., just off the A1A behind the Ron Jon Surf Shop (© **800/343-5307** or 321/799-3460; www.theinnatcocoabeach.com), is almost entirely couples-oriented, presenting itself as more of a personalized inn than a traditional hotel. Almost all of its 50 comfortable rooms face the ocean and include rocking chairs on their balconies, king- or queen-size beds, TVs, and large bathrooms. A bar off the lobby operates on the honor system (just sign for what you take), and two lobby dogs and four tropical birds in cages around the property add to the homey, low-key atmosphere. Rates: $135 to $225.

Located near Lori Wilson Park on the A1A (and, for you '60s TV fans, near a street called I Dream of Jeannie Lane), the **Cocoa Beach Hilton,** 1550 N. Atlantic Ave./A1A (© **800/526-2609** or 321/799-0003; www.cocoabeachhilton. com), is the most upscale of the mainstream beachfront hotels, though it looks like a downtown business hotel that's been transplanted to the seashore. Rooms are spacious but have smallish picture windows only, and none offer a balcony. Rates: $145 to $182.

WHERE TO DINE

In the heart of Cocoa Beach, the Fischer Family restaurants, **Bernard's Surf, Fischer's Seafood Bar & Grill,** and **Rusty's Seafood & Oyster Bar** (all at © **321/ 783-2033;** www.bernardssurf.com), are all bunched up together at 2 S. Atlantic Ave., at Minuteman Causeway Road. At Bernard's, opened in 1948, photos testify to the many astronauts—and Russian cosmonauts, too—who have celebrated their safe return to Earth with the restaurant's steak and seafood, the latter provided by the Fischer family's own boats. Fischer's Seafood Bar & Grill is a Cheers-like lounge popular with the locals, serving fried combo platters, shrimp, crab claw meat, and the like. Rusty's is another casual option, with spicy seafood gumbo, raw or steamed oysters, burgers and sandwiches, pasta, and so on. **Another Rusty's branch** is on the south side of Port Canaveral harbor at 628 Glen Cheek Dr. (© **321/783-2033**), serving the same menu and boasting views of the fishing boats and cruise ships heading in and out of the port. Bernard's main courses $17 to $50; Fischer's main courses $7 to $15, sandwiches and salads $4 to $8; Rusty's main courses $15 to $20, sandwiches and salads $5 to $9.

The Mango Tree, 118 N. Atlantic Ave./A1A, between N. 1st and N. 2nd streets (© **321/799-0513**), is the most beautiful and sophisticated restaurant in Cocoa Beach, serving gourmet seafood, pasta, chicken, and continental dishes in a plantation-home atmosphere. Dinner main courses $15 to $39.

In downtown Cocoa Beach, the **Heidelberg Restaurant,** 7 N. Orlando Ave./ A1A at the Minuteman Causeway (© **321/783-6806**), serves German and Continental dinner cuisine such as beef filet stroganoff, goulash, roast duck, sauerbraten, and grilled loin pork chops, in a middling-elegant atmosphere. The adjoining Heidi's Jazz Club (see "Port Canaveral After Dark," below) has music nightly except Mondays. Dinner main courses $16 to $23.

PORT CANAVERAL AFTER DARK

The **Cocoa Beach Pier,** 401 Meade Ave., off the A1A, a ½-mile north of State Road 520 (© **321/783-7549;** www.cocoabeachpier.com), juts out 800 feet over the Atlantic, offering a casual beer-and-fruity-drinks atmosphere, an open-air bar with live music most nights, an ice-cream shop, sit-down seafood restaurants, and an arcade, plus beach equipment rentals and volleyball right next door on the sand.

At the Heidelberg restaurant (see "Where to Dine," above), **Heidi's Jazz Club,** 7 N. Orlando Ave./A1A at the Minuteman Causeway (© **321/783-4559;** www. heidisjazzclub.com), offers live jazz and blues Tuesday through Sunday, with featured performers on selected Friday and Saturday evenings and an open jam session Sundays at 7pm. Check out their website for a schedule of performances.

4 Tampa & St. Petersburg

Tampa was a sleepy port until Cuban immigrants founded Ybor City's cigar industry in the 1880s. A few years later, Henry B. Plant built a railroad to carry tourists into town and constructed his garish Tampa Bay Hotel (now the Henry B. Plant Museum). During the Spanish-American War, Teddy Roosevelt trained his Rough Riders here and walked the Ybor City streets with Cuban revolutionary José Marti. A land boom in the 1920s gave the city its charming, Victorian-style Hyde Park suburb (now a gentrified area, just across the Hillsborough River from downtown), and the go-go 1980s and 1990s brought skyscrapers, a convention center, a performing-arts center, and lots of shopping and dining options to the downtown area.

On the western shore of Tampa Bay, St. Petersburg is the picturesque and pleasant opposite of busy, industrial, business-filled Tampa. Originally conceived and built primarily for tourists and wintering snowbirds, it's got a nice downtown area, some quality museums, and a few good restaurants.

The Port of Tampa is set amid a complicated network of channels and harbors near historic Ybor City and its deepwater Ybor Channel. Ships sailing from here head primarily to the western Caribbean, the Yucatán, and Central America.

GETTING TO TAMPA & THE PORT

The **Tampa Port Authority** is located at 1101 Channelside Dr. (© **813/905-7678;** www.tampaport.com). The Garrison Seaport Center's Cruise Terminal 2 is located at 651 Channelside Dr.; Terminal 3, 815 Channelside Dr.; the Garrison Seaport Center Terminal 6 is at 1333 East McKay St.; and Terminal 7, 2303 Guy N. Verger Blvd.

BY AIR **Tampa International Airport** (© 813/870-8700; www.tampaairport. com) lies 5 miles west of downtown Tampa, near the junction of Florida 60 and Memorial Highway. If you haven't arranged for transfers with the cruise line, the port is an easy 30-minute taxi ride away; the fare is $17 per person via **Central Florida Limo** (© 813/396-3730). **Travel Ways** (© 800/888-1428) also runs a bus service, which costs $16 per person from the airport to the Garrison Seaport Center cruise terminals.

BY CAR Tampa lies 188 miles southwest of Jacksonville, 50 miles north of Sarasota, and 245 miles northwest of Miami. **From I-75 and I-4:** To Terminals 2 and 6 take I-4 West to Exit 1 (Ybor City), go South on 21st Street, then turn right on Adamo Drive (Hwy. 60) and then left on Channelside Drive; for Terminal 7 go south on 21st Street (21st St. merges with 22nd St. after crossing Adamo Dr.), turn right on Maritime Boulevard, and then go left on Guy N. Verger to Hooker's Point. From Tampa International Airport: To Terminals 2 and 6, follow signs to I-275 North, go to I-4 East and then to Exit 1 (Ybor City), go South on 21st Street, turn right on Adamo Drive (Hwy. 60), and then turn left on Channelside Drive; for Terminal 7, use directions from I-75 above. The port has ample parking (at $8 per day), with good security.

EXPLORING TAMPA

Tampa is best explored by car, as only the commercial district can be covered on foot. If you want to go to the beach, you'll have to head to neighboring St. Petersburg.

VISITOR INFORMATION Contact the **Tampa/Hillsborough Convention and Visitors Association, Inc. (THCVA),** 400 N. Tampa St., Suite 1010, Tampa, FL 33602 (© **800/44-TAMPA** or 813/223-2752; www.visittampabay. com). You can also stop by the **Tampa Bay Visitor Information Center,** 3601 E. Busch Blvd. (© **813/985-3601**), north of downtown in the Busch Gardens area.

GETTING AROUND Taxis in Tampa do not normally cruise the streets for fares; instead, they line up at public loading places, such as the airport, cruise terminal, and major hotels. **Yellow Cab** (© **813/253-0121**) or **United Cab** (© **813/253-2424** or 813/251-5555) charge about $1.75 per mile.

The **Hillsborough Area Regional Transit/HARTline** (© **813/254-HART**) provides regularly scheduled bus service between downtown Tampa and the suburbs. Fares are $1.15 for local service and $1.50 for express routes; exact change is required.

ATTRACTIONS
BUSCH GARDENS

Yes, admission prices are high, but **Busch Gardens** remains Tampa Bay's most popular attraction. The 335-acre family entertainment park, at 3605 E. Bougainvilla Ave. (© **888/800-5447** or 813/987-5171; www.buschgardens. com), features thrill rides, animal habitats, live entertainment, shops, restaurants, and games. The park's zoo ranks among the best in the country, with nearly 3,400 animals.

Montu, the world's tallest and longest inverted roller coaster, is part of **Egypt,** one of the park's themed areas, which also includes a replica of King Tutankhamen's tomb and a sand-dig area for kids. **Timbuktu** is a replica of the ancient desert trading center, complete with African craftspeople at work. It also features a sandstorm ride, a boat-swing ride, a roller coaster, and a video-game arcade. **Morocco,** a walled area with exotic architecture, has Moroccan craft demonstrations and a sultan's tent with snake charmers. **The Congo** features white-water raft rides; **Kumba,** the largest steel roller coaster in the southeastern United States; and **Claw Island,** a display of rare white Bengal tigers in a natural setting.

Rhino Rally is the newest addition. It's an off-road adventure in 16-passenger "Ralliers," or Land Rovers, that travel a bumpy course with views of Asian elephants, buffalo, antelope, and more. Hang on to your hat when a flash flood whisks away the bridge—and your vehicle.

The **Serengeti Plain** is an open area with more than 500 African animals roaming in herds. This 80-acre natural grassy veldt can be viewed from a tram, the Trans-Veldt Railway, or the **Skyride,** a sky tram. **Nairobi** is home to a natural habitat for various species of gorillas and chimpanzees, a baby-animal nursery, a petting zoo, reptile displays, and Curiosity Caverns, where visitors can observe animals active at night. **Bird Gardens,** the original core of Busch Gardens, offers rich foliage, lagoons, and a free-flight aviary holding hundreds of

ATTRACTIONS & SHOPPING
Busch Gardens **3**
Centro Ybor **6**
Florida Aquarium **15**
Henry B. Plant Museum **12**
Old Hyde Park Village **7**
Tampa Museum of Art **11**
Ybor City State Museum **6**

ACCOMMODATIONS
Grand Hyatt Tampa Bay **9**
Hyatt Regency Tampa **14**
La Quintana Inn & Suites **2**
Renaissance Vinoy Resort **10**
Tampa Mariott Waterside **13**

DINING & NIGHTLIFE
Armani's **9**

Bern's Steak House **8**
Columbia Restaurant **5**
The Masquerade **6**
Oystercatchers **9**
Seminole Indian Casino **4**
Side Splitter's Comedy Club **6**
The Skipper Dome/
   Skipper's Smokehouse **1**

exotic birds, including golden and American bald eagles, hawks, owls, and falcons. This area also features **Land of the Dragons,** a children's land and water play area.

The **Crown Colony** area encompasses the **Crown Colony House Restaurant,** overlooking the Serengeti Plain; stables with a team of Clydesdale horses; and the Anheuser-Busch hospitality center. Akbar's Adventure Tours, which offers a flight simulator, is located here.

To get to the Gardens, take Interstate 275 northeast of downtown to Busch Boulevard (Exit 33), and go east 2 miles to the entrance on 40th Street (McKinley Ave.). Admission is $52 for adults and $43 for kids 3 to 9 (plus 7% tax). Parking is $7. Park hours are at least 10am to 6pm; hours are extended during summer. See the website for opening and closing times.

OTHER ATTRACTIONS

Only steps from the Garrison Seaport Center, the **Florida Aquarium** (© 813/ 273-4000; www.flaquarium.net) celebrates the role of water in the development and maintenance of Florida's topography and ecosystems, with more than 10,000 aquatic plants and animals. One exhibit follows a drop of water as it bubbles through Florida limestone and winds its way to the sea. Admission is $16 for ages 12 and older, $14 for seniors, and $11 for children 3 to 12. Children 2 and under are admitted free.

Thirteen silver minarets and distinctive Moorish architecture make the stunning **Henry B. Plant Museum,** 401 W. Kennedy Blvd. (© 813/254-1891; www.plantmuseum.com), the focal point of the Tampa skyline. This national historic landmark, built in 1891 as the Tampa Bay Hotel, is filled with European and Oriental furnishings and decorative arts from the original hotel collection.

Ybor City is only about a mile or so from the cruise ship docks. It's Tampa's historic Latin enclave and one of only three national historic districts in Florida. Once known as the cigar capital of the world, Ybor offers a charming slice of the past with its Spanish architecture, antique street lamps, wrought-iron balconies, ornate grillwork, and renovated cigar factories. Stroll along 7th Avenue, the main artery (closed to traffic at night), where you'll find cigar shops, boutiques, nightclubs, and the famous 100-year-old Columbia Restaurant (see "Where to Dine," later).

The **Ybor City Museum State Park,** 1818 9th Ave., between 18th and 19th streets (© 813/247-6323; www.ybormuseum.org), relates the city's history, with special attention paid to the importance of the cigar to the area. Among other exhibits, you'll find a collection of cigar labels, cigar memorabilia, and works by local artisans. Admission is $2 per person. Children under 6 are admitted free. The museum is open daily from 9am to 5pm.

At **Centro Ybor,** a shopping/entertainment complex between 7th and 8th avenues and 16th and 17th streets (© 813/242-4660; www.thecentroybor. com), you'll find a multiscreen cinema, several restaurants, a comedy club, a large open-air bar, a bunch of typical mall-type stores, and GameWorks, a high-tech entertainment center designed by Steven Spielberg's Dreamworks and Universal Studios. The Ybor City Chamber of Commerce has its Cigar Museum & Visitor Center here (on 8th Ave. next to Centro Espanol).

The permanent collection of the **Tampa Museum of Art,** 600 N. Ashley Dr. (© 813/274-8130; www.tampamuseum.com), is especially strong in ancient Greek, Etruscan, and Roman artifacts, as well as 20th-century art. The museum grounds, fronting the Hillsborough River, contain a sculpture garden and a decorative fountain. It's open 10am to 5pm Tuesday to Saturday (till 8pm every third Thurs), and 1 to 5pm on Sunday. Admission is $7 adults, $6 seniors, $3 for students with ID cards and children over 6, and free for kids under 6.

ORGANIZED TOURS

BY BUS **Swiss Chalet Tours,** 3601 E. Busch Blvd. (© **813/985-3601**), operates guided tours of Tampa, Ybor City, and the surrounding region. Four-hour (10am–2pm) tours run most every day, and cost $40 for adults, $35 for children 3 to 12. Seven-hour tours, which also run virtually every day (10am–5pm), visit Tampa, Clearwater, and St. Petersburg. Cost is $70 for adults and $65 for children. Reservations for both tours must be made 1 day in advance.

ON FOOT **Ybor City** walking tours are available through the Ybor City Museum (see "Other Attractions," above). Tours are $5 for ages 6 and older.

HITTING THE BEACH

Start at **St. Petersburg,** across the bay, for a north-to-south string of interconnected white sandy shores. Most beaches have restrooms, refreshment stands, and picnic areas. You can either park on the street at meters (usually 25¢ for each half-hour) or at one of the four major parking lots located from north to south at Sand Key Park in Clearwater, beside Gulf Boulevard (also known as Rte. 699), just south of the Clearwater Pass Bridge; Redington Shores Beach Park, beside Gulf Boulevard at 182nd Street; Treasure Island Park, on Gulf Boulevard just north of 108th Avenue; and St. Pete Beach Park, beside Gulf Boulevard at 46th Street.

SHOPPING

On and around **7th Avenue in Ybor City,** you'll find a variety of interesting boutiques and shops, plus lots of cigar stores selling handmade stogies.

Some 60 upscale shops, plus restaurants and movie theaters, are located at **Old Hyde Park Village,** an outdoor, European-style market at Swann and Dakota avenues near Bayshore Boulevard (© **813/251-3500;** http://oldhyde parkvillage.com). There's nothing particularly "Tampa" about it, but if you need a new Brooks Brothers suit or Ann Taylor dress for your cruise, it'll do.

WHERE TO STAY

TAMPA Tampa has two Hyatts. The **Grand Hyatt Tampa Bay,** 6200 Courtney Campbell Causeway (© **800/233-1234** or 813/874-1234; http://grand tampabay.hyatt.com), sits in a 35-acre wildlife preserve at the Tampa end of the long causeway traversing Tampa Bay, about 2 miles from the airport and 8 miles from downtown. In addition to regular rooms and suites, 45 Spanish-style town houses/villas are set about a ½-mile from the main hotel building. Rates: $180 to $395. **The Hyatt Regency Tampa,** Two Tampa City Center at 211 N. Tampa St. (© **800/233-1234** or 813/225-1234; http://tamparegency.hyatt.com), sits in Tampa's commercial center and caters mostly to the corporate crowd. Rates: $195 to $375. At the other big downtown hotel, the **Tampa Marriott Waterside,** 700 S. Florida Ave. (© **800/228-9290** or 813/221-4900; www.marriott hotels.com), about half of the rooms have balconies overlooking the bay or city (the best views are high up on the south side). Rates: $129 to $189.

La Quinta Inn & Suites, 3701 E. Fowler Ave. (© **800/687-6667** or 813/ 910-7500; www.laquinta.com), is a motel with a pinch of upscale. Rooms have coffeemakers and dataports, and the place is located only 1½ miles from Busch Gardens. Rates: $85 to $115.

ST. PETERSBURG Overlooking Tampa Bay, the **Renaissance Vinoy Resort,** 501 Fifth Ave. NE, at Beach Drive (© **800/HOTELS1** or 727/894-1000;

www.renaissancehotels.com), is the grande dame of the region's hotels. Built as the grand Vinoy Park in 1925, this elegant Spanish-style establishment reopened in 1992 after a meticulous $93-million restoration. Many of the guest rooms offer lovely views of the bay. Accommodations in the newer wing ("The Tower") are slightly larger than those in the hotel's original core. Rates: $199 to $349.

WHERE TO DINE

On the 14th floor of the Grand Hyatt Tampa, **Armani's,** 6200 Courtney Campbell Causeway (© **813/207-6800**), is a stylish northern Italian restaurant with a panoramic view of the city skyline and the bay. Jackets are recommended but not required. Dinner main courses: $18 to $35. At **Bern's Steak House,** 1208 S. Howard Ave. (© **813/251-2421**), the steaks are close to perfect. You order according to thickness and weight. Dinner main courses: $27 to $60.

In Ybor City, the nearly 100-year-old **Columbia Restaurant,** 2117 7th Ave. E., between 21st and 22nd streets (© **813/248-4961**), occupies an attractive tile-sheathed building that fills an entire city block about a mile from the cruise docks. The aura is pre-Castro Cuba and the food is primarily Cuban. The simpler your dish is, the better it's likely to be. Filet mignon; roasted pork; and black beans, yellow rice, and plantains are flavorful and well prepared. Catch a flamenco show on the dance floor Monday through Saturday. Dinner main courses: $15 to $25.

The best fish in Tampa is served at **Oystercatchers,** in the Grand Hyatt Tampa complex, 6200 Courtney Campbell Causeway (© **813/207-6815**). Pick your desired fish from a glass-fronted buffet, or enjoy mesquite-grilled steaks, chicken rollatini, and shellfish. Dinner main courses: $20 to $30.

TAMPA AFTER DARK

Nightfall transforms Ybor City, Tampa's century-old Latin Quarter, into a orgy of music, ethnic food, poetry readings, and after-midnight coffee and dessert. Seventh Avenue, one of Ybor City's main arteries, is closed to all but pedestrian traffic Wednesday through Saturday evenings. **The Masquerade,** 1503 E. 7th Ave. (© **813/247-3319**), housed in a 1940s movie palace, is just one of the many nightclubs that pepper the streets here. Other options include **Side Splitters Comedy Club,** 12938 N. Dale Mabry Hwy. (© **813/960-1197**), which features stand-up pros most nights of the week. Ticket prices are $12 for general admission and $15 for preferred admission.

In North Tampa, **Skipper's Smokehouse,** 910 Skipper Rd., at the corner of Nebraska Avenue (© **813/971-0666;** www.skipperssmokehouse.com), is a favorite evening spot, with an all-purpose restaurant and bar where oysters and fresh shellfish are sold by the dozen and half-dozen. You'll find live music back in the Skipper Dome, a sprawling deck sheltered by a canopy of oak trees.

Northeast of town, at Exit 6 off the I-4, the **Seminole Casino,** 5223 N. Orient Rd., at Hillsborough Road (© **813/621-1302;** http://tampa.seminolehardrock. com), is open 24 hours every day of the year, offering poker, bingo, and slots.

For more on Tampa nightlife, the **Tampa/Hillsborough Arts Council** maintains **Artsline** (© **813/229-ARTS**), a 24-hour information service about current and upcoming cultural events.

5 New Orleans

New Orleans may be best known as a world-class party town, but by some yardsticks, it's also the busiest seaport in the nation, visited by thousands of cargo vessels transporting grain, ore, machinery, and building supplies, in addition to

Airport ✈
Cruise Ship Dock

ACCOMMODATIONS
McKendrick-
Breaux House **3**
Windsor Court Hotel **5**
DINING & NIGHTLIFE
Commander's Palace **2**
Mother's Restaurant **4**
Snug Harbor **6**
Tipitina's **1**

**ATTRACTIONS
& SHOPPING**
Aquarium of the
Americas **5**
Lafayette Cemetery
No. 1 **2**

a number of cruise ships bound for ports in the western Caribbean, including Cancún, Playa del Carmen, and Cozumel. You can watch the parade of cargo ships pass by as you steam downriver to the ocean, against the backdrop of Louisiana's Mississippi River delta.

GETTING TO NEW ORLEANS & THE PORT

The **Julia Street Cruise Ship Terminal** sits at the foot of Julia Street on the Mississippi River, in the convention center district, a 10-minute walk or a short streetcar or taxi ride away from the edge of the French Quarter. For information, call the **Port of New Orleans** at © 504/522-2551 or check out www.portno.com.

BY AIR **New Orleans International Airport** (© **504/464-0831**) is about 15 miles northwest of the port. Cruise line representatives meet all passengers who have booked transfers through the line. For those who haven't, a taxi to the port costs about $28 for two passengers and takes about 45 minutes. **Airport Shuttle** (© **866/596-2699** or 504/592-0555) runs vans at 10- to 12-minute intervals from outside the airport's baggage claim to the port and other points in town. It costs $13 per passenger each way; free for children under 5.

BY CAR Take the I-10 downtown. Then take the Tchoupitoulas/St. Peters Street exit, the last one before you cross the Mississippi. Stay to the right, and head toward the New Orleans Convention Center. Turn right onto Convention Center Boulevard, then left onto Henderson Street, which will take you to Port of New Orleans Place. Turn left and continue on to the Cruise Ship Terminal. You can park your car in long-term parking at the port; inquire through your cruise line. You must present a boarding pass or ticket before parking.

EXPLORING NEW ORLEANS

The French Quarter is the oldest part of the city and still the most popular area for sightseeing. Many visitors never leave its confines, but we encourage you to venture outside the Quarter to feel the pulse of the city's commerce, see river activities that keep the city alive, stroll through spacious parks, drive or walk by the impressive homes of the Garden District, and get a firsthand view of the bayou/lake connection that explains why New Orleans grew up here in the first place.

VISITOR INFORMATION Contact or visit the **New Orleans Metropolitan Convention and Visitors Bureau,** 2020 St. Charles Ave. (© **800/672-6124** or 504/566-5011; www.neworleanscvb.com), for brochures, pamphlets, and information..

GETTING AROUND Taxis are plentiful. If you're not near a taxi stand, call **United Cabs** (© **504/522-9771**) and a car will come in 5 to 10 minutes. The meter begins at $2.50 plus $1 for each additional person, and goes to $1.20 per mile thereafter.

Streetcar lines run the length of St. Charles Avenue. The cars, with wooden bench seats, operate 24 hours a day and cost $1.25 per ride (you must have exact change). A transfer from streetcar to bus costs 25¢. You can board the streetcar at the corner of Canal and Carondelet streets in the French Quarter, or at intervals along St. Charles Avenue. A VisiTour Pass, which gives you unlimited rides on all streetcar and bus lines, sells for $5 for 1 day, $12 for 3 days. You can buy passes through selected hotel information counters and retail stores; you'll find a list at www.norta.com.

Where the trolleys don't run, a **city bus** will. For route information, call © **504/248-3900** or pick up a map at the **Regional Transit Authority** office

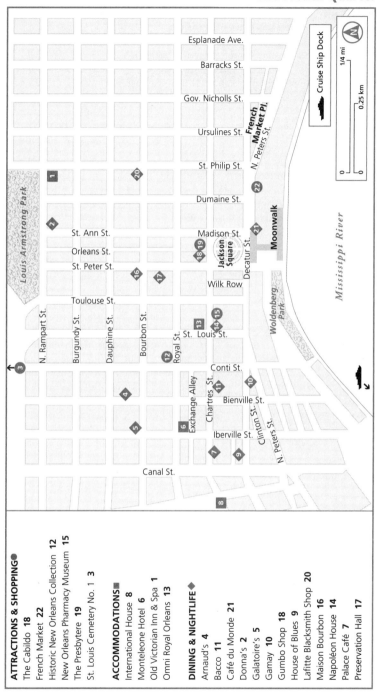

The French Quarter

Esplanade Ave.
Barracks St.
Gov. Nicholls St.
Ursulines St.
St. Philip St.
Dumaine St.
St. Ann St.
Madison St.
Orleans St.
St. Peter St.
Wilk Row
Toulouse St.
St. Louis St.
Conti St.
Bienville St.
Iberville St.
Canal St.

Louis Armstrong Park

French Market Pl.
N. Peters St.

Jackson Square

Moonwalk

Woldenberg Park

Mississippi River

N. Rampart St.
Burgundy St.
Dauphine St.
Bourbon St.
Royal St.
Exchange Alley
Chartres St.
Decatur St.
Clinton St.
N. Peters St.

Cruise Ship Dock

1/4 mi
0.25 km

ATTRACTIONS & SHOPPING ●
The Cabildo **18**
French Market **22**
Historic New Orleans Collection **12**
New Orleans Pharmacy Museum **15**
The Presbytere **19**
St. Louis Cemetery No. 1 **3**

ACCOMMODATIONS ■
International House **8**
Monteleone Hotel **6**
Old Victorian Inn & Spa **1**
Omni Royal Orleans **13**

DINING & NIGHTLIFE ◆
Arnaud's **4**
Bacco **11**
Café du Monde **21**
Donna's **2**
Galatoire's **5**
Gamay **10**
Gumbo Shop **18**
House of Blues **9**
Lafitte Blacksmith Shop **20**
Maison Bourbon **16**
Napoléon House **14**
Palace Café **7**
Preservation Hall **17**

(2817 Canal St.). Most buses charge $1.25 per ride (plus 25¢ for a transfer), although some express buses charge $1.50.

The Vieux Carré Minibus takes you to French Quarter sights. The route is posted along Canal and Bourbon streets. The minibus operates weekdays between 6am and 6:30pm and costs $2.

From Jackson Square (at Decatur St.), you can take a 2¼-mile, 30-minute horse-drawn carriage ride through the French Quarter. **Royal Carriage Tour Co.** (© **504/943-8820**) offers group tours for $10 per person in open-topped surreys suitable for up to eight passengers at a time, daily from 9am to midnight. Private rides for up to four passengers in a Cinderella carriage go for $50 a pop.

ATTRACTIONS

At the well-designed **Aquarium of the Americas,** 1 Canal St., at the Mississippi River (© **800/774-7394** or 504/581-4629), a 400,000-gallon tank holds a kaleidoscope of species from the deep waters of the nearby Gulf of Mexico. Admission is $15 for adults, $11 for seniors, $8 for children under 12; open 9:30am to 6pm Sunday through Thursday, 9:30am to 7pm Friday and Saturday.

Incorporating seven historic buildings connected by a brick courtyard, the **Historic New Orleans Collection,** 533 Royal St., between St. Louis and Toulouse streets (© **504/523-4662;** www.hnoc.org), evokes the New Orleans of 200 years ago. The oldest building in the complex escaped the tragic fire of 1794. The others hold exhibitions about Louisiana's culture and history. All are open from 10am to 4:30pm Tuesday through Saturday. Admission is free.

Founded in 1950, the **New Orleans Pharmacy Museum,** 514 Chartres St., at St. Louis Street (© **504/565-8027;** www.pharmacymuseum.org), is just what the name implies. In 1823, the first licensed pharmacist in the United States, Louis J. Dufilho Jr., opened an apothecary shop here. Today you'll find old apothecary bottles, voodoo potions, pill tiles, and suppository molds, as well as the old glass cosmetics counter and a jar of leeches, in case you feel the need to be bled. It's open Tuesday through Sunday 10am to 5pm; admission is $2 adults, $1 seniors and students, free for children under 12.

Constructed from 1795 through 1799 as the Spanish government seat in New Orleans, **The Cabildo,** 701 Chartres St., at Jackson Square (© **800/568-6968** or 504/568-6968), was the site of the signing of the Louisiana Purchase transfer. The building is now the center of the Louisiana State Museum's facilities in the French Quarter, with a multiroom exhibition that traces the history of Louisiana from exploration through Reconstruction, covering all aspects of life, including antebellum music, mourning and burial customs, immigrants, and the changing roles of women in the South. It's open Tuesday through Sunday 9am to 5pm; admission $5 adults, $4 students and seniors, free for children under 12.

Also on Jackson Square, **The Presbytère,** 751 Chartres St. (© **800/568-6968** or 504/568-6968), was planned as housing for clergy but is now a Mardi Gras museum that traces the history of the annual event, with everything from elaborate Mardi Gras Indian costumes to Rex Queen jewelry from the turn of the century on display. A re-creation of a float allows you to pretend you are throwing beads to a crowd on a screen in front of you. The museum is open Tuesday through Sunday 9am to 5pm; admission $5 adults, $4 seniors and students, free for children under 12

New Orleans' cemeteries are a bit peculiar: Since the city is prone to flooding, bodies have been interred aboveground since the city's earliest days, in sometimes very elaborate tombs that are definitely worth a visit. **St. Louis Cemetery No. 1,** Basin Street between Conti and St. Louis streets, at the top of the French Quarter, is the oldest extant cemetery (1789) in the area and the most iconic. The acid-dropping scene from *Easy Rider* was shot here, prompting the city to declare that no film would ever, ever, ever be shot again in one of its cemeteries. In the Garden District, **Lafayette Cemetery No. 1,** 1427 Sixth St., right across the street from Commander's Palace Restaurant, is another old cemetery that's been beautifully restored. Though both of these cemeteries are usually full of visitors during the day, you should exercise caution when touring, as they've seen some crime over the years.

ORGANIZED TOURS

ON FOOT   There are a lot of tours offered in New Orleans, but **Historic New Orleans Walking Tours** (© **504/947-2120;** www.tourneworleans.com) are the tours to take for authenticity. The company offers tours of the French Quarter and the Garden District (including Lafayette Cemetery), plus a cemetery and voodoo tour. Prices are about $10 to $15 per person.

BY BUS   **Gray Line,** 1 Toulouse St. (© **800/535-7786** or 504/587-0861), offers a 2-hour bus tour that gives a fast overview of the city. Tours cost $24 for adults and $12 for children, and require advance booking.

SHOPPING

Despite what you may think while making your first walk down **Bourbon Street,** there's more to New Orleans shopping than tourist traps selling cheap T-shirts, alligator snow globes, and other souvenir items—although there are plenty of those too (most of them with an absolutely mind-boggling selection of hot sauces). The city's antiques stores are especially good.

On Decatur Street across from Jackson Square, **The French Market** has shops selling candy, cookware, fashion, crafts, toys, New Orleans memorabilia, and candles. There's a lot of kitsch, but some good buys are mixed in, and it's always fun to stroll through and grab a few beignets at **Café du Monde** (see "Snacks & Sweets," below). The French Market is open from 10am to 6pm; Café du Monde is open 24 hours.

From Camp Street down to the river on Julia Street, you'll find many of the city's best **contemporary art galleries.** Of course, some of the works are a bit pricey, but there are good deals to be had if you're collecting, and fine art to be seen if you're not.

Magazine Street is the Garden District's premier shopping street, with more than 140 shops among the 19th-century brick storefronts and cottages. You'll find antiques stores, art galleries, boutiques, craft shops, and more. The greatest concentration of stores is between Felicity and Washington streets, but if you're so inclined, you could shop your way from here all the way to Audubon Park, hopping over the dry patches on the city bus. Be sure to pick up a copy of *Shopper's Dream,* a free guide and map to most of the stores. It's available all along the street.

WHERE TO STAY

In the Garden District, the **McKendrick-Breaux House,** 1474 Magazine St. (© **888/570-1700** or 504/586-1700; fax 504/522-7138; www.mckendrick-breaux.com), was built at the end of the Civil War by a wealthy plumber and Scottish immigrant. Today, it's one of the best guesthouses for value. It's been completely restored to its original charming state, and each room furnished with antiques, family collectibles, and fresh flowers. Rates: $125 to $195.

In the Central Business District, just outside the French Quarter and close to the cruise ship terminal, the **International House,** 221 Camp St., just west of Canal (© **800/633-5770** or 504/553-9550; www.ihhotel.com), is a modern, minimalist hotel housed in an old beaux arts bank building. Rooms are simple, with high ceilings, ceiling fans, modern bathrooms, dataports, wireless Internet, CD players with CDs, and photos and knickknacks that remind you that you're in New Orleans. It's all corridors and dark and chic. Rates: $159 to $219.

About 7 blocks from the cruise ship terminal is the atmospheric **Hotel Monteleone,** 214 Royal St., between Iberville and Bienville streets (© **800/535-9595** or 504/523-3341; www.hotelmonteleone.com), the oldest hotel in the city and also the largest hotel in the French Quarter—because of its size you can almost always get a reservation here, even when other places are booked. Everyone who stays here loves it, probably because its staff is among the most helpful in town. Decor and floor layouts are slightly different in each of the rooms, so ask to see a few different ones. Rates: $199 to $510.

Three streets from Bourbon in the French Quarter, the **Olde Victorian Inn and Spa,** 914 N. Rampart St. (© **800/725-2446** or 504/522-2446; www.olde victorianinn.com) was formerly known as P. J. Holbrook's and is now owned by Keith and Andre West-Harrison (and their four dogs and one cat). The new owners have retained the former decor. The inn is a beautifully restored 1840s home, with antiques and reproductions. Some rooms have balconies, and most have fireplaces. The inn can arrange wedding packages that include a service in its courtyard; you can head off for your honeymoon cruise from there! The "spa" in the name refers to the inn's recently opened day spa. Rates: $120 to $185.

The **Omni Royal Orleans,** 621 St. Louis St., between Royal and Chartres streets (© **800/843-6664** or 504/529-5333; www.omnihotels.com), is an elegant hotel located smack in the center of the Quarter. The lobby is a small sea of marble, and the rooms are sizable and elegant, full of muted tones and plush furniture, with windows that let you gaze out over the Quarter. Service varies, but can be exceptional. Rates: $206 to $269.

In the Central Business District, the **Windsor Court Hotel,** 300 Gravier St. (© **800/262-2662** or 504/523-6000; www.windsorcourthotel.com), was named "Best Hotel in North America" by *Condé Nast Traveler,* so feel free to hold it to a high standard. Accommodations are exceptionally spacious and classy, with large bay windows or a private balcony overlooking the river or the city. Downstairs, two corridors display original 17th-, 18th-, and 19th-century art. A plush reading area with international newspapers is on the second floor. Rates: $180 to $450.

WHERE TO DINE

Essentially, New Orleans is one giant restaurant. In 1997, a U.S. survey named New Orleans "the fattest city in the country," which makes sense once you've tasted what's being whipped up at 3 or 4 or 8 or 40 of the city's best restaurants. We've profiled many of the best below. Most of them are in the French Quarter.

In business since 1918 and still mighty fine, the legendary **Arnaud's,** 813 Bienville St. (© **504/523-2847;** www.arnauds.com), is set in three interconnected, once-private houses from the 1700s. The restaurant's three Belle Epoque dining rooms are lush with Edwardian embellishments. Especially delicious menu items include snapper or trout topped with crabmeat, filet mignon, oysters stewed in cream, roasted duck in blueberry sauce, and a classic bananas foster. Dinner main courses: $22 to $35.

Bacco, 310 Chartres St., between Bienville and Conti streets (© **504/522-2426;** www.bacco.com), a great New Orleans bistro, has an elegant setting of pink faux-marble floors and Venetian chandeliers. You can feast on wood-fired pizzas, regional seafood, and such specialties as black-truffle fettuccine and lobster ravioli. Dinner main courses: $19 to $25.

Galatoire's, 209 Bourbon St., at Iberville Street (© **504/525-2021**), feels like a bistro in turn-of-the-20th-century Paris, and is one of the city's most legendary places—it's one of the spots that locals go to for a good meal. Menu items include trout (meunière or amandine), rémoulade of shrimp, oysters en brochette, a savory Creole-style bouillabaisse, and eggplant stuffed with a purée of seafood. Dinner main courses: $18 to $28.

Louisiana Heritage Cafe, in the Bienville House hotel, 320 Decatur St., at Conti Street (© **504/299-8800**), serves contemporary Creole cuisine in a formal setting. Entrees include the garlic shrimp and saffron pasta, and a Gulf fish of the day. Dinner main courses: $10 to $20.

The Gumbo Shop, 630 St. Peter St., at Royal Street (© **504/525-1486**), is a cheap and convenient place to get solid, classic Creole food. The menu reads like a textbook list of traditional local food: red beans and rice, shrimp Creole, crawfish étouffée. The seafood gumbo with okra is a meal in itself, and do try the jambalaya. Dinner main courses: $7 to $19.

Not far outside the Quarter, **Mother's Restaurant,** 401 Poydras St., at Tchoupitoulas Street (© **504/523-9656**), has long lines and zero atmosphere, but damn, those po' boys. Customers have been flocking here since 1938 for homemade biscuits and red-bean omelets at breakfast, po' boys at lunch, and soft-shell crabs and jambalaya at dinner. Everything's between $5 and $21.

Napoleon House, 500 Chartres St., at the corner of St. Louis Street (© **504/524-9752**), would have been the home of the lieutenant himself if some locals' wild plan to bring him here to live out his exile had panned out. A landmark 1797 building with an incredible atmosphere, this place is a hangout for drinking and good times, but also serves food. The specialty is Italian muffuletta, with ham, Genoa salami, pastrami, Swiss cheese, and provolone. Dinner main courses: $12 to $24.

Right on the border of the French Quarter, the open kitchen at **Palace Café,** 605 Canal St., between Royal and Chartres streets (© **504/523-1661**), serves contemporary Creole food with a big emphasis on seafood: catfish pecan meunière, andouille-crusted fish of the day, and lots more. Don't miss the white-chocolate bread pudding. Dinner main courses: $19 to $28.

Outside the Quarter, at the corner of Washington Avenue and Coliseum Street in the Garden District, **Commander's Palace,** 1403 Washington Ave. (© **504/899-8221**), still reigns as one of the finest dining choices not only in New Orleans, but in the whole United States—the James Beard Foundation voted it the country's best restaurant in 1996. The cuisine is haute Creole. Try anything with shrimp or crawfish, or the Mississippi quail, or . . . oh, just try anything. Dinner main courses: $26 to $38.

SNACKS & SWEETS

Café du Monde, 800 Decatur St., right on the river (© **504/581-2914**), is basically a 24-hour coffee shop that specializes in beignets—square, really yummy French doughnut–type things, hot and covered in powdered sugar. This is a great spot for people-watching, but if you don't want to wait for a table, you can always get a bag of beignets to go. Grab lots of napkins. Premoistened tow-elettes would be a good idea, too.

NEW ORLEANS AFTER DARK

Life in "The Big Easy" is conducive to all manner of nighttime entertainment, usually raucous. There's a reason why jazz was born in this town.

Do what most people do: Start at one end of **Bourbon Street** (say, around Iberville St.), walk down to the other end, and then turn around and do it again. Along the way, you'll hear R & B, blues, and jazz pouring out of dozens of bars, be beckoned by touts from the numerous strip clubs, and see one tiny little storefront stall after another sporting hand-lettered signs that say OUR BEER IS CHEAPER THAN NEXT DOOR. It's a scene. Bacchanalian? Yes. Will you spend time in purgatory for it? Maybe, but it's loads of fun. Grab yourself a big $2 beer or one of the famous rum-based Hurricanes—preferably in a yard-long green plas-tic vessel shaped like a Roswell alien—and join the party.

Most of the places in this section have a cover charge that varies depending on who's performing; some are free.

Preservation Hall, 726 St. Peter St., just off Bourbon (© **504/522-2841** during the day, 504/523-8939 after 8pm; www.preservationhall.com), is a delib-erately shabby little hall with very few places to sit and no air-conditioning. Nonetheless, people usually pack the place to see the house band, a bunch of mostly older musicians who have been at this for eons. Don't request "When the Saints Go Marching In" 'cause the band won't play it—even classics get to be old smelly hats when you've played them 45,000 times. There's a $5 admission fee.

Close by, **Maison Bourbon,** 641 Bourbon St. (© **504/522-8818**), presents authentic and often fantastic Dixieland and traditional jazz. Stepping into the brick-walled room, or even just peering in from the street, takes you away from the mayhem outside. There's a one-drink minimum.

Lafitte's Blacksmith Shop, 941 Bourbon St. (© **504/523-0066**), is a French Quarter pub housed in an 18th-century Creole blacksmith shop that looks like only faith keeps it standing. Tennessee Williams used to hang out here.

If you're looking to get away from the Bourbon scene and hear some real brass-band jazz, head up to **Donna's,** 800 N. Rampart St., at the top of St. Ann Street (© **504/596-6914;** www.donnasbarandgrill.com). There's no better place to hear the authentic sounds that made New Orleans famous. The cover varies, but is always reasonable.

Jazz, blues, and Dixieland pour out of the nostalgia-laden bar and concert hall **Tipitina's,** way out in the Uptown neighborhood at 501 Napoleon Ave. (© **504/ 891-8477;** www.tipitinas.com).

House of Blues, 225 Decatur St. (© **504/529-2583**), is one of the city's largest live-music venues. You stand and move among the several bars that pep-per the club. There's also a restaurant.

One block beyond Esplanade, on the periphery of the French Quarter, **Snug Harbor,** 626 Frenchman St. (© **504/949-0696;** www.snugjazz.com), is a jazz bistro, a classic spot to hear modern jazz in a cozy setting. Sometimes R & B combos and blues are added to the program. There's a full dinner menu in the restaurant, but only appetizers are served in the club.

6 Alternative Home Ports

Whether it's because of convenience or an aversion to flying (that is, the cost of flying or the fear of it), the cruise lines realize that lots of you love the idea of hopping on a cruise within driving distance of your home. That's why you can now cruise to the Caribbean from the big Florida cruise ports or from ports up and down the Eastern seaboard and throughout the Gulf of Mexico. In addition to the primary alternative ports below, ships are also sailing from Houston (www. portofhouston.com); Norfolk, Virginia (www.cruisenorfolk.org); Baltimore (www.mpa.state.md.us); Jacksonville, Florida (www.jaxport.com); and Philadelphia (www.cruisephilly.com).

GALVESTON, TEXAS
Galveston is an island some 50 miles south of Houston, just off the mainland. It was one of the first big alternative ports developed for Caribbean-bound megaships. Ships departing from Galveston can reach the open sea in about 30 minutes, compared to the several hours of lag time from the Port of Houston— which, like New Orleans, sits inland, on the edge of the Houston Ship Channel, above Galveston Bay. (The Port of Houston does have one advantage: It's closer to the airports. It takes 45–90 min. to travel between the Port of Galveston and the airports, depending on which airport you're using. Currently, Royal Olympia Cruises' Olympia Voyager and NCL's Norwegian Sea are sailing out of Houston to the western Caribbean.)

Until recently, the Port of Galveston offered just one 132,000-square-foot cruise ship terminal, but in late 2002, a warehouse adjacent to Terminal One was converted into a second terminal, offering facilities and services for 4-, 5-, 7-, 10-, 11- and 12-night sailings. Within walking distance of the terminal is the historic Strand District, Galveston's revitalized downtown, with shops, art galleries, museums, and eateries lining its quaint brick streets.

GETTING TO GALVESTON & THE PORT
The **Texas Cruise Ship Terminal** at the Port of Galveston is at Harborside Drive and 25th Street, on Galveston Island. It's reached via I-45 south from Houston. For information, call ℭ **409/766-6113** or check out www.portof galveston.com or www.galveston.com.

BY PLANE   You'll fly into one of two Houston airports: **William P. Hobby Airport** (south of downtown Houston, and about 31 miles, or a 45-min. drive from the terminal) or **George Bush Intercontinental Airport** (just north of downtown Houston, and about 54 miles, or an 80-min. drive from the terminal). Information on both is available at the Houston Airport System website: www.houstonairportsystem.org. Bush is the larger airport and is international. If you've arranged air transportation and/or transfers through the cruise line a cruise line representative will direct you to shuttle buses that will take you to the port. Taxis are also available. **United Cab** (ℭ 713/699-0000) charges $75 per carload from Hobby Airport and $119 from George Bush Intercontinental Airport. The following taxi companies provide service from the port to the airports only (not the other way around): **Busy Bee** (ℭ 409/762-6666) for $70 to Hobby Airport and $125 to George Bush (each additional passenger is $5); and **Yellow Cab Company** (ℭ 409/763-3333) for $70 to Hobby and $110 to Bush. **Galveston Limousine Service** (ℭ 800/640-4826 or 409/744-5466) provides the same service, charging $30 per person to/from Hobby and $35 to/from Bush. Round-trip rates are $50 and $60, respectively. All three companies require reservations.

BY CAR   I-45 is the main artery for those arriving from the north. To get to the terminal, follow I-45 South to Exit 1C (at Harborside Dr./Hwy. 275); it's the first exit after the causeway. Turn left (east) onto Harborside Drive and continue for about 5 miles to the cruise terminal.

Long-term parking at the port is $40 for a 4-night cruise, $45 for a 5-night cruise, $60 for a 7-night cruise, $75 for a 10-night cruise, $80 for an 11-night cruise, and $85 for 12-night cruise. The lots are a ½-mile from the cruise ship terminal, and shuttle buses transport passengers between the lots and the terminal, where porters are available to carry luggage.

NEW YORK CITY

Up until the 1950s, New York City was one of the biggest ports in the world for both cargo and passenger vessels; its famous skyline and the Statue of Liberty offering a dramatic approach that no other ports could match. So many ships parked their noses against Manhattan's West side that it was dubbed Luxury Liner Row. All the greats were there, from the *Normandie* to *Queen Mary* and *France,* their horns echoing across midtown. All that ended when the jet plane put the liners out of business, allowing people to cross the Atlantic in half a day rather than a week. Never again would the Port of New York see as much traffic, though today it's reclaiming a bit of its former glory as a cruise home port.

Joining a handful of lines that have long based ships in NYC for summer and/or fall cruises to Bermuda, New England, and Canada, are several Caribbean-bound ships, including NCL's *Norwegian Dawn,* (which offers 7-night round-trip cruises year-round to Florida and the Bahamas).

Like the ports of New Orleans, San Francisco, and Charleston, New York's cruise ship piers are in the heart of town. Passengers are a short stroll away from 42nd Street and Times Square and a slightly longer one from Fifth Avenue, Central Park, and many other sites. Much of the Big Apple can be explored on foot (Manhattan is only about 2 miles wide by 13 miles long, with most visitors remaining in its bottom half). If you need a break, hail one of the ubiquitous yellow taxis (meters start at $2 and increase 30¢ every ⅕-mile or 20¢ per 90 seconds when stuck in traffic) or hop on the red double-decker Gray Line tour buses that crisscross the city (© **800/669-0051** or 212/445-0848; www.grayline newyork.com); you can join the tour loop at the Circle Line terminal just a few steps south of the cruise ship piers.

GETTING TO NEW YORK CITY & THE PORT

The **New York City Passenger Ship Terminal** is at 711 12th Ave., between 46th and 54th streets, on the Hudson River waterfront. It's reached via the Henry Hudson Parkway (also known as the West Side Hwy.) via the 54th Street vehicle ramp. Frequently congested on turnaround days, at press time the city had announced a $50 million initiative to significantly improve the port facilities, improving passenger circulation and reducing roadway congestion. For information, call © **212/246-5450** or check out www.nypst.com.

As this book went to press, Royal Caribbean was gearing up for its first season offering cruises from its new **Cape Liberty Cruise Port,** across the Hudson from New York, in Bayonne, New Jersey. We know: It doesn't have the same romance. But it does have the advantage of being less congested, and of offering a great view of the NYC skyline and the Statue of Liberty. The 430-acre man-made peninsula was originally constructed in the late 1930s as a port for international shipping, and was taken over by the U.S. Navy in 1942. It was deeded to the Bayonne Local Redevelopment Authority in December 2002, after the closing of the Navy base. The new port's location—just off the New Jersey Turnpike and I-278, and approximately 15 minutes from the Newark airport—makes it easily accessible for those coming from New Jersey, Long Island, and the New York boroughs of Brooklyn and Staten Island. Passengers coming from Manhattan can connect via a nearby light rail that links with both Amtrak and the PATH subway. Royal Caribbean is also considering a ferry service from Manhattan to the port.

BY PLANE   You'll fly into one of three New York area airports. **John F. Kennedy (JFK) International** is east of Manhattan in the southeastern section of Queens County, 15 miles from midtown Manhattan and a 30- to 60-minute drive from the piers, depending on traffic. **LaGuardia Airport** is also east of Manhattan in Queens, 8 miles from midtown Manhattan and a 20- to 40-minute drive from the piers. **Newark International Airport** is west of Manhattan in Essex and Union counties, New Jersey, about 16 miles from midtown Manhattan and a 30- to 60-minute drive from NYC. Information on all three is at the **Port Authority of New York & New Jersey** website, www.panynj.gov. Kennedy and Newark are the larger airports and accommodate both domestic and international flights. If you've arranged air transportation and/or transfers through the cruise, a cruise line representative will direct you to shuttle buses that take you to the port. Taxis are also available. Yellow New York City taxis are usually lined up in great numbers at the airports waiting for fares. From JFK to Manhattan, yellow taxis charge a flat fee of $35 per carload, plus tolls and tip; there is no flat fee from Newark or LaGuardia. If you're traveling via yellow taxi to any of the airports, pay the amount on the meter (to Newark, a $10 surcharge is added to metered fare).

Carmel Car Service (© 800/9-CARMEL or 212/666-6666) charges $29 per carload from Manhattan (including the cruise ship piers) to LaGuardia, $39 to JFK, and $36 to Newark; to Manhattan, the rates vary depending on time of day: $27 to $34 from LaGuardia, $35 to $41 from JFK, and $36 to $44 to Newark. Freelance (also known "gypsy") drivers may solicit you in the airport; to avoid being gouged, it's better to stick with a car service or the official NYC yellow taxis.

Super Shuttle (© 212/258-3826; www.supershuttle.com) vans are another good way to get between the airports and the piers. Fares are $15 to LaGuardia and $19 to JFK or Newark per person either way (so it's no bargain if you're a group of three or more). Twenty-four-hour advance reservations are recommended.

BY CAR   Manhattan's Henry Hudson Parkway/West Side Highway is the main artery into the port. To get to the terminals at 48th, 50th, and 52nd streets, cars should enter via the vehicle ramp at 54th Street, directly off the highway.

Long-term parking at the port is $18 a day if parking for multiple days, or $15 for up to 10 hours. If you want to park for 9 days or more, the monthly rate is $170. The lots are on top of the three terminals, with escalators leading down. Payment is accepted in cash or travelers checks only.

CHARLESTON, SOUTH CAROLINA

One of the most important seaports and cultural centers of America's colonial period, Charleston is one of the best preserved cities in the U.S., boasting 73 pre–Revolutionary War buildings, 136 structures from the late 18th century, and more than 600 buildings built before the 1840s. Horse-drawn carriages carry visitors through cobblestone, gas-lit streets, as the fragrances of jasmine and wisteria fill the air. Cruise passengers can walk right from the cruise ship docks to the heart of the city, which is filled with lovely 18th-century architecture. Highlights include the **Old City Market** at East Bay and Market streets, a 3-block collection of boutiques and crafts stalls; **Fort Sumter** in Charleston Harbor, where the first shots of the Civil War were fired; and innumerable **antique-filled colonial homes and manicured gardens.**

In 2004, Carnival's *Carnival Victory* and NCL's *Norwegian Majesty* are home porting in Charleston, with Crystal's *Crystal Symphony,* Silversea's *Silver Whisper,* Radisson's *Seven Seas Navigator,* Celebrity's *Galaxy,* and Clipper's *Nantucket Clipper* also using the city as a port of call on several coastal itineraries.

GETTING TO CHARLESTON & THE PORT
The Port of Charleston's 18,000-square-foot cruise ship terminal is located in the peninsular city at 196 Concord St., at the foot of Market Street, in the heart of the historic district.

BY PLANE   The **Charleston International Airport** (© 843/767-7009; www. chs-airport.com) is located in North Charleston, 12 miles from the cruise ship terminal. If you've made arrangements for transfers through your cruise line, a representative will meet your arriving flight and direct you to shuttle buses. Taxis are available at a rate of approximately $20 for one or two passengers, with each additional person charged an additional $10. Shuttle service is available through the Airport **Limo/Taxi Association** (© 800/750-1311 or 843/607-5456), but because the per-person rate is $10, you may as well get a taxi.

BY CAR   The Port of Charleston is located 12 miles from Charleston International Airport. From I-95 North or South, take I-26 (SE) toward Charleston. Exit at East Bay Street, turn left onto Market Street, then right onto Concord Street. The entrance to the terminal will be on your left. From U.S. Highway 17, exit at East Bay Street, turn right off the exit ramp, then left onto Market, then right onto Concord. The entrance will be on your left. From Charleston Airport, exit onto I-526 and connect to I-26 (Charleston). Continue to East Bay Street-Morrison Drive exit (219-B) and turn left at the bottom of the ramp. Continue onto Morrison Drive, which becomes East Bay Street. Turn left onto Calhoun Street, then right onto Washington Street, which will connect to Concord Street and the terminal.

Parking lots are located near the terminal, with port police on hand to direct you. A shuttle bus is available to take you and your luggage right to the pier. Parking is $8 per day.

SAN JUAN, PUERTO RICO
In addition to being the embarkation port for a number of ships, San Juan is also a major port of call, so see "Puerto Rico," in chapter 5, for all information.

The Ports of Call

The Caribbean is the classic cruise destination, tailored to people who want nice white-sand beaches, tiki bars serving tropical drinks, some hot island music, and sun, sun, sun. Culture and history also have their place. In general, western Caribbean itineraries offer opportunities for visiting the ruins of Mayan cities and temple sites on the mainland, while eastern Caribbean itineraries are more likely to dock at ports that offer reminders of British, French, Spanish, and Dutch colonial history. Panama Canal itineraries mix the lore of that massive construction effort with access to rich Central American culture. And of course, there's gorgeous scenery all over the Caribbean, from the lush jungles of Dominica to the arid moonscape of Aruba.

Here's the good news: There are hardly any lousy Caribbean islands, though depending on your likes and dislikes, you'll appreciate some more than others. Some—especially St. Thomas and Nassau—are much more touristy and commercial than others, though their large variety of bustling stores will appeal to shoppers. Others—Virgin Gorda, St. John, Jost Van Dyke, and Les Saintes, for instance—are quieter and more natural and will appeal to those who want to walk along a calm beach or take a drive along a lonely, winding road amid lush tropical foliage. Destinations like St. Barts and Bequia offer a low-key yachting-port atmosphere, while ports like Key West and Cozumel are all about whooping it up.

1 Port Strategies & Tips

SHORE EXCURSIONS VS. GOING IT ON YOUR OWN

Participating in the shore excursions offered by the cruise lines can be a wonderful and carefree way to get to know the islands, and to experience everything from island tours, snorkeling, and sailing excursions (often with a rum-punch party theme) to more physically challenging pursuits like bicycle tours, hiking, kayaking, and horseback riding. But do you really *need* to sign up for them? The answer is, not everywhere. At some ports—Aruba, Curaçao, Bequia, and San Juan, Puerto Rico, for instance—your best bet is experiencing the island on your own. In the following section, we'll advise you on which islands are good bets for solo exploring; tell you whether you should go it on foot or by taxi, motor scooter, ferry, or other form of transportation; and detail the best sights to see. One downside to exploring independently is that you'll be forgoing the kind of narrative you'd get from a guide, so you may miss out on some of the historical, cultural, and other nuances of a particular island. On the other hand, you may find your own fascinating details, things that an organized tour might pass over. In some ports, touring on your own could be an inefficient use of your time, involving lots of hassles and planning, maybe costing more, and possibly incurring some risk (because of poor roads or driving conditions, for instance). In

---

Tips **Booking Shore Excursions Early**

If you want to arrange a private custom-designed excursion for your family or group of friends, or just want to save a little money on a snorkeling trip, Florida-based **Port Promotions** (www.shoreexcursions.com) organizes shore excursions and allows you to book them online as late as a week before your cruise. You'll get a confirmation via e-mail. Port Promotions often uses the same tour companies that the cruise lines do, though groups tend to be smaller and rates for Caribbean tours are about 10% cheaper. If you change your mind before the excursion, you can e-mail or call Port Promotions to get a refund.

---

these cases, the shore excursions offered by the cruise lines are the way to go. Under each port review we'll describe the best excursions available. See the following page for a chart rating various aspects of each island—dining, shopping, activities close to the port, beaches and watersports. This is a good tool for deciding which ports interest you at a glance.

Keep in mind that **shore excursion prices** vary from line to line, even for the exact same tour; the prices we've listed are typical and are adult rates; children's rates for many excursions are also offered, so just ask. Also note that some cruise lines may not offer all these tours, while others may offer even more. Note also that in some cases the excursions fill up fast, especially on the megaships, so don't dawdle in signing up. When you receive your cruise documents, you'll probably receive a pamphlet with a listing of the excursions offered for your itinerary. Look it over, make your selections, and sign up ASAP. A few lines, like Royal Caribbean, Celebrity, and Princess, allow you to sign up precruise, using your booking code on their websites; where this is not the case, sign up on the first or second day of your cruise. In some cases, if a tour offered by your ship is booked up, you can try to book it independently once you get to port. The popular Atlantis submarine tour, for example—offered at Grand Cayman, Nassau, St. Thomas, and other islands—usually has an office/agent in the cruise terminals or nearby.

If you want to **rent a car** in port, make reservations in advance. **Avis** (© 800/331-1212; www.avis.com), **Budget** (© 800/472-3325; www.drivebudget.com), and **Hertz** (© 800/654-3001; www.hertz.com) all have offices on most of the Caribbean islands in this chapter; **Dollar** (© 800/800-4000; www.dollar.com) and **National** (© 800/227-7368; www.nationalcar.com) are less well represented in the region. See "Getting Around" in the individual port listings to see which companies have offices there. Also note that in certain ports we advise against renting at all.

DOCKING, DOLLARS & OTHER PORT DETAILS

ARRIVING IN PORT Most cruise ships arrive in port sometime before 10am, though this will vary slightly from line to line and port to port. If you're a U.S. citizen, you'll rarely have to clear Customs or Immigration, because your ship's purser has your passport or other ID and will have done all the paperwork for you. When local officials give the word, you just go ashore. In most cases you can walk down the gangway right onto the pier, but occasionally (if your ship is too big for the island's docks, for example, or if you've arrived on a busy day and all the pier space is full) your ship will have to anchor offshore and ferry passengers to land via a small boat called a tender. In either case, you might have to wait in line to get ashore, but the wait will be longer if you have to tender in. Once ashore, even if you've come by tender, you aren't stuck there—tenders run back and forth on a regular basis, so you can return to the ship at any time for lunch, a nap, or whatever. Tenders all look pretty much alike, so you might be confused as to which one's heading to your ship, but officers are on duty to check your ID and make sure you get to the right boat.

SCHEDULING YOUR TIME ASHORE   All shore excursions are carefully organized to coincide with your time in port. If you're going it on your own, you can count on finding taxi drivers at the pier when your ship docks. In most cases it's a good idea to arrange with the driver to pick you up at a certain time to bring you back to the port. In most ports you can also rent a car, moped/scooter, or bicycle to get around.

CALLING HOME   Prices for calling home from a cruise ship are sky high (anywhere from $4–$15 a min.), so it's a better idea to call from land, when you're in port. Most phones in port will take any phone card, but for some phones you'll need to purchase a local calling card from a vendor in port. We've included information on where to find phones in all the port reviews. Country codes are as follows: United States and Canada, 1 (from most Caribbean islands, it's just like dialing between states); Australia, 61; New Zealand, 64; the United Kingdom, 44; and the Republic of Ireland, 353. Another option is using your ship's Internet center to keep in touch with folks at home via e-mail. It'll still cost you, but not nearly as much as you'd spend on phone calls. You'll also find Internet centers close to the docks in most ports.

SHOPPING TIPS   You'll find it all here, from jewelry (lots and lots of jewelry), perfume (ditto), and electronics to indigenous arts and handicrafts to the cheesiest tourist gimcracks. Prices vary by port. Some—such as the U.S. Virgin Islands, St. Barts, St. Martin, and Aruba—are pretty pricey, while ports like Cozumel, Jamaica, and the Grenadines are cheaper. **Duty-free merchandise** can save you as little as 5% to as much as 50%, so if you have particular goods you're thinking of buying this way, it pays to check prices at your local discount retailer before you leave home so you'll know whether you're really getting a bargain. Many ports offer particularly good deals on **liquor,** though keep in mind that you'll pay tax when coming back into the U.S. if you buy more than your legal limit (see the section on U.S. Customs in chapter 3 for more info).

When shopping, be aware that some items you may see offered may not be allowed by U.S. Customs. You may be eyeing that gorgeous piece of **black-coral jewelry,** for instance, but laws prohibiting the trade in endangered species make it illegal to bring many products made from coral and other marine animals back to the United States. (Remember, corals aren't rocks: They're living animals—a single branch of coral contains thousands of tiny coral animals, called polyps.) Sea turtles, too, are highly endangered, and sea horses, while not yet protected by

---

(*Tips* **Don't Forget Cash When Going Ashore**

It's happened to both of us and it's happened to our friends, so it can happen to you, too: After a few days of living cash-free aboard ship, it doesn't even cross your mind to grab the greenbacks when you're going ashore. You get there and realize you're penniless. It's soooo frustrating, especially if you've had to take a tender in from offshore. Don't let it happen to you.

Frommer's Ratings at a Glance: Caribbean Ports of Call

Ratings Guide   **1** = poor   **2** = fair   **3** = good   **4** = excellent   **5** = outstanding

Ports	Review on Page	Overall Experience	Shore Excursions	Activities Close to Port	Beaches & Watersports	Shopping	Dining/Bars
Antigua	92	4	3	4	5	2	4
Aruba	99	5	3	4	5	4	4
Freeport, Bahamas	114	3	2	2	3	3	3
Nassau, Bahamas	106	4	3	4	4	3	3
Barbados	119	4	3	3	3	3	3
Belize	126	4	5	2	4	2	3
Bequia	133	4	2	4	4	2	4
Bonaire	139	3	4	3	5	2	3
Tortola, British Virgin Islands	148	4	3	3	3	2	3
Virgin Gorda, British Virgin Islands	152	5	3	4	4	2	3
Cozumel, Mexico	159	4	5	4	2	4	3
Curaçao	168	4	3	4	2	3	3
Dominica	174	3	4	3	2	3	3
Grand Cayman	181	5	5	4	5	4	3
Grenada	186	5	3	4	3	3	3
Guadeloupe	191	4	4	5	4	4	5
Ocho Rios, Jamaica	201	4	5	4	3	2	3
Montego Bay, Jamaica	205	4	5	4	3	3	3
Key West	208	4	4	5	2	3	4
Les Saintes	215	4	2	5	3	2	3
Martinique	220	4	3	3	4	3	3
Nevis	229	4	1	4	4	2	2
Playa del Carmen, Mexico	164	4	5	3	3	2	3
San Juan, Puerto Rico	236	5	2	5	3	4	4
St. Barts	250	4	3	4	4	4	3
St. Croix, U.S. Virgin Islands	294	4	4	4	4	5	3
St. John, U.S. Virgin Islands	290	4	3	4	4	2	2
St. Kitts	255	3	3	1	3	2	3
St. Lucia	259	4	4	3	4	2	3
St. Martin	266	4	3	4	4	4	4
St. Thomas, U.S. Virgin Islands	282	4	4	4	4	5	3
Tobago	278	4	3	1	4	2	2
Trinidad	274	2	2	1	2	2	3

laws, are currently threatened with extinction. The shopkeeper selling items made from these creatures probably won't tell you they're questionable from a Customs standpoint, but the Customs agent sure will, and may fine you or at the least confiscate the item if he catches you with it. Better to just buy a cheap underwater camera and take pictures of underwater beauties on a snorkeling expedition—you get the memories, the evidence, and a little exercise to boot.

Cuban cigars are also prohibited by U.S. Customs. You'll see them all over the islands, but be aware that, *legally* speaking, you have to smoke 'em before you head for home.

REBOARDING   Most passengers start heading back to the ship around 4pm or not much later than 5. By 6 you're often sailing off to your next destination. In some cases—for instance, in Nassau, New Orleans, St. Barts, and the British Virgin Islands—the ship may stay in port until after midnight so that passengers can stay ashore and enjoy the island's nightlife. When actually walking back aboard, you'll have to present your shipboard ID to be scanned (except aboard some small ships, which are less formal).

If a shore excursion runs late, the ship will be held until the excursion's participants are back on board. It occasionally happens, though, that a passenger goes off on his or her own, has a little too much fun, and misses the boat. If it happens to you, don't panic: The cruise line's port agent (whose offices will be at or close to the pier) will be able to get you back aboard, though it'll cost you—you'll either have to charter a boat or pay for a flight to the next port of call.

2 A Brief History of the Caribbean

Caribbean history reads like a Hollywood blockbuster—brutal conquests, devastating plagues, swashbuckling pirates, new frontiers, monumental sea battles, slave insurrections, and violent revolutions. Grab your popcorn.

PRE-COLUMBIAN CULTURES   Every schoolchild learns that in 1492 Columbus sailed the ocean blue. He was a johnny-come-lately, of course—people lived in the Caribbean for hundreds, even thousands of years before Europeans arrived. Three major groups, all originally from South America, were there when Columbus arrived.

The least advanced of the native peoples, the **Ciboney,** were probably the first to arrive. Living primarily in rock shelters and caves, they formed small family groups, hunted turtles and reptiles, and collected shellfish, wild fruits, and herbs. Their rudimentary tools were made of stone.

The more advanced **Arawak** and **Carib** peoples had frequent contact with each other and shared many of the same material technologies. They farmed, hunted, and fished, and both groups used similar methods to construct canoes, build huts, weave cloth, and make pottery. Both peoples cultivated root plants—yucca, yams, arrowroot, peanuts, peppers, and gourds—and seed crops like maize, beans, and squash. Pineapple and guava, shellfish, fish, iguanas, birds, and snakes provided additional sustenance. Men generally hunted and fished, while women farmed, cooked, wove cloth, and made household pottery and baskets.

The Arawak, by all accounts, were peaceful, gentle, and friendly. Women enjoyed considerable status, religion was based on the belief that spirits inhabited both humans and natural objects, and islands were divided into provinces ruled by chiefs.

Carib authority was less centralized. Independent villages were presided over by village chiefs, who came together to elect war chiefs for each island. Men lived together in communal houses and kept their wives, who they treated as servants, in separate huts. Because they resisted Spain's efforts to enslave them, the Carib were vilified as bloodthirsty savages by the Spanish. In fact, the word "cannibal" comes from the Spanish name for the tribe—*caribal.* There is no evidence that the Carib practiced cannibalism—the Spanish may have made the claim to justify their assault on the tribe. The Carib were more aggressive than the Arawak, who were frequently on the receiving end of Carib raids. However, when the French and English settled the Lesser Antilles (most of the Caribbean islands except Cuba, Jamaica and Hispaniolia) in the 1630s, the Carib were friendly and provided food for the starving adventurers—they became violent only after the Europeans attacked them.

EUROPEAN "DISCOVERY" OF THE ISLANDS   On October 12, 1492, Columbus became the first European to reach the New World, landing on Watling's Island in the Bahamas. This exploratory first voyage was followed in 1493 by a second and much larger expedition to establish a permanent foothold in the islands. On his second expedition, along with 1,500 men, Columbus brought horses, sheep, cattle, and hogs, as well as plants grown in Europe such as wheat, barley, grapes, and sugarcane. Landing first on Dominica, the fleet passed through and named the islands of the Lesser Antilles before arriving in Hispaniola (where Haiti and the Dominican Republic are located) in November 1494. Before returning to Spain, Columbus sighted Jamaica and explored Cuba.

ENSLAVEMENT OF THE INDIANS   The Spanish crown distributed land on the islands to individual settlers, who were expected to cultivate it for 4 years. In return, they received the use of the property in perpetuity. By the time Columbus returned on his third voyage in 1498, the system had been distorted considerably, with Indian communities forced to work the land as slave laborers. Without this slave system, the colonial economies certainly would have failed. The Spanish not only enslaved the local population, but eventually, if unintentionally, almost completely obliterated it by bringing in diseases that the native islanders had no immunity to.

DISEASE AND DECIMATION   Prior to the 15th century, the peoples of Europe and Africa rarely mingled, and the indigenous peoples of the Americas existed in total isolation. Consequently, a distinctive disease environment developed on each continent. Until the Europeans and Africans arrived, a host of illnesses—among them smallpox, measles, typhus, yellow fever, malaria, and tuberculosis—were unknown in the New World. The native peoples had no natural immunity to these diseases, and when exposed to them, they died in staggering numbers. In 1492, as many as six million Arawak and Carib Indians lived in the Caribbean. Within 20 years, almost all were dead. Europeans and African slaves gave each other diseases as well, and as many as a third of both groups died during their first 2 years on the islands.

GOLD FEVER   The Spanish were interested in only one thing in the New World: gold. Wherever gold was found, settlers rushed in, and the meager gold sources on any given island were quickly exhausted. Undaunted, the Spanish would move on to another island, with Indian slaves in tow. Eventually, they searched farther, into Mexico, Panama, and Peru, where they hit the jackpot: the unparalleled treasures of the Aztec and Inca.

Once the enormous value of the gold and silver in Mexico and Peru became clear, the Spanish ignored the Antilles except as a source of slaves. King Ferdinand authorized slaving expeditions to the Lesser Antilles and the Curaçao group in 1511. By 1520, the northern (or Leeward) islands from the Virgins to Barbuda (located next to Antigua), except for St. Kitts and Nevis, were depopulated. The inhabitants of the Curaçao group, Barbados, St. Lucia, and Tobago were also forcibly removed, and on the remaining islands, the Carib retreated to the mountainous interiors, where they resisted would-be enslavers with considerable skill.

TREASURE SHIPS AND PIRATES   The islands remained important to Spain not only as sources of slaves, but because Spanish treasure fleets had to pass by them on their way from Mexico and Peru to Seville, the sole port in Spain authorized to receive the gold, silver, and other riches from the New World. Rulers of other European states, envious of Spain's wealth, encouraged their subjects to plunder Spanish ships. Piracy became an accepted business, and thousands of buccaneer ships, sailing from ports in France, Britain, and the Netherlands, attacked Spanish ships, as well as ports in the Caribbean and along the coast of Central America. **Sir Francis Drake** took the greatest booty, capturing an entire year's yield of Peruvian silver in 1573. To protect its treasure fleets from pirates, Spain closed its American empire to outside trade, forbidding its American colonies from trading with any other European powers. Spain also limited ocean crossings to Europe—only two heavily guarded convoys made the trip each year. While great forts were built on gold- and silver-loaded islands along the fleet route, other island settlements remained unprotected, and had to fend for themselves when buccaneers came onto their shores to help themselves to food, water, and any other supplies that they needed on their long journey. Spain's focus on Peru and Mexico precluded state development of the Caribbean colonies, and for 3 centuries, most inhabitants of the forgotten islands earned modest livings as farmers and ranchers.

COLONISTS FROM NORTHERN EUROPE   The British, French, and Dutch established permanent colonies on the islands in the 1620s, initially concentrating on the smaller, still unoccupied islands of the eastern Caribbean, and moving west into the Greater Antilles (Cuba, Jamaica, and Hispaniola) after 1650. The success of these efforts often depended on events in Europe, and islands, like chips in a poker game, often changed hands during wars on the Continent. Governments, more interested in European affairs and with no money to spend on colonial development, played only a limited role in the initial settlement and economic development of the islands. Individual adventurers, often acting for groups of merchants, established the first Dutch, French, and British colonies. Governments gave adventurers exclusive licenses to exploit specific areas in return for a share of the profit.

In 1618, the Dutch began to challenge Spanish control of the Caribbean by establishing its own colonies and trade in the region. During the 17th century, the Netherlands led all other European nations in manufacturing, commerce, and finance capitalism, and the nation soon dominated trade with the Far East, Africa, and the Caribbean. The **Dutch West India Company,** chartered in 1621, had a state-granted 25-year monopoly in the Americas. Between 1625 and 1635, Dutch maritime forces changed the balance of power in the Caribbean, making it possible for Dutch traders to control most of the region's commerce for decades. The Dutch established colonies on Sint Maarten, St. Eustatius, Saba, Curaçao, Aruba, and Bonaire. Eventually, the Dutch West India Company's fortunes waned and its monopoly expired after investors became displeased by the venture's profits. Individual traders then moved in to fill the void, and the Dutch West India Company reorganized to focus on the trade in West African slaves and goods to Caribbean colonies settled and controlled by other European powers.

New waves of British and French marauders followed the Dutch to the Caribbean. Tropical products such as **tobacco** and **sugar** were fetching high prices in Europe, and few investments at home promised comparable profits.

The prospect of economic gain was the primary lure, but adventurers, fame seekers, and religious nationalists had their own motives for going to the Caribbean. The British and French claimed many of the same islands, but speaking in very general terms, the British settled St. Kitts, Barbados, Nevis, Antigua, Montserrat, Anguilla, the British Virgin Islands, and Jamaica, while the French established colonies on Guadeloupe, Martinique, St. Christophe (the French name for St. Kitts), and what is today Haiti. The Danish (St. Thomas, St. John, and St. Croix) and Swedish (St. Barts) came later and in much smaller numbers.

ENORMOUS SUGAR PROFITS   The Caribbean enjoyed relative peace and prosperity for much of the 1700s, and the region's economy—especially the sugar industry—grew rapidly. During the 18th century, the islands produced 80% to 90% of the sugar consumed in western Europe. Demand encouraged planters to develop large-scale plantations and ushered in a new era of slavery. Profits and associated tax revenues convinced British and French politicians that both sugar and slavery were essential to their national economies.

SLAVERY ON AN UNPRECEDENTED SCALE   Economically, socially, and politically, slavery dominated the sugar islands to an extent never matched in human history. By the 1750s, almost 9 out of 10 people on all the islands where sugar was grown were slaves. Conditions were brutal: Heat, disease, and backbreaking work killed slaves before they could reproduce, and sugar estates could operate only by constantly importing enormous numbers of new slaves from Africa. Except for the Spanish, all the colonial powers supported and were directly involved in the slave trade. The genocide began even before the human cargo from Africa arrived on the islands. The trip across the Atlantic—the Middle Passage, as it was known—claimed the lives of millions. Shackled together, subsisting on tainted water and food of minimal nutritional value, and exposed to disease, 20% of the slaves died aboard ship. As many as another third, already weakened by confinement and malnutrition, perished in their first few years on the islands. And three out of four babies born to slaves died before the age of 5.

ENGLAND & FRANCE COMPETE FOR DOMINANCE   From 1740, Great Britain and France fought throughout the world to gain commercial and colonial supremacy. The Caribbean was a major theater of battle, but the struggle was worldwide in scope, affecting Europe, North America, Africa, and India as well. Caribbean islands, often used as bargaining chips, changed flags frequently as the balance of world power shifted between France and England. But the swing of the pendulum affected Caribbean societies and economies only superficially. Soldiers, rather than civilians, fought battles. Crops and plantations were largely unscathed, and planters essentially maintained power over island politics regardless of which flag happened to be flying at any particular time. And slaves remained slaves whether an island was designated as British or French.

Islands held by both sides were vulnerable to attack, as neither the British nor the French were willing to spend the huge sums needed to protect them. The British maintained two permanent ports in the region; France had none, electing instead to send ships from Europe for specific purposes. The French fleets arrived fresh from the dockyard and in good shape, while the British ships quickly rotted under the tropical conditions. Once they arrived in the region, however, the French fleets quickly ran out of food, while British ships obtained provisions from their permanent naval stations. Disease also played a role: Any victory had to be won almost immediately, as a long siege led to staggering death rates from illnesses.

SLAVE RESISTANCE   During the height of the slave era, blacks outnumbered whites 10 to 1 on most islands. Individual slaves frequently ran away, and groups of slaves planned escapes and uprisings. In fact, slaves rebelled much more frequently in the Caribbean than in the United States, and thousands joined in widespread insurrection on dozens of occasions, destroying plantations and killing slave owners. But only the 1791 revolt on Saint-Domingue (now Haiti), led by **Toussaint L'Ouverture,** culminated in permanent liberation, with the establishment of an independent Haiti in 1804. On other islands, maroons—escaped slaves who banded together and formed their own independent communities—sought refuge in mountains and areas of dense brush and broken terrain. As planters cut down forests to create new cane estates, maroons fled to Dominica and St. Vincent, two lush, mountainous islands designated as Carib territory. Escaped slaves on the flatter, drier islands had no hiding places at all.

ABOLITION OF SLAVERY & INFLUX OF INDENTURED SERVANTS
Slavery dominated every facet of life in the Caribbean islands—it made sugar plantations possible, shaped social and familial relations, and dominated the laws and politics of the region. The abolition of slavery, therefore, represented a cataclysmic change in island life. In 1833, pressured by more frequent slave rebellions, and by the large segment of the British population who increasingly found slavery morally repugnant, cruel, and economically inefficient, England permanently ended slavery in its Caribbean colonies. Inspired by the success of British abolitionists, French intellectuals pressed for emancipation, winning the fight in 1848. The Dutch abolished slavery in 1863. Many freed slaves moved off the plantations to squat on vacant land, and the loss of free labor temporarily crippled sugar production. To fill the labor void, planters recruited indentured workers (who labored under contract), primarily from India, but also from China, Indochina, and Africa's west coast.

INDEPENDENCE & ECONOMIC CHALLENGES   At the end of the 19th century, the United States succeeded the European powers as the main economic and political force in the Caribbean. Under the centralized political systems in place until the 1950s, laws governing the region continued to be made in London, Paris, and the Hague, but after almost a century of economic decline on the islands, it was American capital that provided the means to rebuild the sugar, coffee, and banana industries. And American military power, protecting American commercial interests in the region, intervened in Cuba, Haiti, and the Dominican Republic.

In the years between the two world wars, islandwide political movements developed, paving the way for independence. Since World War II, some islands have become integral parts of larger nations with constitutional arrangements that give their peoples management of local affairs. Puerto Rico and the Virgin Islands entered into relationships with the United States, the French Antilles were integrated into France, and the Dutch West Indies became an autonomous part of the Kingdom of the Netherlands. The major British colonies have become totally independent states, while smaller islands remaining within the British sphere enjoy home rule.

The Caribbean islands have different languages, political systems, and cultural traditions, but all face similar economic problems as they search for new sources of income to replace the declining sugar industry. Tourism is now the region's main business.

3 The Cruise Lines' Private Islands

Royal Caribbean, Princess, Disney, Holland America, Norwegian, and Costa all have private islands (or parts of islands) that are included as port of calls on many of their Caribbean and Bahamas itineraries. While few offer any kind of true Caribbean culture, they do offer cruisers a guaranteed beach day with all the trimmings and a more private experience than you'd get at most ports' public beaches. Note that aside from Disney's Castaway Cay, none of the islands has a large dock, so passengers are ferried ashore by tender.

CELEBRITY CRUISES   See "Royal Caribbean," below.

COSTA CRUISES   Passengers on Costa's eastern Caribbean itineraries spend 1 day at **Catalina Island,** off the coast of the Dominican Republic. This relaxing patch of paradise offers a long beach fringed by palm trees, with activities such as volleyball, beach Olympics, and snorkeling. The area adjacent to the tender dock is the busiest spot, as is to be expected, but if you walk down the beach a bit you'll find a more private, quiet area (though the coastline gets a little rocky when you get farther out from the dock). The island has a strip of shops hawking jewelry, beachwear, and other souvenirs; a local island vendor rents jet skis and offers banana-boat rides; and the ship's spa staff sets up a cabana to do massages on the beach. Locals often offer massages as well; for $25 each—a fraction of what the ship charges—a local woman gave us a great foot and shoulder massage. Locals also sell coconuts for $2 apiece, hacking off the end and plunking in a straw or two so you can get at the milk. After you're finished, take it back to the vendor and they'll whack the thing to pieces with a machete and scrape out the tender coconut meat for you. Music and a barbecue round out the day.

DISNEY CRUISE LINE   A port of call on all *Disney Magic* and *Disney Wonder* cruises, 1,000-acre, 3-by-2-mile **Castaway Cay** is rimmed with idyllically clear Bahamian water and fine sandy beaches. Disney has developed less than 10% of the island, but in that 10% guests can swim and snorkel, rent bikes and boats, get their hair braided (for 2 bucks!), shop, send postcards, have a massage, or just lounge in a hammock or on the beach. Barbecue burgers, ribs, fish, and chicken are available at Cookie's Bar-B-Q, and several bars are scattered near the beaches.

The island's best quality is its accessibility. Unlike the other private islands, which require ships to anchor offshore and shuttle passengers back and forth on tenders, Castaway Cay's dock allows *Magic* and *Wonder* guests to step right off the ship onto the island. Visitors can then walk or take a shuttle tram to the island's attractions. Families can head to their own beach, lined with lounge chairs and pastel-colored umbrellas, where they can swim, explore a 12-acre snorkeling course, climb around on the offshore water-play structures, or rent a kayak, paddle boat, banana boat, sailboat, or other beach equipment. Teens have a beach of their own, where they can play volleyball, soccer, or tetherball; go on a "Wild Side" bike, snorkel, and kayak adventure; or design, build, and race their own boats. Parents who want some quiet time can drop preteens at **Scuttle's Cove,** a supervised children's activity center for ages 3 to 12, where activities include arts and crafts, music and theater, and scavenger hunts. An "excavation site" at Scuttle's Cove allows kids to go on their own archeological digs and make plaster molds of what they find—including a 35-foot reproduction of a whale skeleton. Meanwhile, Mom and Dad can walk or hop the shuttle to quiet, secluded **Serenity Bay,** a mile-long stretch of beach in the northwest part of the island, at the end of an old airstrip decorated with vintage prop planes for a 1940s feel. Twenty-five- and 50-minute massages are available here in private cabanas open to a sea view on one side (sign up for your appointment at the onboard spa on the first day of your cruise to ensure that you get a spot), and the Castaway Air Bar serves up drinks.

Adult- and child-size bicycles can be rented on the island for $6. A 2½-mile round-trip biking/walking path begins at Serenity Bay, but don't go looking for scenery or wildlife—the most you'll see is the occasional bird or leaping lizard. Parasailing is available for $70 (45 min.; over age 8 only). Beach wheelchairs and all-terrain strollers with canopies are available free of charge.

HOLLAND AMERICA LINE   Located on the Bahamian island of San Salvador, 2,500-acre **Half Moon Cay** is a port of call on most of HAL's Caribbean and Panama Canal cruises. Passengers can take it easy on one of the many beach chairs or under a blue canvas cabana (a boon to shade-worshipers), or do a little windsurfing, snorkeling, kayaking, scuba diving, deep-sea fishing, parasailing, sailboarding, aqua-cycling, or horseback riding. The ship's activities staffs also organize volleyball matches, tug-of-war competitions, and other games for adults, and sandcastle building and treasure hunts for kids and teens. Facilities around the island include a food pavilion, a few bars, an ice-cream stand, a kids' play area that was expanded recently as part of the line's "Signature of Excellence" initiative, a post office selling exclusive Half Moon Cay stamps, a cute chapel for vow-renewal ceremonies, and several "tropical mist stations" to help you keep cool. For a special treat, you can get a massage on the beach from the Steiner spa therapists, who set up a pair of tents on the sand. Choose from options including full body, half body, and scalp massages. Chair massages are also available on the beach at $1 per minute (10-min. minimum).

NORWEGIAN CRUISE LINE   NCL's private island, **Great Stirrup Cay,** is a stretch of palm-studded beachfront in the southern Bahamas. This was the very first private resort developed by a cruise line in the Caribbean. Loaded with bar, lunch, and watersports facilities, the sleepy beach turns into an instant party whenever one of the NCL vessels is in port. Music is either broadcast or performed live, barbecues are fired up, hammocks are strung between palms, and rum punches are spiced and served. Passengers can ride paddleboats, sail one-person Sunfish sailboats, go snorkeling or parasailing, hop on a banana boat, get a massage at one of the beachside stations, or do nothing more than sunbathe all day long.

PRINCESS CRUISES   Most of Princess's eastern and western Caribbean itineraries offer a stop at **Princess Cays,** the line's "private island" (a misnomer; since it's really a 40-acre strip off the southwestern coast of Eleuthera in the Bahamas, pretty much cut off from the rest of the island). A half-mile of shoreline allows passengers to swim, snorkel, and make use of Princess's fleet of Hobie Cats (catamarans), Sunfish sailboats, banana boats, kayaks, and paddle-wheelers. (If you want to rent watersports equipment, be sure to book it aboard the ship or even online before your cruise to ensure that you get what you want.) There's live music, a dance area, and a beach barbecue on the island, and anyone who wants to get away from it all (or sleep off too many rum punches) can head for the several dozen terrific tree-shaded hammocks at the far end of the beach. Princess's local shop sells T-shirts and other clothing plus souvenirs of the mug-and-key-chain variety, and local vendors set up stands around the island to sell conch shells, shell anklets, straw bags, and other crafts, and to offer hair braiding.

ROYAL CARIBBEAN & CELEBRITY CRUISES   Many ships of sister lines Royal Caribbean and Celebrity stop for a day at one of the line's two private beach resorts, **CocoCay** and **Labadee.**

At **CocoCay** (also called Little Stirrup Cay), an otherwise uninhabited 140-acre landfall in the Bahamas's Berry Islands, you'll find lots of beach, hammocks, food, drink, and watersports, plus such activities as limbo contests, water-balloon tosses, relay races, and volleyball tournaments. For snorkelers, they've even built and sank a replica of one of Bluebeard's schooners.

Labadee, an isolated, sun-flooded, 270-acre peninsula along Haiti's north coast, is so completely tourist-oriented that you'd never know it was attached to the rest of poverty-stricken Haiti. Labadee is a rarity among cruise lines' private islands in that it gives you a real glimpse of the island's culture. At the straightforwardly named "Folkloric Show," a large, colorfully costumed troupe performs Haiti's distinctly African brand of dancing, drumming, and song, while bands at the various bars and restaurants perform the kind of acoustic guitar, banjo, and percussion "mento" music that was a precursor to reggae and other Caribbean styles. It's happy stuff, creating a wonderfully relaxed soundtrack for the whole island. Five beaches are spread around the peninsula, and are progressively less crowded the farther you walk from the dock, where enormous tenders make the short trip to and from the ship. In the Columbus Cove area, a children's aqua-park called Arawak Cay is full of floating trampolines, inflatable iceberg-shaped slides, and water seesaws. Kayaking and parasailing are offered from a dock nearby. At the center of the peninsula, the Haitian Market and Artisan's Market are the port's low points, full of cheesy Africanesque statues and carvings, with touts trying to lure you in with "Sir, let me just show you something over here." Steer clear unless you're desperate for a souvenir. When we were here last, a painter near the dock had much more interesting work for sale.

On both Labadee and Coco Cay, organized children's activities include beach parties, volleyball, seashell collecting, and sand-castle building.

4 Antigua

Though it's the largest of the British Leeward Islands, Antigua (pronounced An-*tee*-gah) is still only 23km (14 miles) long and 18km (11 miles) wide, and offers little of the polish or glitz of some Caribbean islands. And that's its greatest asset: serenity. Nice, relaxing beaches are close to port; **St. John's,** the island's capital and main town, is sleepy and undemanding; and the locals, usually friendly, sometimes wary, are easygoing. Sure, there are things to do, but nothing will raise your blood pressure. Close to port, you can shop lazily in historic, restored warehouses that now feature boutiques and restaurants, spend half an hour or so at a museum to get a sense of Antigua's past, or climb a gentle hill to the massive cathedral overlooking town. Not all of St. John's is charming, but the town is full of cobblestone sidewalks, weather-beaten wooden houses, and louvered Caribbean verandas. The island's British legacy is clearly evident: Antigua has been independent since 1981, but driving is on the left, half of the tourists are subjects of the queen, every little village has an Anglican church, and the island's greatest passion is for the sport of cricket.

Away from St. John's, the rolling, rustic island boasts important historic sites and lots of pretty beaches. On the southern coast, **Nelson's Dockyard,** once Britain's main naval station in the Lesser Antilles, is now a well-maintained national park. Tucked away in the arid, grassy interior, **Betty's Hope,** with its picturesque windmills, conjures up Antigua's sugar-plantation past. And the **Wallings Conservation Area,** in the island's southwestern region, is the best example of the moist forests that covered Antigua before Europeans cleared the land for agriculture.

Antigua cashed in on sugar and cotton production for years. Today, tourism is the main industry. Most Antiguans are descendants of African slaves brought over centuries ago to labor in the fields. People of European, Asian, and Middle Eastern extraction are also represented in the population of 68,000.

COMING ASHORE   Most cruise ships dock at **Heritage Quay** (pronounced *key*) in St. John's, the island's only town of any size. Heritage Quay and the adjacent **Redcliffe Quay** are the main shopping areas, but duty-free stores, restaurants, taxis, and other services can be found in the surrounding blocks as well. When several ships are in port, some dock at the **Deep Water Harbour Terminal,** 1.6km (1 mile) from St. John's. From there, you can either walk or take a short taxi ride into town. A handful of smaller vessels drop anchor at **English Harbour,** on the south coast.

Credit card phone booths can be found on the dock, at both quays, and at Deep Water Harbour. If you want a more comfortable, air-conditioned place to make calls, try the Kinko's-like **Comet** (© 268/462-1040) at 14 Redcliffe St. (in Redcliffe Quay), where you can also check your e-mail ($3 for 15 min.). **Cable & Wireless** (© 268/480-4237), on the corner of Long and Thames streets, sells prepaid phone cards for as little as $4.

You'll find **ATMs** at both quays and at the corner of Thames and St. Mary streets.

LANGUAGE   Antigua is a former British colony, so the official language is **English,** often spoken with a musical West Indian lilt.

CURRENCY   Although the **Eastern Caribbean dollar** (EC$2.70 = $1 US; EC$1 = US37¢) is Antigua's official currency, the U.S. dollar is readily accepted by most shopkeepers and cab drivers, and almost all businesses post their prices in U.S. currency. Prices quoted in this section are in U.S. dollars. Credit cards and traveler's checks are accepted by most traveler-oriented businesses as well.

INFORMATION   The **Antigua and Barbuda Department of Tourism,** at Nevis Street and Friendly Alley in St. John's (© **268/462-0480**), is open Monday through Thursday from 8am to 3pm. Before you leave home, contact the Department of Tourism's New York office (© **888/268-4227** or 212/541-4117; www.antigua-barbuda.org).

CALLING FROM THE U.S.   When calling Antigua from the U.S., simply dial "1" before the numbers listed throughout this section.

GETTING AROUND

BY TAXI   Taxis meet every cruise ship. Although meters are nonexistent, rates are fixed by the government and are posted at the taxi stand at the end of Heritage Quay's pedestrian mall. From the cruise ship dock, it's US$10 to Dickenson Bay, US$20 to Betty's Hope, US$22 to Nelson's Dockyard, and US$25 to Devil's Bridge. Settle on a fare (and the currency) before hopping in. Drivers often double as tour guides: For this added service, expect to pay about US$20 per hour for up to four people, with a 2-hour minimum. Tip between 10% and 15% for all rides.

BY BUS   Buses are cheap (little more than US$1 to almost anywhere on the island), but service is erratic. The privately operated vehicles, mostly 12-seat vans (all have license plates beginning with "A" or "B"), run from early morning until about 6pm. If you're adventurous and want to chew the fat with Antiguan villagers, give it a whirl.

There are two bus stations in St. John's: East Bus Station, on Independence Avenue, serves the north and east; West Bus Station, near St. John's market, is the terminus for routes to the south and west (and English Harbour).

BY RENTAL CAR   Driving is on the left side. Most roads are decent, but some are narrow and chock-full of potholes. Inadequate signage is a problem islandwide. On the bright side, you'll never have to worry about traffic jams. **Avis, Budget, Hertz,** and **National** all operate on the island. Your valid driver's license and a local temporary driving permit (US$20, available from all rental agencies) are required.

BEST CRUISE LINE SHORE EXCURSIONS

Nelson's Dockyard at English Harbour (US$42, 3 hr.): After traversing the island's hilly countryside, you'll visit the site of the planet's last surviving, working Georgian dockyard. Many colonial buildings still stand, including forts, residences, and barracks; several have been converted into restaurants, hotels, shops, and museums. The sea vistas are impressive.

Helicopter to Montserrat Volcano (US$225, 2 hr.): In December 1997, the Soufrierre Hills Volcano on Antigua's neighboring island of Montserrat blew its top, spewing lava and ash over a huge area and burying large swaths of the

---

Frommer's Favorite Antigua Experiences

Sand, Sun, and Sloth: It's your choice: A bustling, social strand or a tranquil, private refuge. Either is within easy reach of the dock. (See "Beaches," below.)

Salt, Sailors, and Swashbucklers: Nelson's Dockyard, on Antigua's southern coast, is a must for history buffs. Colonial forts guard the narrow passage into the protected harbor where the British maintained their most important naval station in the Lesser Antilles, beginning in the 1700s. Like a Caribbean version of Colonial Williamsburg, the national park, with its many restored buildings, evokes another era. (See "On Your Own: Beyond the Port Area," below.)

---

island, including the former capital, Plymouth. This trip takes you over both the volcano and the char-broiled highlights of Montserrat's exclusion zone, the area declared off-limits to ground transportation.

Four-Wheel-Drive Island Tour (US$66, 3 hr.): Tour the island's only remaining rainforest in a four-wheel-drive vehicle, and stop at the ruins of forts, sugar mills, and plantation houses. The excursion includes beach time.

Hiking Safari (US$49, 3 hr.): This 6.4km (4-mile) uphill/downhill hike takes you through Antigua's rainforest, offering panoramic views from one of the island's highest peaks (360m/1,200 ft.).

Jolly Roger Cruise (US$39, 3 hr.): Aboard this wooden "pirate ship," you can take in some of the island's coastal sights, snorkel, dance on the poop deck, limbo, and walk the plank.

EXCURSIONS OFFERED BY LOCAL AGENCIES

Catamaran Cruises: Wadadli Cats (© 268/462-4792) offers different all-day catamaran cruises every day except Monday. Prices, which include an open bar, buffet lunch, live music, and snorkeling equipment, range from US$70 to US$100 (children under 12 half price, under 2 free). Check, though, to make sure you'll be back in time to reboard your cruise ship before it leaves. Both companies offer private catamaran charters.

Miscellaneous Tours: Several reputable operators offer outback eco-adventures, Jeep safaris, kayak and snorkeling excursions, and bus tours of the island. Prices are reasonable, and discounts for children under 12 are common. Inquire at **Antigua Destination Planners** (© 268/463-1944), **Paradise Island Tours** (© 268/462-7280), and **Wadadli Island Tours** (© 268/773-0367).

ON YOUR OWN: WITHIN WALKING DISTANCE

St. John's has a number of attractions that are easily accessible on foot. To your right, just as you pass through immigration formalities, is **Redcliffe Quay,** Antigua's most interesting shopping complex. Most of the sugar, coffee, and tobacco produced on the island in years past was stored in the warehouses here, and before slavery was abolished on the island in 1834, the area witnessed slave auctions. The restored buildings, with their stone foundations, wooden-slat sidings, colorful shutters, and red corrugated-metal roofs, now house an array of boutiques and restaurants. For more local color, turn right (south) once you've reached Market Street and walk 5 blocks to the **Public Market.** The roof of the enclosed structure casts a strange color on the vendors' wares below, but this is the best place to sample locally grown fruits and vegetables and to pick up some Antiguan pottery or baskets. The market is at its most animated early in the morning, especially on Fridays and Saturdays. Across the street, next to the West Bus Station, fishermen hawk their catch every morning at the waterfront **Fish Market.** Chances are slim that you'll buy anything here, but stop by for the salty and sometimes saucy scene. Next, retrace your steps on Market Street, walking north to the intersection of Long Street, where you'll find the **Museum of Antigua and Barbuda** (✆ **268/462-1469**). Although it's not the plushest exhibition space in the Caribbean, the museum traces the history of the nation from its geological birth to the present day. Housed in a former courthouse, a neo-classical structure built in 1750, its exhibits include pre-Columbian tools and artifacts, a replica of an Arawak wattle-and-daub hut, African-Caribbean pottery, and sections dedicated to the island's naval, sugar, and slavery eras. It's open Monday to Friday from 8:30am to 4pm, Saturday from 10am to 2pm. Admission is free, but a donation of US$2 is requested. A couple of blocks uphill from the museum, bordered by Church, Long, and Newgate streets, **St. John's Anglican Cathedral** dominates St. John's skyline with its 21m-high (69-ft.), aluminum-capped twin spires. The original St. John's, a simple wooden structure built in 1681, was replaced in 1720 by a brick building, which was destroyed during an 1843 earthquake. Upon its completion in 1847, the present baroque structure was not universally appreciated: Ecclesiastical architects criticized it as being like "a pagan temple with two dumpy pepperpot towers." The cavernous interior is entirely encased in pitch pine, a construction method intended to secure the building from hurricanes and earthquakes.

ON YOUR OWN: BEYOND THE PORT AREA

One of the major historical attractions of the eastern Caribbean, **Nelson's Dockyard National Park** (✆ **268/481-5021** or 268/481-5022) lies 18km (11 miles) southeast of St. John's, along one of the world's best-protected natural harbors. English ships used the site as a refuge from hurricanes as early as 1671, and the dockyard played a major role during the 18th century, an era of privateers, pirates, and great sea battles. Admiral Nelson's headquarters from 1784 to 1787, the restored dockyard today remains the only Georgian naval base still in use. At its heart, the **Dockyard Museum,** housed in a former Naval Officers' House built in 1855, traces the history of the site from its beginnings as a British Navy stronghold through its development into a national park and yachting center. You'll find plenty of nautical memorabilia. Uphill and east of the Dockyard, the **Dow's Hill Interpretation Center** (✆ **268/481-5045**) features an entertaining 15-minute multimedia overview of Antiguan history and an observation platform that affords a 360-degree view of the park. Farther uphill, Palladian arches mark the **Blockhouse,** a military fortification built in 1787 that included officers' quarters and a powder magazine. For an eagle's-eye view of English Harbour, continue to the hill's summit, where you'll discover the **Shirley Heights Lookout.** Fortified to defend the precious cargo in the harbor below, Fort Shirley's barracks, arched walkways, batteries, and powder magazines are scattered around the hilltop. The Lookout, with its view of the French island of Guadeloupe, was the main signal station used to warn of approaching hostile ships.

The grounds of the national park, which represent 10% of Antigua's total land area, are well worth exploring. Bordered on one side by sandy beaches, the park is blanketed in cactus, tamarind, cinnamon, and turpentine trees, and mangroves that shelter African cattle egrets. An array of **nature trails,** which take anywhere from 30 minutes to 5 hours to walk, meander through the vegetation and offer vistas of the coast. One trail climbs to **Fort Berkeley,** built in 1704 to protect the harbor's entrance. Admission to the park, which is US$5 for adults (children under 12 are free), covers the Dockyard, the Dockyard Museum, Dow's Hill Interpretation Center, the Blockhouse, Shirley Heights, and the rest of the park. The complex is open daily from 9am to 5pm, and is within walking distance of the dock at English Harbor. Free guided tours of the dockyard last 15 to 20 minutes; tipping is discretionary.

To see what's billed as the only operational 18th-century sugar mill in the Caribbean, visit **Betty's Hope,** not far from Pares village on the island's east side (© 268/462-1469). On-site are twin mills, the remnants of a boiling house, and a small visitor center, which opens its doors Tuesday through Saturday from 10am till 3pm. Gardeners should be able to spot golden seal bushes, neem trees, and wild tamarinds on the rolling hills. Serene cows saunter lazily on the grounds.

Not far from Betty's Hope, on the extreme eastern tip of the island, **Devil's Bridge** is one Antigua's most picturesque natural wonders. Over the centuries, powerful Atlantic breakers, gathering strength over the course of their 4,830km (2,995-mile) run from Africa, have carved out a natural arch in the limestone coastline and created blowholes through which the surf spurts skyward at high tide.

Another attraction for nature lovers, **Wallings Conservation Area** is Antigua's largest remaining tract of tropical rainforest. Located in the southwest, this lush wilderness area features three hiking trails and numerous opportunities to spot some of Antigua's nonhuman inhabitants: birds (purple-throated caribs, Antillean crested hummingbirds, broadwinged hawks), mammals (mongooses, bats), amphibians (tree frogs), and reptiles (lizards, snakes). Vegetation includes strangler fig, hog plum, black loblolly, mango, and silk cotton trees, as well as numerous epiphytes. If you've spent your day at Nelson's Dockyard, pass through the area on the way back to your ship via the circular Fig Tree Drive. Although full of potholes in places, this is the island's most scenic drive. It winds through the tropical forest, passing fishing villages, frisky goats, and old sugar mills along the way.

SHOPPING
Most shops of interest in St. John's are clustered in Heritage Quay and Redcliffe Quay, and on St. Mary's Street, all within easy walking distance of the cruise ship docks. Duty-free items include English woolens and linens, as well as local pottery, straw work, and rum.

Redcliffe Quay, to your right as you pass through Customs, was a slave-trading and warehouse district before abolition. Tastefully renovated, it now contains interesting specialty shops, including **Jacaranda** on Redcliffe Street (© 268/462-1888), which sells spices and Caribbean art; **The Goldsmitty** on Redcliffe Street (© 268/462-4601), which offers handmade gold jewelry; and **The Map Shop** on St. Mary's Street (© 268/462-3993), which stocks old and new map prints, sea charts, and Caribbean literature.

Located at the cruise dock, **Heritage Quay** is a run-of-the-mill shopping center with 40 duty-free shops and a vendors' hall.

BEACHES
Antiguans claim that the island is home to 365 beaches, one for each day of the year. True or not, all of them are public, and quite a few are spectacular.

Closest to St. John's, **Fort James Beach,** located 5 minutes and a US$7 cab fare from the cruise dock, is popular with both locals and visitors. The cordoned area of the water is always safe, but farther from shore, undercurrents are occasionally strong. Volleyball and cricket are played daily. You can rent umbrellas and beach chairs, and the open-air restaurant/bar allows you to spend every minute outdoors. For a change of pace, hike up the hill to explore the authentically derelict ruins of Fort James, which once protected St. John's harbor. Another restaurant/bar at the summit offers splendid views of the area.

A bit farther north, a US$10 cab ride from the dock, the .8km-long (½-mile) beach at **Dickenson Bay** is the island's most bustling strand, with numerous hotels, restaurants, and watersports. It's the place to watch people, try out some watersports equipment, or just bake in a social environment. The water is calm, drinking and eating options abound, and chairs and umbrellas are available for rent.

Pleasant, picturesque spots on the less-developed southwest coast include unspoiled **Darkwood Beach** and nearby **Turner's Beach.** Showers, snorkeling equipment, and chairs are available. Restaurants serve fresh seafood, while bars keep you hydrated.

If you crave complete peace and quiet, head to Antigua's most beautiful beach, at **Half Moon Bay.** Isolated at the island's southeast extreme, this expanse is virtually undeveloped. Waves at the beach's center are great for bodysurfing, while the quieter eastern side is better for children and for snorkeling. A restaurant and bar are near the parking lot.

SPORTS

GOLF   The 18-hole, par-70 **Cedar Valley Golf Club,** Friar's Hill Road (© **268/462-0161**), is a 10-minute, US$10 taxi ride from the cruise dock. The 6,142-yard golf course has panoramic views of the northern coast. Greens fees for 18 holes are US$35 and use of a cart is an additional US$30. Club rental is US$20.

SCUBA DIVING & SNORKELING   Antigua's dive sites include reefs, wall drops, caves, and shipwrecks. To arrange a dive, contact **Dive Antigua,** at the north end of Dickenson Bay (© **268/462-3483**). A two-tank dive is US$79. Reef snorkeling is US$25.

WATERSPORTS   Tony's Watersports (© **268/462-6326**) and **Sea Sports** (© **268/462-3355**), both located at Dickenson Bay Beach, offer a full range of watersports equipment. Prices are negotiable depending on season and demand, but sample fares are US$35 per half-hour for jet skis and US$25 per lap for water-skiing.

WINDSURFING   Windsurfing Antigua Watersports (© **268/461-9463**), also at Dickenson Bay Beach, specializes in 2-hour introductory lessons (US$60) that are limited to four people. Experienced wind sailors can rent a full rig for the day at US$50, or for half a day at US$40. The operation also rents Sunfish sailboats (US$20 per hr.), kayaks (US$10 per hr.), and snorkel gear (US$10 for the day).

GREAT LOCAL RESTAURANTS & BARS

Lunch menus on the island focus on West Indian cuisine, though you can get sandwiches, salads, and burgers as well. Antigua's **local beer** is Wadadli, the island's Carib name. The **local rum** is Cavalier.

There's no better place to watch the street life of St. John's than the second-floor wraparound veranda at **Hemingway's,** on St. Mary's Street (© **268/462-2763**). Across from Heritage Quay, on the main road leading from the dock, it serves tasty salads, sandwiches, burgers, seafood, and refreshing tropical drinks.

If you've opted to spend all day at the beach, your best bet at Dickenson Bay is **Coconut Grove Restaurant** (© **268/462-1538**), a quiet, open-air beachside refuge at the strand's southern extreme, complete with palm trees and superb seafood. Lunch is about US$19.

If you're in English Harbour, stop for a lunch break at the rustic **Admiral's Inn,** in Nelson's Dockyard (© **268/460-1027**). Built in 1788, this restored brick building originally stored barrels of pitch, turpentine, and lead used to repair ships. The menu changes daily but usually features pumpkin soup and main courses such as local red snapper, grilled steak, and lobster. Lunch is around US$12.

5 Aruba

More of a desert island than a rainforest, Aruba has unwaveringly sunny skies, warm temperatures, and cooling breezes, along with some of the best beaches in the Caribbean—or in the world, for that matter—miles of white sugary sand; turquoise and aqua seas; warm, gentle surf; and plenty of space.

If you tire of lolling on the beach, there's scuba diving, snorkeling, great wind-surfing, and all the other watersports you expect from a sun-and-sea vacation. On land, you can golf, ride a horse, or drive an all-terrain vehicle over the island's wild-and-woolly outback. Away from the beach, Aruba is full of cactus, iguanas, and strange boulder formations. Contrasting sharply with the southern shoreline's beaches, the north coast features craggy limestone cliffs, sand dunes, and crashing breakers.

Focused on shopping? The collection of stores and malls in Oranjestad, the island's capital, can compete with the most impressive offerings in the Caribbean. In between purchases, try your luck at one of the island's dozen **casinos;** two are just steps away from your ship. Or grab a bite to eat: Unlike the so-so fare found in much of the Caribbean, Aruba's culinary offerings are diverse, inventive, and often outstanding.

Aruba's still part of the Netherlands, so there's a Dutch influence, which adds a nice European flavor. Though it has a few small museums, and some centuries-old indigenous rock glyphs and paintings, nobody comes to Aruba for culture or history.

Only 32km (20 miles) long and 9.7km (6 miles) across at its widest point, the island is slightly larger than Washington, D.C. It's the westernmost of the Dutch ABC islands—Aruba, Bonaire, and Curaçao—and lies less than 32km (20 miles) north of Venezuela. Aruba's capital and largest city, **Oranjestad,** is on the island's southern coast, pretty far to the west.

The Arubans are as friendly as can be. With little history of racial or cultural conflicts, locals have no cause for animosity. And everybody speaks English, as well as Dutch, Spanish, and Papiamento, the local patois.

COMING ASHORE   Cruise ships arrive at the **Aruba Port Authority,** a modern terminal with a tourist information booth, phones, ATMs, and plenty of shops. From the pier it's a 5-minute walk to the **shopping districts** of downtown Oranjestad.

Frommer's Favorite Aruba Experiences

Pretend You're Neil Armstrong: Alien boulders and stark terrain mark Aruba's northern coast, making you feel like a visitor to the moon. The roads are unpaved but easy to navigate in an all-terrain vehicle. You can stop at a lighthouse, an old chapel, and the ruins of a gold-smelting factory, but the major attractions are supplied by nature. (See "Best Cruise Line Shore Excursions" and "On Your Own: Touring by Rental Jeep," below)

Make Like Captain Nemo: Submerge yourself 45m (148 ft.) beneath the sea in a modern submarine to marvel at nature's underwater splendor. (See "Best Cruise Line Shore Excursions," below.)

LANGUAGE The official language is **Dutch,** but nearly everybody speaks **English.** The language of the street is often **Papiamento,** a patois that combines various European, African, and indigenous American languages. **Spanish** is also widely spoken.

CURRENCY The **Aruba florin (AFl)** is the official currency, but U.S. dollars are widely accepted, and most items and services are priced in both currencies. Traveler's checks and major credit cards are almost universally accepted as well. The exchange rate is relatively stable at about 1.8 AFl to US$1 (1 AFl = US56¢). Prices quoted in this section are in U.S. dollars.

INFORMATION For information, go to the **Aruba Tourism Authority,** 172 L. G. Smith Blvd., Oranjestad (© **297/58-23777;** www.aruba.com). It's open Monday to Friday from 7am to 4:30pm.

CALLING FROM THE U.S. When calling Aruba from the U.S., dial the international access code (011) before the numbers listed in this section.

GETTING AROUND
BY RENTAL CAR Excellent roads connect major tourist attractions, and all the major rental companies accept valid U.S. or Canadian driver's licenses. Rent a four-wheel-drive vehicle for the rough roads in the outback. **Avis, Budget, Dollar, Hertz,** and **National** all have offices here.

BY MOTORCYCLE OR BIKE Scooters and motorcycles are only practical if you plan to stick to paved roads. They're available at **George's Cycle Center,** L. G. Smith Blvd. 136 (© **297/58-25975**). Scooters rent for $30 per day, while motorcycles go for $45 up to $100 for a Harley. You can rent mountain bikes **at Semver Cycle Rental,** Noord 22 (© **297/58-66851**), where rates start at $25 per day.

BY TAXI Taxis line up at the dock to take you wherever you want to go. Cabs don't have meters, but fares are fixed, and every driver has a copy of the official rate table. Ask what the fare will be before getting in the car. The fare from the cruise terminal to the beach resorts will be $8 to $10. Tip between 15% and 20%. The dispatch office number is © **297/58-22116.**

Most drivers speak good English and are eager to give you a tour of the island. Expect to pay $40 per hour for a maximum of four passengers.

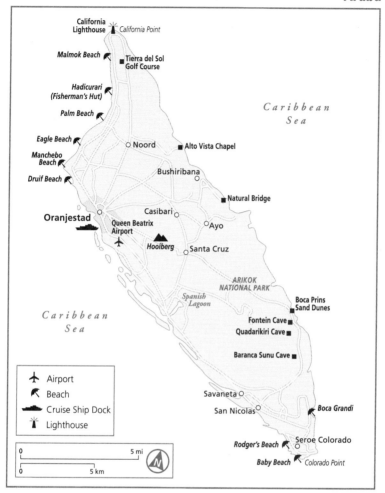

California Lighthouse ☀ California Point

Malmok Beach 🏖 ■ Tierra del Sol Golf Course

Hadicurari (Fisherman's Hut) 🏖

Palm Beach 🏖

Caribbean Sea

Eagle Beach 🏖

Manchebo Beach 🏖

Druif Beach 🏖

○ Noord ■ Alto Vista Chapel

Bushiribana ○

■ Natural Bridge

Casibari ○

Oranjestad

Queen Beatrix Airport ✈ ○Ayo

▲ Hooiberg ○ Santa Cruz

ARIKOK NATIONAL PARK

Spanish Lagoon

Boca Prins Sand Dunes

Caribbean Sea

Fontein Cave ■
Quadarikiri Cave ■

Baranca Sunu Cave ■

✈ Airport
🏖 Beach
⛴ Cruise Ship Dock
☀ Lighthouse

Savaneta ○

San Nicolas ○

🏖 Boca Grandi

0 ————— 5 mi
0 ————— 5 km

Rodger's Beach 🏖 Seroe Colorado ○

Baby Beach 🏖 Colorado Point

BY BUS Aruba has good daily bus service beginning at 6am. The same-day round-trip fare between the beach hotels and Oranjestad is $2; a one-way ride is $1.15. Have exact change. The bus terminal is across the street from the cruise terminal on L. G. Smith Boulevard.

BEST CRUISE LINE SHORE EXCURSIONS

In addition to the tours described here, cruise lines typically offer about a dozen snorkeling, diving, sailing, and other water-oriented tours.

Four-Wheel-Drive Tour ($98, 7 ½ hr.): Take off into Aruba's backcountry in a convoy of four-passenger SUVs. You'll be behind the wheel and have radio contact with your guide. A stop is made for lunch and swimming.

Island Bike Adventure ($47, 3 ½ hr.): Explore Aruba's undeveloped northeast coast by mountain bike, pedaling 10 miles and visiting the Natural Bridge (cut by the sea and wind), the Bushiribana Gold Mine, the Alto Vista Chapel, and the California Lighthouse.

Aruba Pub Crawl ($52, 4 hr.): Travel by antique bus to five different local pubs, including watering holes along the beach, in the countryside, and on Oranjestad's streets, with one free drink included at each. After being dropped off at Carlos and Charlie's, you're on your own to get back to the ship. Good luck.

Atlantis Submarine Journey ($84, 1½ hr.): Cruise 45m (148 ft.) below the sea in a submarine. During the gentle descent, you'll pass by scuba divers, coral reefs, shipwrecks, and hundreds of curious sergeant majors, damselfish, parrotfish, and angelfish.

Aruba Bus Tour ($34, 3 hr.): This air-conditioned bus tour rolls along part of Aruba's wild and woolly windward coastline to the Natural Bridge and the Casibari rock formations, and swings by Aruba's hotel strip.

ON YOUR OWN: WITHIN WALKING DISTANCE

Aruba's capital has a sunny Caribbean atmosphere, with Dutch colonial buildings painted in vivid colors. The main thoroughfare, **Lloyd G. Smith Boulevard,** runs along the waterfront and is crowded with marinas, shopping malls, restaurants, and bars. **Caya G. F. Betico Croes,** or Main Street, is another major shopping street running roughly parallel to the waterfront several blocks inland. The harbor is packed with fishing boats and schooners docked next to stalls where vendors hawk fruits, vegetables, and fish. On the other side of the Seaport Marketplace shopping mall, **Queen Wilhelmina Park,** named after one of Holland's longest-reigning monarchs, features manicured lawns, views of colorful fishing boats, and lush tropical vegetation. If you're looking for a little culture, Oranjestad has a handful of museums that are worth a bit of your time. Squeezed between St. Franciscus Roman Catholic Church and the parish rectory, the small **Archaeological Museum of Aruba,** J. E. Irausquinplein 2A (© 297/58-28979), illustrates the island's Amerindian heritage with pottery vessels, shell and stone tools, burial urns, and skulls and bones. (Free admission; open Mon–Fri 8am–noon and 1–4pm.) To defend the island against pirates, the Dutch erected Fort Zoutman in 1796. In 1867, Willem III Tower, named after the then-reigning Dutch monarch, was added. Since 1992, the complex has housed the modest **Museo Arubano,** Zoutmanstraat z/n (no street number; © 297/58-26099), which displays prehistoric Amerindian artifacts and relics from the Dutch-colonial period. (Admission $1.75; open Mon–Fri 9am–noon and 1–4pm.) The small **Numismatic Museum of Aruba,** Zuidstraat 7, 1 block northeast of Fort Zoutman (© 297/58-28831), may not look promising from the outside, but its meticulous, homemade exhibits tell the history of the world through coins. Dedicated numismatists can spend the better part of the morning perusing the 35,000 different specimens from more than 400 countries, and anyone with a passing interest in coins or history will appreciate this labor of love. (Free admission, donations appreciated; open Mon–Fri 7:30am–3:30pm.)

ON YOUR OWN: TOURING BY RENTAL JEEP

The best way to see Aruba's desertlike terrain is to rent a four-wheel-drive vehicle. Car-rental companies have maps highlighting the best routes to reach the island's attractions. Here's one of the most popular routes:

Following the system of roads that traces the perimeter of the island, start clockwise from Oranjestad. Drive past the hotel strip, toward the island's northwesternmost point. Here, the **California Lighthouse** affords sweeping 360-degree views of spectacular scenery—gentle sand dunes, rocky coral shorelines, and turbulent waves. The picturesque lighthouse got its name from the *California,* a passenger ship that sank off the nearby coast in 1916. The story that this vessel was the only ship to have heard (and ignored) the *Titanic's* distress signal is malarkey. (In fact, the *Californian* [with a final "n"] of *Titanic* infamy was torpedoed by a German submarine off the coast of Greece in 1915.)

From here on, your adventure will take you onto the island's moonlike terrain, past heaps of giant boulders and barren rocky coastline. The well-maintained road that links the hotel strip with Oranjestad deteriorates abruptly into a band of rubble, and the calm, turquoise sea turns rough and rowdy.

By the time you reach the **Alto Vista Chapel,** about 8km (5 miles) from the lighthouse, chances are you'll already be coated with red dust. Don't let that stop you from peeking inside the quaint pale-yellow church that was built in 1750 and renovated 200 years later. Radiating serenity from its cactus-studded perch overlooking the sea, the chapel, Aruba's first, was built by native Indians and Spanish settlers before the island had its own priest.

Farther along the northern coast, you'll approach the hulking ruins of the **Bushiribana Gold Smelter.** Built in 1872, its massive stone walls are reminders of the importance of gold-mining on the island in the 19th century. Unfortunately, the walls have been marred with artless graffiti. Climb the multitiered interior for impressive sea views.

Within view of the smelter, **Natural Bridge** is Aruba's most photographed attraction. Rising 7.5m (25 ft.) above the sea and spanning 30m (98 ft.) of rock-strewn waters, this limestone arch has been carved out over the centuries by the relentless pounding of the surf. Because the bridge acts as a buffer between the sandy beach and open ocean, many people come here to swim and picnic.

Next, head toward the center of the island and the bizarre **Ayó and Casibari rock formations.** Looking like something out of *The Flintstones,* the gargantuan Ayó rocks served Aruba's early inhabitants as a dwelling or religious site. The reddish-brown petroglyphs on the boulders suggest mystical significance. Although the Casibari boulders weigh several tons each, they look freshly scattered by some cyclopean dice roller. Look for the formations that resemble birds and dragons, and climb the trail to the top of the highest rock mound for a panorama of the area.

Farther east, back along the northern coast, **Arikok National Park,** Aruba's showcase ecological preserve, sprawls over roughly 20% of the island. Its premier attractions are a series of caves that punctuate the cliff sides of the area's mesas. The most popular, **Fontein Cave,** has brownish-red drawings left by Amerindians and graffiti etched by early European settlers. Stalagmites and stalactites here look like human heads and bison; park rangers stationed at the cave will point them out. The cave is an important roosting place for long-tongued bats, which nap in the damp inner sanctum. Nearby **Quadirikiri Cave** boasts two large chambers with roof openings that allow sunlight in, making flashlights unnecessary. Hundreds of small bats use the 30m-long (98-ft.) tunnel to reach their nests deeper in the cave. You'll need a flashlight to explore the 90m-long (295-ft.) passageway of **Baranca Sunu,** another cave in the area commonly known as the Tunnel of Love because of its heart-shaped entrance. Helmets and lights can be rented at the entrance for $6.

Heading southeast toward Aruba's behemoth oil refinery, you'll eventually come to **Baby Beach,** at the island's easternmost point. Like a great big bathtub, this shallow bowl of warm turquoise water is protected by an almost complete circle of rock, and is a great place for a dip after a sweaty day behind the wheel.

SHOPPING

Although Aruba boasts plenty of shopping, don't expect prices to be fabulously cut-rate: The days of Caribbean bargains are waning. Nevertheless, the island's low 3.3% duty can make prices on items such as jewelry and fragrances attractive. What's more, there's no sales tax.

Because the island is part of the Netherlands, **Dutch goods** such as Delft porcelain, chocolate, and cheese are especially good buys. Items from **Indonesia,** another former Dutch colony, are reasonably priced, too. **Skin and hair-care** products made from locally produced aloe are also popular and practical. If you're looking for **big-ticket items,** Aruba offers the usual array of watches, cameras, gold and diamond jewelry, Cuban cigars, premium liquor, English and German china, porcelain, French and American fragrances, and crystal.

Aruba's retail activity centers on Oranjestad. About 1km (½-mile) long, **Caya G. F. Betico Croes,** better known as Main Street, is the city's major shopping venue. Downtown also teems with several contiguous shopping malls that stretch for several blocks along the harbor front. **Seaport Mall** and **Seaport Marketplace** feature more than 130 stores, 2 casinos, 20 restaurants and cafes, and a movie theater. Just down the road, **Royal Plaza Mall** is chock-full of popular restaurants and upscale boutiques.

BEACHES

All of Aruba's beaches are public, but chairs and shade huts are hotel property. If you use them, expect to be charged. Shade huts located at beaches where there are no hotels, such as Baby Beach, Arashi, and Malmok, are free of charge. Visitors can rent chairs at Eagle and Bay beaches.

Palm Beach, home of Aruba's glamorous high-rise hotels, is the best spot for people-watching. This stretch of sea and white sand is also great for swimming, sunbathing, sailing, fishing, and snorkeling. It can get crowded, and with two piers and numerous watersports operators, it's also busier and noisier than Aruba's other beaches.

Separated from Palm Beach by a limestone outcrop, **Eagle Beach** stretches as far as the eye can see. The sugar-white sand and gentle surf are ideal for swimming, and although the nearby hotels offer watersports and beach activities, the atmosphere on the beach is relaxed and quiet. A couple of bars punctuate the expansive strand, and shaded picnic areas are provided for the public.

Baby Beach, at Aruba's easternmost tip, is a prime destination for families with young children. The protection of rock breakwaters makes this shallow bowl of warm turquoise water perfect for inexperienced swimmers. Giant sea-grape bushes offer protection from the sun. The beach has a refreshment stand and washrooms, but no other facilities.

SPORTS

SCUBA DIVING & SNORKELING   Aruba is no Bonaire, but it still offers enough coral reefs, marine life, and wrecks to keep scuba divers and snorkelers busy. The best snorkeling sites are around Malmok Beach and Boca Catalina, where the water is calm and shallow and marine life is plentiful. Dive sites stretch along the entire southern coast, but most divers head for the German freighter *Antilla,* which was scuttled during World War II off the island's northwestern tip, near Palm Beach. The island's largest watersports operators, **Pelican Adventures** (© **297/58-63271**) and **Red Sail Sports** (© **297/58-61603**), offer sailing, wind-surfing, and water-skiing in addition to snorkeling and scuba diving. Two-tank dives are $80; one-tank dives are $58. Two-and-a-half-hour snorkeling trips are $33 and half-day (4½ hr.) snorkeling excursions sell are $59.

WINDSURFING Aruba's world-class windsurfing conditions attract wind sailors from around the world. Malmok Beach is the island's most popular windsurfing spot. Used by novices and pros alike, it has slightly gusty offshore winds, minimal current, and moderate chop. Boca Grandi, on the extreme eastern coast, is for advanced wave sailors only. **Aruba Boardsailing Productions** (© **297/58-63940**) offers 2-hour beginner lessons with equipment for $55. Equipment is $30 for 2 hours, $45 for half a day, and $55 for a full day.

GAMBLING

Aruba boasts 11 casinos, most of them casually elegant. Slot machines gear up at 10am; table games such as baccarat, blackjack, poker, roulette, and craps can start as early as noon; and bingo starts in the afternoon.

Two casinos are steps from the dock. At the Aruba Renaissance Beach Resort, the **Crystal Casino,** L. G. Smith Blvd. 82 (© **297/58-36000**), is one of Aruba's only 24-hour casinos and probably its most elegant. In addition to slots and an array of table games, it features a race and sports book room with a satellite linkup and wagering based on Las Vegas odds. The **Seaport Casino,** L. G. Smith Blvd. 9 (© **297/58-36000**), also in downtown Oranjestad, fits in well with the surrounding shopping mall; you might think it's just another store.

GREAT LOCAL RESTAURANTS & BARS

Opulence and first-rate French cuisine make **Chez Mathilde,** Havenstraat 23 (© **297/58-34968**), the perfect choice for special occasions. Main courses include pan-fried trout, wild boar, and ostrich. It's pricey, but you deserve it. Lunch is about $30.

Hip and happy **Cuba's Cookin',** Wilhelminastraat 27 (© **297/58-80627**), serves flavorful Cuban dishes that a re expertly prepared. Kid-friendly **Waterfront Crabhouse,** Seaport Market, L. G. Smith Boulevard (© **297/58-35858**), offers grilled-cheese sandwiches and "psketti." The more sophisticated adult fare includes red snapper, Maine lobster, and crab. Lunch will about $10.

6 Bahamas: Nassau & Freeport

Technically, the 700 islands of the Bahamas aren't in the Caribbean—they're in the Atlantic Ocean, just north of the Caribbean and less than 161km (100 miles) from Miami. However, because they're an important port of call on the cruise ship circuit and are part of the West Indies, they're almost always lumped together with their island neighbors to the south.

If you're a seasoned cruiser, chances are you've been to the Bahamas already and might prefer an itinerary that includes more far-flung ports. If you're new to the region, the Bahamas are a great introduction, with everything you'd expect from a fun-in-the-sun vacation—postcard-perfect beaches, a full range of water activities, and warm temperatures year-round. There's a well-developed tourist infrastructure—things work here—and economic conditions are the envy of most other West Indian islands, so you won't see the kind of poverty that plagues some Caribbean islands. In many ways, the Bahamas isn't much different from, say, some parts of Florida, but if you're looking for something on the exotic side, you'll be able to see and experience colonial sights, British influences, and West Indian color—you'll know right away you're not in Kansas anymore.

The Bahamas became an independent commonwealth of Great Britain in 1973. Tourism and offshore banking account for the islands' current prosperity. About 85% of Bahamians are descended from African slaves; people of European extraction make up most of the rest of the population.

LANGUAGE   English is the official language of the Bahamas. Most people in the tourism industry speak a standard American version of the language at work. You'll also hear an island lilt and a vocabulary that reflects British, Arawak, and African influences.

CURRENCY   The Bahamas's legal tender is the **Bahamian dollar** (B$1), whose value is always the same as that of the U.S. dollar. Both currencies are accepted everywhere on the islands, and most stores accept traveler's checks and major credit cards.

CALLING FROM THE U.S.   Calling the Bahamas from the United States is as simple as phoning between states: Just dial "1" before the numbers listed throughout this section.

NASSAU

Located 298km (185 miles) southeast of Miami, the town of Nassau is the cultural, social, political, and economic center of the Bahamas. With its beaches, shopping, resorts, casinos, historic landmarks, and water and land activities, it's also the island chain's most visited destination—one million travelers a year make their way to the town, and Nassau is one of the world's busiest cruise ship ports. The Nassau/Paradise Island area comprises two separate islands. Nassau is on the northeastern shore of the 34km-long (21-mile) island of New Providence, while tiny Paradise Island, linked to New Providence by bridges, protects Nassau harbor for a 4.8km (3-mile) stretch. Although the area accounts for only 2% of the nation's land area, its 175,000 residents represent 60% of the Bahamian population.

COMING ASHORE   The cruise ship docks at Prince George Wharf are in the center of town, near Rawson Square and adjacent to the main shopping areas. Your best bet for making long-distance phone calls is the Bahamas Telecommunications (BATELCO) phone center on East Street, about 4 blocks inland from Rawson Square.

INFORMATION   The **Ministry of Tourism Office** is located in the British Colonial Hilton, 1 Bay St. (© **242/322-7500**), and is open Monday through Friday 9am to 5pm. A smaller booth at Rawson Square is near the dock. For information before you go, call the **Tourist Office** in the U.S. (© **800/4-BAHAMAS;** www.bahamas.com).

GETTING AROUND

Unless you hire a horse-drawn carriage, the only way to see old Nassau is on foot. The major attractions and stores are pretty concentrated, so walking is the most convenient mode of transportation anyway. If you're really fit, you can even trek over to Cable Beach or Paradise Island.

BY TAXI   Practical for longer trips, taxis are required to have working meters, but some drivers insist on flat rates. The initial meter fare is $3, and each additional quarter-mile for the first two passengers is 40¢; for third and fourth passengers, add $3 each to the meter reading. Also, a surcharge is added for luggage stowed in the trunk. Tip your driver 15%. You can hire a five-passenger cab at

Nassau

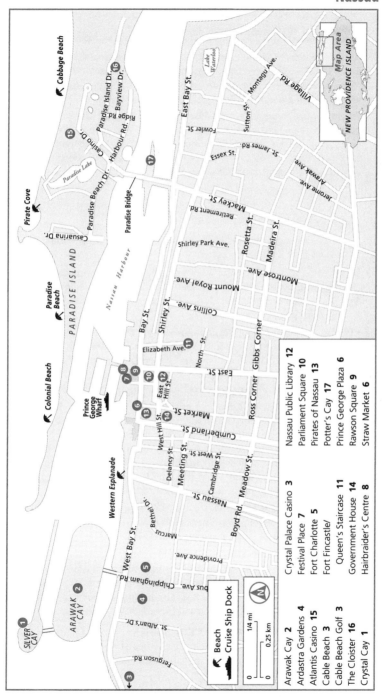

Arawak Cay **2**
Ardastra Gardens **4**
Atlantis Casino **15**
Cable Beach **3**
Cable Beach Golf **3**
The Cloister **16**
Crystal Cay **1**

Crystal Palace Casino **3**
Festival Place **7**
Fort Charlotte **5**
Fort Fincastle/
    Queen's Staircase **11**
Government House **14**
Hairbraider's Centre **8**

Nassau Public Library **12**
Parliament Square **10**
Pirates of Nassau **13**
Potter's Cay **17**
Prince George Plaza **6**
Rawson Square **9**
Straw Market **6**

Frommer's Favorite Nassau Experiences

Gorging on Fresh Conch at Arawak Cay: This small man-made island across the West Bay Street shore has the freshest conch around. For a true island experience, wash it down with the local cocktail—coconut water, milk, and gin. (See "Great Local Restaurants & Bars," below.)

Taking a Walk Through Colonial History: Nassau has numerous forts, government buildings, and private establishments that keep the flavor of the islands' colonial past alive. Shops and boutiques abut the historic attractions, so you can get some culture and feed your shopping addiction at the same time. (See "On Your Own: Within Walking Distance," below.)

$45 per hour. Taxis can be hailed on the street or taken from stands. **Radio cabs** can be ordered at © **242/323-5111.**

BY JITNEY Jitneys, medium-size buses that travel set routes throughout the city, are the least expensive means of transport. The fare is $1 for adults, 75¢ for children, and exact change is required. Buses operate from early in the morning until about 7pm.

BY FERRY Ferries run from the end of Casuarina Drive on Paradise Island across the harbor to Rawson Square for $3 per person. Water taxis also operate during the day between Paradise Island and Prince George Wharf for $4 per person.

BY HORSE-DRAWN CARRIAGE Horse-drawn surreys are the regal (if touristy) way to see Nassau. Agree on a price before you start your ride. The average charge for a 25-minute tour is $10 per person. The maximum load is two adults plus one child under the age of 12 (or three small adults—if you've been spending too much time at the ship's buffet, you don't qualify). The colorfully painted surreys are available daily from 9am to 4:30pm, except when the horses rest—usually from 1 to 3pm May through October, 1 to 2pm November through April. You'll find surreys in front of the cruise port building.

BY MOTOR SCOOTER/MOPED To rent a motorscooter (also known as a moped), contact **Ursa Investment,** Prince George Wharf (© **242/326-8329**). Mopeds run about $20 an hour or $50 for a full day.

BY RENTAL CAR Most vehicles have left-hand steering, and driving is British-style. If you're used to driving on the right, it may take some time to adjust. Thankfully, traffic is seldom heavy except downtown near the port. Rental-car license plates carry the letters "SD" (which stands for "suicide driver" according to joking Bahamians). Avis, Budget, Dollar, and Hertz all have offices here.

BEST CRUISE LINE SHORE EXCURSIONS

In addition to the excursions below, cruise lines typically offer a variety of snorkeling, diving, and boat tours. Avoid the city bus tours, which are dull, dull, dull.

Harbor Cruise & Atlantis Resort ($42, 2½ hr.): A tour boat with a local guide shows you the sights (such as they are) from the water, then drops you at the fanciful Atlantis Resort for a brief tour that includes a visit to Predator Lagoon, home to sharks, barracuda, and other toothy fish.

Thriller Powerboat Tour ($42, 1 hr.): This is a thrill-seeker's excursion, with high-speed boats roaring around the waters off Nassau, scaring the fish out of their wits. Not our personal favorite way to see . . . well, anything, but it sure is fast. Vroom.

EXCURSIONS OFFERED BY LOCAL AGENCIES

Guided Walking Tours: These 1 hour tours, arranged by the **Ministry of Tourism** (© 242/326-9772), depart from the Welcome Center on Prince George Dock, and usually begin every hour from 10am to 2pm. Make reservations in advance. The tours include descriptions of some of the city's oldest buildings, with information on Nassau's history, customs, and traditions. The cost is $10.

Scuba Diving, Sea Scootering & Shark Dives: Unpretentious and friendly **Nassau Scuba Centre,** Coral Harbour (© **242/362-1964;** www.divenassau. com), offers transportation to and from Prince Georges Wharf for cruise ship visitors, with dives at 9am and 1pm. Two-tank dives run about $75; snorkeling is $37, including equipment. For certified divers, shark dives allow you to either watch a divemaster feed sharks ($120) or don a chain-mail shark suit and feed them yourself (for a hefty $425). **Stuart Cove,** Southwest Bay Street, South Ocean (© **800/879-9832** in the U.S., or 242/362-4171; www.stuartcove.com), offers more options, including personal submarine excursions, which allow nondivers to move about underwater without scuba equipment ($95). The operation can be a mob scene, though, and the service is less personal than that at Nassau Scuba. The company also offers two-tank dives for certified divers ($80–$125) and snorkel excursions ($40). All programs are 3½ hours long. For both outfitters, we recommend that you reserve ahead.

Walking on the Ocean Floor: If you loved *Captain Nemo* and *20,000 Leagues Under the Sea,* you won't want to miss **Hartley's Undersea Walk,** East Bay Street (© **242/393-8234;** www.underseawalk.com). As part of a 3½-hour yacht cruise ($125 per person), you'll don a breathing helmet and spend about 20 minutes walking along the ocean bottom through a "garden" of tropical fish, sponges, and other undersea life. You don't have to be able to swim, and you can wear your glasses, but some people find the high-pitched pinging noise annoying. Ships depart from the Nassau Yacht Haven Tuesday through Saturday at 9:30am and 1:30pm. Check-in times are 9am and 1pm, respectively.

Yacht Cruises: Located at the Paradise Island Bridge, **Nassau Cruises** (© **242/ 363-3333**) has three luxurious yachts that head for the secluded beaches of Blue Lagoon Island, 6.5km (4 miles) east of Paradise Island. The boats leave Monday, Tuesday, Friday, and Saturday at 10 and 11:30am and return at 2pm and 4pm. A day pass ($25 for adults and $15 for children) covers the boat ride only. An all-inclusive day pass ($65 for adults and $35 for children) includes transportation to the dock, the boat ride, lunch, one rum punch for adults, and all nonmotorized watersports.

ON YOUR OWN: WITHIN WALKING DISTANCE

Walking is the best way to see the major sites of Nassau and to get a feel for the city's character and history (and to shop, shop, shop). Start at Prince George Wharf, where your ship is docked.

As you exit from the cruise ship wharf into the main port area, you'll have no choice but to pass through **Festival Place,** a barnlike hall full of little shops and stalls selling arts and crafts, T-shirts, hot sauces, and other touristy items. Outside, hawkers will encourage you to have your hair braided at the **Hairbraider's Centre.** This government-sponsored open-air pavilion attracts braiding experts from all over the island. If you're looking for a Bo Derek look, here's your chance. If you're not, a simple "no thanks" keeps the touts at bay.

Just across Bay Street from Rawson Square (inland from the wharf) are the flamingo-pink government buildings of **Parliament Square,** constructed in 1815. The House of Assembly, old colonial Secretary's Office, and Supreme Court flank a statue of Queen Victoria, while a bust on the north side of the square honors Sir Milo B. Butler, the Bahamas's first governor-general.

Built as a prison in 1798, the **Nassau Public Library,** located a block inland from Parliament Square, facing Shirley Street, is one of the city's oldest buildings and surely one of the more interesting libraries anywhere. Its octagonal shape was copied from a munitions storage facility, and the decidedly unpenitentiary pink paint was added after 1889, when the building reopened as a library. The books, historical prints, colonial documents, and Arawak Indian artifacts are kept in former cells.

Slaves carved the **Queen's Staircase** out of a solid limestone cliff in 1793. Originally designed as an escape route for soldiers at Fort Fincastle, each step now represents a year in Queen Victoria's 65-year reign. Lush plants and a waterfall stand guard over the staircase, which is located a few blocks up from the library on East Street. The staircase leads to Fort Fincastle, on Elizabeth Avenue, built in 1793 by Lord Dunmore, the royal governor. At the fort, an elevator climbs a 38m-high (125-ft.) water tower; from the top, you can look down on the entire arrowhead-shaped fort. Walk around on your own or hire a guide. (*Note:* You may find some of them aggressive.)

Walking downhill from Fort Fincastle and back toward the waterfront, turn left on East Hill Street past Market Street. On the left stands Government House, the official residence of the governor-general, built in 1801. Tropical foliage lines the grounds leading to the colonial mansion, and a statue of Columbus stands over the hillside steps.

This one's for kids, but young-at-heart parents may also enjoy the corny **Pirates of Nassau Museum** at King and George streets, downhill from Government House (© **242/356-3759;** www.pirates-of-nassau.com). Step aboard an embattled pirate ship and come face to face with Captain Teach and his fearsome crew as they guide you through the age of piracy in the lawless Nassau of 1716. It's open 9am to 5:30pm daily, except on Sunday, when it closes at 1pm; admission is a steep $12 for adults—only worth it if you're with kids, as each adult may bring two children under 12 free, and each additional child is $6. Admission includes a 45-minute tour.

On Bay Street, not far from the Pirates of Nassau, is the **Straw Market,** full of stalls selling some authentic Bahamian items and lots and lots of objects that are actually made in Asia. There are better places to get the real thing (see "Shopping," later in this section), but enjoy the scene anyway. Hours are roughly 7:30am to 7pm.

If you're up for more walking, **Potter's Cay,** under the Paradise Island Bridge, provides more market color. Sloops from the less populated Out Islands bring in their fresh catch. Freshly grown herbs and vegetables are also sold, along with limes, papayas, pineapples, and bananas. Stalls sell conch in several forms: raw and marinated in lime juice, as spicy deep-fried fritters, and in salad and soup.

ON YOUR OWN: BEYOND THE PORT AREA

About 1.6km (1 mile) west of downtown Nassau, just off West Bay Street, **Fort Charlotte** covers more than 40 hilltop hectares (99 acres). The Bahamas's largest fort, it offers impressive views of Paradise Island, Nassau, and the harbor. The complex, constructed in 1788, features a moat, dungeons, underground passageways, and 42 cannons.

Parading pink flamingos are the main attraction at the lush 2-hectare (5-acre) **Ardastra Gardens,** Chippingham Road, about 1.6km (1 mile) west of downtown Nassau (© 242/323-5806). The graceful birds obey their drillmaster's orders, and with their long-legged precision and discipline, they give the Rockettes a run for their money. The performances, accompanied by informative commentary, are presented daily at 10:30am, 2:10pm, and 4pm. Lory parrot feedings can be viewed at 11am, 1:30pm, and 3:30pm. The other exotic wildlife here—boa constrictors, honey bears, macaws, and capuchin monkeys—are less talented but fascinating in their own right. Paths meander through tropical foliage that's sure to enchant gardeners. The gardens are open daily from 9am to 5pm, with gates closing at 4:30pm. Admission is $12 per person.

The Cloister, on Casino Drive on Paradise Island (© 242/363-3000), is part of a monastery built in the 13th century by French monks. In the 1920s, William Randolph Hearst bought it, had it disassembled, and moved it from France to his estate in San Simeon, California. The stones were stored for years because no one knew how to properly reassemble them. In 1962, Huntington Hartford, the A&P grocery store heir and developer of Paradise Island, bought the structure from Hearst and hired a sculptor to reconstruct it on the island. It's quite an anomaly on tropical Paradise Island, but it's a serene spot. The adjacent **Versailles Gardens** feature formal vistas, tropical flowers, and classic bronze and marble statuary. The Cloister is only open to guests staying at the Ocean Club, Comfort Suites Paradise Island, Atlantis Paradise Island, or Harborside Resort at Atlantis. Visitors are welcome to walk through when no wedding ceremonies are taking place. There is no admission fee.

The mythical lost city of Atlantis submerged under Bahamian waters? Sure, it sounds hokey, and all the grandiloquent hype makes you want to hate the place, but **The Dig** and **Marine Habitat** at the Atlantis Paradise Island megaresort actually end up exceeding expectations. Drawing on age-old myths of the lost city, The Dig is a fantastic world of faux ancient ruins flooded by the sea. The interconnected passageways, boulevards, and chambers, now inhabited by piranhas, hammerhead sharks, stingrays, and morays, are visible through huge glass windows. Purported to be the largest man-made marine habitat in the world—"second only to Mother Nature"—the resort's sprawling 11-million-gallon lagoon system boasts more than 200 sea species and 50,000 individual creatures. Tickets for the guided "Discovery Tour" of the marine attractions are available at the resort's guest services desks for $25 for adults, $19 for children under 12. (**Note:** This tour does not include use of the resort's beach or water slide, which are reserved for guests only.) For information, call © **242/363-3000** or check out www.atlantis.com.

GAMBLING

If you think your ship's casino is as good as most land-based facilities, you haven't been to the impressive, 9,290-sq.-m (100,000-sq.-ft.) **Atlantis Casino** in the Atlantis Paradise Island megaresort (© **242/363-3000**). This is the largest gaming and entertainment complex in the Caribbean. Two astounding glass sculptures, the Temple of the Sun and the Temple of the Moon, anchor the vast facility and tie in with the resort's Lost City of Atlantis theme. Open daily until 4am, the casino boasts almost 1,000 slot machines and 78 gaming tables for baccarat, roulette, craps, blackjack, and Caribbean stud poker. Unlike most other casinos, the Atlantis makes no attempt at hiding what's going on outside: Huge windows provide panoramas of the adjacent marina and lagoons.

The 3,250-sq.-m (34,983-sq.-ft.) **Crystal Palace Casino,** West Bay Street, Cable Beach (© **242/327-6200**), screams 1980s with its pink and purple decor. The only casino on New Providence Island, it's part of the Wyndham Nassau Resort. Despite tough competition from the Atlantis Casino, it stacks up well against most other casinos in the Caribbean, with 750 slot machines and more than 100 gaming tables. The oval-shaped bar extends onto the gaming floor, and the lounge offers live entertainment. It's open every day, 24 hours.

Taxis will take you to either casino from the cruise pier.

SHOPPING

In 1992, the Bahamas abolished import duties on 11 luxury-good categories, including china, crystal, fine linens, jewelry, leather goods, photographic equipment, watches, and fragrances. Even so, you can end up spending more on an item in the Bahamas than you would at home. True bargains are rare, as is finding much that's really worth buying. The principal shopping area is **Bay Street** and the adjacent blocks, which are almost the first areas you see when you leave your ship. Here you'll find duty-free luxury-goods stores, such as Colombian Emeralds and Solomon's Mines, plus hundreds of other shops selling T-shirts, tourist gimcracks, duty-free booze and cigars, and recordings of Junkanoo music.

In the crowded aisles of the **Straw Market** on Bay Street, you can watch craftspeople weave and plait straw hats, handbags, dolls, place mats, and other items; be aware, though, that many of the items for sale here aren't of the best quality, nor even made locally (much of the stock is imported from Asia). Welcome to the global market, folks! It's tourist central, so most shopkeepers are willing to bargain, though some won't budge. If you want really beautiful hand-made straw work, walk a few blocks to **The Plait Lady,** at Victoria and Bay streets. The merchandise here is vastly superior to what's peddled in the Straw Market, and it's 100% Bahamian-made. Both **Island Tings,** Bay Street between East Street and Elizabeth Avenue, and **Seagrape,** West Bay Street at the Travelers' Rest restaurant (10 min. west of Cable Beach by car), offer Bahamian arts and crafts, Junkanoo masks, and jewelry.

Marlborough Antiques, across the street from the Hilton British Colonial on Marlborough Street, has an eclectic and interesting collection of antiques and books.

Bahamas Rum Cake Factory, at 602 E. Bay St., carries an array of Bahamian food products, including hot sauces, spices, and the eponymous dessert, which you can buy as they come out of the oven. If you can't get enough of the local rum, try a milkshake with a shot. And if you get home and want more, you can arrange worldwide cake delivery through its website, www.bahamasrumcakefactory.com.

BEACHES

On New Providence Island, sun worshippers make the pilgrimage to **Cable Beach,** which offers various watersports and easy access to shops, a casino, bars, and restaurants. The beach stretches for 6.4km (4 miles), and the waters can change quickly from rough to calm and clear. It's 8km (5 miles) from the port—a $10 taxi ride or $1 on the no. 10 bus.

More convenient for cruise ship passengers but inferior to Cable Beach, the **Western Esplanade** sweeps westward from the Hilton British Colonial hotel. Facilities include restrooms, changing facilities, and a snack bar. In the months preceding the Junkanoo carnival (celebrated on the new year), local bands practice their carnival routines here.

Paradise Beach on Paradise Island is a ferry ride away from Prince George Wharf (see "By Ferry" under "Getting Around," above). The price of admission ($3 for adults, $1 for children) includes use of the showers and a locker. An extra $10 deposit is required for towels. Paradise Island has a number of smaller beaches as well, including **Pirate's Cove Beach** and **Cabbage Beach.** Bordered by casuarinas, palms, and sea grapes, Cabbage Beach's broad sands stretch for 3.2km (2 miles), but it's likely to be crowded with guests from the nearby resorts. Tranquillity seekers find something approaching solitude on the northwestern end of the island, accessible by boat or foot only.

SPORTS
GOLF   South Ocean Golf Course, Southwest Bay Road (© **242/362-4391**), is the best course on New Providence Island and one of the best in the Bahamas. Located 30 minutes from Nassau, this 18-hole, 6,707-yard, par-72 beauty has some first-rate holes with a backdrop of trees, shrubs, ravines, and undulating hills. Greens fees are $100 per person with cart. Although not as challenging, the 6,453-yard, par-71 **Cable Beach Golf Course,** Cable Beach, West Bay Road (© **242/327-6000**), has lakes and ponds tucked picturesquely throughout, and the length encourages strong hitters to shave strokes with long, well-placed drives. Greens fees are $140 per person for 18 holes, including cart.

GREAT LOCAL RESTAURANTS & BARS
Conch, Bahamian "rock lobster," and boiled fish are local specialties; pigeon peas and rice are popular side dishes. The **local beer** is Kalik, and Nassau's **local rum** is Bacardi.

ON ARAWAK CAY   You'll get all the conch you can eat on **Arawak Cay,** a small man-made island across West Bay Street from Ardastra Gardens and Fort Charlotte. Join the locals in munching on conch with hot sauce, and wash it down with a coconut water–and–gin cocktail. Gorging on the cay is a local tradition and a real Bahamian experience.

IN NASSAU   If you want fancy, **Graycliff Restaurant,** West Hill Street, next to Government House (© **242/322-2796**), is one of the most elegant restaurants in the West Indies. It was built in the 1740s by a former privateer, and became Nassau's first inn in 1844. During the American Civil War, its cellar served as a jail for war prisoners. Polly Leach, a friend of Al Capone, owned the house some time later, as did Lord and Lady Dudley, friends of the Duke and Duchess of Windsor. Royalty and celebrities have eaten in the elegant surroundings for decades, enjoying its extensive wine list and hand-rolled cigars. The continental lunches and dinners (jacket recommended) are expensive, but worth it if you've squirreled away for a really special meal. Call ahead for reservations. Lunch is about $30.

Much more modest, **Bahamian Kitchen,** Trinity Place, off Market Street, next to Trinity Church (© **242/325-0702**), is one of the best places for good, down-home Bahamian food at modest prices. Specialties include lobster Bahamian style, fried red snapper, and curried chicken. Lunch is $8.

Near Ardastra Gardens, **The Shoal,** Nassau Street (© **242/323-4400**), is a local favorite and a featured restaurant in the Ministry of Tourism's "Real Taste of the Bahamas" program, which highlights independent establishments that serve indigenous cuisine. Every cab driver knows the place, which really hops on Sunday mornings. Try the boiled fish breakfast.

Café Matisse, on Bank Lane at Bay Street, behind Parliament Square (© **242/356-7012**), is housed in an old colonial home, and features antique tile floors, Matisse prints, and a serene outdoor courtyard. The extensive menu includes seafood, pastas, and pizzas. It's an unbeatable respite from shopping and sightseeing in downtown Nassau. Lunch is $15.

ON PARADISE ISLAND Among the 30-plus pricey restaurants and bars in the **Atlantis Paradise Island** resort, on Casino Drive (© **242/363-3000**), two merit special mention. **Seagrapes** serves an affordable buffet of tropical dishes, with a special emphasis on Cuban, Caribbean, and Cajun cuisines. Lunch is $20. **Five Twins,** just off the casino floor, features an elegantly minimalist sushi and satay bar. The lighting is soothingly dim, and the black-and-white marble floor complements the black lacquer dinnerware and scarlet napkins. Don't pass up the tropical-fruit soup dessert. The restaurant is not open for lunch.

FREEPORT/LUCAYA

Freeport/Lucaya, on Grand Bahama Island (often referred to as GBI), is the second most popular destination in the Bahamas. Technically, Freeport is the landlocked section of town while adjacent Lucaya hugs the waterfront. Originally intended as two separate developments, the two have grown together over the years, and though they offer none of Nassau's colonial charm, they do offer plenty of sun, surf, golf, tennis, and watersports—though the frenzy of the gambling and shopping scenes here might be too much for some visitors.

It wasn't until the 19th century that the first permanent settlers arrived on the island. Most earned a living as fishermen or by harvesting timber. GBI remained sparsely populated until 1955, when American developer Wallace Groves joined British industrialist Sir Charles Hayward to build the tax-free city of Freeport for tourism and manufacturing. Today, tourism remains the lifeblood of the island's 50,000 residents.

COMING ASHORE Your ship docks at a dreary port on Grand Bahama Island in the middle of nowhere, a $10 taxi ride from Freeport and the International Bazaar, where you'll find most of the action.

There are long-distance phones in the port terminal.

INFORMATION Information is available from the **Grand Bahama Tourism Board,** located in the International Bazaar in the Lucaya area (© **800/448-3386** or 242/352-8044). Another information booth is located at Port Lucaya (© **242/373-8988**). For information before you go, call the **Bahamas Tourism Board in New York** (© **800/4-BAHAMAS**) or visit the website at www.bahamas.com.

GETTING AROUND

Once you get to Freeport by taxi, you can explore the center of town on foot. If you want to make excursions to the west or east ends of the island, your best bet is to rent a car.

BY TAXI The government sets taxi rates, which start at $3 and increase 40¢ for each additional ¼ mile. Cabs wait at the dock, or you can call **Freeport Taxi Company** (© **242/352-6666**) or **Grand Bahama Taxi Union** (© **242/352-7101**).

West Beach Rd.

Taino Beach

GRAND BAHAMA ISLAND

McLeans Town

Lucayan National Park

Freeport/Lucaya

West End

Settlers Way East

Balao Rd.

East Indianman

Fiddlers Green

Sargeant Major Dr.

Seahorse Rd.

Midshipmans Rd.

Lucayan Beach

Royal Palm Way

Silver Point Beach

Settlers Way

Coral Rd.

Explorers Way

Pioneers Way East

Adventurers Way

East Sunrise Hwy.

Beachway Dr.

San Salvadore

L U C A Y A

Bahama Reef Blvd.

Northwest Providence Channel

FREEPORT

Logwood Rd.

Pioneers Way

Cadwallader Jones

West Atlantic Dr.

East Atlantic Dr.

East Mall Dr.

West Sunrise Hwy.

The Mall South

East Beach

Confederates Walk

Santa Maria Av. Hawksbill St.

Pinta Av.

Xanadu Beach

Queen's Hwy.

Regency Blvd.

Shaftesbury

Ellis

Lightfoot

1 mi

1 km

0

0

Austin's Calypso Bar **1**
Becky's Restaurant **4**
Casino at Bahamia **2**
Count Basie Square **10**
The Country Club
  at Bahamia **2**
Fortune Hills Golf
  & Country Club **12**
Garden of the Groves **11**
Geneva's Place **2**
International Bazaar **3**
Lucayan National Park **11**
Lucayan Park Golf
  & Country Club **7**
Our Lucaya Beach
  & Golf Resort **8**
The Pepper Pot **6**
Peterson Cay
  National Park **11**
Port Lucaya Marketplace **9**
Rand Nature Centre **5**
The Star Club **1**
Straw Market **3**
UNEXSO Dive Shop **9**

115

Frommer's Favorite Freeport/Lucaya Experiences

Touring Lucayan National Park: About 19km (12 miles) from Lucaya, this park boasts one of the loveliest beaches on Grand Bahama, as well as caves, mangroves, and nature walks through various ecological zones. (See "Best Cruise Line Shore Excursions," below.)

Visiting the Star Club: Built in the 1940s, this gem has hosted many famous guests over the years. A salty old joint, it's now the island's only after-hours bar. It's a watering hole Ernest Hemingway would have loved. (See "Great Local Restaurants & Bars," below.)

BY RENTAL CAR   Roads are good on GBI, and traffic is light. Remember that driving is on the left side. Avis, Dollar, and Hertz all have offices here.

BY MOTOR SCOOTER OR BICYCLE   You can rent scooters or bicycles at the island's major hotels, including **The Royal Oasis Beach & Golf Resort,** West Sunrise Highway (© **242/350-7000**). A two-seat scooter requires a $100 deposit and rents for about $45 a day; bikes rent for $20 a day.

BY BUS   Public bus service runs from the International Bazaar to downtown Freeport, and from the Pub on the Mall to the Lucaya area. The typical fare is 75¢ to $1.

BEST CRUISE LINE SHORE EXCURSIONS

Sanctuary Bay Dolphin Encounter ($80, 3¼ hr.): Pat a dolphin on the nose! On this excursion you can watch, touch, and photograph Flipper, or at least one of his relatives. See the UNEXSO information below for more elaborate dolphin excursions that you can arrange on your own.

Kayaking Nature Adventure ($75, 6 hr.): Visit a protected island creek, kayak through a mangrove forest, explore the island's caves, and take a guided nature walk into Lucayan National Park. The excursion includes lunch and beach time.

EXCURSIONS OFFERED BY LOCAL AGENCIES

Kayak & Bike Tours: Kayak Nature Tours (© **242/373-2485;** www.grand bahamanaturetours.com) offers three worthwhile and recommended excursions that fit in the time frame that cruisers have. The first, to Lucayan National Park, features sea kayaking through mangroves, a nature hike, a stop at two caves, and a swim and picnic lunch at Gold Rock Beach ($69, 6 hr.). The second, to Peterson Cay National Park, includes sea kayaking to the small offshore cay, guided snorkeling, beach time, and lunch ($69, 5 hr.). The other features a leisurely bicycle ride along Taíno Beach and the Settlement of Smith Point. The tour includes a visit to Sanctuary Bay, a guided walk through the tropical landscape of Garden of the Groves, and lunch ($79, 6 hr.). Guides on each of the tours are personable, informative, and professional.

Scuba, Snorkeling, Shark Dives & Dolphin Swims: In the Bahamas, reef diving takes a back seat to theme-park-style "adventure" programs, including shark-feeding dives and swim-with-dolphins adventures. One of the premier diving and snorkeling outfitters in the Caribbean, the **Underwater Explorers Society (UNEXSO),** at Lucaya Beach (© **800/992-3483** or 242/373-1244; www. unexso.com), offers reef and wreck dives. Two-tank reef dives are $50, 3-hour learn-to-dive courses are $69. UNEXSO also allows divers to swim alongside dolphins in the open ocean. Several different programs are available: During **The Close Encounter** ($69 adults, $35 children 4–12, under 4 free) you will observe the sea mammals from an observation deck while listening to an informative presentation. Then, you can wade into the waist-high water and touch the creatures. The highlight of the **Swim with the Dolphins** experience ($159; minimum age 10, under 16 must be accompanied by an adult) is swimming alongside the animals in protected waters after a briefing on dolphin behavior. The open-ocean **Ultimate Dolphins Experience** ($269; minimum age 10, under 16 must be accompanied by an adult) allows you to dive with bottlenose dolphins in shallow waters. These programs are exceedingly popular, so advance reservations are a must.

Party/Snorkel Cruises: Superior Watersports, in Freeport (© 242/373-7863) offers daily 5-hour party/snorkeling cruises that include equipment, lunch, and unlimited rum punch ($59 for adults, $39 for children 2–12). **Paradise Watersport,** at Club Fortuna (© 242/374-6676 or 242/373-4001) offers snorkeling cruises on a 14m (48-ft.) catamaran ($35 adults, $16 children under 12) and glass-bottom boat rides ($23 adults, $15 children under 12).

ON YOUR OWN: BEYOND THE PORT AREA

Nothing of note is within walking distance of the port. You must take a cab over to Freeport/Lucaya for all attractions.

One of the island's top attractions, the 4.8-hectare (12-acre) **Garden of the Groves** was once the private meditation garden of Freeport's founder, Wallace Groves. The tranquil park features waterfalls, flowering shrubs, about 10,000 trees, tropical birds, Bahamian raccoons, Vietnamese potbellied pigs, and West African pygmy goats. The serene hilltop chapel overlooking the pond is a popular place for exchanging vows. The garden is located at the intersection of Midshipman Road and Magellan Drive, Freeport (© 242/373-5668), and is open Monday through Sunday 9am to 4pm; $9.95 for adults, $6.95 for ages 3 to 10.

A couple of miles east of downtown Freeport, the 40-hectare (99-acre) **Rand Nature Centre** serves as the regional headquarters of the Bahamas National Trust. Pineland nature trails meander past native flora and wild birds, including the Bahama parrot and other animals. Other highlights include native animal displays (don't miss the boa constrictors), an education center, and a gift shop. It's located on East Settlers Way, Freeport (© 242/352-5438), and is open Monday through Friday 9am to 4pm; $5 for adults, $3 for ages 5 to 12.

Peterson Cay National Park, approximately 24km (15 miles) east of Freeport and .8km (½ mile) offshore, is accessible by boat only. Coral reefs ringing the tiny island make for great snorkeling and diving, and the serene location is perfect for a picnic. For information, contact the Rand Nature Centre (© 242/352-5438).

If your ship's in port late, don't miss the free nightly concert at **Count Basie Square,** in the center of Port Lucaya's waterfront restaurant-and-shopping complex. The legendary jazz bandleader who lends his name to the square had a home on Grand Bahama, and the square's vine-covered bandstand attracts steel-drum bands, small Junkanoo groups, and gospel singers.

SHOPPING

The International Bazaar, at East Mall Drive and East Sunrise Highway, next to the Casino at Bahamia, is pure 1960s Bahamian kitsch, and though relentlessly cheerful, it's a little long in the tooth. Each area of the 4-hectare (10-acre),

100-shop complex attempts to capture the ambience of a different region of the globe. Stereotypes abound. You'll find Japanese items in the "Ginza," sidewalk cafes on the "Left Bank," silk saris in "India," woodcarvings and dashikis in "Africa," serapes and piñatas in "Spain," and everything from high-end luxury goods to T-shirts throughout. Some items here run about 40% less than in the United States, though certainly not all. Buses marked INTERNATIONAL BAZAAR deliver passengers to the center's much-photographed Torii Gate, a Japanese symbol of welcome.

The **Straw Market,** beside the International Bazaar, features items with a Bahamian touch—baskets, hats, handbags, and place mats. Quality varies, so look around before buying.

The **Port Lucaya Marketplace,** on Seahorse Road near the UNEXSO Dive Shop, is a 2.4-hectare (6-acre) shopping-and-dining complex much like the International Bazaar. Steel-drum bands and strolling musicians add to the festive atmosphere. Many of the restaurants and shops overlook a 50-slip marina, and the boardwalk along the water is ideal for watching the dolphins at UNEXSO (www.unexso.com). If you're in need of a wet suit, an underwater camera, or more prosaic items such as swimsuits, sunglasses, and hats, hit the UNEXSO Dive Shop.

BEACHES

Grand Bahama Island has miles of white-sand beaches. **Xanadu Beach,** immediately east of Freeport at the Xanadu Beach Resort, is the premier stretch in the Lucaya area, offering lots of watersports equipment. It can get crowded at times. Taíno Beach, Churchill Beach, and Fortune Beach are all conveniently located on the Lucaya oceanfront. A 20-minute ride east of Lucaya, **Gold Rock Beach** may be the island's best. Hidden away in Lucayan National Park, it has barbecue pits, picnic tables, and a spectacular low tide. **Barbary Beach,** slightly closer to Lucaya, is great for seashell hunters, and white spider lilies in the area bloom spectacularly in May and June.

SPORTS

GOLF With more links than any other island in the Bahamas, Grand Bahama is becoming a prime golf destination. The **Country Club at Bahamia,** The Mall South (© **242/352-6721**), has two championship courses. **The Emerald Course** has plenty of trees along the fairways, as well as an abundance of water hazards and bunkers. Its toughest hole is the ninth, a par-5 with 545 yards from the blue tees to the hole. The **Ruby Course** has a total of 6,750 yards if played from the championship tees. Greens fees on both courses for 18 holes are $85, including cart.

Our Lucaya Beach & Golf Resort, Royal Palm Way, F-42500, Lucaya (© **242/373-2002;** www.ourlucaya.com) offers two courses. The par-72 **Lucayan** course, designed by Dick Wilson, features well-protected elevated greens, fairways lined with tropical foliage, and doglegs. The par-72 links-style **Reef** course, designed by Robert Trent Jones Jr., is 6,909 yards from the championship tees, with water traps on 13 of 18 holes. Greens fees are $120 for 18 holes, including cart. Club rentals are $30.

The course at **Lucayan Park Golf & Country Club,** at Lucaya Beach (© **242/373-1066**), was recently made over and is known for its entrance and its hanging boulder sculpture. Greens are fast, and the course has a couple of par-5 holes more than 500 yards long. Total distance from the blue tees is 6,824 yards; par is 72. Greens fees are $120 per person for 18 holes, including cart.

Fortune Hills Golf & Country Club, Richmond Park, Lucaya (© 242/373-4500), was designed as an 18-hole course, but the back nine holes were never completed. You can replay the front nine for a total of 6,916 yards from the blue tees; par is 72. Greens fees are $51 per person, including cart.

WATERSPORTS   Paradise Watersport at Club Fortuna (© 242/374-6676), offers water-skiing ($30 for 30 min.) and parasailing ($50). Water-skiing lessons are $50 for 1 hour.

GAMBLING

The 1,860-sq.-m (20,021-sq.-ft.) **Casino at Bahamia,** on the Mall at West Sunrise Highway (© 242/350-7000), offers gaming, dining, and live entertainment. The exterior looks like a Moroccan palace—a fanciful Kismet sort of conceit that's perfect next to the kitsch of the International Bazaar. Serious gamblers appreciate the variety of games: full-service sports book, double odds, craps, blackjack, minibaccarat, roulette, Caribbean stud poker, big six wheel, and hundreds of slots and video poker games.

GREAT LOCAL RESTAURANTS & BARS

The **most popular Bahamian beer** is Kalik. Bahamian Hammerhead, another brand, is brewed on Grand Bahama. GBI's **local rums** include Don Lorenzo and Ricardo.

If you'd like a taste of the Bahamas the way they used to be, head for the **Star Club,** on Bayshore Road, on the island's West End (© 242/346-6207). Built in the 1940s, the Star was Grand Bahama's first hotel, and over the years it has hosted many famous guests. The joint's still run by the family of the late Austin Henry Grant Jr., a former Bahamian senator and West End legend. You can order Bahamian chicken in the bag, burgers, fish and chips, "fresh sexy" ceviche conch salad, or cooked conch in chowder or fritters. But come for the good times and to mix with the locals, not for the food. Lunch is $8. Next door, Austin's Calypso Bar is a colorful old dive if ever there was one.

At Freeport Harbor, near the cruise ship dock, **Pier 1** (© 242/352-6674) serves clam chowder, fresh oysters, baby shark, sand crabs, a fresh fish of the day, and more in several dining rooms. There's also a nice high-ceilinged bar. Lunch is $10. **Geneva's Place,** East Mall Drive and Kipling Lane (© 242/352-5085), offers traditional Bahamian meals. It's one of the best places to sample conch, whether it be stewed, cracked, fried, or part of a savory conch chowder. Lunch is $8. **The Pepper Pot,** East Sunrise Highway at Coral Road (© 242/373-7655), a 5-minute drive east of the International Bazaar, in a tiny shopping mall, serves takeout portions of the best carrot cake on the island, as well as a savory conch chowder, fish, pork chops, chicken souse (a traditional soup), cracked conch, sandwiches, and hamburgers. Lunch is $6. **Becky's Restaurant,** near the International Bazaar, East Sunrise Highway (© 242/352-8717), offers authentic Bahamian cuisine prepared in the time-tested style of the Out Islands. Try the souse, stewed fish, and johnnycakes. Lunch is $9.

7 Barbados

No port of call in the southern Caribbean can compete with Barbados when it comes to natural beauty, attractions, and fine dining. With all it offers, you'll think the island is much bigger than it is. But what really put Barbados on world travelers' maps is its seemingly endless stretches of pink- and white-sandy beaches, among the best in the entire Caribbean Basin.

Frommer's Favorite Barbados Experiences

Renting a Car for a Barbados Road Trip: Seventeenth-century churches, tropical flowers, snorkeling, great views, and more are just a rental-car ride away. (See "On Your Own: Beyond the Port Area," below.)

Visiting Gun Hill Signal Station: If you've got less time, hire a taxi or rent a car and go to Gun Hill for panoramic views of the island. (See "On Your Own: Beyond the Port Area," below.)

Taking a Submarine Trip: Sightseeing submarines make several dives daily. (See "Best Cruise Line Shore Excursions," below.)

This Atlantic outpost was one of the most staunchly loyal members of the British Commonwealth for over 300 years, and although it gained its independence in 1966, Britishisms still remain—the accent is British, driving is on the left, cricket is a popular sport, and Queen Elizabeth II is still officially the head of state.

Originally operated on a plantation economy that made its aristocracy rich, the island is the most easterly in the Caribbean, floating in the mid-Atlantic like a great coral reef. Topography varies from rolling hills and savage waves on the eastern (Atlantic) coast to densely populated flatlands, rows of hotels and apartments, and sheltered beaches in the southwest.

The people in Barbados are called Bajans, and you'll see this term used everywhere.

COMING ASHORE   The cruise ship pier, a short drive from Bridgetown, the capital, is one of the best docking facilities in the southern Caribbean. You can walk right into the modern cruise ship terminal, which has car rentals, taxi services, sightseeing tours, and a tourist information office, plus shops and scads of vendors (see "Shopping," below).

If you want to go into Bridgetown, about 1.6km (1 mile) from the port, instead of to the beach, you can take a hot, dusty walk of 10 to 15 minutes, or catch a taxi. The one-way fare ranges from US$4 on up. Buses pass by the Harbour frequently. Bus fares are BD$1.50 (US75¢).

At a huge phone center in the cruise terminal, you can make credit card calls to the U.S. and other international destinations. You'll also find fax facilities and phone cards and stamps for sale.

LANGUAGE   English is spoken with an island lilt.

CURRENCY   The Barbados dollar (BD$) is the official currency, and is available in $100, $20, $10, and $5 notes and $1, 25¢, and 10¢ silver coins, plus 5¢ and 1¢ copper coins. The exchange rate is BD$2.03 to US$1 (BD$1 = US 49¢). Unless otherwise noted, prices in this section are given in U.S. dollars. Most stores take traveler's checks or U.S. dollars, so don't bother to convert money if you're here for only a day.

INFORMATION   The **Barbados Tourism Authority** is on Harbour Road (P.O. Box 242), Bridgetown, Barbados, W.I. (© **888/BARBADOS** or 246/427-2623; www.barbados.org). Its cruise terminal office, which is very well run, is always open when a cruise ship is in port.

Travel Tip: He who finds the best hotel deal has more to spend on facials involving knobbly vegetables.

Hello, the Roaming Gnome here. I've been nabbed from the garden and taken round the world. The people who took me are so terribly clever. They find the best offerings on Travelocity. For very little cha-ching. And that means I get to be pampered and exfoliated till I'm pink as a bunny's doodah.

travelocity®

1-888-TRAVELOCITY / travelocity.com / America Online Keyword: Travel

Barbados

Map Legend:
- ✈ Airport
- 🏖 Beach
- ⛪ Church
- 🚢 Cruise Ship Dock
- 🗼 Lighthouse

Scale: 0 — 5 mi / 0 — 5 km

**Map labels:**

North Point
Archer's Bay
River Bay
Stroud Bay
Harrison Point
Cuckold Point
Gay's Cove
ST. LUCY
Fairfield
Pico Teneriffe
Maycock's Bay 1B
Coleton 1C
Half Moon Fort
Morgan Lewis Beach
Six Men's Bay
Heywoods Beach
ST. PETER
Greeland 2
St. Andrew's Church
ATLANTIC OCEAN
Speightstown
ST. ANDREW
SCOTLAND
Mullins Beach
Chalky Mount
Cattlewash
Gibbs Beach
Gold Coast
Lower Carlton 1 2A
Turner's Hall Woods
Bathsheba
Tent Bay
ST. JAMES
Church Point
4 ST. JOSEPH
Martin's Bay
Congor Rocks
FOLKSTONE UNDERWATER PARK
Welchman Hall 3 3A
Hackleton's Cliff
Consett Bay
Holetown 1A
3
Culpepper Island
Sunset Crest
Blackmans
ST. JOHN
Ragged Point Lighthouse
Paynes Bay
ST. THOMAS
5
Lazaretto
6
3B
Prospect
2A 2
Locust Hall
Three Houses
Kitridge Point
Paradise Beach
Warrens
7 8 4
Brighton Beach
ST. MICHAEL
ST. GEORGE
Bushy Park
Sandford
ST. PHILIP
Bottom Bay
Black Rock
3
2
4B
Marchfield
Long Bay
5
Deep Water Harbour
4
5
Beachy Head
Queen's Park
7
Crane Beach
Bridgetown
6
CHRISTCHURCH
Carlisle Bay
9
6
Tom Adams Hwy.
Needham's Point
Hastings
St. Lawrence
Grantley Adams International Airport
Worthing
Maxwell
7
Rockley Beach
Sandy Beach
Casuarina Beach
Oistins
Long Bay
South Point
Silver Sands Beach

Caribbean Sea

- Barbados Wildlife Reserve **1**
- Brown Sugar Restaurant **9**
- Earthworks Pottery/Potters House Gallery **6**
- Flower Forest of Barbados **4**
- Francia Plantation **7**
- Gun Hill Signal Station **8**
- Harrison's Cave **5**
- St. James Church **2**
- Welchman Hall Gully **3**

PUERTO RICO
ATLANTIC OCEAN
LESSER ANTILLES
Caribbean Sea
Barbados

CALLING FROM THE U.S.   When calling Barbados from the United States, you need only dial a "1" before the telephone numbers listed here.

GETTING AROUND

BY TAXI   Taxis are not metered, but their rates are fixed by the government. Even so, drivers may try to get more money out of you, so make sure you settle on the rate before getting in. Taxis are identified by the letter "Z" on their license plates, and you'll find them just outside of the terminal.

BY BUS   Blue-and-yellow public buses fan out from Bridgetown every 20 minutes or so onto the major routes; their destinations are marked on the front. Buses going south and east leave from Fairchild Street, and those going north and west depart from Lower Green and the Princess Alice Highway. Fares are BD$1.50 (US75¢) and exact change is required.

   Privately owned minibuses run shorter distances and travel more frequently. These bright yellow buses display destinations on the bottom-left corner of the windshield. In Bridgetown, board at River Road, Temple Yard, and Probyn Street. Fare is about BD$1.50 (US75¢).

BY RENTAL CAR   While it's a good way to see the island if you've got an adventurous streak and an easygoing attitude, before you decide to rent a car, keep in mind that driving is on the left side of the road and that signs are totally inadequate (boy, could we tell you stories!). Hertz has an office here. Rental cars all have an "H" on their license plates (meaning "hired"), so everyone will know you're a visitor.

BEST CRUISE LINE SHORE EXCURSIONS

It's not easy to get around Barbados quickly and conveniently, so a shore excursion is a good idea here.

Kayak & Turtle Encounter (US$69, 3½ hr.): A boat ride along the west coast brings you to the beach, where you'll clamber into your kayak for a 45-minute paddle along the shore. Once at the snorkel site, you'll be able to swim with and feed sea turtles.

Mount Gay Rum Distillery & Banks Beer Tour (US$42, 3½ hr.): Talk about getting in the spirit. This excursion takes you for a tour and tipple at Barbados's number-one rum distillery, then head for the Banks Brewery for the yeasty side of things.

Rainforest Hike & Cave Exploration (US$74, 4 hr.): A guide leads your group through one of Barbados's rainforest gullies, then down into a natural cave.

Harrison's Cave (US$58, 4 hr.): Most cruise lines offer a tour to Harrison's Cave in the center of the island (see "On Your Own: Beyond the Port Area," below, for details).

Horseback Riding (US$89, 3½ hr.): Horse treks through the heart of the island wind past old plantation houses, sugar-cane fields, old sugar factories, small villages, and, if you're lucky, green monkeys scouting for food.

TOURING THROUGH LOCAL OPERATORS

Island Tours/Eco-Tours: Since most cruise lines don't really offer a comprehensive island tour, many passengers rely on one of the local tour companies. **Bajan Tours,** Glenayre, Locust Hall, St. George (© **800/550-6288,** ext. 2225 from the U.S.; www.funbarbados.com/Tours/bajantrs.cfm), offers an island tour that leaves between 8:30 and 9am and returns to the ship before departure. It covers all of the island's highlights. On Friday, the company conducts a heritage tour, focusing mainly on the island's major plantations and museums. On Tuesday and Wednesday it offers an eco-tour, which takes in the natural beauty of the island. Call ahead for information and to reserve a spot. The cost is generally around US$56 per person.

Taxi Tours: If you can afford it, touring by taxi is far more relaxing than the standardized bus tour. Nearly all Bajan taxi drivers are familiar with their island and like to show off their knowledge to visitors. The standard rate is about US$20 per hour per taxi (for one to four passengers). You might want to try contacting taxi owner/driver **Aaron Francis** (© 246/431-9059). He's a gem—friendly, reliable, and knowledgeable.

ON YOUR OWN: WITHIN WALKING DISTANCE

About the only thing you can walk to is the cruise terminal. The modern, pleasant complex has an array of duty-free shops and retail stores, plus many vendors selling arts and crafts, jewelry, liquor, china, crystal, electronics, perfume, and leather goods.

ON YOUR OWN: BEYOND THE PORT AREA

We don't recommend wasting too much time in Bridgetown—it's hot, dry, and dusty, and the honking horns of traffic jams only add to its woes. So, unless you want to go shopping, you should spend your time exploring all the beauty the island has to offer. The tourist office in the cruise terminal is very helpful if you want to go somewhere on your own.

Welchman Hall Gully, St. Thomas (Hwy. 2 from Bridgetown; © 246/438-6671), is a lush tropical garden owned by the Barbados National Trust. It's 13km (8 miles) from the port (reachable by bus) and features some plants that were here when the English settlers landed in 1627.

All cruise ship excursions visit **Harrison's Cave,** Welchman Hall, St. Thomas (© 246/438-6640), Barbados's top tourist attraction. Here you can see a beautiful underground world from aboard an electric tram and trailer. Admission is US$16 for adults and US$6 for children. If you'd like to go on your own, a taxi ride takes about 30 minutes and costs at least US$40 round-trip.

About 1.6km (1 mile) from Harrison's Cave is the **Flower Forest,** Richmond Plantation, St. Joseph (© 246/433-8152). This old sugar plantation stands 255m (836 ft.) above sea level near the western edge of the "Scotland district," in one of the most scenic parts of Barbados. The entrance fee is US$7.50.

A fine home still owned and occupied by descendants of the original owner, the **Francia Plantation,** St. George (© 246/429-0474), stands on a wooded hillside overlooking the St. George Valley, about 16km (10 miles) from the port. You can explore several rooms. It's open 10am to 4pm Monday through Friday. Admission is US$6 for adults, US$3 for children. One-way taxi fare is about US$15.

Built in 1818, the **Gun Hill Signal Station,** Highway 4 (© 246/429-1358), one of two such stations owned and operated by the Barbados National Trust, is strategically placed on the highland of St. George and commands a wonderful panoramic view from east to west. It's 19km (12 miles) from the port; the one-way taxi ride costs about US$15, and the entrance fee is US$4.60, kids 6 to 12 US$2.30. It's open Monday through Saturday 9am to 5pm.

If it's wildlife you want, head for the **Barbados Wildlife Reserve** (© 246/422-8826), in St. Peter Parish on the northern end of the island. It's not exactly

Animal Kingdom, but you'll see turtles, rabbits, iguanas, peacocks, green monkeys, and a caged python on this 1.6-hectare (4-acre) site.

Maybe it's the party life you crave. If so, don't miss the **Mount Gay Rum Tour** in Bridgetown (© 246/425-9066; www.mountgay.com). You'll get a 40-minute soup-to-nuts introduction to rum in an air-conditioned rum shop (rumor has it that of all the rum shops on the island, this is the only one with A/C). Tours are offered every hour Monday to Friday from 9am to 3:45pm. The cost is US$6 per person. They also offer a "with lunch" tour for US$14.

SHOPPING

The shopping-mall-size cruise terminal contains duty-free shops, retail stores, a convenience store, and a plethora of vendors selling arts and crafts, jewelry, liquor, china, crystal, electronics, perfume, and leather goods. Vendors sell great local hot sauce, as well as yummy Punch de Crème (you can get a free sample before buying), a creamy rum drink. For rum cake, an island specialty, the family-owned **Calypso Island Bakery** has a shop in the terminal (© 246/426-1702). The shrink-wrapped cakes last up to 6 months and make great gifts. In general, though, you'll find a wider selection of merchandise and better prices in **Bridgetown**—last time we were there, T-shirts in the terminal were going for US$15 apiece, a roll of film was US$5, and a liter of J&B (yellow label) was anywhere from US$11 to US$15.

Good duty-free buys include cameras, watches, crystal, gold jewelry, bone china, cosmetics and perfumes, and liquor (including locally produced Barbados rum and liqueurs), along with tobacco products and British-made cashmere sweaters, tweeds, and sportswear. **Cave Shepherd,** Broad Street, Bridgetown (© 246/431-2121), is the largest department store on Barbados and the best place to shop for duty-free merchandise.

Among Barbados handcrafts, you'll find lots of black-coral jewelry, but beware—because black coral is endangered, it's illegal to bring it back to the United States. We suggest looking, but not buying. Local clay potters turn out different products, some based on designs that are centuries old. Check out the **Potters House Gallery** (© 246/425-3463) and **Earthworks Pottery** (© 246/425-0223; www.earthworks-pottery.com), both on Edghill Heights, in St. Thomas parish. Crafts include wall hangings made from grasses and dried flowers, straw mats, baskets, and bags with raffia embroidery. Bajan leatherwork includes handbags, belts, and sandals.

In Bridgetown, a standout store is **Articrafts,** on Broad Street, for Bajan arts and crafts, straw work, handbags, and bamboo items.

BEACHES

Beaches on the island's western side—the luxury resort area called the Gold Coast—are far preferable to those on the surf-pounded Atlantic side, which are dangerous for swimming. The government requires that there be access to all beaches, via roads along the property line or through the hotel entrance, so all Barbados beaches are open to the public, even those in front of the big resort hotels and private homes.

ON THE WEST COAST (GOLD COAST)   Take your pick of the west coast beaches, which are about a 15-minute, US$8 taxi ride from the cruise terminal. **Payne's Bay,** with access from the Coach House (© 246/432-1163) or Mannie's Suga Suga restaurant (© 246/419-4511), is a good beach for watersports, especially snorkeling. There's a parking area here. This beach can get rather crowded, but the beautiful bay makes it worth it. Directly south of Payne's Bay, at Fresh Water Bay, is a trio of fine beaches: **Brighton Beach, Brandon's Beach,** and **Paradise Beach.**

Church Point lies north of St. James Church, opening onto Heron Bay, site of the **Colony Club Hotel** (© **246/422-2335**). Although this beach can get crowded, it's one of the most scenic bays in Barbados, and the swimming is ideal. Retreat under some shade trees when you've had enough sun. You can also order drinks at the Colony Club's beach terrace.

Snorkelers in particular seek out the glassy blue waters by Mullins Beach. There are some shady areas, and you can park on the main road.

ON THE SOUTH COAST Depending on traffic, south-coast beaches are usually easy to reach from the cruise terminal. Figure on about a US$10 taxi fare. **Sandy Beach,** reached from the parking lot on the Worthing main road, has tranquil waters opening onto a lagoon. This is a family favorite, with lots of screaming and yelling, especially on weekends. Food and drink are sold here.

Windsurfers are particularly fond of the trade winds that sweep across **Casuarina Beach** even on the hottest summer days. Access is from Maxwell Coast Road, across the property of Casuarina Beach Hotel (© **246/428-3600**). This is one of the wider beaches on Barbados. The hotel has food and drink.

Silver Sands Beach is to the east of the town of Oistins, near the very southernmost point of Barbados, directly east of South Point Lighthouse and near the Silver Rock Resort (© **246/428-2866**). This white-sandy beach is a favorite with many Bajans, who probably want to keep it a secret from as many visitors as possible. Windsurfing is good here, but not as good as at Casuarina Beach. You can buy drinks at Silver Rock Resort's pool bar, called **Jibbooms** (© **246/428-2866**).

ON THE SOUTHEAST COAST The southeast coast is known for its big waves, especially at **Crane Beach,** a white-sandy stretch backed by cliffs and palms that often appears in travel-magazine articles about Barbados. The Crane Beach Hotel (© **246/423-6220**) towers above it from the cliffs, and Prince Andrew owns a house here. The beach offers excellent bodysurfing, but this is real ocean swimming, not the calm Caribbean, so be careful. At US$20 from the cruise pier, the one-way taxi fare is relatively steep, so try to share the ride with other cruise passengers.

SPORTS

GOLF The 18-hole, par-72 championship course at the west coast's **Sandy Lane Golf Club,** St. James (© **246/432-1311;** www.sandylane.com), is open to all. Greens fees are US$200 for 18 holes. Carts and caddies are required and cost US$35. Make reservations the day before you arrive in Barbados or before you leave home. The course is a 20- to 25-minute taxi ride from the cruise terminal. The one-way fare is about US$20.

WINDSURFING Experts say that Barbados windsurfing is as good as any this side of Hawaii. In fact, it's a very big business between November and April, when thousands of windsurfers from all over the world come here. **Silver Sands** is rated the best spot in the Caribbean for advanced windsurfing (skill rating 5–6). **Club Mistral,** at the Silver Sands Resort in Christ Church (© **246/428-6001;** www.clubmistralbarbados.com), gives lessons and rents boards. Windsurfing rentals are US$55 for 3 hours, and US$75 for 9 hours. To reach the club, take a taxi from the cruise terminal; it's a US$15 one-way fare.

GREAT LOCAL RESTAURANTS & BARS

Two tips for you: Be sure to try the tasty local delicacy, flying fish (you can even get it in burger form), and, because this is a British-flavored island, the custom in restaurants is that you won't get your bill until you ask for it.

Try **Mustors** (© **246/426-5175**), on McGregor Street. It's a favorite with locals and serves authentic Barbadian lunch fare. Lunch is about US$7. For pub grub, try the hopping **Whistling Frog Pub** (© **246/420-5021**), located at the Gap Hotel near the Turtle Beach Resort. Lunch will run you about US$10.

Brown Sugar, Aquatic Gap (off Bay St.), St. Michael, just below Bridgetown on Carlisle Bay (© **246/426-7684**), is an alfresco restaurant in a turn-of-the-century bungalow. The chefs prepare some of the tastiest Bajan specialties on the island. Of the main dishes, Creole-broiled pepper chicken is popular, as are the stuffed crab backs. There's a great lunch buffet for less than US$20 per person.

8 Belize

Located on the northeastern tip of Central America, bordering Mexico on the north, Guatemala to the west and south, and the Caribbean to the east, Belize combines Central American and Caribbean cultures. The area offers both ancient Mayan ruins and a 298km (185-mile) coral reef that runs the entire length of the country—it's the largest in the Western Hemisphere and the second largest in the world, supporting a tremendous number of patch reefs, shoals, and more than 1,000 islands called cayes (pronounced *keys*), the largest and most populous being Ambergris Caye. (Both Ambergris Caye and Caye Caulker are popular with visitors, offering a barefoot informality.) The country is noted for its eco-friendly ways and, unlike many other Caribbean countries, is serious in its dedication to conservation: One-fifth of Belize's total landmass is dedicated as nature reserves, and 7,770 sq. km (3,030 sq. miles) of its waters are protected as well.

Previously known as British Honduras, Belize gained its independence from England in 1981. It has a parliamentary democracy and is a member of the British Commonwealth. Belmopan is the capital, but **Belize City** is the economic center of the country. Trying to choose which natural or man-made wonder to explore will be the most stress you'll feel in this very laid-back, diverse, stable, and English-speaking nation, whose population of about 216,000 comprises Creoles, Garifuna (Black Carib Indians), mestizos (a mix of Spanish and Indian), Spanish, Maya, English, Lebanese, Chinese, and Eastern Indians. The country has the highest concentration of **Mayan sites** among all Central American nations, including Altun Ha, Caracol, Cerros, Lamanai, Lubaantun, and Xunantunich (plus Tikal is nearby in Guatemala). During the classic period (A.D. 250–900), there were a million Maya in Belize, and although the civilization began to decline after A.D. 900, some Mayan centers were occupied until contact with the Spanish in the 1500s. Today, Belize has joined with El Salvador, Guatemala, Honduras, and Mexico to establish Mundo Maya (World of the Maya), a program dedicated to the preservation of Mayan culture.

The country gained dubious celebrity in recent years as the setting for the reality TV show *Temptation Island* (even though it's not, in fact, an island), but adventurous travelers have been vacationing here for years. However, it's only in the past several years, as Belize has gradually developed its tourism infrastructure, that cruise lines have added the country to their ever-expanding itineraries. Although Belize is a year-round destination, the waters are especially clear from April to June; and the dry season, lasting from February to May, coincides nicely with the cruise high season.

Belize

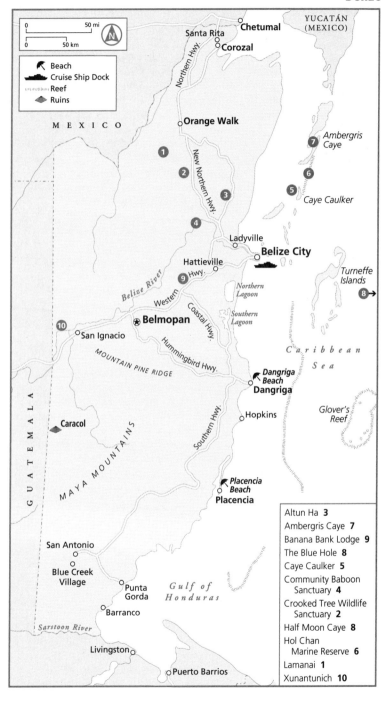

0   50 mi

0   50 km

Beach
Cruise Ship Dock
Reef
Ruins

YUCATÁN
(MEXICO)

Chetumal

Santa Rita
Corozal

M E X I C O

Northern Hwy.

Orange Walk

1

New Northern Hwy.

2

3

Ambergris
Caye

7

6

5

Caye Caulker

4

Ladyville

Belize City

Hattieville

9

Hwy.

Belize River

Western

Coastal Hwy.

Northern
Lagoon

Southern
Lagoon

Turneffe
Islands

8 →

10

San Ignacio

Belmopan

MOUNTAIN PINE RIDGE

Hummingbird Hwy.

C a r i b b e a n

S e a

Dangriga
Beach
Dangriga

G U A T E M A L A

Caracol

M A Y A   M O U N T A I N S

Southern Hwy.

Hopkins

Glover's
Reef

Placencia
Beach
Placencia

San Antonio

Blue Creek
Village

Punta
Gorda

Barranco

Sarstoon River

Gulf of
Honduras

Livingston

Puerto Barrios

Altun Ha **3**
Ambergris Caye **7**
Banana Bank Lodge **9**
The Blue Hole **8**
Caye Caulker **5**
Community Baboon
   Sanctuary **4**
Crooked Tree Wildlife
   Sanctuary **2**
Half Moon Caye **8**
Hol Chan
   Marine Reserve **6**
Lamanai **1**
Xunantunich **10**

127

Frommer's Favorite Belize Experiences

Visiting Lamanai: Satisfying to both the archaeology buff and the wildlife enthusiast, a visit to this Mayan site gives you both land and water experiences. And how could you pass up wonderful photo ops and howler monkeys? (See "Best Cruise Line Shore Excursions," below.)

Snorkeling or Diving at Hol Chan Marine Reserve & Shark Ray Alley: The reef is what it's all about when it comes to the waters of Belize: Friendly fish and playful stingrays make for an extremely memorable day. (See "Best Cruise Line Shore Excursions," below.)

Going Horseback Riding: Whether you're an experienced rider or have always wanted to give it a try, Banana Bank Lodge is definitely the place to go. (See "Excursions Offered by Local Agencies," below.)

Tubing in Caves: Glide down the Caves Branch River in an inner tube while wearing miner-style flashlight headbands. (See "Best Cruise Line Shore Excursions," below.)

Xunantunich: This western Belize Mayan site boasts one of the largest temples in the country; if you're sturdy enough to climb to the top, you're rewarded with amazing panoramic views of Belize and nearby Guatemala. (See "Best Cruise Line Shore Excursions," below.)

COMING ASHORE   A new multimillion-dollar, 450-sq.-m (4,844-sq.-ft.) pier called Belize Tourism Village opened in Belize City in October 2001. While big ships still can't pull alongside because of shallow waters, and must tender in passengers from anchorages offshore (a 20- to 30-min. trip each way), the spiffy pier area now offers a new shopping complex, with restaurants, tourist information, and even a tranquil Mayan-themed courtyard. Smaller ships, like Windstar's, skip Belize City completely and anchor offshore from the cayes and other parts of the mainland, such as the southern Dangriga and Placencia.

LANGUAGE   **English** is the official language of Belize, although Spanish, Creole, Garifuna, and Mayan are spoken throughout the country as well.

CURRENCY   The Belize dollar (BZ$) has a fixed exchange rate of BZ$2 to US$1 (BZ$1 = US50¢), so even after a few too many rum punches, you won't have to take out your calculator here. Most establishments, as well as taxis and vendors on the street, take U.S. dollars, and most places take credit cards too. In especially touristy areas, just be sure to ask if the price quoted is in U.S. or BZ dollars.

INFORMATION   If you want information before you leave home, contact the **Belize Tourism Board** (© **800/624-0686** or 501/223-1913; www.travel belize.org) or the **Belize Tourism Industry Association** (© **501/227-5717**). The **Belize Audubon Society** (© **501/223-4987**) also has a huge presence, not only for bird-watching but for all areas of nature conservation; the organization manages many of the country's reserves.

CALLING FROM THE U.S.   To make a call from the U.S. to Belize, dial the international access code (011), the country code (501), and then the number of the establishment.

GETTING AROUND

BY TAXI   Taxis are available at the pier, in town, and in resort areas, and are easily recognized by their green license plates. Although the taxis have no meters, the drivers do charge somewhat standard fares; ask what your fare will be prior to hiring a taxi.

BY WATER TAXI   From the **Marine Terminal** in Belize City (① **501/203-1969**), water-taxi service runs to Ambergris Caye, Caye Caulker, and various other cayes. Boats leave at 9am, 10:30am, noon, 1:30pm, 3pm, and 4:30pm. The ride from Belize City to San Pedro, the main town on Ambergris Caye, is approximately 80 minutes and costs US$25 round-trip.

BY PLANE   Local airlines **Tropic Air** (① 800/422-3435 or 501/226-2012; www.tropicair.com) and **Maya Island Air** (① 800/225-6732 or 501/226-2435; www.mayaislandair.com) offer hourly flights to Ambergris Caye, Caye Caulker, Placencia, and Dangriga. The flight to Ambergris Caye takes approximately 20 minutes, and, because you fly so low, you get a breathtaking view of the surrounding cayes and atolls. Keep your eyes open for stingrays and dolphins swimming below you. Flights leave from Belize City going to San Pedro approximately every 90 minutes until 5pm and cost approximately US$93 round-trip. The term "puddle jumper" really applies here: The planes can be as small as six-seaters, and you may even get to sit next to the pilot.

BY RENTAL CAR   Not recommended. Although most of the major roads and highways are paved, lots of patches are in need of repair, which makes for a very bumpy ride.

BEST CRUISE LINE SHORE EXCURSIONS

Lamanai (US$87, 7½ hr.): Lamanai is one of the largest ceremonial centers in Belize. In the original Mayan language, its name means "submerged crocodile," and you will see various crocodile carvings throughout the site. Starting with a 45-minute drive up the Northern Highway to Tower Hill, you'll board a riverboat and head up the New River. Along the way, through the mangroves, your guide will point out crocodiles basking in the sun, a variety of birds (including jacanas and hawks), delicate water lilies, and other exotic flowers such as black orchids. You'll pass local fisherman and, surprisingly, Mennonite farms—Mennonites from Canada and Mexico began arriving in Belize in 1958 in search of land and a more isolated and simple life, and today their community numbers around 7,000. Landing at the Lamanai grounds, you'll have lunch and then tour the series of temples. There are more than 700 structures, most of them still buried beneath mounds of earth. For a view above the thick jungle, you can climb some of the temples—look in the trees for toucans and spider monkeys playing or napping. You won't mistake the roar of the howler monkey. Your guide may tell you about the red gumbo-limbo tree, whose bark becomes red and then peels off—it's jokingly referred to as the tourist tree. A small archaeological museum is at the site, and there are a few stands to buy souvenirs.

Altun Ha (US$45, 4 hr.): Meaning "water of the rock," Altun Ha is a relatively small site of temples and tombs that was rediscovered in 1957 during expansion of the Northern Highway. This is one of the most extensively excavated sites, and was an important trading post during the classical Mayan period. Many treasures were found here, including a carved jade head representing Kinich Ahau, the Mayan sun god (not on display). It has become one of the country's national symbols, and is depicted on the nation's currency. The tour includes lunch. There is a small gift shop on-site.

Xunantunich (US$90, 8 hr.): This site, also called **Maiden of the Rock,** is located near the Guatemalan border, overlooking the Mopan River. Xunantunich was a major ceremonial center during the classic Mayan period. After crossing the river by hand-cranked ferry, you can explore six major plazas surrounded by more than 25 temples and palaces, including El Castillo (the castle), the largest of the temples. Be sure to climb to the top—it's well worth it for the amazing panoramic view. There's a new visitor's center with old excavation photos, a scale model, and a few exhibits and souvenir shops. Afterwards, you'll head to San Ignacio for lunch and enjoy a marimba band.

Hol Chan Marine Reserve & Shark Ray Alley (US$92, 8 hr.): You'll head north for an hour-long speedboat ride to Hol Chan (Mayan for "little channel"), 6.4km (4 miles) southeast of San Pedro on Ambergris Caye, snorkel the reef for about an hour, and then head off to the Shark Ray Alley dive site, about 5 minutes away, where you'll see and pet dozens of southern stingrays and nurse sharks. Guides bring goodies for them to eat, and they stick around till the food is gone. Remember to bring a disposable underwater camera—if you're going to pet a stingray, you may as well capture it on film! Lunch is on San Pedro, where you can find yourself a rum punch, go shopping, or just hang out at the beach.

Cave Tubing (US$96, 6½ hr.): Upon arrival at Jaguar Paw, you'll take a 45-minute hike down a jungle trail where your guide will point out various plants and trees used by the ancient Maya for medicinal purposes. When you get to the cave, your guide will hand out flashlights and inner tubes and set you afloat, propelled by the current, through the cave system. On several occasions, you'll emerge into the sunlight before entering another cave. The float lasts about 2 hours, after which you'll have lunch. Bring a change of clothes.

Belize City Tour (US$38, 3 hr.): It's hardly one of the most exciting tours and definitely isn't a great way to see the natural side of Belize, but if you want to do something quick and easy, this is the tour. It will give you a feel for the city, its colonial architecture, and its culture through a visit to the Belize Maritime Museum and Terminal, the Government House Museum, and St. John's Cathedral, which was built in 1812, making it the oldest Anglican cathedral in Central America. Around lunchtime, the Mennonite farmers and craftsman are out selling their handmade furniture. Their denim overalls, checked shirts, and straw cowboy hats make them easily recognizable. If you want to combine your city tour with a little nature, the **"City & Sanctuary"** (US$49, 4hr.) tour adds a visit to the **Belize Zoo** (© 220-8004). First created as a haven for animals who were injured and couldn't be returned to the wild, the zoo now houses an impressive array of large cats, primates, reptiles, and birds.

EXCURSIONS OFFERED BY LOCAL AGENCIES

Taxi Tours: Generally, the excursions offered by the cruise lines are the way to go in Belize, but if you crave a more personalized experience, you can hire a taxi driver who doubles as a guide (make sure you tell the driver that you want a tour before getting into the taxi and negotiating a price). Tour guides must be licensed by the Belize Tourism Board and are recognizable with a photo ID. Of the many operators, one of the larger ones is **Cruise Solutions** (© 501/223-0748), which offers a wide variety of tours all around the country and can arrange custom tours as well. For a tour of Belize City, try to snag **Lasalle Tillet**

of **S&L Travel & Tours** (© **501/227-7593** or 501/227-5145; fax 501/227-7594). Everyone in town seems to know him, and you'll enjoy his cheerful demeanor and insightful information.

Horseback Tours: Banana Bank Lodge (© **501/820-2020;** www.bananabank.com), located in Belmopan, about an hour's drive from the pier, offers 7-hour tours through the jungle, plains, and riverbank. Larger-than-life cowboy-owner John Carr greets each of his guests personally and makes your riding experience a memorable one. The US$90 per-person cost includes a delicious traditional lunch and a tour of the lodge's grounds. Well-trained horses are matched to each rider's ability.

Fishing Excursions: Belize is a fishing mecca, with an abundance of game fish that guarantees excellent sport. The estuaries, inlets, and mouths to the many rivers are known for their tarpon, snook, and jacks; the lagoons and grass flats are known for bonefish, permit, and barracuda; the coral reefs support grouper, snapper, jacks, and barracuda; and the deeper waters offshore are home to sailfish, marlin, bonito, and pompano. One of the largest operations is the **Belize River Lodge** (© **888/275-4843;** www.belizeriverlodge.com), which offers a half-day fishing package that includes lunch and drinks (US$388 for up to two guests). A favorite local fishing guide is **Richard Young Jr.** (© **501/227-4385**). Most guides and boatmen speak English.

ON YOUR OWN: WITHIN WALKING DISTANCE

Belize City is the hub of the country but is not home to the country's major attractions. The **historic harbor district** right around the pier is small and quaint. You'll find a few restaurants, and the **Baron Bliss Park and Lighthouse** is just a short stroll away. After sailing from Portugal, Baron Bliss arrived sick with food poisoning, and remained aboard his yacht for 2 months; local fisherman and administrators treated him kindly and taught him about Belize. He died soon after arriving, but not before changing his will and leaving $2 million to Belize in a trust fund. That money made possible the building of the Bliss Institute Library and Museum and a number of health clinics and markets around the country, as well as helping with the Belize City water system. The baron is considered Belize's greatest benefactor, and Baron Bliss Day, a national holiday, is celebrated on March 9.

Outside of the immediate port area, much of the rest of the city is run down and poor, with narrow, crowded streets and many old colonial structures that are in need of repair. However, since tourism is an important industry in Belize, the country is making an effort to spruce up the city and reduce crime, instituting a squad of Tourism Police to patrol popular tourist areas. Its officers are dressed in brown uniforms.

ON YOUR OWN: BEYOND THE PORT AREA

A 20-minute flight will get you to **Ambergris Caye,** the largest of Belize's 200 offshore islands and the inspiration for the Madonna song "La Isla Bonita." You know: "Last night I dreamt of San Pedro . . . tropical island breeze . . . all of nature wild and free . . ." blah blah blah? The thing is, she got it about right. They have a motto here: "No shoes, no shirt . . . no problem," and that's really true. Everyone drives around in golf carts, and you can too (for about US$35 for an afternoon, from rental places located along the main streets and near the little airport). Once in San Pedro (the island's main town), the beach is functions as the main street, offering plenty of shopping, restaurants, bars, and watersports.

Slightly smaller **Caye Caulker** is Belize's second most popular caye, and is even more laid-back, with plenty of beachfront restaurants and bars. Despite the growth of tourism, the island retains a small-village feel not found in areas with large-scale tourist development. Almost all of the businesses are locally owned, and you'll rarely see vehicles larger than golf carts on the streets. You can just hang out on the beach or plunge into one of the island's watersports, including snorkeling, scuba, fishing, kayaking, windsurfing, sailing, or manatee-watching. Birding is also popular.

The **Community Baboon Sanctuary,** located about 48m (30 miles) west of Belize City off the Northern Highway in the Belize District (© **501/220-2181**), offers a guided tour along forest trails. Through a grassroots effort, the villagers and landowners committed to preserving the habitat necessary to ensure a healthy population of black howler monkeys (locally known as baboons). Passengers interested in birding should tour the **Crooked Tree Wildlife Sanctuary** (© **501/209-7084** or 501/614-5658). Located approximately 35 minutes from Belize City, the sanctuary provides a habitat for more than 360 species of birds.

Back in Belize City, if you want to do some gambling, the **Princess Hotel-Casino** is located a couple of kilometers (a mile or two) from the cruise pier, on Newtown Barricks Road (© **501/223-2670**); the casino is about 10 minutes and US$5 by taxi from the pier.

SHOPPING

In general, the best buys in Belize are wooden and slate carvings, Mayan calendars, pottery, ceramics, and furniture made by the Mennonites. At the pier, the new **Tourism Village** offers shops specializing in local souvenirs such as mahogany bowls, jewelry, clothes, assorted carvings, and artwork. A local favorite is Marie Sharp's hot sauces and jams. They're served everywhere and can be purchased to take home. On Ambergris Caye, you'll find a variety of slightly upscale gift shops, and the excursion sites all have local goods available.

BEACHES

Compared to many other islands in the Caribbean, the beaches of Belize are neither the biggest nor the widest, but they are relaxing, with very clear water. Areas that offer the best beach sunbathing are in the cayes, including Ambergris Caye, Caye Caulker, and Tobacco Caye; and on the mainland to the south in Dangriga and Placencia. There are no beaches near Belize City.

SPORTS

WATERSPORTS   If you don't opt for one of your ship's dive excursions, local dive shops can customize an experience for you. Hugh Parkey's **Belize Dive Connection** (© **888/223-5403** or 501/223-4526; www.belizediving.com) is conveniently located on the Radisson Pier and offers day scuba dives and snorkel trips with a yummy lunch catered by the Fort Street Restaurant. In San Pedro, **Aqua Dives** (© **800/641-2994** or 501/226-3415; www.aquadives.com) is located on the beachfront and will plan your diving or snorkeling adventure.

In the center of Lighthouse Reef Atoll, about 80km (50 miles) due east of Belize City, the **"Blue Hole"** was originally a cave. The roof fell in some 10,000 years ago as the land receded into the sea, leaving an almost perfectly circular hole 300m (984 ft.) in diameter and 124m (407 ft.) deep. Popularized by a Jacques Cousteau television special, it's become the most famous dive site in all of Belize. **Half Moon Caye,** located at the southeast corner of Lighthouse Reef Atoll, was the first reserve to be established by the Natural Parks System Act of

1981, which specifically protected the Red-footed Booby bird and its rookery. Some 98 other species of birds have been recorded on the Caye.

One of the newest national parks in Belize is **Laughing Bird Caye,** located 21km (13 miles) southeast of Placencia Village in the Stann Creek District. Although the caye was named for the large number of laughing gulls that used to live here, the birds have virtually abandoned their rookery because of excessive human encroachment. Since Laughing Bird Caye is a shelf atoll with deep channels, the scuba-diving and snorkeling opportunities are outstanding.

Many dive excursions include a barbecue lunch on Goff's Caye. Part of the Central Main Reef, it's a popular dive site itself.

GREAT LOCAL RESTAURANTS & BARS

The **local beer** is Belikan, and you can order it most anywhere. If you visit Altun Ha you'll recognize the site as the beer's logo (or vice versa).

IN BELIZE CITY   Around the Tourism Village you'll find many pleasant restaurants within walking distance. Stroll to The Great House Hotel at 13 Cork St. to find **The Smokey Mermaid** (© 501/223-4759), situated in a lovely mango tree–shaded patio garden. One of its specialties is the yucca-crusted snapper with a fruity salsa topping. For dessert, be sure to try the coconut pie. The lunch special is US$10. **Chateau Caribbean,** 6 Marine Parade (© 501/223-0800), offers Caribbean and Asian specialties. Lunch runs approximately US$13. At the **Radisson Hotel** (© 800/333-3333 or 501/223-3333), you have several dining choices either inside or on a deck outside overlooking the Caribbean. A buffet lunch is about US$12, while sandwiches and burgers can be had for about US$7.

IN SAN PEDRO, AMBERGRIS CAYE   Most of the restaurants and bars here are on the beach, so you can just stroll along and stop at whatever place strikes your fancy.

ON CAYE CAULKER   Caye Caulker has about 25 restaurants, also mostly on the beach, offering Belizean and international cuisine, including fresh seafood. Lobster, conch, and red snapper are seasonal specialties.

FARTHER OUT   Heading west of Belize City, the very rustic **Cheers Bar & Restaurant** (© 501/804-9311) is kind of in the middle of nowhere on the Western Highway at mile 31 (about 3km/2 miles from the Belize Zoo and 26km/16 miles from Banana Bank Lodge), but the food is good, it has a nice outdoor patio, and it's frequented by travelers and locals. Leave behind a memento T-shirt to say you were here—there are dozens of them from all over the world. Still farther west, about 5km (3 miles) from Xunantunich, you'll find **Eva's Restaurant** at 22 Burns St., San Ignacio, (© 501/804-2267), where you can enjoy a tasty lunch and check your e-mail as well.

9 Bequia

Bequia (meaning "Island of the Cloud" in the original Carib, and inexplicably pronounced *beck*-wee) is the largest island in the St. Vincent Grenadines, with a population of around 5,000. Sun-drenched, windswept, peaceful, and green (though arid), it's a popular stop for small-ship lines such as Clipper, ACCL, Star Clippers, Windjammer, and the more upscale Seabourn, SeaDream, and Windstar, which join the many yachts in Admiralty Bay throughout the yachting season.

Very much a tourism-oriented island, Bequia is nevertheless anything but touristy. You'll find a few of the requisite cheesy gift shops in the main town,

Frommer's Favorite Bequia Experiences

Strolling Along the Belmont Walkway: In the evenings, this walkway at water's edge makes for a terrifically romantic stroll as you make your way from one nightspot to the next. You might even pick up the company of one of the friendly port dogs, who seem more interested in companionship than panhandling. (See "On Your Own: Within Walking Distance," below.)

Visiting Brother King's Old Hegg Turtle Sanctuary: Wanna see baby turtles? This is your place. You'll see hundreds of the critters in the main swimming pool and in their own little private cubbyholes, and hear about the sanctuary's conservation efforts. Donations are gladly accepted. (See "On Your Own: Beyond the Port Area," below.)

Visiting the Lower Bay and Princess Margaret Beach: South of Port Elizabeth, this stretch of sand is frequently described by cruisers as "the best beach I've ever experienced." It's a little chunk of paradise, backed by waving palms and fronted by yachts bobbing at anchor in the distance. (See "Beaches," below.)

Port Elizabeth, but none of the typical cruise-port giants such as Little Switzerland. Instead, the town offers one of the most attractive port settings in the Caribbean, with restaurants, cozy bars, a produce market, and craft shops strung along and around the Belmont Walkway, a path that skirts so close to the calm bay waters that at high tide you have to skip across rocks to avoid getting your feet wet. Many ships spend the night here or make late departures, allowing passengers to take in the nightlife.

The island has a rich seafaring tradition, including fishing, sailing, boat building (though most of the handmade boats that you'll see are scale models made for the yachting set), and even whaling, though this is whaling of a token, almost ritualistic sort—only about one whale is taken in any given year.

COMING ASHORE Ships dock right in the center of the island's main town, Port Elizabeth, a stone's throw from the restaurants, bars, and shops that line the waterfront.

LANGUAGE The official and daily-use language is **English.**

CURRENCY The **Eastern Caribbean dollar** (EC$2.70 = US$1; EC$1 = US37¢) is used on Bequia; however, U.S. dollars are accepted by all businesses. It's always a good idea to ask if you're not sure which currency a price tag refers to. Rates quoted in this section are given in U.S. dollars.

INFORMATION A small tourist information booth is right on the beach by the cruise dock, but frankly, you can almost see everything there is to do from the same spot. It's a pretty small island. For information before you go, contact the **Bequia Tourist Association** (© 784/458-3286; www.bequiatourism.com) or the **St. Vincent & The Grenadines Department of Tourism** (© 800/729-1726 or 212/687-4981 in the U.S., 784/457-1502; www.svgtourism.com).

CALLING FROM THE U.S. To place a call to Bequia you need only dial a "1" before the numbers listed in this section.

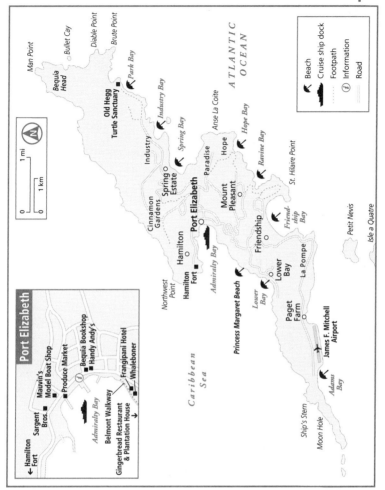

GETTING AROUND

Ships dock right in Port Elizabeth, putting you within walking distance of all the town sights. The popular Princess Margaret Beach is within walking distance as well.

BY TAXI You'll find plenty of taxis lined up right at the cruise dock to take you around the island. The fare is approximately US$20 per hour, or US$5 per person per hour for groups of more than four.

BY MINIBUS The entire island of Bequia is served by a fleet of small, unofficial dollar-cab minibuses that cruise regular routes, picking up passengers when flagged down (some obvious bus stops are also scattered around). Tell the driver where you want to go and he'll tell you a price.

BY RENTAL CAR Rentals are available at **Handy Andy's Rentals,** on the Main Road in Port Elizabeth, to the right of the dock if you're facing inland (© **784/458-3722;** http://handyandybequia.tripod.com). A Jeep Wrangler rents for US$60 daily. **Phil's Car Rental** (℗ 784/458-3304), located at the cruise ship dock, has Geo Trackers and Suzuki Sidekicks for rent for approximately US$70 per day.

BY BICYCLE **Handy Andy's** (see above) also rents Mongoose mountain bikes for US$10.

BEST CRUISE LINE SHORE EXCURSIONS

Bequia is very much a "relax and have a drink" kind of island, rather than one with a lot of definable, tourable attractions. Standard island tours (US$35, 3 hr.) offer an overview and still allow you plenty of time to poke around or go to the beach. Most other excursions are sailing trips around the island and to neighboring Mustique and Tobago Cays, but we'd advise not missing Bequia. It's a lovely place.

Sailing Excursion to Mustique (US$90, 7–8 hr.): Sail aboard a schooner to exclusive (i.e. rich people own it) Mustique, just southeast of Bequia, for strolling, shopping, snorkeling, or simply lying on the beach. Complimentary drinks are included aboard ship. A shorter version of this tour travels between islands by powerboat rather than sailing ship—less romantic, but speedier (US$70, 3–4 hr.).

ON YOUR OWN: WITHIN WALKING DISTANCE

In theory, almost the entire island of Bequia is within walking distance, but only for serious walkers. We decided to test this theory out by walking from Port Elizabeth to Hamilton Fort, just north of town, then backtracking through the port and down to the tiny old whaling village of Paget Farm, near the airport on Bequia's southern tip. As the crow flies it's not much of a distance, but curving roads and hilly terrain made it a real journey that took about 4 to 5 hours round-trip, with no significant stops. If your ship is in port late and you're in good shape, it's a great way to see the island (including lovely Friendship Bay, on the east coast) and meet some of the local people along the way. Bring water.

For those wanting something less strenuous, strolling around Port Elizabeth itself is close to idyllic. The **Belmont Walkway** runs south from the docks right at the water's edge (meaning at high tide, parts of it are actually under a few inches of water), fronting many restaurants, shops, and bars. This area is particularly romantic in the evenings.

Heading north from the docks along the Main Road, you'll find a homey produce market that also stocks some souvenir items. Across the street, **Mauvin's Model Boat Shop** (℗ 784/458-3669) is one of the visible reminders of the island's boat-building tradition, though now the money seems to lie in crafting scale models of real boats for sale to the yachting crowd. Farther along the Main Road, **Sargent Bros. Model Boat Shop** (℗ 784/458-3344) is a larger shop offering the same type of merchandise. The workshop is a little more accessible here, so you can easily see the craftsmen creating their wares (all the work is done by hand; no power tools are employed at all), and see models in various stages of construction. At both shops, the models are beautiful, lovingly constructed, and signed by the craftsman—but they're not what you'd call cheap: Prices start

---

Use Your Ship's Facilities

Since Bequia is an extremely dry island and is very conscious of water conservation, it has few public washrooms. You'd be well advised to use your ship's bathroom facilities before coming ashore.

around $110 for a tiny model, and can go up as high as $10,000 for something really fabulous.

If you continue walking along the Main Road, you'll pass through an area with many boating supply stores and a few bars and food stands obviously geared to the local fishing and sailing trades. It's a quiet, pretty walk, even though it may well be the most "industrial" part of the island. Eventually you'll come upon a concrete walkway hanging above the water along the coast. From here, the going gets rough—many sections of the walkway have been cracked and heaved drastically off-kilter by hurricanes, and it's patched here and there with planks and other makeshift materials. At the end of the walkway the road starts curving uphill and inland through a quiet residential area, and all the way up to Hamilton Fort, perched above Admiralty Bay and offering a lovely view of Port Elizabeth, though that's about all it offers—a few tiny fragments of battlements and five plugged canons are all that remain of the old fort. A taxi can take you here by another route if you want to avoid the walk (a good idea unless you're in decent shape and very sure-footed).

ON YOUR OWN: BEYOND THE PORT AREA

At Park Beach, on the island's northeast coast, 3.2km (2 miles) east of Port Elizabeth, **Brother King's Old Hegg Turtle Sanctuary** (℃ 784/458-3596) offers a chance to see conservation in action. Founded in 1995 by the eponymous King and dedicated to raising and releasing Hawksbill turtle hatchlings, the sanctuary is a real labor of love. A main concrete swimming pool and small plastic kiddy pools allow maturing hatchlings to socialize. Brother King and his assistants are on hand to tell you about their conservation efforts, and will gladly accept donations to help keep the place going.

Aside from this and the activities in Port Elizabeth, most of the island's other attractions are beaches, so turn to that section, below.

SHOPPING

You'll find most shopping worth doing within walking distance of the docks in Port Elizabeth. Heading south from the pier, one of the first businesses you'll come to is the **Bequia Bookshop** (℃ 784/458-3905), selling books on the island's and region's cultures and history; books of poetry and prose by local authors; yachting guides; and a selection of other fiction and nonfiction titles; as well as truly beautiful scrimshaw pocket knives, pendants, money clips, necklaces, and pins, all made from polished domesticated camel bone rather than the traditional whale bone.

Sam McDowell, the artist who creates these scrimshaw items, opens his **Banana Patch Studio** for visitors by appointment. Located in the little village of Paget Farm on the southern part of the island, near the airport, the studio displays Sam's scrimshaw and whaling-themed paintings, as well as his wife Donna's shellwork. Call or fax ℃ 784/458-3865 for an appointment.

You'll find several generic gift shops farther along, some fronting off the Belmont Walkway, including **Solana's,** for Caribelle batiks, T-shirts, and so on.

Heading in the other direction, north from the docks, you'll find the two model-boat shops described above, as well as a couple of open-air souvenir/crafts stalls, a produce market, and **Kennie's Music Shop** (℃ 784/527-1614), for island sounds on CD.

BEACHES

Beaches are one of the big draws on Bequia, and all are open to the public. The best on the list is **Princess Margaret Beach,** a golden-sand stretch lying just

A Quiet Day on Union Island

Some small ships stop for a day at quiet, tranquil (very quiet, very tranquil) Union Island, the southernmost port of entry in the St. Vincent Grenadines. Think of your stop here as a "recovery day" rather than a whiz-bang exciting day in port: There are few facilities (none whatsoever in Chatham Bay, where ships usually tender passengers to land), few people, and few opportunities to do anything more than swim, snorkel, and do a little beachcombing. You'll likely see hundreds of conch-shell pieces along the beach, since a number of local fishermen are based here. (You can always tell if the conch was naturally thrown up on the beach or caught, since the latter have a small gash in the shell—the method the fishermen use to sever the muscle by which the conch beast holds onto its shell home.) Some enterprising fishermen set out the best shells they find (conch and otherwise) on small tables, offering them to tourists for a couple bucks—you miss out on the personal thrill of finding them yourself, but they're some mighty nice shells.

Snorkeling is decent in Chatham Bay, though the waters don't yield the diversity you'll see elsewhere in the eastern Caribbean.

south of Port Elizabeth. To get there, take the Belmont Walkway to its end; from there, take the dirt path over the hill. Lower Bay beach is a little farther down along the same stretch of coast.

On the northeast coast, the **beach at Industry Bay** is, despite its name, windswept and gorgeous, a scene straight out of a romance novel. Trees on the hills surrounding the bay grow up to a certain height and then level out, growing sideways due to the constant wind off the Atlantic. The small, three-room **Crescent Beach Inn** (② 784/458-3400) lies along this stretch, in case you want to come back after your cruise and stay a while. Along the southeast coast is Friendship Bay, an area that draws many European visitors.

Do not under any circumstances pick or eat the small green apples you'll see growing in some spots. These are manchineel, and are extremely poisonous.

SPORTS

Besides walking (see above) and biking (mountain bikes are available to rent from Handy Andy's Rentals right by the cruise dock), the sports here, like the rest of life on the island, center on the water. **Dive Bequia** (② 784/458-3504; www.dive-bequia.com) and **Bequia Dive Adventure** (② 784/458-3826; www.bequiadiveadventures.com), located along Belmont Walkway right by the docks, specialize in diving and snorkeling.

GREAT LOCAL RESTAURANTS & BARS

The coastal stretch along the Belmont Walkway is chockablock with restaurants and bars. The **local beer** of St. Vincent and the Grenadines is Hairoun, which is decent but not up to the level of St. Lucia's Piton. The **local rum** is Sunset.

The **Frangipani Hotel Restaurant and Bar** (② 784/458-3255) is right on the water along the walkway. Lunch (served 10am–5pm) includes sandwiches, salads, and seafood platters. Dinner specialties include conch chowder, baked chicken with rice-and-coconut stuffing, and an array of fresh fish. On Thursday nights the bar hosts an excellent steel band. It's a lovely scene, with yachters, locals, cruisers from ships that have stayed late in port, and a coterie of friendly local dogs all getting to know one another over drinks or settling down for the restaurant's special barbecue. Lunch is about US$9.

Farther along the walkway, the **Whaleboner Bar & Restaurant** (© **784/458-3233**) serves a nice thin-crust pizza (with toppings such as lobster, shrimp, and generic "fish"), sandwiches, fish and chips, and cold beer, either indoors or at tables in their shaded, oceanview front yard. It's a perfect casual resting-up spot after walking around the island. Lunch is about US$10.

The **Gingerbread Restaurant & Bar,** also right along the waterfront (© **784/ 458-3800**), has a beautiful balcony dining room that's open throughout the day, and a downstairs cafe that serves coffee, tea, and Italian ice cream at outside tables. Lunch is about US$12. **Plantation House** (© **784/458-3425**), farther along the waterfront, is the premier dining spot on the island, and serves informal lunches between noon and 2:30pm for around US$18. Service and cuisine are both first-rate. Reservations are recommended.

10 Bonaire

Ever wonder what's going on under all that water you've been cruising on for days? There's no better place to find out than the island of Bonaire—"Divers Paradise," as the slogan on the island's license plates says. Avid divers have flocked to this unspoiled treasure for years for its pristine waters, stunning coral reefs (which encircle the island just feet from shore), and vibrant marine life—it's simply one of the best places in the Caribbean for diving and snorkeling.

The island also offers other adventure activities such as mountain biking, kayaking, and windsurfing; if these options sound too strenuous, why not just marvel at the sun-basking iguanas, fluorescent lora parrots, wild donkeys, graceful flamingos, and feral goats? As for flora, you're likely to see more cacti in Bonaire than anywhere outside of the deserts of Mexico and the Southwest. Sprawling bushes of exotic succulents and permanently windswept divi-divi trees also abound. If you'd rather join the iguanas and just bake in the sun, Bonaire's beaches are intimate and uncrowded. In fact, the entire island is cozy and manageable. In no time at all, you'll feel it's your very own private resort.

Relying on your high-school language lessons, you might think Bonaire was colonized by the French and named for its "good air," but you'd be wrong: The name actually comes from the Caiquetio word "bonay," which means "low country." Located 81km (50 miles) north of Venezuela and 48km (30 miles) east of Curaçao, this untrampled, boomerang-shaped refuge is one of the southernmost Caribbean islands, and forms the "B" in the ABC chain, along with Aruba and Curaçao. Thirty-nine kilometers (24 miles) long and 5km to 11km (3–7 miles) wide at various points, it's large enough to require a motorized vehicle if you want to explore, but small enough that you won't get lost.

The Caiquetios, members of the Arawak tribe who sailed from the coast of Venezuela a thousand years ago, were Bonaire's first human inhabitants. Europeans arrived 500 years later, in 1499, when Alonso de Ojeda and Amerigo Vespucci claimed the island for Spain. The Spanish enslaved the indigenous people and moved them to other Caribbean islands. Later, the Europeans used the island to raise cows, goats, horses, and donkeys. The Dutch gained control in the 1630s, and on the back of African slave labor, Bonaire became an important salt producer.

With the discovery of oil in Venezuela early in the 20th century, Aruba and Curaçao became refining centers, and Bonaire, too, got a piece of the pie. Tourism, the island's major industry today, developed after World War II, when Bonaire won self-rule from the Netherlands (though it remains a Dutch protectorate). The people of Bonaire are a mix of African, Dutch, and South American ancestries. You'll also meet expatriates from the U.S., Britain, and Australia.

COMING ASHORE   Cruise ships dock in the port of **Kralendijk** (*crawl*-en-dike), the island's capital, commercial center, and largest town (pop. about 2,500). The dock leads to Wilhelmina Park, a pleasant public space named after a former Dutch queen. **Queen Beatrix Way,** the brick-paved path along the waterfront, is lined with open-air restaurants and bars. Most of the town's shopping is a block inland on **Kaya Grandi.**

Your best bet for making long-distance phone calls is the 24-hour central phone company office (Telbo) at Kaya Libertador Simón Bolívar 8.

LANGUAGE   Almost everyone in Bonaire speaks **English,** which, along with Dutch, is a required course in the local schools. **Papiamentu** is the local patois and language of the street, a rich blend of Dutch, Spanish, Portuguese, French, English, Caribbean Indian, and several African languages. Given the island's proximity to Venezuela, you're likely to hear **Spanish** as well.

CURRENCY   Bonaire's official currency is the euro (exchange rate at press time: 1€ = US$1.22; $1 = .82€). Each euro is divisible by 100 cents. Don't waste your time exchanging money, though, since the U.S. dollar is as widely accepted as the local currency. Prices quoted in this section are in U.S. dollars. Change may be a mixture of dollars and euros. If you need cash, several ATMs are located along Kaya Grandi. Traveler's checks and credit cards are widely accepted.

INFORMATION   The **Tourism Corporation Bonaire** is located at Kaya Grandi 2 in Kralendijk (© **599/717-8322** or 800/BONAIRE; fax 599/717-8408; www.infoBonaire.com).

CALLING FROM THE U.S.   When calling Bonaire from the United States, dial the international access code (011) before the numbers listed in this section.

GETTING AROUND
BY RENTAL CAR   Highway signs are in Dutch and sometimes English, with easy-to-understand international symbols. Driving is on the right, the same as in the States and most of Europe. A valid driver's license is acceptable for renting and driving a car. Avis, Budget, Hertz, and National, as well as a number of local companies, all have offices here.

BY TAXI   Taxis greet cruise ship passengers at the pier. Although the cars are unmetered, the government establishes rates, and drivers should produce a price list upon request. Most cabs can be hired for a tour of the island, with as many as four passengers allowed to go along for the ride. Negotiate a price before leaving, but expect to pay about $30 per hour. You can get more information from the **Taxi Central Dispatch** office (© **599/717-8100**).

BY SCOOTER OR MOPED   If you plan to stick relatively close to the port area, scooters and mopeds are practical options. They can be rented from **Hot Shot Scooter/Rento Fun Drive,** Kaya Grandi 47 (© **599/717-2408**) or **Macho Scooter Rentals** at the Plaza Resort Bonaire, J. A. Abraham Blvd. 80 (© **599/717-2500**). Mopeds are about $19 a day; two-seat scooters run about $27.

BY BICYCLE For getting around town or exploring the nearby coast, try bicycling. The coastal terrain is essentially flat, but the sun can be brutal even before noon. Plan your excursion as early in the day as possible. **Cycle Bonaire,** Kaya L. D. Gerharts 11D (© **599/717-7558**), rents 21-speed mountain bikes ($15–$20) and arranges half- ($55) and full-day ($65) tours.

BEST CRUISE LINE SHORE EXCURSIONS
One-Tank Scuba Excursion for Certified Divers ($94, 3½–4 hr.): Dive in the island's famous Bonaire Marine Park.

Two-Site Snorkeling ($59, 3 hr.): The snorkeling here is some of the best you'll find in the Caribbean, and this tour takes you to two different sites around Bonaire and uninhabited Klein Bonaire, just off the west coast.

Bike Tour ($79, 3 hr.): This scenic 7½-mile ride along the northern shoreline's mostly flat and downhill terrain affords riders views of Bonaire's flora and fauna,

Frommer's Favorite Bonaire Experiences

Scuba Diving: Diving in Bonaire is said to be easier than anywhere else on Earth. The island's leeward coast has more than 80 dive sites, and whether you're diving from a boat or right from shore, you'll see spectacular coral formations and as many types of fish as anywhere in the Caribbean. If you're not certified to dive, you can take a half-day resort course to see firsthand what divers rave about. If you'd rather just stick to snorkeling, abundant marine life is perfectly visible just beneath the crystal-clear water.

Mountain Biking Along the Western Coast: Bike along the coast on a road carved through lava and limestone, and bordered with cactus. The road north from the island's capital and main town, Kralendijk, is relatively flat and passes several uncrowded beaches—perfect for cooling off. If you're looking for more of a challenge, pedal uphill to Bonaire's oldest town, Rincon. (See "Best Cruise Line Shore Excursions," below.)

Exploring Washington-Slagbaai National Park: This preserve is home to a variety of exotic wildlife and vegetation and offers spectacular coastal views. At times, the towering cacti, iguanas, and thousands of jittery lizards make you think you're in Arizona; but the humidity, flamingos, and beaches make it clear you're not. (See "On Your Own: Beyond the Port Area," below.)

Making New Friends at the Donkey Sanctuary: Miss your pooch back home? Why not lavish your love on some deserving surrogates? Donkeys were first brought to Bonaire centuries ago as beasts of burden; when more efficient modes of transport replaced them, many reverted to feral ways in the outback. More than 40 of them, most of them orphaned or injured by cars, call this oasis near the airport home, and greet you as you enter the gate, accompanying you around the tidy, brightly colored grounds. After recuperation and rehabilitation, they're returned to the wild. If you're moved by the animals' unconditional affection, you can adopt one; as a new parent, you'll receive photos and letters from your adoptee twice a year. The sanctuary is located at Punt Vierkant 5, just south of the airport in Kralendijk (© 599/9-560-7607; www.bonairenature.com/donkey), and is open Tuesday through Sunday from 10am to 4pm. There's no admission charge, but donations are appreciated. The souvenir shop has donkey shirts, donkey bags, and donkey art.

including cacti and pink flamingos. The tour winds down at Dos Pos, a former fruit plantation.

North Tour & Donkey Sanctuary ($49, 3 hr.): This bus tours explores northern coastal Bonaire, visiting the flamingos at Goto Lake, the island's oldest settlement at Rincon, and the Donkey Sanctuary (see above). If you've got a thing for donkeys, this is the tour for you.

ON YOUR OWN: WITHIN WALKING DISTANCE

You can walk the length of **Kralendijk** in an hour or less. It's a sleepy town, but its residents like it that way, thank you. The **tourist office,** Kaya Grandi 2, has walking-tour maps, but because Bonaire has always been off the beaten track, Kralendijk's highlights are modest and few. You'll probably want to stroll along the seafront with its views and restaurants, and along **Kaya Grandi,** the island's major shopping district. Just south of the town dock is **Fort Oranje,** a tiny fortress that has a cannon dating from the time of Napoleon. The town has some charming Dutch Caribbean architecture—gabled roofs you might see in Amsterdam, but in cheerful Caribbean colors, especially sunny ochre and terra cotta. If your ship arrives early enough, you can visit the waterfront produce market.

ON YOUR OWN: BEYOND THE PORT AREA

As a day visitor, you'll probably choose to explore either the northern or southern part of the island. The coastal road north of Kralendijk is one of the most beautiful in the Antilles. Turquoise, azure, and cobalt waters stretch to the horizon on your left, while pink-coral and black-volcanic cliffs loom on your right. Towering cacti, intimate coastal coves, strange rock formations, and panoramic vistas add to the beauty. The north also boasts Washington-Slagbaai National Park, an impressive, 5,400-hectare (13,338-acre) preserve that occupies the northwestern portion of the island, and Rincon, Bonaire's "other" town and oldest settlement.

NORTH OF KRALENDIJK   Soon after leaving Kralendijk, on the coast road, across from the Bonaire Caribbean Club, you'll find **Barcadera,** an old cave once used to trap goats. Take the stone steps down to the cave and examine the stalactites.

Just past the Radio Nederland towers, **1,000 Steps Beach** and dive site offers lovely views: picturesque coves, craggy coastline, and tropical waters of changing hues. Actually, there are only 67 steps; it just feels like a thousand if you're schlepping dive gear.

At the Kaya Karpata intersection, you'll see a mustard-colored building on your right. It's what's left of the aloe-processing facilities of Landhuis Karpata, a 100-year-old former plantation. The modest exhibits here explain the cultivation, harvesting, and processing of aloe, once a major export crop.

Thirty or 40 arduous minutes after turning right on Kaya Karpata, you'll arrive in **Rincon,** the original Spanish settlement on the island, founded in 1527. The town eventually became the home of African slaves who worked the island's plantations and salt pans. Nestled in a valley away from either coast, Rincon was hidden from marauding pirates, who plagued the Caribbean for decades. Today, the quiet and picturesque village is home to Bonaire's oldest church, a handsome ochre-and-white structure.

The pride of Bonaire, located on the island's northern tip, **Washington-Slagbaai National Park** is one of the Caribbean's first national parks. Formerly two separate plantations that produced aloe and charcoal and raised goats, it now showcases the island's geology, animals, and vegetation. The park boasts more than 190 species of birds; thousands of kadushi, yatu, and prickly pear cactus; and herds of wild goats, foraging donkeys, flocks of flamingos, and what seems like billions of lizards. The scenery includes stark, desertlike hills, quiet beaches, secluded caverns, and wave-battered cliffs. You have two options: Either take the shorter 24km (15-mile) route around the park, marked with green arrows, or take the longer 35km (22-mile) track, marked with yellow arrows. You'll have plenty of opportunities to hike, swim, or snorkel either way. Admission is $10 for adults, $2 for children under 15, and the park is open from 8am to 5pm daily except for major holidays; last entry is at 2:45 pm. Guide booklets and maps are available at the gate, where there's also a small museum and a visitor center. The unpaved roads are well marked and safe, but rugged; jeeps trump small cars.

On your way back to Kralendijk, take the Kaminda Onima, which traces the island's northeastern coast to **Onima,** the site of 500-year-old Caiquetio Indian inscriptions. Some of the red and brown drawings depict turtles and rain; others appear to have religious significance. You'll be able to recognize snakes, human hands, and the sun among the roughly 75 inscriptions.

Before returning to Kralendijk, call on **Sherman Gibbs.** You'll find his monument to the beauty of common objects on Kaminda Tras di Montaña, the road leading back to Kralendijk. Eccentric is one way to describe Mr. Gibbs; genius is another. If you're familiar with the Watts Tower in Los Angeles, you know "junk" can be transformed into something beautiful. Sherman, who's as gentle as his pet iguanas, combines old detergent bottles, boat motors, buoys, car seats, and just about anything else that strikes his fancy to create a wondrously happy sanctuary. The wind and old fan blades power his TV.

SOUTH OF KRALENDIJK   Just minutes south of town, dazzlingly bright salt pyramids dominate the horizon. These hills, looking more like alpine snow-drifts than sodium mounds, are created when seawater is forced into lakes by the tide and then evaporates, leaving crystallized salt behind. Farther from the road, abandoned saltworks have been set aside as a flamingo sanctuary. Bonaire is one of the world's few nesting places for pink flamingos, a species that until recently was seriously threatened by extinction. Thanks to the reserve, the island's flamingo population during the breeding season now swells to roughly 10,000, rivaling the island's human population of 14,000. The sanctuary is completely off-limits to the public because the birds are extremely wary of humans and disturbances of any kind. But even from the road you can spot a pink haze on the horizon, and with binoculars you can see the graceful birds feeding in the briny pink-and-purple waters.

At the island's southern tip, restored slave huts stand as monuments to the inhumanity of the island's slave era. Each hut, no bigger than a large doghouse, provided crude nighttime shelter for slaves brought from Africa by the Dutch West Indies Company to cut dyewood, cultivate maize, and harvest solar salt. On Friday afternoons, the slaves trekked 7 hours in the oppressive heat to their homes and families in Rincon for the weekend, returning to the salt pans on Sunday evenings.

Located on the eastern side of the island's southern tip, the classically picturesque **Willemstoren Lighthouse,** Bonaire's first, was built in 1837. It's fully automated today and usually closed to visitors, but its magnificent setting is the real draw. Odd little bundles of driftwood, bleached coral, and rocks in the area look like something out of *The Blair Witch Project,* but they're actually constructed by fishermen to mark where boats have been left.

A few minutes up the east coast is Lac Bay, a lagoon that's every bit as tranquil as the nearby windward sea is furious. The calm, shallow waters and steady breezes make the area ideal for windsurfing, and various fish come here to hatch their young. Deep inside the lagoon, mangrove trees with Edward Scissorhands roots lunge out of the water. If it weren't for the relentlessly cheerful sun, they might seem sinister. Wild donkeys, goats, and flamingos pepper the countryside along the way.

SHOPPING

Don't expect to be caught up in a duty-free frenzy in Bonaire. You'll be able to hit every store in Kralendijk before lunch, and you'll probably find greater selections and better prices at other ports. The island is a great place to buy certain items, though. Consider top-of-the-line dive watches and underwater cameras. Or how about jewelry with marine themes?

You'll find most shops on **Kaya Grandi,** on the adjacent streets, or in small malls. For Tag-Heuer dive watches, Cuban cigars, Lladró porcelain, Daum crystal, and Kosta Boda glass, try **Littman Jewelers** at Kaya Grandi 33. In the centrally located **Harborside Mall,** Little Holland has silk neckties, Nautica menswear, blue Delft porcelain, and an even more impressive array of Cuban cigars. If you're an aficionado, you'll love the shop's climate-controlled cigar room with its Montecristos, H. Upmanns, Romeo & Julietas, and Cohibas. **Sparky's,** in the same mall, carries perfume and other cosmetics, including Lancôme, Esteé Lauder, Chanel, Calvin Klein, and Ralph Lauren.

Benetton, at Kaya Grandi 49, has smart casual wear at discounts of 20% to 30%. If batik shirts, bathing suits, or souvenir T-shirts are what you want, try **Best Buddies,** Kaya Grandi 32; **Boutique Gina,** Kaya Grandi 16; **Bye-Bye Bonaire,** Harborside Mall; or **Island Fashions,** Kaya Grandi 5.

On a hot day, nothing beats the frozen-food section at **Cultimara Supermarket,** Kaya L. D. Gerharts 13. The store offers free coffee, a wide assortment of Dutch cheeses and chocolates, straight-from-the-oven breads and pastries, and various products from the Caribbean, Europe, South America, and the United States.

BEACHES

Bonaire's beaches are narrow and full of coral, but they're clean, intimate, and uncrowded. Swimming on the tranquil, leeward coast is never a problem, but the east coast is rough and dangerous. **Pink Beach,** south of Kralendijk, is the island's best strand. Aptly named, the sand here turns a rosy hue as the sun sets. No refreshment stands or equipment rentals mar the panoramic setting, so bring your own drinks and towels. Bring sun protection too: The few palm trees offer little shade. The southern end has less exposed rock. Crowded with Bonaireans on weekends, the beach is yours alone during the week.

The water at **Lac Bay Beach** is only 1 to 2 feet deep, making it especially popular with families. In a protected area of Bonaire's southeast coast, it offers windsurfing concessions and snack bars. Trees provide shade. Across the bay, white-sand **Sorobon Beach** is the island's only nude beach. It's part of the Sorobon Beach Resort, which means that as a nonguest, you'll pay for the privilege of disrobing.

North of Kralendijk, **Nukove Beach** is a small white-sand cove carved out of a limestone cliff. A narrow sand channel cuts through an otherwise impenetrable wall of elkhorn coral, giving divers and snorkelers access to the sea.

Washington-Slagbaai National Park has a number of beaches. **Boca Slagbaai,** once a plantation harbor, draws divers, snorkelers, and picnickers. Be careful venturing into the water barefoot, though: The coral bottom can be sharp. The island's northernmost beach, **Boca Cocolishi,** is a perfect spot to picnic. The calm, shallow basin is good for snorkeling, but stay very close to shore. Algae makes the water purplish, and the sand, formed by coral and mollusk shells, is black. At **Playa Chikitu,** the water is too treacherous for swimming but the cove is secluded, and the sand dunes and crashing waves are beautiful. On one side of **Playa Funchi,** flamingos nest in the lagoon; on the other, there's excellent snorkeling.

Klein Bonaire, the small uninhabited island about 1km (½ mile) west of Kralendijk, boasts **No Name Beach,** which features a 270m (886-ft.) white-sand strip. Parrotfish and yellowtail snappers patrol the finger, brain, and mustard hill corals, attracting snorkelers and divers. There are no facilities or shade on Klein Bonaire.

SPORTS

KAYAKING   For a peaceful, relaxing time, kayak through the mangroves in Lac Bay Cai. Proceed at your own pace in the calm waters, but take time to observe the hundreds of baby fish and the bizarre tree roots. Bring protection from the sun and the ravenous mosquitoes. Divers and snorkelers can tow a lightweight sea kayak behind them as they explore the waters of the leeward coast. Kayak rentals and guided trips through the mangroves are available from **Bonaire Dive and Adventure,** at the southern end of Sand Dollar Condominium Resort, Kaya Gobernador N. Debrot 77A (② **599/717-2229;** www. bonairekayaking.com), and, in Sorobon, from **Jibe City** (② **599/717-5233**). Kayak rentals are $20 for one person and $25 for two for a half-day. In December 2002, Bonaire Boating/ABC Yachting (② **599/790-5353**) opened the **Mangrove Information & Kayak Center.** It's located on Kaminda Lac, the road to Lac Bay Cai, and provides information about the mangrove forest in addition to offering guided mangrove tours.

MOUNTAIN BIKING   Bonaire has miles of roads, paved and unpaved, flat and hilly. The truly athletic can even follow goat paths. Take water, a map, a wide-brimmed hat, and plenty of sunscreen. **Bonaire Dive and Adventure** (see above) conducts guided bike tours through the *kunuku* (outback) and Washington-Slagbaai National Park for $65 per person.

SCUBA DIVING AND SNORKELING   Bonaire has 80 marked dive sites and a rich marine ecosystem that includes brain, elkhorn, staghorn, mountainous star, gorgonian, and black coral; anemones, sea cucumbers, and sea sponges; parrotfish, surgeonfish, angelfish, grouper, blennies, frogfish, and yellowtails; and morays and sea snakes. Dive shops are numerous and highly professional. Expect to pay $45 to $55 for a one-tank boat dive (equipment extra) and $120 to $120 for an introductory resort course (equipment included). **Great Adventures Bonaire** at Harbour Village Beach Club, Kaya Gobernador N. Debrot 72 (② **599/717-7500,** ext. 286; www.harbourvillage.com), is the island's poshest operation, upscale but unpretentious and friendly, offering two of the island's most beautiful boats. The Sand Dollar Condominium resort's "Sand Penny" children's program is a godsend for parents who want to dive without worrying about the kids. **Captain Don's Habitat,** Kaya Gobernador N. Debrot 103 (② **800/327-6709** or 305/438-4222 in the U.S. for Maduro Dive Fanta-Seas, Captain Don's North American representative; www.habitatdiveresorts.com), attracts diving fanatics, including disciples of Captain Don Stewart, an island icon and the driving force behind the Bonaire Marine Park. The full-service outfitter offers a photo shop and lab, and equipment repair.

Thanks to shallow-water coral reefs, snorkelers can also enjoy Bonaire's awesome marine environment. The island's **Guided Snorkeling Program** includes a slide-show introduction to reef fish, corals, and sponges; an in-water demonstration of snorkeling skills; and a guided tour of one of several snorkeling sites. The cost is $25 per person. Equipment rental is about $10 more. You can arrange a tour through any of the dive shops listed above or through **Buddy Dive Resort,** Kaya Gobernador N. Debrot 85 (© 599/717-5080); **Bon Bini Divers,** at the Lions Dive and Beach Resort Bonaire, Kaya Gobernador N. Debrot 90 (© **866/546-6734** or 599/717-5425); or **Dive Inn,** Kaya C. E. B. Hellmund 27 (© **599/717-8761**).

WINDSURFING   Shallow waters, steady breezes, and protection from choppy waters make Lac Bay perfect for beginners and pros. Sorobon has two equipment-rental centers: **Jibe City** (© **599/717-5233**) and **Bonaire Windsurf Place** (© **599/717-2288**). Boards and sails are $40 for half a day, $60 for a full day. Beginner's lessons are $45, including equipment.

GREAT LOCAL RESTAURANTS & BARS

Kralendijk offers a variety of culinary options at generally reasonable prices. One of Bonaire's most popular restaurants, **Capriccio,** Kaya Isla Riba 1 (© **599/717-7230**), serves impeccably fresh northern Italian cuisine on the harbor front. Originally from Padua and Milan, the restaurateurs offer savory salads, homemade pastas, straight-from-the-oven focaccia, thin-crust pizzas, and more substantial fare such as mahimahi braised in onion, olives, and sun-dried tomatoes, and braised duck in port-wine sauce. Lunch is around $12. **Zeezicht Seaside Restaurant,** Kaya Jan N. E. Craane 12 (© **599/717-8434**), is a local favorite, also on the downtown waterfront. Ceviche, conch sandwiches, and a gumbo of conch, fish, shrimp, and oysters are on the menu; and mermaids, fishing nets, and pirates adorn the walls. Lunch is about $6. To sample traditional Bonairean food in an unpretentious setting, try **Bon Awa,** Kaya Nikiboko Zuid 8 (© **599/ 717-5157**), with its outside tables, killer hot sauce, and outstanding homemade ice cream.

11 British Virgin Islands: Tortola & Virgin Gorda

With small bays and hidden coves that were once havens for pirates, the BVIs are among the world's loveliest cruising regions, consisting of some 40 islands located in the northeastern corner of the Caribbean, about 97km (60 miles) east of Puerto Rico. Only Tortola, Virgin Gorda, and Jost Van Dyke (plus Anegada, 26km/16 miles to the north) are of significant size. The other islets, most of them tiny rocks and cays, have names such as Fallen Jerusalem and Ginger. Norman Island is said to have been the prototype for Robert Louis Stevenson's Treasure Island, and Blackbeard inspired a famous ditty by marooning 15 pirates and a bottle of rum on the rocky cay known as Deadman Bay. Yo-ho-ho.

Columbus came this way in 1493, but the British Virgins apparently made little impression on him. Although the Spanish and Dutch contested it, the English officially annexed Tortola in 1672. Today, these islands are a British territory, with their own elected government and a population of about 21,000.

The vegetation is varied and depends on the rainfall. Palms and mangoes grow in profusion in some parts, while other places are arid and studded with cacti.

Smaller cruise lines such as Seabourn, Windstar, and Windjammer Barefoot Cruises call at Tortola and the more scenic Virgin Gorda and Jost Van Dyke. Unlike port calls at St. Thomas and other major ports, visits here are less bound by rigid scheduling.

LANGUAGE   **English** is spoken here.

CURRENCY   The **U.S. dollar** is the legal currency, much to the surprise of arriving Brits who find no one willing to accept their pounds.

CALLING FROM THE U.S.   When calling the BVIs from the United States, you need only dial a "1" before the numbers listed here.

TORTOLA

Road Town, the colony's capital, sits about midway along the southern shore of 62-sq.-km (24-sq.-mile) Tortola. Once a sleepy village, it's become a bustling center since **Wickhams Cay,** a 28-hectare (69-acre) landfill development and marina, brought in a massive yacht-chartering business.

Rugged mountain peaks characterize the island's entire southern coast. On the northern coast are beautiful bays with white-sandy beaches, banana trees, mangoes, and clusters of palms.

If your ship isn't scheduled to visit Virgin Gorda but you want to see the island, you can catch a boat, ferry, or launch here and be on the island in no time, since it's only a 19km (12-mile) trip.

COMING ASHORE   Visiting cruise ships dock at **Wickhams Cay,** a pleasant 5-minute walk from Main Street in Road Town. You should have no trouble finding your way around.

INFORMATION   The **BVI Tourist Board** office is on Wickhams Cay 1 (© **284/494-3134**) in the Akara Building and is open Monday to Friday from 8:30am to 4:30pm. You can pick up a copy of the *Welcome Tourist Guide* here. For info before you go, log on to www.bvitouristboard.com.

GETTING AROUND

BY TAXI   Open-air and sedan-style taxis meet every arriving cruise ship. To call a taxi in Road Town, call the **BVI Taxi Association** (© **284/494-2322**). Three other local taxi services, **Quality Taxi** (© **284/494-8397**), **Road Town Taxi Association** (© **284/494-8755**), and the **Waterfront Taxi Association** (© **284/494-3456**), are within walking distance of the cruise pier.

BY BUS   **Scato's Bus Service** (© **284/494-2365**) picks up passengers (mostly locals) who hail the bus. Fares for a trek across the island are about $2 to $4.

BY RENTAL CAR   We don't recommend driving here, as driving is on the left. But if you're intent on it, Avis, Dollar, Hertz, and ITGO (the local Budget operator) all have offices here.

BEST CRUISE LINE SHORE EXCURSIONS

Town & Country Tour ($34, 3½ hr.): Tour the island in an open-air minibus, visiting the Botanical Gardens, Cane Garden Bay, Bomba's Surfside Shack at Capoons Bay, and Soper's Hole.

Norman Island Snorkeling ($50, 3 hr.): Cross the Sir Frances Drake Channel by boat to Normal Island, one of the BVI's prime snorkel sites, full of coral formations, colorful fish, and a group of caves at Treasure Point, where pirate treasure is reputed to have been hidden.

Forest Walk & Botanical Gardens ($34, 3½ hr.): Safari buses take you to Tortola's interior for a 1-mile hike through the Sage Mountain rainforest to the highest point in the Virgin Islands, then head down the Ridge Road for a brief stop at the Botanical Gardens.

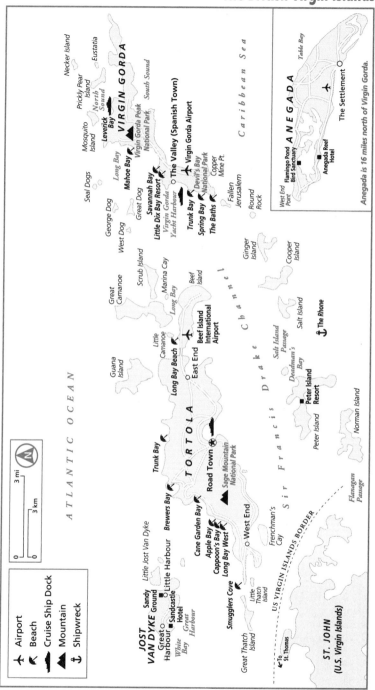

The British Virgin Islands

Legend

- ✈ Airport
- ✔ Beach
- ⏏ Cruise Ship Dock
- ▲ Mountain
- ⚓ Shipwreck

Scale
0 3 mi
0 3 km

ATLANTIC OCEAN

Caribbean Sea

ANEGADA
- Table Bay
- The Settlement
- West End Point
- Flamingo Pond Bird Sanctuary
- Anegada Reef Hotel

Anegada is 16 miles north of Virgin Gorda.

VIRGIN GORDA
- Necker Island
- Eustatia
- Prickly Pear Island
- North Sound
- Mosquito Island
- South Sound
- Leverick Bay
- Virgin Gorda Peak National Park
- Virgin Gorda Airport
- The Valley (Spanish Town)
- Long Bay
- Mahoe Bay
- Savannah Bay
- Little Dix Bay Resort
- Devil's Bay National Park
- Copper Mine Pt.
- Virgin Gorda Yacht Harbour
- Trunk Bay
- Spring Bay
- The Baths
- Fallen Jerusalem
- Round Rock

- Seal Dogs
- George Dog
- Great Dog
- West Dog
- Scrub Island
- Marina Cay
- Long Bay
- Great Camanoe
- Little Camanoe
- Beef Island
- Beef Island International Airport
- Long Bay Beach
- East End

- Ginger Island
- Cooper Island
- Salt Island
- Salt Island Passage
- ⚓ The Rhone
- Deadman's Bay
- Peter Island Resort
- Peter Island
- Norman Island

- Drake Channel
- Sir Francis Drake Channel

TORTOLA
- Trunk Bay
- Brewers Bay
- Cane Garden Bay
- Apple Bay
- Cappoon's Bay
- Long Bay West
- Smugglers Cove
- West End
- Frenchman's Cay
- Road Town ✈
- Sage Mountain National Park

JOST VAN DYKE
- Little Jost Van Dyke
- Sandy Ground
- Little Harbour
- Sandcastle Hotel
- Great Harbour
- White Bay
- Great Thatch Island
- Little Thatch Island

- Flanagan Passage
- US VIRGIN ISLANDS BORDER
- ← To St. Thomas
- **ST. JOHN (U.S. Virgin Islands)**

149

Frommer's Favorite Tortola Experiences

Visiting Bomba's Surfside Shack: The oldest, most memorable bar on Tortola may not look like much, but it's the best party on the island. (See "Great Local Restaurants & Bars," below.)

Spending a Day at Cane Garden Bay: It's the best beach on the island, with palm trees, sand, and a great local restaurant (shack) for lunch and drinks. (See "Beaches," below.)

Hiking up Sage Mountain: This is one of the best ways to learn about Tortola's natural character. Organized shore excursions usually include hiking trips to the 534m (1,751-ft.) peak, beginning with a ride along mountain roads in an open-air safari bus. (See "On Your Own: Beyond the Port Area," below.)

Taking an Island Tour: Open-air safari buses take you on a scenic journey around the extremely hilly island. Take your ship's organized tour (see "Best Cruise Line Shore Excursions," below), or take a 2- to 3-hour taxi tour from the pier, with beach stops, for about $15 per person.

Scuba Diving at the HMS *Rhône* ($125, 3½ hr.): This is a guided dive to a British ship sunk in an 1867 hurricane, her bow lying almost fully intact in 80 feet of water. All divers must be certified and must have dived within the last 2 years.

EXCURSIONS OFFERED BY LOCAL AGENCIES

Bus Tours/Snorkeling/Glass-Bottom Boat Tours: Since the shore excursions here are very modest, you might consider calling **Travel Plan Tours,** Romasco Place, Wickham's Cay, Road Town (© **284/494-2872**), which will take one to three people on a 3-hour guided tour of the island (about $23 a person, if there is a minimum of two people), a snorkeling excursion (about $28 a person for groups of 10 or more), or an all-day catamaran sailing excursion ($95 per person, including lunch).

Taxi Tours: You can take a 2- to 3-hour taxi tour for about $60 for up to three people. For a taxi in Road Town, call © **284/494-2322.**

ON YOUR OWN: WITHIN WALKING DISTANCE

Besides the handful of shops on Main and Upper Main streets in Road Town, there's also a **Botanic Garden** (© **284/494-4557**) right in the middle of town, across from the police station. It's open daily from 8am to 6pm and features a wide variety of flowers and plants, including a section on medicinal plants.

ON YOUR OWN: BEYOND THE PORT AREA

You mainly have nature to look at on Tortola. The big attraction is **Mount Sage National Park,** which rises to 534m (1,751 ft.) (the highest point in the BVIs and USVIs) and covers 37 hectares (91 acres). The park was established in 1964 to protect those remnants of Tortola's original forests not burned or cleared during the island's plantation era; and is both the oldest national park in the British Virgin Islands and the best present-day example of the territory's native moist forests. You'll find a lush forest of mango, papaya, breadfruit, birchberry, mountain guava, guavaberry, and coconut trees here, all of which have edible fruit. Many of the plants and trees are labeled. This is a great place to enjoy a picnic while overlooking neighboring islets and cays. Any taxi driver can take you to the mountain. Before going, stop at the tourist office (see above) and pick up a brochure with a map and an outline of the park's trails. The two main hikes are the Rain Forest Trail and the Mahogany Forest Trail. For a quiet beach day, head to **Smuggler's Cove**, a secluded, picture-perfect spot with white sand and calm turquoise water. ***Note:*** At press time, there is no fee for park admission, but the BVI National Parks Trust plans to implement one soon. Call © 284/494-2069 or 284/494-6177 or log on to www.bvinationalparkstrust.org for more information.

SHOPPING

Shopping on Tortola is a minor activity compared to shopping at other Caribbean ports. Only British goods are imported without duty, and they are the best buys, especially English china. You'll also find West Indian art, terracotta pottery, wicker and rattan home furnishings, Mexican glassware, dhurrie rugs, baskets, and ceramics. Most stores are on Main Street in Road Town.

The **Pusser's Company Store,** Main Street, Road Town (© **284/494-2467;** www.pussers.com), offers a selection of classic travel and adventure clothing, along with unusual accessories and Pusser's famous (though not terribly good) rum, which was served aboard British Navy ships for over 300 years. A good, cheap gift item is packets of Pusser's coasters, on which is written the recipe for that classic Caribbean rum specialty, the Painkiller. The **Sunny Caribee Herb and Spice Company,** also on Main Street (© **284/494-2178;** www.sunnycaribbee.com), is a good spot for Caribbean spices, seasonings, teas, condiments, and handicrafts. You can buy two world-famous specialties here: West Indian Hangover Cure and Arawak Love Potion.

BEACHES

Most of the beaches are a 20-minute taxi ride from the cruise dock. Figure on about $15 per person one-way (some will charge less, about $5 per person if you've got a group), but discuss it with the driver before setting out. You can also ask the driver to pick you up at a designated time.

The finest beach is at **Cane Garden Bay,** which reminds us of the famous Magens Bay Beach on the north shore of St. Thomas. It's on the northwest side of the island, across the mountains from Road Town; it's worth the effort needed to get there, and is so special you might want to take a taxi here in the morning and not head back to your cruise ship until departure time. Plan to have lunch here at **Rhymer's** (© **284/495-4639**), where the chef will cook some conch or whelk, or perhaps some barbecue spareribs. The beach bar and restaurant is open daily from 8am to 9pm, serving breakfast, lunch, and dinner, with main courses ranging from $15 to $25. Showers are available, and Rhymer's rents towels.

Surfers like **Apple Bay,** also on the northwest side, but you'll have to watch out for sharks (no joke: On a recent trip a friend saw one while surfing, and its dorsal fins were visible from the shore). A hotel here called **Sebastians** (© **284/ 495-4212**) caters to the surfing crowd that visits in January and February, but the beach is ideal year-round. **Brewers Bay,** site of a campground, is on the northwest shore near Cane Garden Bay and is good for beach strolling and swimming. Both snorkelers and surfers come here. **Smugglers Cove** (sometimes known as Lower Belmont Bay) is a wide crescent of white sand wrapped around calm, sky-blue water, located at the extreme western end of Tortola, opposite the offshore island of Great Thatch and very close to St. John's in the U.S. Virgin Islands. Snorkelers and surfers also like this beach.

SPORTS

SCUBA DIVING *Skin Diver* magazine has called the wreckage of the RMS *Rhône,* which sank in 1867 near the western point of Salt Island, the world's most fantastic shipwreck dive. It teems with marine life and coral formations, and was featured in the motion picture *The Deep. Chikuzen,* an 81m (266-ft.) steel-hulled refrigerator ship that sank off the island's east end in 1981, is another intriguing dive site off Tortola, although it's no *Rhône.* The hull, still intact under about 24m (79 ft.) of water, is now home to a vast array of tropical marine life, including yellowtail, barracuda, black-tip sharks, octopus, and drum fish. **Underwater Safaris** (② 284/494-3235) can take you to all the best sites. It offers a complete PADI and NAUI training facility and is associated with The Moorings yacht charter company. Underwater Safaris' Road Town office is a 5-minute, $4 taxi ride from the docks. Two-tank dives sell for $84, while a one-tank dive costs $58. Equipment rental is $10.

GREAT LOCAL RESTAURANTS & BARS

On Cappoon's Bay, **Bomba's Surfside Shack** (② 284/495-4148) is the oldest, most memorable bar on Tortola, sitting on a 6m-wide (20-ft.) strip of coastline near the West End. It's the "junk palace" of the island, covered with Day-Glo graffiti and laced with wire and rejected odds and ends of plywood, driftwood, and abandoned rubber tires. They must've spent their decorating budget on the sound system, which thumps mightily. It's open daily from 10am to midnight (or later, depending on business). Lunch is about $10 .

Standing on the waterfront across from the ferry dock, **Pusser's Road Town Pub** (② 284/494-3897) serves Caribbean fare, English pub grub, and good pizzas. The drink to have here is the famous Pusser's Rum, the same blend of five West Indian rums that the Royal Navy served to its men for more than 300 years. Honestly, it's not the world's greatest rum, but sometimes you just have to do things for the experience. Lunch is about $19. **Capriccio di Mare,** Waterfront Drive (② 284/494-5369), is the most authentic-looking Italian cafe in the Virgin Islands, serving fresh pastas with succulent sauces, well-stuffed sandwiches, and great pizza. Lunch is about $10. For a fine *roti* (curries wrapped in flat bread) sans atmosphere—it's sparsely furnished and not too attractive—try **Roti Palace** (② 284/494-4196), in Road Town. Lunch is about $8. **Callaloo,** at the Prospect Reef Resort (② 284/494-3311), is very romantic if it's a balmy day and the tropical breezes are blowing. Begin with the conch fritters or shrimp cocktail, and don't pass on the house salad, which has a zesty papaya dressing. Main dishes include fresh fish. Lunch is about $15. At **Pusser's Landing,** Frenchman's Cay, on the West End (② 284/495-4554), you can enjoy grilled fish such as mahimahi, or West Indian roast chicken. Try the mango soufflé for dessert. Lunch is about $10. **Quito's Gazebo** (② 284/495-4837), on Cane Garden Bay, is owned by local recording star Quito Rhymer. It's a good place for West Indian fish dishes. Quito performs Thursday to Sunday and Tuesday. Lunch is about $11 .

VIRGIN GORDA

Instead of visiting Tortola, some small cruise ships put in at lovely Virgin Gorda, famous for its boulder-strewn beach known as The Baths. The third-largest island in the colony, it got its name ("Fat Virgin") from Christopher Columbus, who thought the mountain framing it looked like a protruding stomach. At 16km (10 miles) long and 3.2km (2 miles) wide, the island is about 19km (12 miles) east of Road Town, so it's easy to take a ferry here if your ship only visits Tortola (cruise lines offer shore excursions that do this trip too).

Frommer's Favorite Virgin Gorda Experiences

Visiting The Baths: House-size boulders and clear waters make for excellent swimming and snorkeling in a fabulous setting. (See "Best Cruise Line Shore Excursions" and "Beaches," both below.)

Spending a Beach Day in Spring Bay or Trunk Bay: Located near The Baths, Spring Bay has one of the best beaches on the island, with white sand, clear water, and good snorkeling. Trunk Bay, a wide sand beach that can be reached by boat or via a rough path from Spring Bay, is another good bet. (See "Beaches," below.)

Taking an Island Tour: Open-air safari buses do a good job of showing guests this beautiful island. (See "Best Cruise Line Shore Excursions," below.)

The island was a fairly desolate agricultural community until Little Dix Bay Hotel opened here in the early 1960s. Other major hotels followed, but privacy and solitude still reign supreme on Virgin Gorda.

COMING ASHORE   Virgin Gorda doesn't have a pier or landing facilities to suit any of the large ships. Most vessels anchor offshore and tender passengers in to St. Thomas Bay, the port area and yacht harbor for Spanish Town. Ferries from Tortola also berth here.

GETTING AROUND   Taxis are available and will take visitors to The Baths and area beaches for about $5 per person each way. For a tour of the island, contact Andy Flax of the **Virgin Gorda Tours Association** (c/o the Fischers Cove Beach Hotel, © 284/495-5252). It'll run you about $40 per couple, and they'll pick you up at the dock if given at least 24-hour notice. Another good option is to call **Speedy's**, also known as Virgin Gorda Transport (© 284/495-5240). The Virgin Gorda Tourist Association gives island tours for about $40 per couple and will pick visitors up at the dock if provided with 24-hour notice.

BEST CRUISE LINE SHORE EXCURSIONS
The Baths Excursion ($40, 3–4 hr.): All cruise lines stopping here offer this trip. (See "Beaches," below, for details.)

Island Tour ($45, 3–4 hr.): The open-air safari buses travel around this stunning island, traveling from Leverick Bay, ascending at least partway up Gorda Peak, and stopping at the quaint capital, Spanish Town.

ON YOUR OWN: WITHIN WALKING DISTANCE
The **Virgin Gorda Yacht Harbour** at St. Thomas Bay has several restaurants and shops.

ON YOUR OWN: BEYOND THE PORT AREA
You might also consider cabbing it up to glamorous **Little Dix Bay Resort** (© 284/495-5555), established by Laurence Rockefeller in 1965, to enjoy a lunch buffet at an outdoor pavilion that shows off Virgin Gorda's beautiful hills, bays, and sky. Aside from this, most people head for The Baths, which really is spectacular (see "Beaches," below).

A Slice of Paradise: Jost Van Dyke

Covering only 10 sq. km (4 sq. miles), mountainous Jost Van Dyke is truly an offbeat, rarely visited retreat—unless you count the small yachts dotting Great Harbour. With no cruise pier, passengers are shuttled ashore via tender. Small-ship lines such as Windjammer Barefoot Cruises will sometimes throw an afternoon beach party on the beach at White Bay, with the crew lugging ashore a picnic lunch for a leisurely afternoon of eating, drinking, and swimming. If your ship stays late, don't miss a trip to **Foxy's** (© **284/495-9258**), a well-known watering hole at the far end of Great Harbour that's popular with the yachting set as well as locals. It's your classic island beach bar, with music pounding and drinks flowing into the wee hours.

SHOPPING
The only shopping of note here is right at the Yacht Harbor complex, with a few dive shops, boutiques, and handicraft shops. **DIVE BVI** (© **284/495-5513**) sells diving equipment and offers diving instruction for all ability levels. **Margo's Jewelry Boutique** (© **284/495-5237**) sells handcrafted gold and silver items. The **Virgin Gorda Craft Shop** (© **284/495-5137**) features locally made items. The **Wine Cellar** (© **284/495-5250**) offers oven-baked French bread and pastries, cookies, and sandwiches. The **Blue Banana Boutique** (© **284/495-6633**) sells women's swimwear and beachwear.

BEACHES
The major reason cruise ships come to Virgin Gorda is to visit **The Baths,** where geologists believe ice-age eruptions caused house-size boulders to topple onto one another to form the saltwater grottoes we see today. The pools around The Baths are excellent for swimming and snorkeling (equipment can be rented on the beach), and a crawl between and among the boulders, which in places are very cavelike, is more than a little bit fun. A cafe sits just above the beach for a quick snack or a cool drink. **Devil's Bay,** a great beach just south of The Baths, is usually less crowded. Just north of The Baths is **Spring Bay,** one of the best of the island's beaches, with white sand, clear water, and good snorkeling. Nearby is **The Crawl,** a natural pool formed by rocks that's great for novice snorkelers; a marked path leads there from Spring Bay. **Trunk Bay,** just to the north, is a wide sand beach that can be reached via a rough path from Spring Bay.

   Devil's Bay National Park can be reached by a trail from The Baths. The walk to the secluded coral-sand beach takes about 15 minutes through a natural setting of boulders and dry coastal vegetation.

SPORTS
WATERSPORTS   Kilbrides Sunchaser Scuba, at the Bitter End Resort at North Sound (© **800/932-4286** in the U.S., or 284/495-9638; www.sun chaserscuba.com), offers diving at more than 20 BVI sites, including the wreck of the RMS *Rhône.* Morning two-tank dives are $85. Afternoon dives are $60. The excursions last about 4½ hours. Wet suits rent for $5.

GREAT LOCAL RESTAURANTS & BARS

At the end of the waterfront shopping plaza in Spanish Town, **Bath and Turtle Pub,** Virgin Gorda Yacht Harbour (© **284/495-5239**), is the island's most popular bar and pub. You can join the regulars over midmorning guava coladas or peach daiquiris and order fried fish fingers, very spicy chili, pizzas, Reubens or tuna melts, steak, lobster, and daily seafood specials such as conch fritters. Lunch is about $13. **Mad Dog** (© **284/495-5830**) is a hot-dog stop near The Baths that also serves BLTs, beer, and frozen piña coladas. Lunch is about $4.

12 Cozumel & the Yucatán Peninsula

Check this statistic: On some days, up to 16 ships visit Cozumel simultaneously, counting those that anchor offshore and tender passengers into shore. All that activity can make the port town of San Miguel seem more like Times Square than the sleepy, refreshingly gritty Mexican port town it once was. **San Miguel** has developed at a faster rate in the past few years than just about any other Caribbean port on the map, so if you haven't been there in a while, you may not recognize the place. Still, crowds and shiny, Miami-wannabe boutiques aside, Cozumel's allure remains its proximity to the ancient Mayan ruins at **Tulum** and **Chichén-Itzá** on the mainland of the Yucatán Peninsula. Besides the ruins, the island's beaches are a big draw, along with diving and shopping for silver jewelry, local handicrafts, and T-shirts from the town's notorious beer pit, Carlos 'n Charlie's.

To see the ruins, you must take a rocky 45-minute ferry ride between Cozumel and Playa del Carmen, on the mainland, though a few cruise ships call directly on Playa del Carmen, anchoring just offshore. In recent years, a handful of other Yucatán ports have come onto the scene, including Costa Maya near the sleepy fishing village of Mahajual, just over 161km (100 miles) south of Playa del Carmen. Details on both Playa and Costa Maya are included later in this section. A few ships also call at Calica, just south of Playa, where there's little more than a pier, and at Progreso, on the Gulf coast of the Yucatán, where the Mayan ruins and colonial architecture of nearby Merida are the big draw. At press time, Carnival was still negotiating final terms for a new port and pier called the Port of Cancun at Xcaret, just down the road from Playa del Carmen.

LANGUAGE **Spanish** is the tongue of the land, although **English** is spoken in most places that cater to tourists.

CURRENCY The Mexican currency is the **nuevo peso** (new peso). Its symbol is the "$" sign, but it's hardly the equivalent of the U.S. dollar—the exchange rate is about $11 pesos to US$1 ($1 peso = about US9¢). The main tourist stores gladly accept U.S. dollars, credit cards, and traveler's checks; but if you want to change money, many banks are within a block or so of the downtown tender and ferry pier. Unless otherwise specified, prices in this section are given in U.S. dollars.

CALLING FROM THE U.S. When calling from the U.S., you need to dial the international access code (011) and 52 before the numbers listed here.

MAYAN RUINS & OTHER MAINLAND ATTRACTIONS

Because all of the sites listed here are quite far from the cruise piers, most cruise passengers visit them as part of **shore excursions.** Admission to the sites is included in the excursion prices, which typically runs from US$100 to US$130 for Chichén-Itzá and around US$75 for Tulum or Cobá. Chichén-Itzá and Cobá are all-day excursions. Visits to smaller Tulum are often paired with a visit to the Xel-Ha Eco Park, making it a full-day trek (US$99). Guests are usually served free and refreshingly cooooolllldddd Mexican beer on the bus back after exploring the ruins.

CHICHÉN ITZÁ   The largest and most fabled of the Yucatán ruins, Chichén-Itzá (meaning "Mouth of the Well of the Itza Family") was founded in A.D. 445 by the Mayans and later inhabited by the Toltecs of central Mexico. At its height, the city had about 50,000 residents, but it was mysteriously abandoned only 2 centuries after its founding. After lying dormant for 2 more centuries, the site was resettled and enjoyed prosperity again until the early 13th century, when it was once more relinquished to the surrounding jungle. The area covers 18 square km (7 sq. miles), so you can see only a fraction of it on a day trip. The following are some of the highlights:

The best known of Chichén-Itzá's ruins is the magnificent **El Castillo pyramid** (also called the Pyramid of Kukulkán), which was built with the Maya calendar in mind. The four stairways leading up to the central platform each have 91 steps, making a total of 364; when you add the top central platform you get the 365 days of the solar year. On either side of each stairway are nine terraces, which makes 18 on each face of the pyramid, equaling the number of months in the Maya solar calendar. On the facing of these terraces are 52 panels that represent the 52-year cycle when both the solar and religious calendars would become realigned. The pyramid's position is such that on the **spring** and **fall equinoxes,** light striking the pyramid gives the illusion of a snake slithering down the steps to join its gigantic stone head mounted at the base.

Northwest of El Castillo is Chichén's main **Ball Court (Juego de Pelota),** the largest and best preserved such Mayan ruin anywhere. Carved on both walls of the ball court are scenes showing Mayan figures dressed as ball players and decked out in heavy protective padding. The carved scene also shows a headless player kneeling with blood shooting from his neck; another player holding the head looks on. Here's the way it worked: Players on two teams tried to knock a hard rubber ball through one of the two stone rings placed high on either wall, using only their elbows, knees, and hips. According to legend, the losing players paid for defeat with their lives. However, some experts say the victors were the only appropriate sacrifices for the gods. Note the lack of bleacher seating. As the games were played as a ritual, for the entertainment of the gods, only a single judge looked on.

Temples are located at both ends of the ball court. The **North Temple** has sculptured pillars and more sculptures inside, as well as badly ruined murals. The acoustics of the ball court are so good that from the North Temple, a person speaking can be heard clearly at the opposite end, about 136m (446 ft.) away. Near the southeastern corner of the main ball court is the **Temple of the Jaguars,** a small temple with serpent columns and carved panels showing warriors and jaguars. Up the steps and inside the temple, a mural was found that chronicles a battle in a Maya village. To the right of the ball court is the **Temple of the Skulls (Tzompantli).** Notice the rows of skulls carved into the stone platform. When a sacrificial victim's head was cut off, it was impaled on a pole and displayed in a tidy row with others. Also carved into the stone are pictures of eagles tearing hearts from human victims.

Follow the dirt road (actually an ancient *sacbé,* or causeway, made from a white, compacted, claylike soil that made the way visible at night) that heads north from the Platform of Venus. After about 5 minutes you'll come to the

The Yucatán's Upper Caribbean Coast

To Progreso

El Cuyo

Holbox

Isla Holbox

Isla Contoy

RÍO LAGARTOS
NATURE RESERVE

Chiquilá

Isla Mujeres

Punta Sam

Cancún

Puerto
Juárez

Buenaventura

QUINTANA ROO
STATE

Isla Cancun

YUCATÁN
STATE

✈

Croco-Cun

Jardín
Botanico

Puerto
Morelos

180

180
D

180
D

Nuevo Xcan

307

180
D

180

Punta
Bete

To Valladolid
& Chichén Itzá

Chemax

Xcaret
Calica

Playa del
Carmen

Pamul

San Gervasio

Xpuha

Cobá

Puerto Aventuras

San Miguel
de Cozumel

Akumal

Yalku
Lagoon

El Cedral

ISLA DE
COZUMEL

Xelha Lagoon
National Park

Chankanaab
Nature Park

Tancah

Tulum

Chunyaxche

Muyil

Caribbean Sea

Boca Paila

Chumpón

Vigia Chíco

Punta Allen

Peninsula
Vigia Grande

Bahia de la
Ascensión

Felipe Carrillo
Puerto

SIAN KA'AN
BIOSPHERE RESERVE

To Chetumal
& Costa Maya

0	25 mi
0	25 km

N

✈ Airport

⛴ Cruise Ship Dock

---- Ferry Route

|||| Reef

◈ Ruins

Sacred Cenote, a great natural well that may have given Chichén Itzá its name. This well was used for ceremonial purposes, not for drinking water. According to legend, sacrificial victims adorned with gold and other riches were drowned in this pool to honor the rain god Chaac. In the early in the 20th century, American consul and Harvard professor Edward Thompson bought the ruins of Chichén-Itzá and explored the cenote with dredges and divers, unearthing (and exporting) a fortune in gold and jade.

Due east of El Castillo is one of the most impressive structures at Chichén: the **Temple of the Warriors,** named for the carvings of warriors marching along its walls. It's also called the Group of the Thousand Columns for the rows of broken square pillars that flank it. A figure of high priest Chaac-Mool sits at the top of the temple, surrounded by impressive columns carved in relief to look like enormous feathered serpents. According to scholars, Chaac-Mool would tear out a sacrificial victim's heart here and then throw the body down the steps, where another priest would strip off his or her skin. The high priest would then dress himself in the skin, cross to a nearby platform, and dance. Lovely, huh? South of the temple is another group of columns (these ones round) that were once an important **market,** controlling the trade in salt on the Yucatan.

South of the Market, a cluster of interesting ruins include the **Observatory (El Caracol),** a complex building with a circular tower through whose slits astronomers could observe the cardinal directions and the approach of the all-important spring and autumn equinoxes; the **Edifice of the Nuns (Edificio de las Monjas),** which was named for its resemblance to a European convent; and the **Church (La Iglesia),** one of the oldest buildings at Chichén, named for its beautiful decorations. Its ceiling, with a Mayan false arch, is a stone replica of the thatched ceilings that were typical in Mayan homes of the period.

TULUM   About 130km (81 miles) south of Cancún and about a 30-minute drive from Playa del Carmen, the small walled city of Tulum is the single most visited Mayan ruin due to its proximity to the ports. It was the only Mayan city built on the coast and the only one inhabited when the Spanish conquistadors arrived in the 1500s. From its dramatic perch atop seaside cliffs, you can see wonderful panoramic views of the Caribbean. Tulum consists of 60 individual structures. Though nowhere near as large and impressive as Chichén-Itzá, the two cities share a similar prominent feature: a ruin topped with a temple to Kukulkán, the primary Mayan/Olmec god. Other important structures include the Temple of the Frescoes, the Temple of the Descending God, the House of Columns, and the House of the Cenote, which is a well. There's also a sliver of silky beach at the site, so bring your bathing suit for a quick refreshing dip. Visitor facilities include a well-stocked bookstore and a soon-to-open museum.

COBÁ   A 35-minute drive northwest of Tulum puts you at Cobá, site of one of the most important city-states in the Mayan empire. Cobá flourished from A.D. 300 to 1000, with its population numbering perhaps as many as 40,000. Excavation work began in 1972, and archaeologists estimate that only 5% of this dead city has yet been uncovered. The site lies on four lakes. Its 32 rural hectares (81 acres) provide excellent exploration opportunities for hikers. Cobá's pyramid, Nohoch Mul, is the tallest in the Yucatán.

XCARET ECOLOGICAL PARK   Lying about 6,4km (4 miles) south of Playa del Carmen on the coast, Xcaret (pronounced *Ish*-car-et) is a 100-hectare (250-acre) ecological theme park with small Mayan ruins scattered about the lushly landscaped acres. Visitors can put on life jackets for a river ride, which takes them through currents running through a series of caves. You can also snorkel through the caves (something we recommend highly) as well as swim with dolphins, though this is not included in the cost of the excursions. The park has a botanical garden, an aquarium, a sea-turtle breeding and release facility, a dive shop, a rotating observation tower, a Mayan village, and two theaters that put on worthwhile cultural shows. Excursions run about US$88, and take up a full day from Cozumel.

XEL-HA ECO PARK   Farther south of Xcaret, Xel-Ha (pronounced *shell*-ha) features a sprawling natural lagoon filled with sparkling blue-green water and surrounded by lush foliage. The use of inner tubes and life vests are included in the admission price, and you can spend a great couple of hours wending your way from one end of the snaking body of calm water to the other, accompanied by schools of tropical fish. Snorkeling gear is available for rental. Xel-Ha has dolphins too. You'll find shops, restaurants, and lots of beach chairs here.

COZUMEL

The ancient Mayans, who lived here for 12 centuries, would be shocked by the million cruise passengers who now visit Cozumel each year. Their presence has greatly changed San Miguel, the only town, which now has fast-food joints and a Hard Rock Cafe. Development, however, hasn't touched much of the island's natural beauty. Ashore, away from San Miguel, you'll see abundant wildlife, including armadillos, brightly colored tropical birds, and lizards. Offshore, the government has set aside 32km (20 miles) of coral reefs as an underwater national park, including the stunning Palancar Reef, the world's second-largest natural coral formation.

COMING ASHORE   It seems like the whole coast of San Miguel is a cruise ship berth these days. The newest berth is **Punta Langosta,** right in the center of town, which puts you just steps from the shops, restaurants, and cafes across the street. (The ferries to Playa del Carmen dock about .4km/¼ mile away.) Other ships pull alongside the well-accoutered **International Pier** (3.2km/2 miles south of San Miguel) or the **Puerto Maya pier** (another kilometer or so farther south), both a US$4 to US$5 taxi ride from town or a 30- to 45-minute walk from the heart of San Miguel. The beaches are close to the International Pier.

You can make telephone calls in Cozumel from the Punta Langosta pier or from the Global Communications phone center on the International Pier for a few bucks a minute, or from a kiosk inside the terminal. Keep in mind, there are often lines for the phones. In town, try the Calling Station, Avenida Rafael Melgar 27, at the corner of Calle 3 in San Miguel, 3 blocks from the ferry pier.

INFORMATION   **The Department of Tourism Office,** on the second floor of Plaza del Sol (© **987/872-0972**), distributes the *Vacation Guide to Cozumel* and *Cozumel Island's Restaurant Guide;* both have island maps. It's open Monday to Friday from 8:30am to 5pm, and Saturday from 9am to 1pm. The Tourism booth at the ferry pier is open Monday to Saturday, from 8:30am to 4pm. For info before you go, call © **800/44-MEXICO** or surf to www.islacozumel.com.mx.

GETTING AROUND

The town of San Miguel is so small you can walk anywhere you want to go. Essentially, there's only one large road in Cozumel—it starts at the northern tip of the island, hugs the western shoreline, and then loops around the southern tip and returns to the capital.

Frommer's Favorite Cozumel Experiences

Visiting the Mayan Ruins at Chichén-Itzá or Tulum: Chichén-Itzá is the largest and most fabled of the Yucatán ruins—and the flight there, in a small plane, only adds to the experience of exploring the site. A few hours a day, you can climb a narrow staircase inside the main temple's inner pyramid to sneak a claustrophobic peek at a stunning jaguar throne inlaid with turquoise spots and eyes. Tulum is perched dramatically above the ocean (and in the middle of "iguana central"—they're everywhere), and tours there often include a stop at the beautiful Xel-Ha Lagoon for some swimming. (See "Mayan Ruins & Other Mainland Attractions," above.)

Swimming with the Dolphins at Chankanaab: Book on your own for this once-in-a-lifetime opportunity to be kissed, splashed, towed, and pushed through the wake like a water-skier by some of the friendliest locals you'll ever meet. For the not-so-bold, the less expensive Dolphin Encounter (which is offered as a shore excursion), allows you to get up close and personal with two friendly dolphins, minus the aquatic acrobatics. The encounter program does not include the overpriced but irresistible video, complete with music and slow motion close-ups. (See "On Your Own: Beyond the Port Area," below.)

Signing Up for a Jeep Trek: Explore Cozumel's jungles and sandy back roads on a fun self-drive, caravan-style adventure, and then stop at a beach for lunch and swimming. (See "Best Cruise Line Shore Excursions," below.)

If you're driving in Cozumel, it's helpful to know that the roads parallel to the sea are called avenues, and these have the right of way. The ones running from the sea are called streets, and you have to stop at each street to give way.

BY TAXI   Taxi service is available 24 hours a day; however, like many other things in the Miami of the Yucatán, it's no bargain. The average fare from San Miguel to most major resorts and beaches is about US$15; between the International terminal and downtown it's about US$6. More distant island rides cost US$20 and up. It's customary to overcharge cruise ship passengers, so settle on a fare before getting in—occasionally you can bargain it down. It's easy to find a cab at the pier, but you can also call ⓒ **987/872-0236.**

BY RENTAL CAR   If you want to drive yourself, four-wheel-drive vehicles or open-air jeeps are the best rental choice. Avis, Budget, and Hertz all have offices here. **Rent-a-Car,** Avenida 5A at Calle 20A (ⓒ **800/527-0700** in the U.S., or 987/872-0903), 2 blocks from the ferry pier, rents cars and four-wheel drive vehicles. A four-door economy car rents for about US$35 a day, with a Geo Tracker going for US$45 and up, plus insurance and gas. *Note:* Most rental cars in the Caribbean have manual transmissions, so if you need an automatic, be sure to specify that when renting.

BY MOPED   Mopeds are a popular means of getting about despite heavy traffic, hidden stop signs, potholed roads, and a high accident rate. The best and most convenient rentals are at **Auto Rent** (ⓒ **987/872-0844**) in the Hotel El

Cid La Ceiba, right next to the International Pier. The cost is about US$35 per day, including helmet rental; Mexican law requires that you wear a helmet.

BY FERRY   A number of passenger ferries link Cozumel with Playa del Carmen, all of them with ticket booths at the main pier. The most comfortable are the big speedboats and water-jet catamarans run by **Cruceros Maritimos,** which make the trip in 25 to 45 minute and run Monday to Saturday from 6am to 10pm. One-way fares cost about US$8 per person. You'll get a ferry schedule when you buy your ticket.

BEST CRUISE LINE SHORE EXCURSIONS

See "Mayan Ruins & Other Mainland Attractions" for details on the big mainland excursions. In addition to those below, the cruise lines also offer dozens of different snorkeling, party-boat, and underwater excursions in Cozumel.

Jeep Trek (US$86, 4½ hr.): Hop in a four-seat Jeep, draw straws to see who gets to drive, and explore the natural side of Cozumel. Much of the roller-coaster-like route is off-road, and the Jeeps travel in a convoy, stopping eventually at a lovely secluded beach for swimming and a picnic lunch.

Horseback-Riding Tours (US$85, 3–4 hr.): Worthwhile horseback-riding tours offer a chance to see Cozumel's landscape. However, although they tout visits to Mayan ruins, don't get your hopes up—there's little more than a few refrigerator-size rocks here and there on Cozumel. A bus transports riders to a ranch, where the ride begins.

ON YOUR OWN: WITHIN WALKING DISTANCE

For walkers, the classic grid layout makes getting around the town of San Miguel easy. Directly across from the downtown tender docks, the main square—**Plaza del Sol** (also called *la plaza* or *el parque*)—is excellent for people-watching. **Avenida Rafael Melgar,** the principal street along the waterfront, runs along the western shore of the island, which is the site of the best resorts and beaches. Most of the shops and restaurants are on Rafael Melgar, although many well-stocked duty-free shops line the Malecón, the seaside promenade.

Only 3 blocks from the ferry pier on Agenda Rafael Melgar between Calles 4 and 6 N., the **Museo de la Isla de Cozumel** (© 987/872-1434) has two floors of exhibits displayed in what was Cozumel's first luxury hotel. Exhibits cover everything from pre-Hispanic times to the colonial era to the present. Included are many swords and nautical artifacts; one of the displays showcases endangered species. The highlight is a reproduction of a Mayan house. It's open daily from 9am to 5pm, and sometimes later; admission is $3.

ON YOUR OWN: BEYOND THE PORT AREA

You can rent a motor scooter and zip around most of the island, including its wild and natural side. Stop for lunch at a beachside open-air seafood restaurant for some grilled fish and a cool drink. Scooters can be rented from several outfits, including Auto Rent (see "By Moped," above).

Outside of San Miguel is the **Chankanaab Nature Park,** where an archaeological park, botanical garden, and wildlife sanctuary compliment a saltwater lagoon, offshore reefs, and underwater caves. More than 10 countries have contributed seedlings and cuttings to the botanical garden here. Some 60 species of marine life occupy the lagoon, including sea turtles and captive dolphins (that you can swim with for a mere US$120). Reproductions of Mayan dwellings are scattered throughout the park. There's also a wide white-sand beach with thatch umbrellas and a changing area with lockers and showers. Both scuba divers and snorkelers enjoy examining the sunken ship offshore (there are four dive shops here). The park also has a restaurant and snack stand. It's all located at Carretera Sur, km. 9 (no phone). It's open daily from 9am to 5pm. Admission is US$7, free for children 9 and under. The 10-minute taxi ride from the downtown tender and ferry pier (Muelle Fiscal) costs about US$10.

Mayan ruins on Cozumel are very minor compared to those on the mainland. The most notable of the two is at **San Gervasio,** reached by driving west across the island to the army air base, and then turning right and continuing north 6.4km (4 miles) to San Gervasio. This was once a ceremonial center and capital of Cozumel. The Mayans dedicated the area to Ixchel, the fertility goddess. The ruins cost US$3.50 to visit, plus US$1 for entrance to the access road. For US$12, guides will show people what's left, including several broken columns and lintels. It's open daily from 8am to 5pm.

Another meager ruin is **El Cedral,** which lies 3.2km (2 miles) inland at the turnoff at km. 17.5, east of Playa San Francisco. It's the island's oldest structure, with traces of original Mayan wall paintings. The Spanish tore much of it down, and the U.S. Army nearly finished the job when it built an airfield here in World War II. Little remains now except a Mayan arch and a few small ruins covered in heavy growth. Guides at the site will show you around for a fee.

SHOPPING
You can walk from the ferry pier to the best shops in San Miguel (they start right across the street from the Punta Langosta pier, and are 3.2km–4.8km/2–3 miles by taxi or foot from the International and Puerto Maya cruise ship piers). Because of the influx of cruise ship passengers, prices are relatively high here, but you can and should bargain. Silver jewelry is big business, and it's generally sold by weight. You can find some nice pieces, but again, don't expect much of a bargain. **Heritage,** Avenida Rafael Melgar 341, is one of the most important jewelers in Cozumel, and the exclusive distributor of Rolex watches on the Mexican Riviera. **Rachat & Romero,** Avenida Rafael Melgar 101, has a wide variety of loose stones, which they can mount while you wait.

Wall-to-wall shops along the waterfront in San Miguel offer all manner of souvenirs. Shops also line the perimeter of **Plaza del Sol,** adjacent to the downtown ferry pier (.4km/¼ mile or so north of the Punta Langosta pier), and several shopping arcades are accessible from the plaza, including the pleasant, tree-lined **Plaza Confetti** and the peach-painted **Villa Mar complex,** with several good silver jewelry shops.

Agencia Publicaciones Gracia, Avenida 5A, a block from the downtown tender and ferry pier, is Cozumel's best source for English-language books, guidebooks, newspapers, and magazines. **Cinco Soleils** at Avenida Rafael Melagar and Calle 8 is well stocked with beautiful, if pricey, handmade local goods. There is also a small tequila bar and coffee shop to reenergize the weary shopper.

If you're docking at the International Pier, a bunch of nice shops in the terminal sell everything from Mexican blankets to jewelry, T-shirts, and handicrafts of all kinds. Again, prices aren't cheap—a roll of film went for US$9 at the terminal last time we were there. The pier at Puerta Maya has just undergone a major expansion and now boasts a wide selection of well-stocked gift shops.

BEACHES
Cozumel's best powdery white-sand beach, **Playa San Francisco,** stretches for some 4.8km (3 miles) along the southwestern shoreline. It was once one of the most idyllic beaches in Mexico, but resort development is threatening to destroy

its old character. You can rent equipment for watersports here, and have lunch at one of the many restaurants and bars on the shoreline. There's no admission to the beach, and it's about a US$10 taxi ride south of San Miguel's downtown pier. If you land at the International Pier, you're practically at the beach already.

Playa del Sol, about 1.6km (1 mile) south of Playa del San Francisco, is a fine beach but has a big reputation, so it's likely to be wall-to-wall with your fellow cruisers. **Playa Bonita** (sometimes called "Punta Chiqueros") is one of the least crowded beaches; it lies on the east (windward) side of the island and is difficult to reach unless you rent a vehicle or throw yourself at the mercy of a taxi driver. It sits in a moon-shaped cove sheltered from the Caribbean Sea by an offshore reef. Waves are only moderate, the sand is powdery, and the water is clear.

You may want to consider **Parque Chankanaab,** a parklike beach area lined with thatched umbrellas and contoured plastic chaise longues. While the water is rough here and not ideal for swimming, the beach and scenery are very nice and the place is popular with locals. Admission is US$10, and you can swim with dolphins (for a fee, of course) or rent snorkeling equipment. There's also a restaurant and bar. This beach is about a 15-minute, US$12 taxi ride from the downtown pier.

If you don't want to go far, two hotel beaches are a stone's throw north of the International Pier (facing the water, they're on the right), and they welcome day visitors to use their small beach, cabanas, pools, and changing facilities. **El Cid La Ceiba** charges US$10 per person for the day, and the **Park Royale** charges US$25 per person for the day (9am–5pm), which includes all drinks, snacks, and lunch.

SPORTS

SCUBA DIVING   Black coral in profusion, hundreds of species of rainbow-hued tropical fish, and underwater visibility that can reach 75m (246 ft.) make Cozumel one of the best (if not the best) diving destinations in the Caribbean. Cruisers might want to confine their adventures to the finest spot, **Palancar Reef.** Lying about 1.6km (1 mile) offshore, this fabulous water world features gigantic elephant-ear sponges and black coral, as well as deep caves, canyons, and tunnels. It's a favorite of divers from all over the world. The best scuba outfitters are **Aqua Safari,** Avenida Rafael Melgar at Calle 5, next to the Vista del Mar Hotel (© **987/872-0101;** www.aquasafari.com), and **Diving Adventures,** Calle 51 Sur no. 2, near the corner of Avenida Rafael Melgar (© **888/338-0388** from the U.S., or 987/872-3009; www.divingadventures.net).

SNORKELING   The shallow reefs at Playa San Francisco and Chankanaab Bay are among the best snorkeling spots. You'll see a world of sea creatures parading by, everything from parrotfish to conch. The best outfitter is **Cozumel Snorkeling Center,** Calle Primera Sur (© **987/872-0539**), which offers a 3-hour snorkeling tour (US$40 per person), including all equipment and refreshments. They can also arrange parasailing. In addition, you can just rent snorkeling equipment at Chankanaab.

GREAT LOCAL RESTAURANTS & BARS

The **local beer** is Sol. On a hot day, a bottle of the stuff is manna from heaven.

Carlos 'n Charlie's, Avenida Rafael Melgar 551, right across from the Punta Langosta pier (© **987/872-0191;** www.carlosn-charlies.com), is Mexico's equivalent of the Hard Rock Cafe, but much wilder. Though it moved into these more sterile Houlihan's-style digs a few years ago, the music still blares, and dancing tourists pound back yard-long glasses of beer as if they're going out of style—just like they did at the old sawdust-covered Carlos 'n Charlie's that once roared just down the road. Many a cruise passenger has stumbled back from this place clutching a souvenir glass as though it were the Holy Grail—dubious proof of a visit to Mexico. People come here for good times and the spicy, tasty ribs. You can dine surprisingly well on Yucatán specialties and the best chicken and beef fajitas in Cozumel.

Another party spot is the **Hard Rock Cozumel** itself, at Avenida Rafael Melgar 2A (© **529/872-5273;** www.hardrock.com), which serves the hard stuff as well as burgers and grilled beef or chicken fajitas. Yet another is **Fat Tuesday,** at the end of the International Pier (© **987/872-5130**), where you'll find lots of crew members on their day or night off (you can even hear their revelry from the ship). Join the fun and guzzle a 16-ounce margarita for US$5 a pop or a 24-ounce version for US$7. There's another Fat Tuesdays near the ferry pier at the entrance to the Villa Mar complex, right next to Plaza del Sol. A half block from the pier, **Las Palmeras,** Avenida Rafael Melgar (© **987/872-0532**), is ideal for casual eating. If you arrive in time, it serves one of the best breakfasts in town; for lunch, it offers tempting seafood dishes or Mexican specialties.

On the main drag in town is **Lobster's Cove** (© **987/872-4022**), offering tasty seafood and Mexican dishes. Just north of the ferry pier, **El Capi Naveg-ante,** Avenida 10A #312 at Calles 3 and 4, 5 blocks from the downtown tender and ferry pier (© **987/872-1730**), offers the freshest fish in San Miguel, as well as a great lobster soufflé. **La Choza,** Calle Rosada Salas 200 at Avenida 10A Sur, 2 blocks from the downtown tender and ferry pier (© **987/872-0958**), offers real local cooking that's a favorite of the town's savvy foodies.

PLAYA DEL CARMEN

Some cruise ships spend a day at Cozumel and then anchor offshore at Playa del Carmen for another day, but most ferry passengers to Playa from Cozumel for tours to Tulum and Chichén-Itzá, then head on to spend the day tied up at Cozumel.

The famed white-sand beach here was relatively untouched by tourists not many years ago, but today the pleasure-seeking hordes have replaced the Indian families who used to gather coconuts for copra (dried coconut meat). Shops have sprung up like weeds, but if you can tolerate the crowds, the snorkeling is still excellent over the offshore reefs. Turtle-watching is another local pastime.

COMING ASHORE   Some cruise ships anchor offshore or at the pier of Cozumel, then send passengers over to Playa del Carmen by tender. Others dock at the **Puerto Calica Cruise Pier** (a former dock for freighters carrying cement), 13km (8 miles) south of Playa del Carmen. Taxis meet each arriving ship here, and drivers transport visitors into the center of Playa del Carmen—which is a good thing since there's nothing to do at Calica save for making a phone call or buying a soda.

GETTING AROUND

BY TAXI   Taxis are readily available to take you anywhere, but you can walk to the center of town, to the beach, and to most major shops.

BY RENTAL CAR   If you decide to rent a car for the day, Avis, Budget, Hertz, and National all have offices here.

BEST CRUISE LINE SHORE EXCURSIONS

Most visitors head for the Mayan ruins or one of the local eco-parks the moment they reach shore (see "Mayan Ruins & Other Mainland Attractions," on p. 155).

Frommer's Favorite Playa del Carmen Experiences

Taking a Tour of Tulum or Chichén-Itzá: Both of the tours described in the Cozumel section, under "Mayan Ruins & Other Mainland Attractions ," earlier in this chapter, are also offered from here.

Spending a Day in Xel-Ha: You'll find yourself floating around the lagoon on an inner tube without a care in the world. See "Mayan Ruins & Other Mainland Attractions," earlier in this chapter.

Spending a Day in Xcaret: How does snorkeling through a cool underwater cave sound? See "Mayan Ruins & Other Mainland Attractions," earlier in this chapter.

ON YOUR OWN: WITHIN WALKING DISTANCE

From the pier, you can walk to the center of Playa del Carmen, to the beach, and to the small but ever expanding shopping district, which has some pretty trendy boutiques and hip restaurants.

ON YOUR OWN: BEYOND THE PORT AREA

Other than the beach and shopping, the only major attractions are **Xcaret** and **Xel-Ha** (both open daily). The easiest way to get to either is to sign up for your ship's organized excursion (p. 167), which includes transportation; otherwise, if you're docked in Cozumel, you'll have to get ferry tickets on your own to get between the island and Playa del Carmen. If you come independently, general admission for **Xcaret** (© 998/881-2400; www.xcaret.net) is a steep US$49 for adults, US$25 for children 5 to 12 (free for kids 5 and under). The **Xel-Ha** eco-park (© 984/875-6000; www.xel-ha.com.mx), just a few miles farther south of Xcaret (and pronounced *shell*-ha), features a sprawling natural lagoon filled with sparkling blue-green water and surrounded by lush foliage. The use of inner tubes and life vests are included in the admission price, and you can spend a great couple of hours floating your way from one end of the calm body of water to the other, stopping to see schools of tropical fish. Snorkeling gear is available for rent. Xel-Ha also has dolphins. Shops, restaurants, and lots of beach chairs pepper the area. Admission is US$25 for adults and US$15 for kids 4 to 11; children under 4 are free. Buses from Playa del Carmen come here frequently; a taxi costs about US$40 one-way.

SHOPPING

Most shops are along Avenida 5, which has pedestrian-only stretch near the dock. The **Rincon del Sol** plaza is a tree-filled courtyard between Calle 4 and Calle 6, built in the colonial Mexican style. It has the best collection of handicraft shops in the area, some of which offer much better quality items than the junky souvenirs peddled elsewhere.

GREAT LOCAL RESTAURANTS & BARS

El Chino, Calle 4, Avenida 15 (© 984/873-0015), is a pristine restaurant known locally for its regional Yucatán specialties, as well as standard dishes from throughout Mexico. **El Tacolote,** Avenida Juárez (© 984/873-1363), specializes in fresh seafood and the best grilled meats in town, brought to your table fresh from the broiler on a charcoal pan to keep the food warm.

Frommer's Favorite Costa Maya Experiences

Jungle Beach Break: A short bus ride lands you at small but charming Uvero Beach, where you can sunbathe, kayak, rent jet skis or a minispeedboat, or snorkel on the pristine reef. Then again, you may just want to stroll out to the end of the long pier to gaze down at the colorful sea life in the crystal-blue water below. See "Shore Excursions," below.

Kohunlich Mayan Explorer: This fascinating Mayan site offers a noncommercial look at both excavated and unrestored Mayan ruins, including a ball court, foundations of residential buildings, and a monument returned to the site after being stolen by thieves. The high point (literally and figuratively) is a large temple with remarkably well-preserved stucco faces flanking the crumbling steps. Uncleared ruins near the ball courts, just waiting to be unearthed, make you feel like a bona fide explorer. See "Shore Excursions," below.

If you want to stay in the thick of things, there's a **Señor Frog's** (© **984/873-0930**) right at the ferry pier for all the beer and shots you can stomach.

COSTA MAYA

While Cozumel gets the most traffic by far, a handful of other Yucatán ports have entered the scene, including Costa Maya near the sleepy fishing village of Mahajual (just over 161km/100 miles south of Playa del Carmen). Don't confuse Costa Maya with Riviera Maya, which stretches between Cancún and Tulum. Technically, Costa Maya is the region between Punta Herrero and Xcalak near the border with Belize. Millions of dollars have been invested in a pier that opened just a couple of years ago, plus a lavish oceanfront shopping and restaurant complex that caters exclusively to the needs of cruise ship passengers (there are no hotels in the area). Princess, Royal Caribbean, Regal, Carnival, and Norwegian are among the lines that visit the port. The Mayan ruins of nearby Kohunlich and Chacchoben are popular attractions, along with silky white beaches and diving and snorkeling at the Chincorro, Mexico's largest coral atoll.

COMING ASHORE   Literally carved out of the jungle, this amenity-filled pier is the only major form of development for miles around, and has pretty much everything you want: sprawling restaurants (one with a balcony, the other with outdoor seating and a stage for live music), an amphitheater for cultural dance performances, two saltwater pools, a pool bar, a trampoline, and plenty of shops. And a free tram shuttles passengers from their ship down the loooooong .5km (⅓-mile) pier to the port entrance.

GETTING AROUND

BY TAXI   A long line of shiny new taxis line up just outside the pier. Unfortunately, because any attraction of note is far, far away and there are no alternative means of transportation, the prices are steep and non-negotiable. Visiting the Mayan ruins of Kohunlich will set passengers back US$65 per person round-trip, while a round-trip ride to Chacchoben comes in at US$45 per person. With prices like these, we highly recommend you book the shore excursions instead (see below). About the only reasonable fare is to the nearby sleepy fishing village of Mahajual (US$5 per person).

BY RENTAL CAR   No rental-car facilities are in the area, but with only one long, straight, flat road—which is still in the process of being paved—this does not seem to be too much of an inconvenience.

BEST CRUISE LINE SHORE EXCURSIONS

The Mayan Ruins of Kohunlich (US$79, 7 hr.): Located in a secluded jungle setting near the border of Belize, this Mayan city was built between A.D. 200 and 900, spanning the early through the late-classical periods. The trail to the ruins is marked by a tree that was uprooted and replanted upside down—a means of marking sites used by the apparently brilliant, though obviously eccentric, Mexican archaeologist who first explored the site. Check out the Plaza of the Acropolis (where two temples are aligned with the equinox) and the Temple of the Masks from the 6th century, where 1.8m (6-ft.) stucco masks of the Mayan sun god are remarkably well preserved.

The Mayan Ruins of Chacchoben (US$62, 4 hr.): Opened to the public in 1999, this collection of temples dates back to A.D. 360, or the middle of the early classical period, and played an important role as a trading center for wood, jade, and colorful birds. There are more than two dozen structures, and to date, less than 5% of the site has been excavated. The first temple that you'll encounter is the temple of Venus, a tribute to fertility. The pyramids are in an excellent state of preservation, and their distinctive curved edges and soft lines are particularly beautiful. Climbing to the first plateau affords an impressive view of the surrounding area.

Bike & Kayak (US$48, 3 hr.): Starting off on mountain bikes, you pedal along a dirt road past a small mangrove lagoon with views of the coastline, then through the village of Mahajual (don't blink or you'll miss it), and finally arrive at the beach. After a short refreshment break, trade in your helmet for a paddle and pair up with a partner for a kayak trip out along the nearby reef. The small two-person kayaks are easily launched from the shore and are easy to handle. The bike ride back includes another beach stop.

Coral Reef Sail & Snorkel (US$54, 3 hr.): A boat takes you to a nearby coral reef, where you can explore with an expert guide.

Dune Buggy Safari (US$82, 3½ hr.): This is a drive-yourself convoy excursion in honest-to-god dune buggies (how '60s . . .), leaving from Majahaul out onto unpaved roads on the way to La Palapa Beach, where you'll have time to swim or use the kayaks and volleyball court.

Jungle Beach Break (US$36, no set time): A shuttle operates between the nearby Uvero Beach and the pier every 35 minutes, allowing you to come and go as you please. But, would you ever want to leave the snow-white beaches and crystal-blue water, not to mention the chaise longues and umbrellas, open bar, free snorkel gear, paddle boats, and the sea kayaks, jet skis, and power boats you can rent? Changing rooms with showers and a snack bar are on-site (food not included). Parasailing is also available.

YOUR OWN: WITHIN WALKING DISTANCE

If you choose, you could stay right at the one-stop-shop pier complex and still get a taste of the Mayan coast. A 650-seat amphitheatre here offers cultural shows daily, from a pre-Hispanic dance drama to a Mexican folkloric performance.

There are also activities throughout the day in and around the pier, from guacamole-making classes to aqua-aerobics, games, and contests. Check the daily entertainment schedule posted near the restrooms for performance times and activities.

Immediately next to the pier is a lovely private beach club with umbrellas, chairs, hammock swings, and a small restaurant and bar. There's a small fee for day passes. Enter from the parking lot near the bus departure point.

ON YOUR OWN: BEYOND THE PORT AREA

The only town in the area is the Mahajual fishing village, which, until quite recently, did not even have electricity. A single main road is lined with a short row of rustic, screened-in restaurants and a miniscule grocery; across the street is a long white beach lined with fishing boats and noticeably devoid of beach umbrellas and sunbathers. Unless you're just curious, there's no real reason to go.

SHOPPING

Because the port at Costa Maya was constructed with the sole purpose of serving American and European cruise ship passengers, you can bet your last enchilada that shopping abounds. There are some 70 shops in a mall-like setting, some of them familiar to the seasoned cruiser, others unique. **Ultra Femme** specializes in fragrances and cosmetics cheaper than you'll find at the duty-free. If it's gold and jewels you're after, head over to **Tanzanite International** for a wide selection and friendly staff, or to **Diamond International** for some great bargains. Next door, you can haggle over "art in silver" at **Taxco Factory.** For something different, head over to the two nearby *palapas* (small thatched-roof stands), where local artisans craft their wares as potential buyers look on.

GREAT LOCAL RESTAURANTS & BARS

Bandito's Lobster House at the pier serves some of the freshest seviche and tastiest guacamole around. The fish, shrimp, and lobster tacos can be ordered a la carte, so you can sample one of each, while the fire-roasted Baja lobster, whole sea bass, and Mayan fajitas are full meals and come with a slew of sides. Order a fruity tropical teaser or classic margarita to wash it all down. Next door, at **Mamacita's Taqueria,** you can enjoy casual dining and drinks while taking in the excellent views of the coast and port. Try the blackened chicken fundido to start, then the grande baja burrito or the tres taco platter.

PROGRESO/MERIDA

Visited by a fraction of the ships that call at Cozumel, Progreso has one major advantage over its rival: proximity to Chichén-Itzá, which lies only 2 hours south by motorcoach. This makes excursions to the ruins considerably cheaper than they are from Cozumel, averaging about $95 per person. Progreso itself is almost nothing but a port. Ships dock here at the end of a man-made causeway that juts several miles out into the Gulf of Mexico, making it very difficult to visit anything on your own. We recommend taking a tour. Aside from visits to Chichén-Itzá and the smaller Mayan ruins at Uxmal and Dzibilchaltun, cruise passengers can take a tour of Merida, the capital of Yucatan state (about 32k/20 miles away), visit the Celestun Estuary Nature Reserve to see pink flamingos in their natural habitat, or take a jeep trek off-road to two local haciendas.

13 Curaçao

As you sail into the harbor of Willemstad, be sure to look for the quaint "floating bridge," the Queen Emma pontoon bridge, which swings aside to open the

Map legend:
- ✈ Airport
- 🏖 Beach
- 🚢 Cruise Ship Dock
- ⛰ Mountain

narrow channel. Welcome to Curaçao, the largest and most populous of the Netherlands Antilles, just 56km (35 miles) north of the Venezuelan coast.

Curaçao was first discovered by the Spanish around 1499, but in 1634, the Dutch came and prospered. Because much of the island's surface is an arid desert, the settlers ruled out farming and instead developed Curaçao into one of the Dutch Empire's busiest trading posts. In 1915, when the Royal Dutch/Shell Company built one of the world's largest oil refineries to process crude from Venezuela, workers from 50 countries poured onto the island, and today it remains a melting pot, its population descended from a curious mixture of bloodlines, including African, Dutch, Venezuelan, and Pakistani. The oil refineries went into decline after World War II, and by the 1980s tourism had begun to develop, leading to the building of many new hotels. Today, the island retains a Dutch flavor, especially in Willemstad, where the harbor is bordered by rows of picture-postcard, pastel-colored gabled Dutch-colonial houses. While these structures give Willemstad a storybook appearance, the rest of the island

Frommer's Favorite Curaçao Experiences

Visiting Christoffel National Park: Hike up 369m (1,210-ft.) St. Christof-felberg, passing cacti, iguanas, wild goats, many species of birds, and ancient Arawak paintings along the way. With 32km (20 miles) of roads, you can also see the park by car. (See "On Your Own: Beyond the Port Area," below.)

Gazing into the Mirrored Waters of the Hato Caves: Stalagmites and stalactites are mirrored in a mystical underground lake in these caves, whose limestone formations were created by water seeping through the coral. (See "On Your Own: Beyond the Port Area," below.)

looks like the American Southwest, its desertlike landscape dotted with three-pronged cacti, spiny-leafed aloes, and divi-divi trees bent by trade winds.

COMING ASHORE   Cruise ships dock in Willemstad at a megapier just beyond the Queen Emma pontoon bridge, which leads to the duty-free shopping sector and the famous floating market. It's a 5- to 10-minute walk from here to the center of town, or you can take a taxi from the stand. A shopping/ entertainment complex called Riffort Village recently opened in a restored fort nearby. The town itself is easy to navigate on foot. Most of it can be explored in 2 or 3 hours, leaving plenty of time for beaches or watersports. Although the ship terminal has a duty-free shop, save your serious shopping for Willemstad. There's a phone center at the cruise terminal.

LANGUAGE   **Dutch, Spanish,** and **English** are spoken on Curaçao, along with **Papiamento,** a patois that combines the three major tongues with Amerindian and African dialects.

CURRENCY   The official currency is the euro (exchange rate at press time: 1€ = US$1.22; $1 = .82€). Each euro is divisible by 100 cents. Canadian and U.S. dollars are accepted for purchases, so there's no need to change money. Unless otherwise noted, prices in this section are given in U.S. dollars.

INFORMATION   For visitor information, go to the **Curaçao Tourist Board,** Pietermaai (© **599/9-434-8200**). It's open Monday to Friday from 8am to 5pm. For information before you go, call © 800/328-7222 or visit www.Curacao-tourism.com.

CALLING FROM THE U.S.   When calling Curaçao from the United States, you need to dial the international access code (011) before the numbers listed here.

GETTING AROUND

BY TAXI   Taxis are metered, and the best place to flag one down is on the Otrabanda side of the floating bridge, or call © **599/9-869-0747.** Generally, there's no need to tip. Up to four passengers can share the price of an island tour by taxi, which costs about $30 per hour.

BY BUS   A fleet of buses operate from Wilhelmina Plein, near the shopping center, and run to most parts of Curaçao. You can hail a bus at any designated bus stop.

BY RENTAL CAR   Driving is on the right on paved roads. Avis, Budget, and Hertz all have offices here.

BEST CRUISE LINE SHORE EXCURSIONS

Many excursions aren't really worth the price here—you can easily see the town on your own and hop a taxi to the few attractions on the island outside of Willemstad.

Spanish Water Canoe & Snorkeling ($69, 3½ hr.): At Caracas Bay Island, you'll board canoes for a 45-minute paddle alongside mangroves and rock formations, then arrive at Baya Beach where instructors lead snorkeling over a sunken tug boat.

Underwater Animal Encounter ($89, 3 hr.): Ever wanted to hand-feed a shark? Here's your chance. Suit up in scuba gear and dive into the shallow (3.6km/ 12-ft.) water at the Curaçao Seaquarium, where sharks and sea turtles are behind fencing, with holes through which you can hand them their grub while stingrays, parrotfish, and other marine life swim around on your side. Since the water is so shallow, scuba certification isn't required.

ON YOUR OWN: WITHIN WALKING DISTANCE

Willemstad is the major attraction here, and you can see it on foot. After years of restoration, the town's historic center and the island's natural harbor, Schottegat, have been inscribed on UNESCO's World Heritage List. Be sure to watch the **Queen Emma pontoon bridge** move. It's motorized and a man actually drives it to the side of the harbor every so often so that ships and boats can pass through the channel. It's exceedingly cool.

A statue of **Pedro Luis Brion** dominates the square known as Brionplein, at the Otrabanda end of the Queen Emma pontoon bridge. Born in Curaçao in 1782, Brion became the island's favorite son and best-known war hero. He was an admiral of the fleet under Simón Bolívar and fought for the independence of Venezuela and Colombia.

Fort Amsterdam, site of the Governor's Palace and the 1769 Dutch Reformed church, has the task of guarding the waterfront. The church here still has a British cannonball embedded in it. The arches leading to the fort were tunneled under the official residence of the governor. A corner of the fort stands at the intersection of Breedestraat and Handelskade, the starting point for a plunge into the island's major shopping district.

A few minutes' walk from the pontoon bridge, at the north end of Handelskade, is the **Floating Market,** where scores of schooners tie up alongside the canal. Boats arrive here from Venezuela and Colombia, and from other West Indian islands, to sell tropical fruits and vegetables, as well as handicrafts. The modern market's vast concrete cap has not diminished the fun of watching the activity here. Either arrive early or stay late to view marine merchants setting up or storing their wares.

Between the I. H. (Sha) Capriles Kade and Fort Amsterdam, at the corner of Columbusstraat and Hanchi di Snoa, is the **Mikve Israel-Emanuel Synagogue.** Dating from 1651, the Jewish congregation here is the oldest in the New World. Next door, the **Jewish Cultural Historical Museum,** Hanchi Snoa 29 (*©* 599/ 9-461-1633; www.snoa.com), is housed in two buildings dating from 1728 that served as the rabbi's residence and the mikvah (bath) for religious purification purposes. Entry is through the synagogue and admission is $5. Hours are Monday through Friday 9am to 4:30pm, Sunday 10am to 4pm.

You can walk from the Queen Emma pontoon bridge to the **Curaçao Museum,** Van Leeuwenhoekstraat (*©* 599/9-462-6051). The building, constructed in 1853 by the Royal Dutch Army as a military hospital, has been carefully restored and furnished with paintings, objets d'art, and antique furniture, and houses a large collection from the Caiquetio tribes. On the museum grounds is an art gallery for temporary exhibitions of both local and international art. Hours are from 8:30am to 4:30pm Monday through Friday, Sunday from 10am to 4pm. Admission is $3 adults, $1.75 children under 15.

ON YOUR OWN: BEYOND THE PORT AREA

Cacti, bromeliads, rare orchids, iguanas, donkeys, wild goats, and many species of birds thrive in the 1,800-hectare (4,446-acre) **Christoffel National Park** (© **599/9-864-0363**), located about a 30-minute taxi or car ride from the capital near the northwestern tip of Curaçao. The park rises from flat, arid countryside to 369m-high (1,210-ft.) St. Christoffelberg, the tallest point in the Dutch Leewards. Along the way are ancient Arawak paintings and the Piedra di Monton, a rock heap piled by African slaves who cleared this former plantation. Legend said that the slaves could climb to the top of the rock pile, jump off, and fly back home across the Atlantic to Africa. If they had ever tasted a grain of salt, however, they would crash to their deaths. The park has 32km (20 miles) of one-way trail-like roads. The shortest is about 8km (5 miles) long, but takes about 40 minutes to drive because of its rough terrain. One of several hiking trails goes to the top of St. Christoffelberg. It takes about 1½ hours to walk to the summit (come early in the morning before it gets hot). There's also a museum in an old storehouse left over from plantation days. The park is open Monday to Saturday from 7:30am to 4pm and Sunday from 6am to 3pm, and guided tours are available. Admission is $10 per person.

The **Curaçao Seaquarium,** off Bhpor Kibra (© **599/9-461-6666**; www. curacao-sea-aquarium.com), displays more than 400 species of fish, crabs, anemones, and other invertebrates, sponges, and coral. In the "shark and animal encounter," divers, snorkelers, and experienced swimmers are able to feed, film, and photograph sharks, stingrays, lobsters, tarpons, parrotfish, and other marine life in a controlled environment. You can swim with the dolphins for $139 or dive with them for $179. Nonswimmers can see the underwater life from a 14m (46-ft.) semisubmersible observatory. Curaçao's only full-facility, white-sand, palm-shaded beach is on the Seaquarium grounds. Admission is $15 for adults and $7.50 for children 5 to 14. Hours are Monday through Sunday 9 am to 4:30pm.

Stalagmites and stalactites are mirrored in a mystical underground lake in **Hato Caves**, F. D. Rosseveltweg (© **599/9-868-0379**). Long ago, geological forces uplifted this limestone terrace, which was originally a coral reef. The limestone formations were created over thousands of years by water seeping through the coral. After crossing the lake, you enter two caverns known as The Cathedral and La Ventana ("The Window"), where you'll see ancient Indian petroglyphs. The caves are open daily from 10am to 4pm, and professional local guides take visitors through every hour. Admission is $6.50 for adults, $5 for children 4 to 11, and free for kids 3 and under.

SHOPPING

Curaçao is a shopper's paradise, with some 200 stores lining Heerenstraat, Breedestraat, and other streets in the 5-block district called the **Punda.** Many shops occupy the town's old Dutch houses.

The island is famous for its 5-pound "wheelers" of Gouda and Edam cheese. Look for good buys on wooden shoes, French perfumes, Dutch blue Delft souvenirs, finely woven Italian silks, Japanese and German cameras, jewelry, silver, Swiss watches, linens, leather goods, liquor, and island-made rum and liqueurs, especially Curaçao liqueur, some of which has a distinctive blue color. Some stores also offer good buys on intricate lacework imported from everywhere between Portugal and China. If you're a street shopper and want something colorful, consider a carving or flamboyant painting from Haiti or the Dominican Republic; both are hawked by street vendors at any of the main plazas.

Suggested shops include **Bamali,** Breedestraat 2 (© **599/9-461-2258**), for Indonesian-influenced clothing (mostly for women); **Gandelman Jewelers,** Breedestraat 35, Punda (© **599/9-461-1854**), for a large selection of fine jewelry as well as Curaçaoan gold pieces; and **Curaçao Creations,** Klipstraat 10 (© **599/9-462-4516**), for Curaçao handicrafts.

BEACHES

Curaçao has some 38 beaches, ranging from hotel sand patches to secluded coves. The seawater remains an almost-constant 76°F (24°C) year-round, with good underwater visibility, but beaches here just aren't as good as others in the region. Taxi drivers waiting at the cruise dock will take you to any of the beaches, but you'll have to negotiate a fare. To be on the safe side, arrange to have your driver pick you up at a certain time and take you back to the cruise dock.

The Curaçao Seaquarium has the island's only full-facility, white-sand, palm-shaded beach, but you'll have to pay the full aquarium admission to get in (see "On Your Own: Beyond the Port Area," above). The rest of the beaches here are public.

Southeast of Willemstad, **Santa Barbara Beach** sits on land owned by a mining company between the open sea and the island's primary watersports and recreational area, known as Spanish Water. It's got pure-white sand and calm water, a buoy line protects swimmers from boats, and there are restrooms, changing rooms, watersports equipment, and a snack bar. The beach has access to the **Curaçao Underwater Park** (© **599/9-462-4242**), which stretches from the Breezes Resort to the eastern tip of Curaçao and includes some of the island's finest reefs.

Daaibooi is a good beach about 30 minutes from town, in the Willibrordus area on the west side of Curaçao. It's free, but there are no changing facilities.

Blauwbaai (Blue Bay) is the largest and most frequented beach on Curaçao, with enough white sand for everybody. Along with showers and changing facilities, there are plenty of shady places to retreat from the noonday sun. To reach it, take the road that goes past the Holiday Beach Hotel & Casino (© **599/9-462-5400**), heading in the direction of Juliandorp. Follow the sign that tells you to bear left for Blauwbaai and the fishing village of San Michiel.

Westpunt is known for its gigantic cliffs and the Sunday divers who jump from them into the ocean below. This public beach is on the northwestern tip of the island. **Knip Bay,** just south of Westpunt, has beautiful turquoise waters. On weekends, live music and dancing make the beach a lively place. Changing facilities and refreshments are available. **Playa Abao,** with crystal-turquoise water, is situated at the northern tip of the island.

Warning: Beware of stepping on the hard spines of sea urchins, which are sometimes found in these waters. While not fatal, their spines can cause several days of real discomfort. For temporary first aid, try the local remedies of vinegar or lime juice.

GREAT LOCAL RESTAURANTS & BARS

Curaçao's **local beer** is the very Dutch Amstel. The **local drink** is Curaçao liqueur, some of which has a distinctive blue color.

La Pergola, in the Waterfront Arches, Waterfort Straat (© **599/9-461-3482**), is an Italian restaurant where the menu items change virtually every day. Lunch is about $25. **Rijstaffel Indonesia and Holland Club Bar,** Mercuriusstraat 13, Salinja (© **599/9-461-2999**), is the best place on the island to sample the Indonesian *rijstafel,* a traditional "rice table" with tons of zesty side dishes. Lunch is around $13. You'll need a taxi to get to this restaurant, which is in the suburbs near Salinja, near the SuperClubs Breezes Curaçao, southeast of Willemstad.

14 Dominica

First things first. It's pronounced "Dome-*ee*-nee-ka," not "Doe-min-i-ka." And it has nothing to do with the Dominican Republic. The Commonwealth of Dominica is an independent country, and English, not Spanish, is the official language. The only Spanish commonly understood in Dominica is *mal encaminado a Santo Domingo* ("accidentally sent to the Dominican Republic"), the phrase stamped on the many letters that make it to their proper destination only after an erroneous but common detour.

To be sure, Dominica has some rough edges. The island is poor, so don't expect luxury or up-to-the-minute technology around every corner, and not everything man-made is as beautiful as nature's handiwork. Balancing this, though, is the fact that Dominica is the most lush and mountainous island in the eastern Caribbean. About 47km (29 miles) long and 26km (16 miles) wide, and lying between the French islands of Guadeloupe and Martinique, smack-dab in the center of the arc formed by the Antilles, it's blessed with astonishing natural wonders—crystal-pure rivers (one for every day of the year, they say), dramatic waterfalls, volcanic lakes (one gurgles and boils from the heat and tumult in the earth below), and foliage as gargantuan as any H. G. Wells ever imagined on Venus. Volcanic coral reefs, every bit as biologically complex as the rainforests onshore, ring the island, and a bit farther from land, whales mate and calve.

Much of Dominica's beauty is accessible to even the most sedentary visitor. Sitting in a rowboat, you can glide up a river through swampland crowded with mangroves and exotic birds, and impressive waterfalls are minutes from paved roads. You can also wend through astonishingly verdant rainforests along undemanding nature trails.

The island's people—primarily descendants of the West Africans brought over to work the plantations, plus some descendants of Europeans and Indians—are another great natural resource. Friendly and proud of their national independence, Dominica's 72,000 citizens remain, for the most part, unchanged by tourism. Don't be surprised when you're greeted with a smile and an "okay," the island's equivalent of "hi." Unfortunately, in Roseau, the main city, drug dealers offering to sell you some of the local weed may also greet you—tourism might be a still-developing industry here, but some other trades are obviously a little further along.

One portion of the island's population has immeasurable ethnological significance: Concentrated in a territory in the northeast, Dominica's approximately 3,000 Carib Indians are the last remaining descendants of the people who dominated the region when Europeans arrived.

COMING ASHORE   Dominica has two cruise ship ports. The most frequented is in the heart of **Roseau,** the country's capital and largest town. The other is near the northwestern town of **Portsmouth.** Banks, restaurants, a market, a tourism

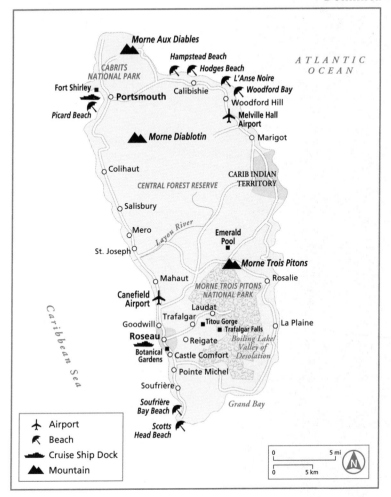

office, and the recommended Dominica Museum line the road opposite Roseau's berth. Portsmouth's port has a tourist welcome center (with an auditorium for speakers and films), shops, and instant access to Fort Shirley and Cabrits National Park.

LANGUAGE   English is Dominica's official language. Almost everyone speaks **Creole** as well, a patois that combines elements of French, English, and African language. Dominica's Creole is similar to those spoken on the neighboring French islands of Guadeloupe and Martinique.

CURRENCY   The Eastern Caribbean dollar (EC$2.70 = US$1; EC$1 = US37¢) is Dominica's official currency, but U.S. dollars are accepted almost everywhere. You're likely to receive change in the local currency. Several ATMs in Roseau, including one at the port, dispense both U.S. and EC dollars. Credit cards and traveler's checks are widely accepted. Unless otherwise specified, prices in this section are given in U.S. dollars.

Frommer's Favorite Dominica Experiences

Hiking to the Emerald Pool: A 15-minute walk through a gorgeous forest brings you to this primeval pool, where you can swim or just take in the beauty of the picture-perfect waterfall, the moss-covered boulders, and the sunlight streaming through branches high overhead. (See "Best Cruise Line Shore Excursions," below.)

Experiencing Carib Culture: Along a rugged portion of Dominica's northeastern coast, the 1,480-hectare (3,656-acre) Carib Territory is home to the world's last surviving Carib Indians. The Caribs today live like most other rural islanders—growing bananas and coconuts, fishing, and operating small shops—but their sturdy baskets of dyed and woven larouma reeds and their wooden canoes carved from the trunks of massive gommier trees are evidence of the people's links to the past. A traditional big house, called the Karbet, serves as a cultural and entertainment center. If you're lucky, you'll witness a performance of the Karifuna Cultural Group, whose youthful members are dedicated to the regeneration of Carib spirit and culture. (See "Best Cruise Line Shore Excursions," below.)

Exploring Fort Shirley/Cabrits National Park: On Dominica's northwestern coast, right by the cruise ship port of Portsmouth, the 104-hectare (257-acre) Cabrits National Park combines stunning mountain scenery, tropical deciduous forest and swampland, volcanic-sand beaches, coral reefs, and the romance of an 18th-century fort. (See "On Your Own: Within Walking Distance," below.)

INFORMATION Dominica's **Division of Tourism** operates branches at the Roseau and Portsmouth cruise ship berths (the Roseau office is located a block from the waterfront at the old post office building on Dame M. E. Charles Blvd.). For information before you leave home, contact the **Dominica Tourist Office** (© 888/645-5637; www.dominica.dm). Several island businesses, including restaurants, tour operators, and other service providers, have joined forces to create another site, **www.delphis.dm/home.htm**, which has scores of links and helpful information.

CALLING FROM THE U.S. When calling Dominica from the United States, simply dial "1" before the numbers listed here.

GETTING AROUND

BY RENTAL CAR Dominica's road system is extensive and relatively well maintained considering the frequent torrential rains, but driving is on the left side, and passage through the mountains can be harrowing. You need a valid driver's license and a Dominican driver's permit, which costs about US$12 and is available through rental agencies. Don't get annoyed when other drivers sound their horns; honking usually indicates an oncoming vehicle (especially at sharp curves) or is meant as a friendly greeting. Avis and Budget have offices here, as do the local agencies **Valley Rent a Car,** with offices in both Roseau and Portsmouth (© 767/448-3233 Roseau, 767/445-5252 Portsmouth), and **Garraway Rent-a-Car,** in downtown Roseau at 17 Old St. (© 767/448-2891). Other options are **Auto Trade Car Rentals** (© 767/440-0415) and **Best Deal Rent a Car** (© 767/449-9204).

BY TAXI   Taxis and public minivans are designated by license plates that begin with the letters "H" or "HA." Fleets of both await cruise ship passengers at the Roseau and Portsmouth docks. Drivers are generally knowledgeable about sites and history, and the standard sightseeing rate is from US$20 per site per person. The vehicles are unmetered, so negotiate a price in advance and make sure everyone's talking about the same currency. You can get more information from the **Dominica Taxi Association** (© 767/449-8533). **Mally's Tour and Taxi Service** (© 767/448-3114), **Julius John's** (© 767/449-1968), and **Alwyn's Taxi and Tour Service** (© 767/235-4260) are three reputable operators.

BEST CRUISE LINE SHORE EXCURSIONS

Trafalgar Falls & Emerald Pool Nature Tour (US$45, 4 hr.): Drive to Morne Bruce for a panoramic view of Roseau and learn about local flora and fauna at the Botanical Gardens. Proceed to a lookout point for a majestic view of Trafalgar Falls. Another drive and a 15-minute walk along a relatively easy trail takes you to the Emerald Pool, named for the moss-covered boulders that enclose it. You can splash in the refreshing water if you like, floating on your back to see the thick rainforest canopy, the 15m (50-foot) waterfall, and the bright blue sky above you.

Carib Indian Territory (US$55, 5 hr.): Along a rugged portion of Dominica's northeastern coast, the 1,480-hectare (3,656-acre) Carib Territory is home to the world's last surviving Carib Indians. The Caribs today live like most other rural islanders—growing bananas and coconuts, fishing, and operating small shops—but their sturdy baskets of dyed and woven larouma reeds and their wooden canoes carved from the trunks of massive gommier trees are evidence of the people's links to the past. The tribe's chief will acquaint you with Carib history, and you'll see a performance by the Karifuna Cultural Group.

Layou Gorge River Tubing (US$65, 3 hr.): A 40-minute drive takes you into the Layou Valley, where tubing guides will take you down the river, lined with tall, overhanging cliffs and lush vegetation.

Jeep Trek & Titou Gorge Swim (US$99, 3½ hr.): A jeep convoy heads up Morne Bruce for a picturesque view, stopping at the Botanical Gardens and the Wotten Waven Sulpher Springs before arriving at the volcanic Titou Gorge, where sheer 6m (20-ft.) black walls, rock outcroppings, caves, and a thundering waterfall provide an exhilarating swimming experience.

Kayak & Snorkel Safari (US$59, 3½ hr.): A guided kayaking trip takes you from Soufrière to your snorkeling site at Scotts Head. The bay here is home to an amazing amount of marine life and coral, and its common to see dolphins and frigate birds feeding.

EXCURSIONS OFFERED BY LOCAL AGENCIES

Nature Tours: Dominica has several excellent tour operators who know the island's many features and intricate terrain like the backs of their hands. One truly outstanding and highly recommended operation is **Ken's Hinterland Adventure Tours,** Fort Young Hotel, Victoria St., Roseau (© 767/448-4850), which offers tours that focus on botany, natural history, bird-watching, and whale-watching.

Carib Indian Excursions: For trips through the Carib Territory, you might want to make arrangements with **NICE** (**Native Indigenous Carib Excursions;** ℭ 767/445-8669). You can't miss with the firsthand knowledge of Carib traditions offered by NICE's operator, former Carib chief Irvince Auguiste.

See "Sports," below, for information on scuba, snorkeling, and kayaking trips.

ON YOUR OWN: WITHIN WALKING DISTANCE

IN ROSEAU   In the early 18th century, the French chose to build their largest settlement at what is now Roseau because the area has the largest expanse of flat land on the leeward coast and is well supplied with fresh water from the nearby Roseau River. The town's name comes from the river reeds (*roseaux* in French) that grow profusely around the estuary. As you come ashore, you'll see the **Dominica Museum,** which faces the bay front. Housed in an old market house dating from 1810, the museum's permanent exhibit provides a clear and interesting overview of the island's geology, history, archaeology, economy, and culture. The displays on pre-Columbian peoples, the slave trade, and the Fighting Maroons—slaves who resisted their white slave owners and established their own communities—are particularly informative. The museum is open Monday to Friday from 9am to 4pm, Saturday from 9am to noon; admission is US$2.

Directly behind the museum is the **Old Market Square.** Vendors of vegetables, fruits, and other merchandise have crowded this cobbled square for centuries, and over the years the location has also witnessed slave auctions, executions, and political meetings and rallies. Today it primarily offers handicrafts and souvenirs. The **Public Market Place** at the mouth of the Roseau River, to your left as you leave the ship, is the Old Market Square's successor as the town's center of commercial activity. It's most colorful on Saturday mornings, when farmers and country vendors from the hills artfully display their fruits, vegetables, root crops, and flowers across the courtyards, sidewalks, and stalls of the marketplace.

It took more than 100 years to build the **Roseau Cathedral of Our Lady of Fair Heaven,** on Virgin Lane. Made of cut volcanic stone in the Gothic-Romanesque revival style, it was finally completed in 1916. The original funds to build the church were raised from levies on French planters, and Caribs erected the first wooden ceiling frame. Convicts on Devil's Island built the pulpit, and one of the stained-glass windows is dedicated to Christopher Columbus. The **Methodist Church** stands next door to the Cathedral on land that once belonged to Catholics who later converted to Methodism. The Protestant church's location and the "conversion" of the land caused such discomfort in the late 1800s that a street riot ensued. Things are calmer today.

On the eastern edge of Roseau, the **Botanical Gardens** lie at the base of Morne Bruce, the mountain overlooking the town. The gardens were established at the end of the 19th century to encourage crop diversification and to provide farmers with correctly propagated seedlings. London's Kew Gardens provided exotic plants collected from every corner of the tropical world, and experiments conducted to see what would grow in Dominica revealed that everything does. Unfortunately, in 1979 Hurricane David destroyed many of the garden's oldest trees. One arboreal victim, an African baobab, still pins the bus it crushed, a monument to the power of the storm. At the garden's aviary you can see sisserou and jacko parrots, part of a captive-breeding program designed to increase the ranks of these endangered species.

IN PORTSMOUTH   The cruise ship dock at Portsmouth leads directly to 104-hectare (257-acre) **Cabrits National Park,** which combines stunning mountain scenery, tropical deciduous forest and swampland, volcanic-sand beaches, coral reefs, and the romance of 18th-century Fort Shirley overlooking the town and Prince Rupert's Bay. Previous visitors to the area include Christopher Columbus, Sir Francis Drake, Admiral Horatio Nelson, and John Smith, who stopped here on his way to Virginia, where he founded Jamestown. Fort Shirley and more than 50 other major structures make up one of the West Indies' most impressive and historic military complexes. Admission is US$2.

ON YOUR OWN: BEYOND THE PORT AREAS

Approximately 15 to 20 minutes by car from Roseau, **Trafalgar Falls** is actually two separate falls referred to as the mother and the father falls. The cascading white torrents dazzle in the sunlight before pummeling black lava boulders below. The surrounding foliage grows in innumerable shades of green. To reach the brisk water of the natural pool at the base of the falls, you'll have to step gingerly along slippery rocks, so the nonballetic shouldn't attempt the climb. The constant mist that tingles the entire area beats any spa treatment. The rainbows are perpetual.

Titou Gorge, near the village of Laudat, offers an exhilarating swimming experience. Wending through the narrow volcanic gorge, you struggle against the cool current like a salmon swimming upstream to spawn. The sheer black walls enclosing the gorge loom 6m (20 ft.) above. At first, they seem sinister, but worn smooth by the water, they're ultimately womblike rather than menacing. Rock outcrops and a small cave provide interludes from the water flow, and eventually you reach the small but thundering waterfall that feeds the torrent.

Emerald Pool sits deep in the rainforest not far from the center of the island. After walking 15 minutes along a relatively easy trail shaded by majestic trees, you reach a 15m (50-ft.) waterfall that crashes into the pool, named for the moss-covered boulders that enclose it. You can splash in the refreshing water if you like, floating on your back to see the thick rainforest canopy and bright blue sky arching over you.

About 6.4km (4 miles) from Portsmouth, in the midst of orange, grapefruit, and banana groves, the **Syndicate Nature Trail** provides an excellent introduction to tropical rainforests. The easy loop trail meanders through a stunningly rich ecosystem that features exotic trees such as the lwoyé kaka and the chantannyé.

Hard-core masochists have an easy choice—the forced march through the **Valley of Desolation** to **Boiling Lake.** Experienced guides say this 6-hour hike is like spending hours on a maximally resistant Stairmaster; one ex-Marine drill sergeant, a master of understatement, referred to it as "arduous." No joke, the trek is part of the Dominican army's basic training (of course, you won't have to carry one of your colleagues along the way). Why would any sane person endure this hell? To breathe in the harsh, sulfuric fumes that have killed all but the hardiest vegetation? Because the idea of baking a potato in the steam rising from the earth is irresistible? Maybe to feel the thrill that comes with the risk that you might break through the thin crust that separates you from hot lava? Or could it be the final destination, the 21m-wide (69-ft.) cauldron of bubbling, slate-blue water of unknown depth? Don't even think of taking a dip in this flooded fumarole: The water temperature ranges from 180°F to 197°F (82°C–92°C). Can we sign you up?

SHOPPING

In addition to the usual duty-free items—jewelry, watches, perfumes, and other luxury goods—Dominica offers handicrafts and art not obtainable anywhere else, most notably Carib Indian baskets made of dyed larouma reeds and balizier (heliconia) leaves. Designs for these items originated in Venezuela's Orinoco River valley and have been handed down from generation to generation since long before the time of Columbus. Dominican designs and materials are similar to those made today in the Orinoco valley—amazing considering that there's been no interaction between the two peoples for more than 500 years. The Carib basket you buy, therefore, is more than a souvenir; it's a link to the pre-Columbian Caribbean. You can buy Carib crafts directly from the craftspeople in the Carib Territory or at various outlets in Roseau. A small, 12-inch basket will cost about US$10, and you can get a bell-shaped model about 22 inches high for US$30 or US$35. Floor mats made from vertiver grass are another Dominican specialty.

At **Tropicrafts,** at the corner of Queen Mary Street and Turkey Lane in Roseau, you can watch local women weave grass mats with designs as varied and complex as those you made as a child with your Spirograph. The large store also stocks Carib baskets, locally made soaps and toiletries, rums, jellies, condiments, woodcarvings, and masks made from the trunks of giant fougère ferns. The **Rainforest Shop,** at 12 Old St. in Roseau, is dedicated to the preservation of Dominica's ecosystem and offers colorful hand-painted items made from recycled materials such as oil drums, coconut shells, and newspapers. The **Crazy Banana,** at 17 Castle St., features Dominican arts and crafts, including straw and ceramic items, as well as jewelry and Cuban cigars. For unique and sometimes whimsical objects, try **Balisier's** at 35 Great George St. Local artist Hilroy Fingal transforms throwaway items such as aluminum cans, perfume bottles, rocks, and coconut shells into things of beauty. His aesthetic is a little like Keith Haring's and every bit as fun. **Earl Etienne's Gallery** at 31 Cork St., is one of the island's oldest craft shops. Etienne, one of Dominica's leading artists, also showcases his paintings here. **Frontline Cooperative,** at 78 Independence, specializes in books about Caribbean peoples, issues, and cooking.

BEACHES

If your sole focus is beaches, you'll likely find Dominica disappointing. Much of the seacoast is rocky, and many sandy beaches have dark, volcanic sand. But there are golden sand beaches as well, primarily on the northern coast. Head for **Woodford Hill Bay, L'Ance Tortue, Pointe Baptiste,** or **Hampstead Beach;** all have honey-colored sand, palm trees, and azure waters protected by reefs or windswept headlands.

SPORTS

FISHING   Dominica is a prime destination for anglers looking to catch marlin, wahoo, yellowfin tuna, or dorado. The island's numerous rivers flow into the Caribbean Sea, providing an abundance of baitfish, including bonito, jacks, and small tuna that attract bigger deepwater species. **Gamefishing Dominica** (© 767/449-6638; www.gamefishingdominica.com) has two boats, a 10m (33-ft.) Luhrs and an 8.4m (28-ft.) Bayliner. Coastline fishing prices start at US$50 per person, with a four-passenger minimum. Deep-water half-day excursions are US$450 for up to six anglers.

SCUBA DIVING   Dominica's lush, beautiful scenery above water is echoed underwater in the surrounding Caribbean and Atlantic. Although the island is drained by hundreds of rivers and streams, the jagged volcanic undersea-scape prevents runoff sediment from clouding the water. Visibility ranges from 18m

(59 ft.) to more than 30m (98 ft.). Most local dive operations surpass international standards set by PADI, NAUI, and SSI, and small, uncrowded excursions are the norm. **Dive Dominica** (© **888/262-6611** in the U.S., or 767/448-2188) is perhaps the island's best operator. Single-tank boat dives run about US$45. First-time dives with instruction run about US$130.

SNORKELING Dominica offers almost 30 top-notch snorkeling areas, including the popular Champagne site. Snorkelers can join a dive-boat party, participate in special snorkel excursions, or explore the coast in a sea kayak, periodically jumping overboard for a look below. The calm water on the island's leeward side is perfect for viewing the riotous colors of the sponges, corals, and 190-plus fish species native to the area. Offshore snorkeling and equipment rental can be arranged through the dive operator listed above. Prices start at approximately US$25.

GREAT LOCAL RESTAURANTS & BARS

Seafood, local root vegetables referred to as "provisions," and Creole recipes are among the highlights of Dominican cuisine. *Crapaud* ("mountain chicken" in English, though it's really mountain frog) is the national delicacy. For a **local beer,** try Kubuli; for a **local rum,** try Soca or Macoucherie.

IN ROSEAU Try **La Robe Créole,** 3 Victoria St. (© 767/448-2896), which gets top marks for its callaloo soup (made from the spinachlike leaves of a local vegetable called dasheen, plus coconut), lobster and conch crepes, and mango chutney. The decor features heavy stone walls, solid ladder-back chairs, and colorful madras tablecloths. Lunch is about US$20. **Guiyave,** 15 Cork St. (© 767/448-2930), an airy restaurant on the second floor of a pistachio-colored wood-frame house, features steamed fish, conch, octopus, and spareribs. Take a table on the veranda and cool off with one of the fresh-squeezed juices. How about soursop, tamarind, sorrel, cherry, or strawberry? The downstairs takeout counter offers chicken patties, spicy *rotis,* and delectable tarts and cakes. Lunch is about US$13. **The Sutton Grille,** 25 Old St. (© 767/449-8700), in the Sutton Place Hotel, boasts an airy dining area ensconced in 100-year-old stone walls. You can choose a table a few steps up from the bustle of downtown Roseau or one set back from the action. The menu, a veritable primer of Creole and other West Indian cookery, also offers a generous sprinkling of international and vegetarian dishes. Lunch is about US$8.

IN PORTSMOUTH If you disembark in Portsmouth, get a table at the **Coconut Beach Restaurant,** near Picard Beach (© 767/445-5393). It overlooks the Caribbean Sea and the twin peaks of Cabrits National Park across Prince Rupert's Bay. The fresh seafood and Creole dishes taste even better with the tang of salt in the air. Lunch is about US$18. **The Purple Turtle** (© 767/445-5296) is closer to the dock and features lobster and crayfish, as well as lighter fare such as *rotis,* sandwiches, and salads. Lunch is about US$10.

15 Grand Cayman

Grand Cayman is the largest of the Cayman Islands, a British colony 773km (479 miles) due south of Miami (Cayman Brac and Little Cayman are the others). It's the top of an underwater mountain, whose side—known as the Cayman Wall—plummets straight down for 150m (492 ft.) before becoming a steep slope that falls away for 1,800m (5,904 ft.) to the ocean floor.

Frommer's Favorite Grand Cayman Experiences

Swimming with Stingrays: At Stingray City, you can hop into the water with dozens of these weird-looking but gentle sea creatures, which will swim right into your arms, like dogs. (See "Best Cruise Line Shore Excursions," below.)

Taking In the Scene on Seven Mile Beach: Grand Cayman's famed stretch of sand is known for its watersports and its translucent aquamarine waters. (See "Beaches," below.)

Despite its "grand" name, the island is only 35km (22 miles) long and 13km (8 miles) across at its widest point. Flat, relatively unattractive, and full of scrubland and swamp, Grand Cayman and its sister islands nevertheless boast more than their share of upscale, expensive private homes and condos, owned by millionaire expatriates from all over who come because of the tiny nation's lenient tax and banking laws. (Enron, the poster child of shady business dealings, reportedly had more than 690 different subsidiaries here to help it avoid paying U.S. taxes.)

Grand Cayman is also popular because of its laid-back civility—so civil that ships aren't allowed to visit on Sunday. George Town is the colony's capital and its commercial hub, and many hotels line the sands of the nation's most famous sunspot, **Seven Mile Beach.** Scuba divers and snorkelers come for the coral reefs and other formations, some of which lie within swimming distance of the shoreline.

COMING ASHORE   Cruise ships anchor off **George Town** and ferry their passengers to a pier on **Harbour Drive.** The short tender ride can be choppy, but the landing point couldn't be more convenient: You're let off right in the heart of the shopping district. There's a tourist information booth at the pier, and taxis line up to meet cruise ship passengers. There's a phone center for credit card calls on Cardinal Avenue, right in downtown.

LANGUAGE   **English** is the official language of the islands.

CURRENCY   The legal tender is the **Cayman Islands dollar** (C 82¢ = US$1; CI$1 = US$1.25), but U.S. dollars are commonly accepted. Be sure to note which currency price tags refer to before making a purchase. Prices in this section are given in U.S. dollars.

INFORMATION   The **Department of Tourism** is in the Pavilion Building, Cricket Square (P.O. Box 67), George Town, Grand Cayman, BWI (© **800/ 346-3313** or 345/949-0623). It's open Monday to Friday from 9am to 5pm. To get info before you go, contact the **Cayman Islands Department of Tourism** in New York (© **212/889-9009;** www.caymanislands.ky).

CALLING FROM THE U.S.   When calling Grand Cayman from the U.S., you need only dial a "1" before the numbers listed here.

GETTING AROUND
BY TAXI   Taxi fares are fixed; typical one-way fares range from US$12 to US$20. **Holiday Taxi** (© **345/947-1066**) offers 24-hour service.

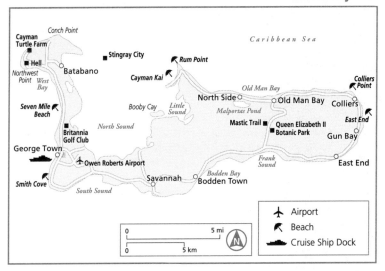

BY RENTAL CAR The roads are good by Caribbean standards, so driving around is relatively easy, as long as you remember to drive on the left side of the road. Avis, Budget, Dollar, and Hertz all have offices here.

BY MOTOR SCOOTER OR BICYCLE The terrain is relatively flat, so motor scooters and bicycles are another way to get around. **Soto Scooters Ltd.,** Seven Mile Beach (② **345/945-4465**), at Coconut Place, offers Honda Elite scooters for about $30 daily, and bicycles for $15 daily.

BEST CRUISE LINE SHORE EXCURSIONS

Cruise lines typically offer about 30 shore excursions here, most of them of the swimming, snorkeling, sailing, submarine, and glass-bottom boat variety.

Stingray City (US$45–US$55, 2–3 hr.): The waters off Grand Cayman are home to Stingray City, one of the world's most unusual underwater attractions. Set in the very shallow waters of North Sound, about 2 miles east of the island's northwestern tip, the site was discovered in the mid-1980s when local fishermen noticed that scores of stingrays were showing up to feed on the offal they dumped overboard. Today, anywhere from 30 to 100 relatively tame stingrays swarm around the hundreds of visiting snorkelers like so many aquatic basset hounds, eager for handouts. Stingrays are terribly gentle creatures, and love to have their bellies rubbed, but never try to grab one by the tail—their barbed stingers can inflict a lot of pain.

Research Submarine Dive (US$395, 1½ hr.): A real research sub takes two passengers at a time down 240m (800 ft.) to explore the Cayman Wall through a 1m (3-ft.) viewing window. Powerful lights illuminate the sponge belt at 120m (400 ft.), and delicate coral and deep-sea creatures can be sighted even further down. Those not quite so adventurous can sign up for the **Atlantis Submarine Excursion** (US$86, 1½ hr.), in which a 48-passenger sub takes you down to 30m (100 ft.) through coral canyons, with an automatic fish feeder drawing swarms of colorful marine creatures.

Island Bicycle Tour (US$69, 3 hr.): A great way to really get a feel for an island—and get some exercise—is via bicycle. You pick up your touring mountain bike at the Beach Club Colony Hotel, ride along the coastline for views of Seven Mile Beach, and then journey inland en route to the north side of the island to ride along the coast again.

EXCURSIONS OFFERED BY LOCAL AGENCIES

Stingray City: If the tours on your ship get booked, about half a dozen entrepreneurs lead expeditions to Stingray City, and usually a few tour agents wait around the terminal in George Town to snare cruise passengers as they debark. One well-known outfit is **Treasure Island Divers** (② 800/872-7552 from the U.S., 345/949-4456; www.tidivers.com), which charges US$30 per person for stingray snorkeling excursions.

Taxi Tours: If you want to see the island, you can grab a taxi in port and take a tour. Taxis should cost about $40 per hour and can hold up to five people. A 3-hour tour covers all the sights in a leisurely fashion. Make sure to stop in the town called Hell and send a postcard home.

ON YOUR OWN: WITHIN WALKING DISTANCE

In George Town, the **Cayman Islands National Museum,** Harbour Drive (② 345/949-8368; www.museum.ky) is housed in a veranda-fronted building that once served as the island's courthouse. Exhibits include Caymanian artifacts collected by Ira Thompson (beginning in the 1930s), and other items relating to the natural, social, and cultural history of the Caymans. There's a gift shop, theater, and cafe. Admission is US$5 for adults and US$2.50 for students and seniors. Hours are 9am to 5pm Monday through Friday, 10am to 2pm on Saturdays.

ON YOUR OWN: BEYOND THE PORT AREA

The only green-sea-turtle farm of its kind in the world, **Cayman Turtle Farm,** Northwest Point (② 345/949-3894; www.turtle.ky), is the island's most popular land-based tourist attraction. Once upon a time a multitude of turtles lived in the waters surrounding the Cayman Islands, but today these creatures are an endangered species. The turtle farm's purpose is twofold: to replenish the waters with hatchlings and yearling turtles and, at the other end of the spectrum, to provide the local market with edible turtle meat. You can peer into 100 circular concrete tanks containing turtles ranging in size from 6 ounces to 600 pounds, or sample turtle dishes at a snack bar and restaurant. The farm is open from 8:30am to 5pm daily. Admission is US$6 for adults, US$3 for children 6 to 12; children under 6 are free.

On 26 hectares (64 acres) of rugged wooded land, **Queen Elizabeth II Botanic Park,** off Frank Sound Road, North Side (② 345/947-9462), offers visitors a 1-hour walk along a short (1.2km/.75-mile) trail through wetlands, swamps, dry thicket, and mahogany trees. You may spot hickatees (the freshwater turtles found only on the Caymans and in Cuba), the rare Grand Cayman parrot, or the anole lizard, with its cobalt-blue throat pouch. There are six rest stations along the trail, plus a visitor center and a canteen. There's also a heritage garden, a floral garden, and a lake. Hours are 9am to 6:30pm daily.

The **Mastic Trail,** west of Frank Sound Road, is a restored 200-year-old footpath through a 2-million-year-old woodland area in the heart of the island. Named for the majestic mastic tree, the trail showcases the reserve's natural attractions, including a native mangrove swamp, traditional agriculture, and an ancient woodland area. You can follow the 3.2km (2-mile) trail on your own, but we recommend taking a 3-hour guided tour. Call © **345/945-6588** to make a reservation. The trail, adjacent to the Botanical Park, is about a 45-minute drive from George Town.

SHOPPING

There's duty-free shopping here for silver, china, crystal, Irish linens, and British woolen goods, but we've found most prices to be similar to those in the United States. You'll also find cigar shops and international chains such as Coach, the leather-goods store. Please don't succumb and purchase turtle or black-coral products. You'll see them everywhere, but it's illegal to bring them back into the United States and most other Western nations.

Some standout shops include **Artifacts Ltd.,** Harbour Drive, on the harbor front, across from the landing dock (© **345/949-2442**), for back issues of Cayman stamps; **The Jewelry Centre,** Cardinal Avenue (© **345/949-0070**), one of the largest jewelry stores in the Caymans; and the **Kennedy Gallery West Shore Centre** (© **345/949-8077**), specializing in paintings and sculptures by local artists.

BEACHES

Grand Cayman's **Seven Mile Beach,** which begins north of George Town, is an easy taxi ride from the cruise dock and has sparkling white sands with a backdrop of Casuarina trees. The beach is really about 8.9km (5½ miles) long, but who are we to quibble with tradition? It's lined with condominiums and plush resorts, and is known for its array of watersports and its translucent aquamarine waters. The average water temperature is a balmy 80°F (27°C).

SPORTS

SCUBA DIVING & SNORKELING   Coral reefs and other formations encircle the island and are filled with marine life. It's easy to dive close to shore, so boats aren't necessary, but plenty of boats and scuba facilities are available, as well as many dive shops renting scuba gear to certified divers. The best dive operation is **Bob Soto's Reef Divers,** P.O. Box 1801, Grand Cayman, BWI (© **800/262-7686** for reservations, or 345/949-2022; www.bobsotosreefdivers. com), with full-service dive shops at Treasure Island, the Scuba Centre on North Church Street, and Soto's Coconut in the Coconut Place Shopping Centre. There are full-day resort courses as well as excursions for experienced divers daily on the west, north, and south walls, plus shore diving from the Scuba Centre. The staff is helpful and highly professional.

GREAT LOCAL RESTAURANTS & BARS

A favorite local beer is Stingray, and a favorite local rum is Tortuga.

Paradise Bar and Grill, on Harbour Drive (© **345/945-1444**), is less than a kilometer's (less than a ½-mile's) walk south of the pier. It's a great open-air seaside cafe for a sandwich, chicken fingers, and a couple of cool Stingray beers or a frozen drink. **Cracked Conch by the Sea,** West Bay Road, near Turtle Bay Farm (© **345/945-5217**), serves some of the island's freshest seafood, including the inevitable conch, plus meat dishes such as beef, jerk pork, and spicy combinations of chicken. Lunch is about US$12. **The Crow's Nest Restaurant,** South Sound, on the southwesternmost tip of the island, a 4-minute drive from George Town (© **345/949-9366**), is one of those places that evokes the Caribbean "the way it used to be." There's no pretense here—you get good, honest Caribbean cookery, including grilled seafood, at great prices. Many dishes are spicy, especially their signature appetizer—fiery coconut shrimp. Lunch is about US$15.

Ottmar's Restaurant and Lounge, West Bay Road (© **345/945-5879**), is one of the island's top restaurants for dinner, offering such dishes as Bavarian cucumber soup; bouillabaisse; French pepper steak; Wiener schnitzel; and chicken Trinidad, stuffed with grapes, nuts, and apples, rolled in coconut flakes, sautéed golden brown, and served in orange-butter sauce.

16 Grenada

The southernmost nation of the British Windwards, Grenada (Gre-*nay*-dah) is one of the lushest places in the Caribbean. Called the "Spice Island," it has extravagant fertility—a result of the gentle climate and volcanic soil—that produces more spices than anywhere else in the world: clove, cinnamon, mace, cocoa, tonka beans, ginger, and a third of the world's supply of nutmeg. The beaches are white and sandy, and the populace (a mixture of English expatriates and islanders of African descent) is friendly. Once a British Crown Colony but now independent, the island nation also incorporates two smaller islands: Carriacou and Petite Martinique, neither of which has many tourist facilities.

St. George's, the country's capital, is one of the most colorful ports in the West Indies. Nearly landlocked in the deep crater of a long-dead volcano, and flanked by old forts, it reminds many visitors of Portofino, Italy. Here you'll see some of the most charming Georgian colonial buildings in the Caribbean, many with red-tile roofs (the tiles were brought by European trade ships as ballast) and pastel walls. Churches dot the hillside of the harbor. Frangipani and flamboyant trees add even more color.

Crisscrossed by nature trails, Grenada's interior is a jungle of palms, oleander, bougainvillea, purple and red hibiscus, crimson anthurium, bananas, breadfruit, bird-song, ferns, and palms. The island's lush tropical scenery and natural bounty attract visitors who want to snorkel, sail, fish, hike on jungle paths, or loll the day away on the 3.2km (2-mile) white-sand Grand Anse Beach, one of the best in the Caribbean.

COMING ASHORE Ships either dock at a pier right in **St. George's** or anchor in the much-photographed harbor and send their passengers to the pier by tender. A tourist information center at the pier dispenses island data. The Carenage (St. George's main street) is only a short walk away from the pier; a taxi into the center of town costs about US$3. To get to Grand Anse, you can take a regular taxi or a water taxi (see "Getting Around," below).

You'll find a pair of credit card phones for international calls inside the small cruise terminal and two more just outside of it. There are six more London-style red phone booths midway around the Carenage, less than a half mile from the terminal.

LANGUAGE **English** is commonly spoken on this island. **Creole English,** a mixture of African, English, and French, is spoken informally by a small percentage of the population.

CURRENCY The official currency is the Eastern Caribbean dollar (EC$2.70 = US$1; EC$1 = US73¢). Always determine which dollars—EC or U.S.—you're talking about when discussing a price. Credit cards and traveler's checks are commonly accepted in tourist areas. Unless otherwise specified, all prices in this section are given in U.S. dollars.

INFORMATION Go to the **Grenada Board of Tourism,** on the Carenage in St. George's (© **800/927-9554** or 473/440-2279), for maps and general

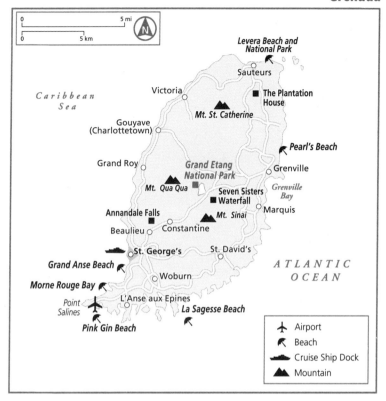

information. It's open Monday to Friday from 9am to 5pm. To get information before you go, contact the **Grenada Tourism Board** in New York (© **212/687-9554;** www.grenadagrenadines.com).

CALLING FROM THE U.S. When calling Grenada from the United States, you need only dial a "1" before the numbers listed here.

GETTING AROUND

St. George's can easily be explored on foot, although parts of the town are steep as the streets rise up from the harbor.

BY TAXI Taxi fares are set by the government. Most cruisers take a cab from the pier to somewhere near St. George's. You can also tap most taxi drivers as a guide for a day's sightseeing. The charge is about US$25 per hour (for a group of one to four persons); be sure to negotiate a price before setting out, and make sure you're both talking about the same currency. From the pier to Grand Anse Beach is about US$12 per carload (of up to four).

BY MINIVAN Minivans, used mostly by locals, charge EC$1 to EC$6 (US75¢–US$4.40). Most minivans depart from Market Square or from the Esplanade area of St. George's. The most popular run is between St. George's and Grand Anse Beach.

BY WATER TAXI Water taxis are an ideal way to get around the harbor and to Grand Anse Beach (the round-trip fare is about US$4) or from one end of

Frommer's Favorite Grenada Experiences

Hiking to the Seven Sisters Waterfalls: This is a hearty walk along a muddy path that winds through the thick, pristine jungle. At the end of the approximately 1.6km-long (1-mile) trail, there's a set of beautiful waterfalls. You can even jump from the tops of two of them into the pools below. (See "Best Cruise Line Shore Excursions," below.)

Visiting Levera National Park: With beaches, coral reefs, a mangrove swamp, a lake, and a bird sanctuary, this is a paradise for hikers, swimmers, and snorkelers alike. (See "On Your Own: Beyond the Port Area," below.)

Taking the Rainforest and Grand Etang Lake Tour: Take a bus to an extinct volcanic crater some 570m (1,870 ft.) above sea level. On the way, drive through rainforests and stop at a spice estate. (See "Best Cruise Line Shore Excursions," below.)

Picnicking at Annandale Falls: A 15m (49-ft.) cascade is the perfect backdrop for a picnic among tropical flora—and you can swim in the falls afterward. (See "On Your Own: Beyond the Port Area," below.)

the Carenage to the other (for another US$2). Look for them on the Carenage by the cruise ship welcome center.

BY RENTAL CAR   We don't recommend driving here, as the roads are very narrow and winding.

BEST CRUISE LINE SHORE EXCURSIONS

Because of Grenada's lush landscape, we recommend spending at least a few hours touring its interior, one of the most scenic in the West Indies.

Hike to Seven Sisters Waterfalls (US$59, 3½ hr.): After a 40-minute hike along a muddy path in the lush Grand Etang rainforest, passengers are free to take a swim in the natural pools or hop off the edge of the cascading waterfalls. It's gorgeous and lots of fun. Don't forget to wear your bathing suit and maybe a pair of Teva-type sandals.

Rainforest/Grand Etang Lake Tour (US$34–US$39, 3–4½ hr.): This is a great way to experience Grenada's lush, cool, dripping-wet tropical interior. Via bus, you travel past the red-tiled roofs of St. George's en route to the bright blue Grand Etang Lake, within an extinct volcanic crater some 570m (1,870 ft.) above sea level. On the way, you drive through rainforests and stop at a spice estate. Some tours include a visit to Annandale Falls and Fort Frederick.

ON YOUR OWN: WITHIN WALKING DISTANCE

In St. George's, you can visit the **Grenada National Museum,** at the corner of Young and Monckton streets (© **473/440-3725**), set in the foundations of an old French army barracks and prison built in 1704. Small but interesting, it houses ancient petroglyphs and other archaeological finds, a rum still, and various Grenada memorabilia, including the island's first telegraph and two notable bathtubs: the wooden barrel used by the fort's prisoners and the carved marble tub used by Joséphine Bonaparte during her adolescence on Martinique. The most comprehensive exhibit illuminates the native culture of Grenada. The museum is open 9am to 4:30pm Monday to Friday, and 10am to 1pm Saturday; admission is US$2.50 for adults and US50¢ for children.

If you're up for a good hike, walk around the historical Carenage from the cruise terminal and head up to **Fort George,** built in 1705 by the French and originally called Fort Royal. (You can pick up a rudimentary walking-tour map from the cruise terminal to help you find interesting sites along the way.) While the fort ruins and the 200- to 300-year-old canons are worth taking a peek at, it's the 360-degree panoramic views of the entire harbor area that are most spectacular, taking in your ship, the sea, and many of the red-tile-roofed buildings dotting the island. Don't forget your camera! Before or after a visit to the fort, be sure to walk along Church Street (which leads right to the fort) as far as St. Johns or Juille Street. Along the way, you'll see lots of quaint 18th- and 19th-century architecture framed by brilliant flowering plants; examples of Grenada's sedan porches, open-ended porches originally used as potte-cocheres to keep residents dry when going between house and carriage; **St. Andrew's Presbyterian Church,** built in 1831 with the help of the Freemasons; **St. George's Anglican Church,** built in 1825 by the British; the **Houses of Parliament;** and the **Roman Catholic Cathedral,** rebuilt in 1884 (the tower dates back to 1818).

ON YOUR OWN: BEYOND THE PORT AREA

You can take a taxi up Richmond Hill to **Fort Frederick,** which the French began building in 1779. The British retook the island in 1783 and completed the fort in 1791. From its battlements you'll have a panoramic view of the harbor and the yacht marina.

Don't miss the mountains northeast of St. George's. If you don't have much time, **Annandale Falls,** a tropical wonderland where a 15m-high (49-ft.) cascade drops into a basin, is just a 15-minute drive away, on the outskirts of the **Grand Etang Forest Reserve.** The overall beauty is almost Tahitian. You can have a picnic surrounded by liana vines, elephant ears, and other tropical flora and spices. Annandale Falls Centre offers gift items, handicrafts, and samples of the island's indigenous spices. Nearby, a trail leads to the falls, where you can enjoy a refreshing swim. If you've got more time and want a less crowded spot, the even better **Seven Sisters Waterfalls** are farther into Grand Etang, an approximately 30-minute drive and then a 1.6km or so (1-mile) hike along a muddy trail. It's well worth the trip and you'll really get a feel for the power and beauty of the tropical forest here. The falls themselves are lovely, and you can even climb to the top and jump off into the pool below. Be careful, though: It's awfully slippery on those rocks. If you want to skip the jumping, you can still enjoy a relaxing swim in the cool water after the sweaty hike.

Opened in 1994, 180-hectare (445-acre) **Levera National Park** has several white-sandy beaches for swimming and snorkeling, although the surf is rough. Offshore are coral reefs and sea-grass beds. Inland, the park contains a mangrove swamp, a lake, and a bird sanctuary—perhaps you'll see a rare tropical parrot. It's a hiker's paradise. The interpretation center (© **473/442-1018**) is open Monday to Sunday from 8am to 4pm. About 24km (15 miles) from the harbor, the park can be reached by taxi, bus, or water taxi.

SHOPPING

The local stores sell luxury imports, mainly from England, at prices that are not quite down at duty-free level. This is no grand Caribbean merchandise mart, so if you're cruising on to such islands as Aruba, St. Martin, or St. Thomas, you might want to postpone serious purchases. On the other hand, you can find some fine local handicrafts, gifts, and art here.

Spice vendors besiege you wherever you go, including just outside of the cruise terminal. If you're not interested, a polite "I just bought some from another vendor" usually works. But you really should take at least a few samples home with you. The spices here are fresher and better than any you're likely to find in your local supermarket, so nearly everybody comes home with a hand-woven basket full of them. Nutmeg products are especially popular. The Grenadians use every part of the nutmeg: They make the outer fruit into a tasty liqueur and a rich jam, and ground the orange membrane around the nut into a different spice called mace. You'll see the outer shells used as gravel to cover trails and parking lots. **Arawak Islands,** Upper Belmont Road, has different fragrances distilled from such island plants as frangipani, wild lilies, cinnamon, nutmeg, and cloves. You'll also find body oils, soaps, an all-natural insect repellent that some clients insist is the most effective (and safest) they're ever used, and some mighty fine hot sauce. We regretted not buying more the last time we were there, but then we found their mail-order website (www.arawak-islands.com).

Some worthwhile shops include **Art Fabrik,** Young Street (© **473/440-0568**), for batik shirts, shifts, shorts, skirts, T-shirts, and the like; **Sea Change Bookstore** (© **473/440-3402**), the **Carenage,** for recent British and American newspapers; and **Tikal,** Young Street (© **473/440-2310**), for handicrafts from Grenada and around the world.

BEACHES
Grenada's **Grand Anse Beach,** with its 3.2km (2 miles) of wide sugar-white sands, is one of the best beaches in the Caribbean, with calm waters and a great view of St. George's to make the scene complete. There are several restaurants beachside, and you can join a banana-boat ride or rent a Sunfish sailboat. From the port, it's about a 10-minute, US$10 taxi ride, although you can also take a water taxi from the pier for only US$4 round-trip.

SPORTS
SCUBA DIVING & SNORKELING   Grenada offers an underwater world rich in marine gardens, exotic fish, and coral formations. Visibility is often up to 36m (118 ft.). Off the coast is the wreck of the nearly 180m (590-ft.) ocean liner *Bianca C.* Novice divers should stick to the west coast; the more experienced might search out the sites along the rougher Atlantic side. **Sanvic's Watersports,** directly on the beach in the Grenada Grand Beach Resort, Grand Anse Beach (© **473/444-4371,** ext. 638), is the premier scuba-diving outfit, also offering snorkeling trips. They will pick you up at the pier in a courtesy bus and bring you back to the cruise ship later. American-run **Eco-Dive,** at Coyaba Beach Resort on Grand Anse Beach (© **473/444-7777**), gives Sanvic's serious competition, offering scuba diving and snorkeling jaunts to reefs and shipwrecks teeming with marine life. Diving instruction is available. (*Note:* Grenada doesn't have a decompression chamber. In the event of an emergency, divers must be taken to the facilities on Barbados or Trinidad.)

GREAT LOCAL RESTAURANTS & BARS
A favorite local beer is Carib; a favorite local rum is Clarkecourt.

Your last chance to enjoy food from old-time island recipes, many now fading from cultural memory, may be at **The Plantation House** (aka the Betty Mascoll Morne Fendue Plantation House), at St. Patrick's (© **473/442-9330**),

40km (25 miles) north of St. George's. The house was built in 1912 of chiseled river rocks held together by a mixture of lime and molasses. Betty Mascoll was born that same year and lived here right up until her recent death. You dine as an upper-class family did in the 1920s. Lunch is likely to include a yam-and-sweet-potato casserole or curried chicken with lots of island-grown spices. The most famous dish is the legendary pepper-pot stew, which includes pork and oxtail, tenderized by the juice of grated cassava. The new proprietor, Dr. Jean Thompson, and the veteran staff need time to prepare, so it's imperative to call ahead. They serve a fixed-price (US$16) lunch Monday to Saturday from 12:30 to 3pm.

The Nutmeg, the Carenage, located right on the harbor over the Sea Change Shop (© 473/440-2539), is a casual hangout for the yachting set and a favorite of expatriates and visitors. The menu is extensive. Lunch is about US$10.

Rudolf's, the Carenage (© 473/440-2241), serves great steak, flying fish, and mahimahi, and prepares conch and shrimp in several different ways. Lunch is about US$16.

17 Guadeloupe

Take the things you love about France—sophistication, great food, and an appreciation of the good things in life—add the best of the Caribbean—nice beaches, a relaxed pace, and warm, friendly people—and combine with efficiency and modern convenience. Voilà! Guadeloupe. And once you leave the crowded, narrow streets of Pointe-à-Pitre, the commercial center and main port, you'll see that the island is more developed and modern than many others in the region.

Guadeloupe's **Creole cuisine,** a mélange of French culinary expertise, African cooking, and Caribbean ingredients, is reason enough to get off the ship, regardless of how much you're enjoying the food on board. And if **shopping** is your favorite sport, you'll have ample opportunity to stock up on French perfumes, clothes, and other luxury products. For the more adventurous, there's a volcano, scuba diving, surfing, and hiking to spectacular mountain waterfalls. Of course, you can always work on your tan at one of the island's many beaches. Or maybe you just want to sit at a sidewalk cafe, sip your espresso while glancing through a copy of *Le Monde,* and watch the world go by.

Guadeloupe, the political entity, is an overseas region of France that includes the islands of St. Barts, St. Martin, Les Saintes, La Désirade, Marie-Galante, and Guadeloupe itself. The name Guadeloupe, however, usually refers to two contiguous islands—Basse-Terre and Grande-Terre—separated by a narrow seawater channel, the Rivière Salée. Nestled between Antigua and Dominica, these two islands are shaped like a 1,373-sq.-km (535-sq.-mile) butterfly. The eastern wing, the limestone island of Grande-Terre, is known for its white-sand beaches, rolling hills, sugar-cane fields, and resort areas. Pointe-à-Pitre, your port of debarkation, is here. The butterfly's larger, volcanic western wing, Basse-Terre, is dominated by the National Park of Guadeloupe, a mountainous rainforest replete with waterfalls and La Soufrière, a brooding, still occasionally troublesome volcano. The capital of Guadeloupe, also called Basse-Terre, is at the southern tip of this western wing.

Almost half of Guadeloupe's population of 410,000 is under the age of 20. About 80% of Guadeloupeans are descended from African slaves, with people of European and East Indian ancestry making up most of the remaining 20%.

Today, sugar and rum are the island's main exports.

COMING ASHORE Cruise ships dock at the modern **Centre Saint-John Perse,** adjacent to downtown Pointe-à-Pitre, Grande-Terre's main city. The terminal has shops, restaurants, cafes, a small tourist office, and phones.

LANGUAGE French is the official language, but you'll often hear islanders speaking a local **Creole** among themselves. Don't expect to get too far with only English unless you're at one of the busier tourist areas. Bring a phrase book. Guadeloupeans are nice people; meet them halfway.

CURRENCY Guadeloupe is an overseas region of France, so the **euro** (€) is now the official currency (exchange rate at press time: 1€ = US$1.22; $1 = .82€). Each euro is divisible by 100 cents. There are numerous **ATMs** *(distributeur de billets)* in downtown Pointe-à-Pitre. You'll have no trouble using your credit cards. Unless otherwise specified, prices in this section are given in U.S. dollars.

INFORMATION The main **tourist office** (Office du Tourisme) in Pointe-à-Pitre is at 5 Square de la Banque, a 5-minute walk from the port (© 590/82-09-30), and is open Monday to Friday from 8am to 5pm, Saturday 8am to noon. If you want information before you leave home, visit www.frenchcaribbean.com.

CALLING FROM THE U.S. When calling Guadeloupe from the United States, dial the international access code (011) and 590 before the numbers listed in this section. The numbers listed already have a 590 prefix, but that's not the same 590: You have to dial 590 twice (bureaucracy in France is just as inscrutable as anywhere). **Telecartes** phone cards make local and international calls easier and less expensive. They're sold at post offices and other outlets marked TELECARTE EN VENTE ICI and are used in phone booths (marked TELECOM) found all over. Many phones accept Visa, MasterCard, and other credit cards for long-distance calls.

GETTING AROUND

BY TAXI Metered taxis await cruise passengers at the Pointe-à-Pitre pier. Rates are regulated, but they can be expensive. Taxis can be hired for private tours, but you'll have a hard time finding a driver who speaks English. Negotiate a price before setting out, and make sure all terms are clear to avoid an unpleasant scene later. One recommended driver is **Alain Narcisse,** an enthusiastic, knowledgeable, English-speaking guide who offers tours of Grande-Terre, northern Basse-Terre, and southern Basse-Terre. He's often booked, so make arrangements in advance by calling © 590/94-55-95. General **radio cab dispatch numbers** include © 590/20-74-74, 590/82-96-69, and 590/83-09-55.

BY BUS Buses are inexpensive, comfortable, and efficient. Almost all play *zouk,* an upbeat local music (at reasonable decibel levels), and some have videos. Signs (ARRET-BUS) indicate bus stops, but you can wave down a driver anywhere along the road. Pay the driver or the conductor as you get off. The fare from Pointe-à-Pitre to Gosier is just over $1.

BY RENTAL CAR Guadeloupe's road system is one of the best in the Caribbean, and traffic regulations and road signs are the same as elsewhere in France. Driving is on the right. Reserve a car before leaving home, especially during the high season. **Avis, Budget, Hertz,** and **Thrifty** all have offices on the island. Your valid driver's license from home will be honored. Almost all rentals have standard transmissions. Be forewarned that Guadeloupeans are skillful but aggressive drivers; don't tarry in the passing lane.

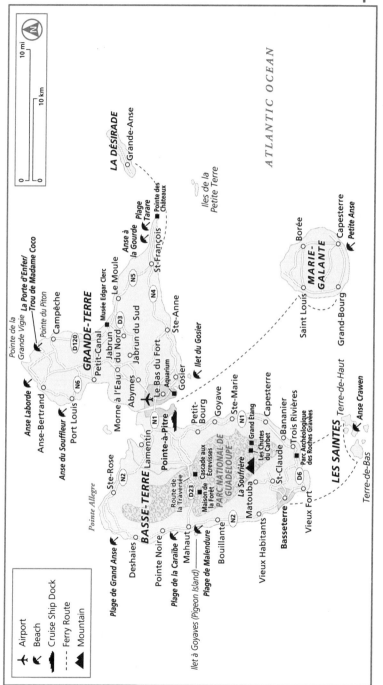

ATLANTIC OCEAN

LA DÉSIRADE

Grande-Anse

Îles de la
Petite Terre

Pointe de la
Grande Vigie
La Porte d'Enfer/
Trou de Madame Coco
Pointe du Piton

Campêche

GRANDE-TERRE

D120

Petit-Canal
Jabrun
du Nord
Musée Edgar Clerc
Le Moule
Morne à l'Eau
D3
N5
Plage
Tarare
Pointe des
Châteaux
Anse à
la Gourde
St-François

Jabrun du Sud
N4
Ste-Anne
Abymes
Le Bas du Fort
Aquarium
Gosier
Îlet du Gosier

Anse Laborde
Anse-Bertrand
N6
Port Louis

MARIE-
GALANTE
Borée
Capesterre
Petite Anse

Saint Louis
Grand-Bourg

Anse du Souffleur

Pointe Allègre

Ste-Rose
N2
Lamentin
Pointe-à-Pitre
N1
Petit-
Bourg
Goyave
Ste-Marie
Grand Étang
N1
Capesterre
Bananier
Trois Rivières
Parc Archéologique
des Roches Gravées

LES SAINTES
Terre-de-Haut
Anse Crawen

Terre-de-Bas

BASSE-TERRE
Deshaies
Route de
la Traversée
D23
Cascade aux
Écrevisses
Maison de
la Forêt
PARC NATIONAL DE
GUADELOUPE
Les Chutes
du Carbet
La Soufrière
Matouba
St-Claude
D6
Vieux Habitants
Basseterre
Vieux Fort

Pointe Noire
N2
Mahaut
Bouillante

Plage de Grand Anse
Plage de la Caraïbe
Plage de Malendure

Îlet à Goyaves (Pigeon Island)

Îlet du Gosier

Legend:
- ✈ Airport
- ⚓ Beach
- Cruise Ship Dock
- --- Ferry Route
- ▲ Mountain

0   10 mi
0   10 km

N

Frommer's Favorite Guadeloupe Experiences

Climbing a Volcano: Draped in thousands of banana trees and other lush foliage, La Soufrière rises 1,440m (4,723 ft.) above the surrounding sea and dominates the island of Basse-Terre. You can drive to a parking area at La Savane à Mulets, then hike the final 450m (1,476 ft; 2 arduous hr.) right to the mouth of the volcano. (See "On Your Own: Beyond the Port Area," below.)

Touring Grande-Terre's Atlantic Coast: Drive out to Grande-Terre's eastern extreme, La Pointe des Châteaux, to watch the Atlantic and Caribbean vent their fury on the rocky shore. Continue up the coast to La Porte d'Enfer and La Pointe de la Grande Vigie for splendid views of limestone cliffs and sparkling aquamarine waters. (See "On Your Own: Beyond the Port Area," below.)

Soaking Up the French-Caribbean Ambience: Walk the streets of Pointe-à-Pitre. Browse through the stores and maybe buy some perfume or "thigh-reducing cream" from one of the upscale pharmacies (look for the neon green cross). Pick up a newspaper; find a shady table at a sidewalk cafe; order a cold, fresh fruit juice; and luxuriate in your blessed life.

BEST CRUISE LINE SHORE EXCURSIONS

La Soufrière Volcano Trek ($59, 5½ hr.): Located in the Parc National de la Guadeloupe, the still-simmering La Soufrière volcano rises to 1,440m (4,723 ft.), flanked by banana plantations and lush vegetation. In 1975, ashes, mud, billowing smoke, and tremors proved that the volcano is still active, and today you can smell sulfurous fumes and feel the heat through the soil as steam spews from the fumaroles. An hour-long uphill hike takes you to the summit, which looks like another planet.

Carbet Falls ($44, 4 hr.): After driving through the banana plantations and rainforests of Basse-Terre's south side, hike 30 minutes to picturesque Carbet Falls, where you're free to swim in the refreshing water. Wear sturdy walking shoes.

Pigeon Island ($55, 4½ hr.): First pass through Guadeloupe's National Park, a lush and mountainous tropical rainforest, on the Route de la Traversée. At Pigeon Island, board a glass-bottom boat for a 90-minute ride around a beautiful coral reef now designated the Cousteau Underwater Reserve. Marvel at the numerous fish, corals, and other marine life.

EXCURSIONS OFFERED BY LOCAL AGENCIES

Hiking Tours: Basse-Terre's **Parc National (National Park)** has 322km (200 miles) of well-marked trails. Some meander through tropical rainforests to waterfalls and mountain pools; others focus on the La Soufrière volcano, geology, animals, and vegetation. Free maps and brochures in English can be obtained from the **National Park Office,** Habitation Beausoleil, Montéran, Boite Postal 13, St-Claude 97120 (© **590/80-24-25**). The park office will also provide visitors with a list of local agencies offering excursions.

Snorkeling Tours: To snorkel in the Cousteau Underwater Reserve, contact **Nautilus** (© **590/98-89-08**) or **Aquarus** (© **590/98-87-30**), both located at the Bouillante town dock, south of Malendure. They offer guided tours in glass-bottom boats several times daily; at least 15 minutes is reserved for snorkeling and refreshments (about 90 min., $25–$30).

ON YOUR OWN: WITHIN WALKING DISTANCE

The little trolley that meets cruise ship passengers at the port is supposed to provide hassle-free transportation around Pointe-à-Pitre. Unfortunately, it's no match for the city's traffic and narrow roads. Unless you enjoy traffic jams, walk. It's a better way to browse, shop, and visit the museums.

Pointe-à-Pitre's narrow streets and congested sidewalks are bustling with activity, and its markets are among the Caribbean's most colorful. The largest, **Marché St. Antoine,** at the corner of rues Frébault and Peynier, is well known for its playful, sassy vendors, who sell tropical produce and spices in madras bags. **Marché de la Darse,** on the waterfront at the foot of place de la Banque, offers exotic fruits, vegetables, and souvenirs. The **place Gourbeyre Flower Market,** next to the cathedral, is ablaze with tropical blooms, including roses de porcelaine and alpinias. Lined with royal palms, scarlet flamboyants, and travelers palms, the renovated **place de la Victoire** commemorates Victor Hugues' defeat of the English in 1794. It's the largest public space in town and is bordered with restaurants and cafes. The nearby **Cathedral of St-Pierre and St-Paul,** built in 1871, has an iron framework designed to withstand earthquakes and hurricanes. Three churches destroyed by successive earthquakes form its foundation. The **Musée Municipal Saint-John Perse,** 9 rue de Nozières, near the corner of rue Achille-René Boisneuf (© **590/90-01-92**), chronicles the life of native son Alexis Léger, who won the Nobel Prize for literature under the nom de plume "Saint-John Perse" in 1960. The museum is housed in one of the city's most beautifully restored colonial mansions, an urban chalet that features ornate friezes, voluted consoles, and wrought-iron galleries. Open windows allow breezes into the main parlor, which is furnished with bourgeois furniture. In addition to many of the poet's personal effects, the museum boasts photographs documenting Guadeloupean life from the turn of the 20th century through the 1930s; you can buy postcards of some of them in the museum gift shop. The museum is open Monday to Friday from 9am to 5pm, Saturday 8:30am to 12:30pm. Admission is about $2 for adults, half price for students.

The **Musée Schoelcher,** 24 rue Peynier (© **590/82-08-04**), tells the story of Victor Schoelcher, the key figure in the move to abolish slavery in Guadeloupe. The powerful exhibit, housed in a renovated mansion, includes a slave-ship model, a miniature guillotine, china from Bordeaux with scenes from *Uncle Tom's Cabin,* and racist caricatures published in Parisian journals. Particularly moving is an 1845 census document that lists slaves as nothing more than plantation animals. It's open Monday to Friday from 9am to 5pm; admission is $2, half that for students and children.

ON YOUR OWN: BEYOND THE PORT AREA

Guadeloupe is too large to tour in 1 day. You'll have to choose among Grande-Terre, northern Basse-Terre, and southern Basse-Terre.

GRANDE-TERRE

The **Aquarium de la Guadeloupe,** near the Bas du Fort Marina just east of Pointe-à-Pitre (© **590/90-92-38**), is compact but has an impressive collection of exotic fish, corals, and sponges from the Caribbean and the Pacific. Come face to face with hugging sea horses, sleeping nurse sharks, and graceful sea turtles. Don't miss the polka-dot grouper known as *mérou de Grace Kelly.* Explanatory markers are in both French and English. The souvenir shop sells hand-painted folk art, jewelry, and fish- and sea-themed trinkets and T-shirts. It's open daily from 9am to 7pm; admission is about $8 for adults, $2.75 for children under 4.

La Pointe des Châteaux (Castle Point), at Grande-Terre's easternmost point, is an impressive seascape spectacle. Angry Atlantic waves bash black-limestone rocks and jagged cliffs with a roughness reminiscent of Brittany's Finistère coast or England's Land's End. Follow the path leading to the point where the land falls off abruptly to the ocean for the best views of the island of La Désirade.

Farther north, La Porte d'Enfer is a quaint little cove and beach protected from the furious Atlantic by an outcrop of limestone cliffs. The name means "Hell's Gate," but swimming close to shore in the turquoise water is usually safe. Don't venture out too far, though; the next cove, Le Trou de Madame Coco (Madame Coco's hole), is where (according to legend) the sea stole Madame Coco and her parasol as she promenaded along the edge. La Pointe de la Grande Vigie, at the northernmost tip of the island, has paths that lead to the edge of spectacular cliffs with dramatic views of Porte de l'Enfer and, on a clear day, the island of Antigua. Cacti and other succulents grow everywhere.

Along the northern coasts of Grande-Terre and Basse-Terre, La Réserve Naturelle du Grand Cul-de-Sac Marin is one of the Caribbean's largest marine reserves.

BASSE-TERRE

Basse-Terre's greatest attraction is the Parc National de la Guadeloupe, 29,600 hectares (74,000 acres) of tropical rainforests, mountains, waterfalls, and ponds. UNESCO designated the park a World Biosphere Reserve in 1992. Its 322km (200 miles) of well-marked trails make it one of the best places for hiking in the entire Caribbean. Pick up information and maps at park entrances. Thirty minutes from Pointe-à-Pitre, La Maison de la Forêt (Forest House; closed Mon) lies on the Route de la Traversée, which bisects the park, and is the starting point for easy walking tours of the surrounding mountainous rainforest. English-language trail-guide booklets describe the plant and animal life. Nearby, the Cascade aux Ecrevisses (Crayfish Falls), a slippery 10-minute walk from the roadside, is nice for a cooling dip. To the south, the steep hike to the three falls of Les Chutes du Carbet (Carbet Falls) is among Guadeloupe's most beautiful excursions (one of the falls drops 20m/66 ft., the second 108m/354 ft., the third 123m/403 ft.). The middle fall, the most dramatic, is the easiest to reach. On the way up, you'll pass Le Grand Etang (the Great Pond), a volcanic lake surrounded by tree-size ferns, giant vining philodendrons, wild bananas, orchids, anthuriums, and pineapples.

The park's single greatest feature is the still-simmering volcano La Soufrière, rising to 1,440m (4,723 ft.) and flanked by banana plantations and lush vegetation. In 1975, ashes, mud, billowing smoke, and tremors proved that the volcano is still active, and today you can smell sulfurous fumes and feel the heat through the soil as steam spews from the fumaroles. The summit is like another planet: Steam rises from two active craters, large rocks form improbable shapes, and roars from the earth make it difficult to hear your companions. Go with an experienced guide (see "Hiking Tours" under "Excursions Offered by Local

Agencies," above). On your way down, don't miss **La Maison du Volcan,** the volcanology museum in St-Claude.

Gardeners should save a couple of hours to visit the **Domaine de Valombreuse** (℡ **590/95-50-50**), a 2.4-hectare (6-acre) floral park with exotic birds, spice gardens, and 300 species of tropical flowers. Created in 1990, and close to the town of Petit Bourg, the park has a riverside restaurant and a superior gift shop. It's open daily from 9am to 6pm; admission is about $10 for adults, $5 for children 6 to 12; children 5 and under are admitted free.

Parc Archéologique des Roches Gravées, on Basse-Terre's southern coast in the town of Trois-Rivières (℡ **590/92-91-88**), has the West Indies' largest collection of Arawak Indian petroglyphs. The animal and human images etched on boulders date from between A.D. 300 and 400. Paths and stone stairways meander through the tranquil grounds, which include avocado, banana, cocoa, coffee, guava, and papaya trees. Explanatory brochures are in French and English. It's open daily from 8:30am to 4:30pm; admission is about $1.50.

SHOPPING

Parlez-vous Chanel? Hermès? Saint Laurent? Baccarat? If you do, you'll find that Guadeloupe has good buys on almost anything French—scarves, perfumes, cosmetics, crystal, and other luxury goods—and many stores offer 20% discounts on items purchased with foreign currency, traveler's checks, or credit cards. You can also find local **handcrafted items,** madras cloth, spices, and rum at any of the local markets.

Right at Pointe-à-Pitre's port, the **Centre Saint-John Perse** has about 20 shops that frequently offer lower prices than can be found elsewhere in town. L'Artisan Parfumeur sells French and American perfumes, as well as tropical scents. **Suzanne Moulin** features original African-inspired jewelry and crafts. **Jean-Louis Padel** specializes in gold jewelry. If you're looking for beach and resort wear, stop by **Vanilla Boutique** and **Brasil Tropique.** For something a little more provocative, look through the delicate lingerie at **Soph't.**

Rue Frébault, directly in front of the port, is one of the best shopping streets for duty-free items. **Rosébleu,** 5 rue Frébault, offers china, crystal, and silver from Christoffle, Kosta Boda, and other high-end manufacturers. **Phoenicia,** 8 rue Frébault and 121 bis rue Frébault, has large selections of French perfumes and cosmetics. For men's and women's fashions, as well as for cosmetics and perfumes, browse through **Vendôme,** 8–10 rue Frébault. Across the street at the intersection of rues Frébault and Delgrès, **Geneviève Lethu** is a French version of Williams-Sonoma, with everything for preparing and serving food. If you find yourself overdosing on froufrou, duck into **Tati,** France's answer to Kmart. It's at the intersection of rues Frébault and Abbé Grégoire. This venerable old department-store chain, famous for its antifashion pink-plaid shopping bags, is great for inexpensive basics.

The French Antilles are where the beguine began, so if you're in the market for French Antillean music or French-language books, there are a couple of large book and music stores across from each other on rue Schoelcher: **Librairie Antillaise** at no. 41 and **Librairie Général** at no. 46. Each has a small selection of English-language books as well.

BEACHES

Beaches on Grande-Terre's southern coast have soft white sand. Those on the Atlantic coast have wilder water and are less crowded. The convenient **Bas du Fort/Gosier hotel area** has mostly man-made strips of sand with rows of beach chairs, watersports shops, and beach bars. Changing facilities and chairs are available for a nominal fee. The tiny, uninhabited **Ilet Gosier,** across Gosier Bay, is a quieter option popular with those who want to bare it all. You can take a fishing boat to the island from Gosier's waterfront. The wide strip of white sand at **Ste-Anne,** about 30 minutes from Pointe-à-Pitre, is lined with shops and food stands. **Plage Tarare,** just before the tip of Pointe des Châteaux, is the most popular nude beach.

On Basse-Terre, the **Plage de Grande Anse** is a long expanse of ochre sand. A pleasant walk north from Deshaies, it offers changing facilities, watersports, boutiques, and outdoor snack bars. Farther south, the gray expanse of **Plage de Malendure** is alive with restaurants, bars, and open-air boutiques. It's the departure point for snorkeling and scuba trips to the **Cousteau Reserve** off Pigeon Island.

SPORTS
SNORKELING   Beachside stands at virtually all the resorts on Grande-Terre's southern coast rent snorkeling equipment for about $8 a day. The St-François reef and the Ilet de Gosier are especially recommended.

GREAT LOCAL RESTAURANTS & BARS
Many restaurants change their hours from time to time and from season to season, so call in advance for reservations and exact hours. Most, but not all, restaurants accept major credit cards.

The **local beer** is Corsaire, while Bonka is the **local coffee. Local rums** come in a variety of flavors—*bois bandé* (made with the bark of the bois bandé tree), shrubb (orange and vanilla), lemon—and are painstakingly nurtured at small rum estates such as Séverin, Longueteau, Damoiseau, Bologne, and Montebello. Local producers compare their slow, time-honored process to that used to make cognac.

ON GRANDE-TERRE
Chez Violetta-La Créole, Perinette, in Gosier (© **590/84-36-80**), was established by the late Violetta Chaville, the island's legendary high priestess of Creole cookery. Her brother continues the family tradition, serving stuffed crabs, cod fritters, and conch fricasée. It's open daily from noon to 3:30pm.

Chez Monia at 4 rue Victor Hugues, off of rue Nozières in Pointe-à-Pitre, serves ice cream that is pure heaven in the midday heat. Flavors *(aromes)* include pear, lemon, kiwi, guava, and champagne. Three scoops in a homemade waffle cone costs about $2. Street vendors also offer superior ice cream, usually flavored with fresh vanilla and coconut, straight from their hand-cranked machines.

ON BASSE-TERRE
In Deshaies, Lucienne Salcède's family has run **Le Karacoli** (© **590/28-41-17**), one of Guadeloupe's best seaside restaurants, for almost 30 years. Sit on the beachfront terrace in the shadow of almond and palm trees and let the waves hypnotize you. In the distance, the island of Montserrat is visible. Try a rum aperitif or two, then bliss out on cod fritters, stuffed christophine, and avocado *féroce* (a peppery purée) before moving on to Creole lobster or conch. It's open daily from noon to 2pm (closed the entire month of Sept). Reservations are imperative on weekends. Lunch is $30.

18 Jamaica

A favorite of North American honeymooners, Jamaica is a mountainous island 145km (90 miles) south of Cuba and about 161km (100 miles) west of Haiti.

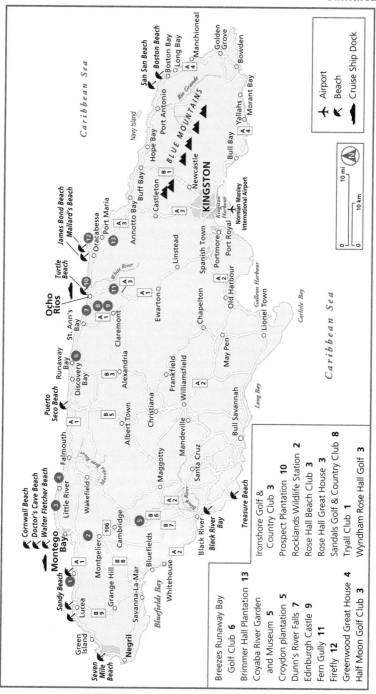

It's the third largest of the Caribbean islands, with some 11,396 sq. km (4,444 sq. miles) of predominantly green terrain, a mountain ridge peaking at 2,220m (7,281 ft.) above sea level, and, on the north coast, many beautiful white-sand beaches rimming the clear blue sea.

One of the most densely populated nations in the Caribbean, with a vivid sense of its own identity, Jamaica has a history rooted in the plantation economy and some of the most impassioned politics in the Western Hemisphere, all of which leads to a sometimes turbulent day-to-day reality. You've probably heard, for instance, that the island's vendors and hawkers can be pushy and the locals not always the most welcoming to tourists, and while there's some truth to this, we've had nothing but positive experiences on many visits to Jamaica. So, keep an open mind.

Most cruise ships dock at **Ocho Rios** on the lush northern coast, although more and more are opting to call at the city of **Montego Bay** ("Mo Bay"), 108km (67 miles) to the west. These ports offer comparable attractions and some of the same shopping possibilities. Don't try to do both ports in one day, however, since the 4-hour round-trip ride leaves time for only superficial visits to each.

LANGUAGE   The official language is **English,** but most Jamaicans speak a richly nuanced patois that's primarily derived from English but includes elements of African, Spanish, Arawak, French, Chinese, Portuguese, and East Indian languages.

CURRENCY   The unit of currency is the **Jamaican dollar,** designated by the same symbol as the U.S. dollar ($). For clarity, we use the symbol J$ to denote prices in Jamaican dollars. The exchange rate is usually US$1 = J$60; J$1 = US2¢. Visitors can pay in U.S. dollars, but always find out if a price is being quoted in Jamaican or U.S. dollars—there's a big difference! Unless otherwise specified, prices in this section are given in U.S. dollars.

INFORMATION   To get more info before you go, call the **Jamaica Tourist Office** in New York (© **800/233-4582** or 212/856-9727; www.jamaica-travel. com). Information booths in the ports are discussed below.

CALLING FROM THE U.S.   When calling Jamaica from the United States, you need only dial a "1" before the numbers listed here.

SHORE EXCURSIONS OFFERED IN BOTH PORTS

Since there's little besides shopping near the docks at either Ocho Rios or Montego Bay, most passengers sign up for shore excursions. The following are usually offered from both ports.

Dunn's River Falls Tour (US$44, 4 hr.): These falls cascade 180m (590 ft.) to the beach and are the most visited attraction in Jamaica, which means they're hopelessly overcrowded when a lot of cruise ships are in port. Tourists are allowed to climb the falls, and it's a ball to slip and slide your way up with the hundreds of others, forming a human chain of sorts. Wear a bathing suit under your clothes, and don't forget your waterproof camera and your aqua-socks. (If you do, most cruise lines will rent you aqua-socks for an extra US$5.) The prettiest part of the falls, known as the Laughing Waters, were used in the James Bond classics *Dr. No* and *Live and Let Die.* This tour usually also visits other local attractions, with time allocated for shopping. (*Note:* The falls are much closer to Ocho Rios than to Mo Bay, so tours from the latter typically cost around US$70 and require a 2¼-hr. drive each way, for a total of 7½ hr.)

Frommer's Favorite Ocho Rios Experiences

Tubing on the White River: Offered by most cruise lines, this trip is just a downright fantastic experience. (See "Shore Excursions Offered in Both Ports," below.)

Riding Horseback Through the Surf: An excursion by horseback includes a ride along the beach and through the surf. (See "Shore Excursions Offered in Both Ports," below.)

River Tubing Safari (US$55, 3½ hr.): This is one of the best excursions we've ever taken. After a scenic van ride deep into the pristine jungles, the group of 20 or so passengers and a couple of guides sit back into big black inner tubes (they have wooden boards covering the bottom so your butt doesn't get scraped on the rocks), and glide a few miles downriver, passing by gorgeous, towering bamboo trees and other lush foliage. It's sometimes peaceful and sometimes exhilarating—especially when you hit the rapids! If you're docking in Ocho Rios, this tour is usually on the White River. If in Montego Bay, it's on the Great River. **Note:** We find this trip much more interesting than the popular **Martha Brae River Rafting,** which takes you down the river on two-seat bamboo rafts. The cost is about the same.

Horseback-Riding Excursion (US$89, 3 hr.): Riders will love this trip; after a 45-minute ride from the stables through fields, you'll gallop along the beach and take your horse bareback into the surf for a thrilling ride.

OCHO RIOS

Once a small banana and fishing port, Ocho Rios is now Jamaica's cruise ship capital, welcoming a couple of ships every day during high season. Though the area has some of the Caribbean's most fabled resorts, and Dunn's River is just a 5-minute taxi ride away, the town itself is not much to see, despite there being a few outdoor local markets within walking distance. Don't expect to shop in the markets without a lot of hassle and a lot of very pushy hawking of merchandise—some of which is likely to be ganja, the locally grown marijuana. (Remember, it may be readily available, but it's still illegal.) In recent years the government has been making an effort to keep things saner around the markets, employing a veritable army of blue-uniformed "resort patrol" officers on bikes to help keep order.

COMING ASHORE   Most cruise ships dock at the **Port of Ocho Rios,** near Dunn's River Falls and adjacent to Island Village and several shopping options. There are bathrooms and a telephone center at the terminal.

INFORMATION   You'll find **tourist board offices** at the Ocean Village Shopping Centre in Ocho Rios (*©* **876/974-2582**), open Monday to Friday from 8:30 am to 4:30 pm and 9 am to 1 pm on Saturdays. There's also a small information stand right at the dock.

GETTING AROUND

BY TAXI   Taxis are your best means of transport, but always agree on a fare before you get in. Your best and safest bet is to get a taxi from the pier; there will be lots of them waiting. Taxis licensed by the government display **JTB** decals, indicating they're official Jamaican Tourist Board taxis. All others are gypsy cabs, which you should avoid. Taxi dispatchers are at the pier and fixed rates are posted. Otherwise, if you're getting into a taxi from somewhere else on the island, always agree to the price first.

BY RENTAL CAR   We don't recommend renting a car here.

BEST CRUISE LINE SHORE EXCURSIONS

In addition to the tours offered from both Jamaican ports (p. 200), Ocho Rios also offers tours to several nearby attractions.

Prospect Plantation & Dunn's River Falls (US$62, 4 hr.): About 3 miles east of town, Prospect Plantation offers a taste of Jamaica's colonial days (sans slavery), with a tractor-drawn jitney taking your among seasonal crops that include bananas, sugar cane, coffee, pineapple, and papaya. The trip includes a stop at Dunn's River Falls (see above).

Coyaba River Garden & Dunn's River Falls (US$44, 3 hr.): About a mile from town, Coyaba River Garden and Museum was built on the grounds of the former Shaw Park plantation, and displays artifacts from the Arawak, Spanish, and English settlements in the area. The gardens are filled with native flora, a cut-stone courtyard, and fountains. Like many of the other tours in Ocho Rios, it hits Dunn's Falls on the way back.

Mountain Biking to Chukka Cove (US$69, 4 hr.): A minivan takes you into the mountains above St. Ann, where you hop on your bike for a ride down back roads, through meadows and woodlands to picturesque Chukka Cove, where you can take a swim.

Dolphin Cove (US$34–US$89, 2 hr.): Various excursions to this beachfront site allow you to gander at, touch, or swim with the resident dolphins. For about US$10 more you can add on an hour and a half at (you guessed it) Dunn's River Falls.

ON YOUR OWN: WITHIN WALKING DISTANCE

Adjacent to the cruise pier, **Island Village** (www.islandjamaica.com) is a 1.6-hectare (4-acre) entertainment and shopping complex developed by Island Records' Chris Blackwell. Attractions include the ReggaeXplosion museum, a museum of Jamaican art, a casino, an outdoor concert venue, an indoor theater, a beach with watersports, shopping (lots of it), and a branch of Jimmy Buffett's Margaritaville.

ON YOUR OWN: BEYOND THE PORT AREA

South of Ocho Rios, **Fern Gully** was originally a riverbed. Today, the main A3 road winds some 210m (689 ft.) through a rainforest filled with wild ferns, hard-wood trees, and lianas. For the botanist, there are hundreds of varieties of ferns; for the less plant-minded, roadside stands sell fruits and vegetables, carved-wood souvenirs, and basketwork. The road runs for about 6.4km (4 miles).

Cruise Booze

If you step inside the small cruise "terminal" in Ocho Rios, you'll find a shop called Cruise Booze, which sets up a tasting station where you can sample a ton of different rums, including a 150-proof white rum.

Near Lydford, southwest of Ocho Rios, are the remains of **Edinburgh Castle.** This was the lair of one of Jamaica's most infamous murderers, a Scot named Lewis Hutchinson, who used to shoot passersby and toss their bodies into a deep pit. The authorities got wind of his activities, and although he tried to escape by canoe, he was captured by the navy and hanged. Rather proud of his achievements (evidence of at least 43 murders was found), he left £100 and instructions for a memorial to be built. It never was, but the 1763 castle ruins remain. To get to Lydford, take the A3 south until you reach a small intersection directly north of Walkers Wood, and then follow the signposts west.

The 1817 **Brimmer Hall Estate,** Port Maria, St. Mary's (© **876/994-2309),** 34km (21 miles) east of Ocho Rios, is a working plantation where you're driven around in a tractor-drawn jitney to see the tropical fruit trees and coffee plants. Knowledgeable guides tell you about the processes necessary to produce the fine fruits of the island. Afterward, you can relax beside the pool and sample a wide variety of drinks, including an interesting one called "Wow!" The Plantation Tour Eating House offers typical Jamaican dishes for lunch. There's also a souvenir shop with a good selection of ceramics, art, straw goods, woodcarvings, rums, liqueurs, and cigars. Tours run daily if there are enough people. Hours are 8am to 4pm weekdays. Admission is US$15 for adults, US$7.50 for children, free for kids under 5.

About 1.6km (1 mile) from the center of Ocho Rios, at an elevation of 126m (413 ft.), **Coyaba River Garden and Museum,** Shaw Park Road (© **876/974-6235;** www.coyabagardens.com), was built on the grounds of the former Shaw Park plantation. The Spanish-style museum displays artifacts from the Arawak, Spanish, and English settlements in the area. The gardens are filled with native flora, a cut-stone courtyard, and fountains. It's open daily from 8am to 6pm. Admission is US$5 for adults, US$2.50 for children.

At the 180m (590-ft.) **Dunn's River Falls,** on the A3 (© **876/974-2857),** you can relax on the beach, splash in the waters at the bottom of the falls, or climb with a guide to the top and drop into the cool pools higher up between the cascades of water. The beach restaurant provides snacks and drinks, and dressing rooms are available. If you're planning to climb the falls, wear aquasocks or sneakers to protect your feet from the sharp rocks and to prevent slipping. At the prettiest part of Dunn's River Falls, known as the Laughing Waters, scenes were shot for the James Bond classics *Dr. No* and *Live and Let Die.*

About 4.8km (3 miles) east of Ocho Rios along the A3, adjoining the 18-hole Prospect Mini Golf Course, the working **Prospect Plantation** (© **876/974-2373)** is often a shore-excursion stop. On your leisurely ride by covered jitney, you'll readily see why this section of Jamaica is called "the garden parish of the island." You'll see pimiento (allspice), banana, cassava, sugar cane, coffee, cocoa, coconut, pineapple, and the famous leucaena "Tree of Life"—plus, for what it's worth, Jamaica's first hydroelectric plant. Horseback riding is available on three scenic trails. The rides vary from 1 to 2¼ hours; you'll need to book a horse at least an hour in advance. Rates are US$20 per person per hour.

Firefly, Grants Pen, 32km (20 miles) east of Ocho Rios above Oracabessa (© **876/725-0920),** was the home of Sir Noël Coward and his longtime companion, Graham Payn, who, as executor of Coward's estate, donated it to the Jamaica National Heritage Trust. The recently restored house is as it was on the day Sir Noël died in 1973. It's open Monday to Thursday from 9am to 5pm. Admission is US$10. Children under 12 are admitted free.

SHOPPING

Shopping in Ocho Rios is not as good as in Montego Bay and other ports, but if your money's burning a hole in your pocket, you can wander around the Ocho Rios Craft Park, opposite the **Ocean Village Shopping Centre** off Main Street. Some 150 stalls stock hats, handbags, place mats, woodcarvings, and paintings, plus the usual T-shirts and jewelry. More luxurious items can be found at **Soni's Plaza** (© 876/974-6455), on Main Street. **Coconut Grove Shopping Plaza** is a collection of low-slung shops linked by walkways and shrubs. The merchandise consists mainly of local craft items. **Island Plaza** shopping complex, right in the heart of Ocho Rios, has paintings by local artists, local handmade crafts (be prepared to do some haggling), carvings, ceramics, and even kitchenware, plus T-shirts, of course. At all of these places, prepare yourself for aggressive selling and fierce haggling. Every vendor asks too much for an item at first, which gives them the leeway to negotiate the price.

To find local handicrafts or art without the hassle of the markets, head for **Beautiful Memories,** 9 Island Plaza (© 876/974-2374), which has a limited but representative sampling of Jamaican art, as well as local crafts, pottery, woodwork, and hand-embroidered items.

If you'd like to flee the hustle and bustle of the Ocho Rios bazaars completely, take a taxi to **Harmony Hall** (© 876/975-4222), Tower Isle, on the A3, 6.4km (4 miles) east of Ocho Rios. One of Jamaica's great houses, the restored house is now a gallery selling paintings and other works by Jamaican artists. The arts and crafts here are of high quality—not the usual junky assortment you might find at the beach.

BEACHES

Mallards Beach, at the Renaissance Jamaica Grand Resort (© 876/974-2201) on Main Street, is shared by hotel guests and cruise ship passengers and tends to be overcrowded. Locals may steer you to the good and less crowded **Turtle Beach,** southwest of Mallards. You might also want to check out the big **James Bond Beach** in Oracabessa, at the east end of Ocho Rios.

SPORTS

GOLF   SuperClubs' 18-hole, par-72 **Breezes Runaway Bay,** at Runaway Beach near Ocho Rios on the north coast (© 876/973-7319), is one of the better courses in the area, although it's nowhere near the courses at Montego Bay. Call ahead to book tee times. Greens fees are US$80 for 18 holes, US$35 for carts, and US$14 for clubs. The 18-hole, par-71 **Sandals Golf & Country Club** at Ocho Rios (© 876/975-0119) is also open to the public, charging US$70 for nine holes and US$100 for 18. Clubs and carts are extra. Caddies, which are required, are US$12 for nine holes and US$17 for 18 holes. The course lies about 210m (689 ft.) above sea level. To get there from the center of Ocho Rios, travel along the main bypass for 3.2km (2 miles) until Mile End Road; turn right at the Texaco station there, and drive for 8km (5 miles).

Tips   Deal or No Deal?

Some so-called duty-free prices are indeed lower than stateside prices, but then the Jamaican government hits you with a 15% "General Consumption Tax." Buyers beware.

Frommer's Favorite Montego Bay Experiences

In addition to these, our favorite shore excursions from Ocho Rios are also offered from Montego Bay.

Visiting Rocklands Wildlife Station: This is the place to go if you want to have a Jamaican doctor bird perch on your finger or feed small doves and finches from your hand. (See "On Your Own: Beyond the Port Area," below.)

Spending a Day at the Rose Hall Beach Club: With a secluded beach, crystal-clear water, a full restaurant, two beach bars, live entertainment, and more, it's well worth the US$8 admission. (See "Beaches," below.)

GREAT LOCAL RESTAURANTS & BARS

The favorite **local beer** is Red Stripe; a favorite **local rum** is Appleton.

Ocho Rios Jerk Centre, on DaCosta Drive (© **876/974-2549**), serves up lip-smacking jerk pork and chicken. Don't expect anything fancy, just come for platters of meat. Lunch is about US$14. For a special lunch out, **Almond Tree Restaurant,** 83 Main St., in the Hibiscus Lodge Hotel, 3 blocks from the Ocho Rios Mall (© **876/974-2813**), is a two-tiered patio restaurant overlooking the Caribbean, with a tree growing through its roof. Lobster thermidor is the most delectable item on the menu. Lunch is about US$20. **Evita's Italian Restaurant,** Eden Bower Road, 5 minutes south of Ocho Rios (© **876/974-2333**), is run by a flamboyant Italian and is the premier Italian restaurant in Ocho Rios. It serves pastas and excellent fish dishes, as well as unique choices such as jerk spaghetti and pasta Viagra (don't ask). Lunch is around US$20. There are probably more great rum bars on Jamaica than churches. Among the best is **Bibi Bips,** 93 Main St. (© **876/974-7438** or 876/865-7482).

MONTEGO BAY

Montego Bay (also referred to as "Mo Bay") is sometimes less of a hassle to explore than the port at Ocho Rios, plus it has better beaches, shopping, and restaurants, as well as some of the best golf courses in the Caribbean, superior even to those on Puerto Rico and the Bahamas. Like Ocho Rios, Montego Bay has its crime, traffic, and annoyances, but there's much more to see and do here.

There's little of interest in the town itself except shopping, although the good stuff in the environs is easily reached by taxi or shore excursion.

COMING ASHORE   Montego Bay has a modern cruise dock with lots of conveniences, including duty-free stores, telephones, tourist information, and plenty of taxis to meet all ships.

INFORMATION   You'll find the **tourist board offices** at Cornwall Beach, St. James (© **876/952-4425**), open Monday to Friday from 9am to 5pm.

GETTING AROUND

BY TAXI   If you don't book a shore excursion, a taxi is the way to get around. See "Getting Around" under "Ocho Rios," above, for taxi information, as the same conditions apply to Mo Bay.

BEST CRUISE LINE SHORE EXCURSIONS

In addition to tour offered from both Jamaica ports, Mo Bay also offers tours to several interesting plantations and great houses.

Rose Hall Great House (US$39, 3½ hr.): This is the most famous plantation home in Jamaica. Built about 2 centuries ago by John Palmer, it gained notoriety from the doings of "Infamous Annie" Palmer, wife of the builder's grandnephew, who supposedly dabbled in witchcraft and took slaves as lovers, killing them when they bored her. Annie also was said to have murdered several of her husbands while they slept, and eventually suffered the same fate herself. For what it's worth, many Jamaicans insist the house is haunted.

Greenwood Great House (US$39, 3½ hr.): More interesting to some than Rose Hall, the Georgian-style building was the residence of Richard Barrett, a first cousin of Elizabeth Barrett Browning. On display are the family's library, portraits, antiques, and period musical instruments.

Croydon Plantation Tour (US$59, 6 hr.): A guided tour of this mountain estate includes a quarter-mile walk over gently sloping terrain, with a lot of great views. Stops are made for refreshments and seasonal fresh fruits, and at the end you get a traditional Jamaican-style lunch.

ON YOUR OWN: WITHIN WALKING DISTANCE

There's nothing really. You'll have to take a taxi to the town for shopping or sign up for an excursion.

ON YOUR OWN: BEYOND THE PORT AREA

It's a unique experience to have a Jamaican doctor bird perch on your finger to drink syrup, or to feed small doves and finches from your hand, or simply to watch dozens of birds flying in for the evening at **Rocklands Wildlife Station,** Anchovy, St. James (© **876/952-2009**). Lisa Salmon, known as the "Bird Lady of Anchovy," established this sanctuary. It's perfect for nature lovers and birdwatchers. Rocklands is about 1.2km (¾ mile) outside Anchovy on the road from Montego Bay. It's open daily from 9am to 5:30pm, and charges US$8 admission for adults and US$4 for children ages 5 to 12.

SHOPPING

The main shopping areas are at **Montego Freeport,** within easy walking distance of the pier; **City Centre,** where most of the duty-free shops are, aside from those at the large hotels; and **Holiday Village Shopping Centre.**

Old Fort Craft Market, a shopping complex with nearly 200 vendors licensed by the Jamaica Tourist Board, fronts Howard Cooke Boulevard up from Gloucester Avenue in the heart of Montego Bay, on the site of Fort Montego. With a varied assortment of handicrafts, this is browsing country. You'll see a selection of wall hangings, hand-woven straw items, and hand-carved wood sculptures, and you can also get your hair braided. Vendors can be extremely aggressive, so be prepared for some major hassles, as well as some serious negotiation. Persistent bargaining on your part will lead to substantial discounts.

You can find the best selection of handmade Jamaican souvenirs at the **Crafts Market,** near Harbour Street in downtown Montego Bay. Straw hats and bags, wooden platters, straw baskets, musical instruments, beads, carved objects, and toys are all available here. That "jipijapa" hat will come in handy if you're going to be out in the island sun.

For the best selection of local folk art—as well an absolutely fantastic, and reasonably priced, collection of Cuban, Jamaican, and Haitian fine art—try the **Gallery of West Indian Art** on 11 Fairfield Rd. (© **876/952-4547**).

Ambiente Art Gallery, 9 Fort St. (© **876/952-7919**), stocks local artwork. At **Blue Mountain Gems Workshop,** at the Holiday Village Shopping Centre (© **876/953-2338**), you can take a tour of the workshops to see the process from raw stone to the finished product available for purchase later. **Klass Kraft Leather Sandals,** 44 Fort St. (© **876/952-5782**), offers sandals and leather accessories made on location.

BEACHES

Doctor's Cave Beach (© **876/952-2566**), on Gloucester Avenue across from the Doctors Cave Beach Hotel (© **876/952-4355;** www.doctorscave.com), helped launch Mo Bay as a resort in the 1940s. Admission to the beach is about $4 for adults, half price for children up to 12. Dressing rooms, chairs, umbrellas, and rafts are available.

One of the premier beaches of Jamaica, **Aquasol Theme Park** (formerly Walter Fletcher Beach), is in the heart of Mo Bay. It's noted for tranquil waters, which makes it a particular favorite for families with children. Changing rooms are available, and lifeguards are on duty. There's also a restaurant for lunch. The beach is open daily, with an admission price of about US$5 for adults, US$3 for children.

You may want to skip the public beaches and head for the **Rose Hall Beach Club** (© **876/680-0969**), lying on the main road 18km (11 miles) east of Montego Bay. It sits on .8km (½ mile) of secure, secluded, white-sandy beach, with crystal-clear water. The club offers a full restaurant, two beach bars, a covered pavilion, an open-air dance area, showers, restrooms, and changing facilities, plus beach volleyball courts, various beach games, and a full watersports activities program. There's also live entertainment. The club is open daily from 9am to 5pm; admission fees are about US$6 for adults, US$3 for children under 12.

SPORTS

GOLF   **Wyndham Rose Hall Golf & Beach Resort,** Rose Hall (© **876/953-2650**), has a noted 18-hole, par-71 course with an unusual and challenging seaside and mountain layout. The 90m-high (295-ft.) 13th tee offers a rare panoramic view of the sea, and the 15th green is next to a 12m (39-ft.) waterfall, once featured in a James Bond movie. A fully stocked pro shop, a clubhouse, and a professional staff are among the amenities. Greens fees are US$120.

The excellent, regal 18-hole, par-72 course at the **Tryall Club** (© **876/956-5660;** www.tryallclub.com), 19km (12 miles) from Montego Bay, has often been the site of major golf tournaments, including the Jamaica Classic Annual and the Johnnie Walker Tournament. Greens fees are US$115 plus US$30 for a cart.

Half Moon, at Rose Hall (© **876/953-2560;** www.halfmoon-resort.com/golf), features an 18-hole, par-72 championship course designed by Robert Trent Jones Sr. Greens fees are US$130, plus US$17 for a mandatory caddy.

Ironshore Golf & Country Club, Ironshore, St. James, Montego Bay (© **876/953-3681**), a well-known, 18-hole, par-72 course, is privately owned but open to the public. Greens fees are US$30 plus US$14 for a mandatory caddy.

HORSEBACK RIDING   The best horseback riding is offered by the helpful staff at the **Rocky Point Riding Stables,** at the Half Moon Club, Rose Hall, Montego Bay (© **876/953-2286**). The stables, built in the colonial Caribbean style in 1992, are the most beautiful in Jamaica.

RAFTING **Mountain Valley Rafting,** 31 Gloucester Ave. (© **876/956-4920**), offers excursions on the Great River, departing from the Lethe Plantation, about 16km (10 miles) south of Montego Bay. Bamboo rafts are designed for two, with a raised dais to sit on. In some cases, a small child can accompany two adults on the same raft, although you should exercise caution when doing so. A half-day experience includes transportation to and from the pier, an hour's rafting, lunch, a garden tour of the Lethe property, and a taste of Jamaican liqueur.

GREAT LOCAL RESTAURANTS & BARS

The Pork Pit, 27 Gloucester Ave., near Walter Fletcher Beach (© **876/952-1046**), is the best place to go for the famous Jamaican jerk pork and jerk chicken. Many beachgoers come over here for a big lunch. Picnic tables encircle the building, and everything is open air and informal. Order half a pound of jerk meat with a baked yam or baked potato and a bottle of Red Stripe beer. Prices are very reasonable. Lunch is about US$10.

The **Native Restaurant,** Gloucester Avenue (© **876/979-2769**), continues to win converts with such appetizers as jerk reggae chicken, ackee and saltfish (an acquired taste), smoked marlin, and steamed fish. The boonoonoonoos, billed as "A Taste of Jamaica," is a big platter with a little bit of everything, including meats and several kinds of fish and vegetables. Lunch is about $20.

19 Key West

No other port of call offers such a sweeping choice of fine dining, easy-to-reach attractions, street entertainment, and roguish bars as does this heavy-drinking, fun-loving town at the very end of the fabled Florida Keys. It's America's southernmost city, located at Mile Marker 0, where U.S. Route 1 begins, but it feels more like a colorful Caribbean outpost mixed with a dash of New Orleans.

You have only a day, so flee the busy cruise docks and touristy Duval Street for a walk through hidden and more secluded byways, such as Simonton, Olivia, or William streets. Or you might want to spend your day playing golf or going diving or snorkeling.

COMING ASHORE Ships dock at **Mallory Square** (Old Town's tourist central), at the nearby Hilton Resort's **Pier B,** and at the U.S. Navy base's **"Outer Mole" pier.** All are on the Gulf side of the island. Passengers arriving at the Navy pier must take an official shuttle bus the short distance to and from Mallory Square, as individuals are not permitted to transit the base on their own.

LANGUAGE Speak **English** here. Remember, you're in the U.S. of A.

CURRENCY **U.S. dollars** are used here.

INFORMATION The **Greater Key West Chamber of Commerce,** 402 Wall St. (© **305/294-5988;** www.keywestchamber.org), lies near the cruise ship docks, and provides information for tours and fishing trips. Pelican Path is a free walking guide that documents the history and architecture of Old Town, and Solares Hill's Walking and Biking Guide to Old Key West contains a bunch of walking tours. To get info before you go, contact the tourism board (© **800/FLA-KEYS;** www.fla-keys.com).

GETTING AROUND

The island is only 4 miles long and 2 miles wide, and getting around is so easy that many locals do without cars, using "conch cruisers" (in other words bicycles) instead. The most popular attractions, including the Harry S Truman Little

Key West

Audubon House
and Tropical Garden **3**
Harry S Truman
Little White House **5**
Hemingway House **8**
Heritage House Museum
and Robert Frost Cottage **6**
Key West Aquarium **4**
Mallory Square/
Mallory Dock **1**
Mel Fisher Maritime
Heritage Society Museum **2**
Nancy Forrester's Secret
Garden **7**

STOCK IS.

5th Ave.
12th Ave.

A1A

1

Duck Ave.
Flagler Ave.

North Roosevelt Blvd.
Northside Dr.

14th St.
Kennedy Dr.
12th St.
10th St.

Patterson Ave.

US NAVAL
RESERVATION

1

7th St.
6th St.
Macmillan St.
2nd St.
1st St.
Harris Ave.
Staples Ave.

Salt
Ponds

South Roosevelt Blvd.

Key West
Municipal Beach

Garrison
Bight

Palm Ave.

1

George St.
Thompson St. Ave.
Bertha St.

Smathers's Beach

ATLANTIC OCEAN

South St.
Flagler St.
Laird St.
Atlantic Blvd.
White St.

White St.
Francis St.
Grinnell St.
Margaret St.
Caroline St.

Olivia St.
Truman Ave.
Virginia St.
Grinnell St.
Reynolds St.

Higgs Memorial Beach

Gulf of Mexico

Key West
Bight

Front St.
Greene St.
Eaton St.
William St.
Fleming St.
Southard
Angela St.
Petronia St.
Fort St.

Windsor
La.
Simonton St.
Duval St.
Whitehead
Amelia
St.

Vernon
St.
United St.

Southernmost Beach

Wisteria Is.

1
5
2
6
4
3
7
8

Fort Zachary
Taylor State Park

✈ Airport
⚓ Cruise Ship Dock

N

0   1/2 mi
0   0.5 km

209

Frommer's Favorite Key West Experiences

Viewing the Sunset from Mallory Dock: More than just a sunset, it's a daily carnival. If your ship is in port late enough, don't miss it. (See "On Your Own: Within Walking Distance," below.)

Taking a Catamaran Party Cruise: The popular Fury catamarans take passengers snorkeling and then back to shore, with music, booze, and a good time. (See " Shore Excursions Offered by the Cruise Lines," below.)

White House and the Key West Art & History Museum, are all within walking distance of Mallory Square—even the farthest (Hemingway House) is only about a mile down Duval.

BY TAXI　Island taxis operate around the clock, but are small and not suited for sightseeing tours. They will, however, take you to the beach and arrange to pick you up at a certain time. You can call one of four services: **Florida Keys Taxi** (✆ 305/294-2227), **Maxi-Taxi Sun Cab System** (✆ 305/294-2222), **Pink Cabs** (✆ 305/296-6666), and **Island Transportation Services** (✆ 305/296-1800). Prices are uniform; the meter starts at about $2.25 and adds 50¢ per ⅓ mile.

BY TRAM　The **Conch Tour Train** (✆ 305/294-5161; www.conchtourtrain.com) is a narrated 90-minute tour that takes you up and down all the most interesting streets and offers commentary on 100 local sites, giving you lots of lore about the town. It's the best way to see lots of Key West in a short time. The depot is located at Mallory Square near the cruise ship docks. Trains depart every 30 minutes. Most ships sell this as an excursion, but you can also do it on your own; departures are daily from 9am to 4:30pm and cost $20 for adults, $10 for children ages 4 to 12, free for children 3 and under. The trip has only one stop where passengers can get on and off (at the Historic Seaport). If you want more flexibility and are booking on your own, try the **Old Town Trolley** (✆ 305/296-6688; www.trolleytours.com). It's less popular than the Conch Tour Train, but it lets you get off and explore a particular attraction, and then reboard another of its trains later. Professional guides spin tall tales about Key West throughout the 90-minute route. The trolleys operate 7 days a week from 9am to 4:30pm, with departures every 30 minutes from convenient spots throughout town. You can board the trolley near the cruise docks (look for signposts). Tours cost about $20 for adults, $10 for children ages 4 to 12, and are free for children under 4.

BY MOTOR SCOOTER OR BICYCLE　One of the largest and best places to rent a bicycle or motorbike is **Keys Moped and Scooter Rental,** 523 Truman Ave., about a block off Duval Street (✆ 305/294-0399). Cruise ship passengers might opt for a 3-hour motor-scooter rental for about $15, the 9am to 5pm rental for $22, or the all day (24-hr.) rental for $30. One-speed, big-wheeled "beach-cruiser" bicycles with soft seats and big baskets for toting beachwear rent for about $4 for 8 hours.

BY BUS　The cheapest way to see the island is by bus, which costs only about 75¢ for adults and 35¢ for seniors and children 6 years and older (kids 5 and under ride free).

BY RENTAL CAR Walking or cycling is better than renting a car here, but if you do want to rent, **Avis, Budget, Dollar,** and **Hertz** all have offices here, as do **Tropical Rent-a-Car,** 1300 Duval St. (© **305/294-8136**), and **Enterprise Rent-a-Car,** 2834 N. Roosevelt Blvd. (© **800/325-8007** or 305/292-0220; www. enterprise.com). If you're visiting in winter, make reservations at least a week in advance.

SHORE EXCURSIONS OFFERED BY THE CRUISE LINES

In addition to the Conch Train Tour described above, most lines offer walking tours and sometimes bike tours for those who like the services of a guide. But, this is really a port to explore on your own.

Catamaran Party Cruises ($45, 3 hr.): The popular Fury catamarans take passengers to a reef for some snorkeling and then finish the trip back to shore with music, booze, and a good time.

EXCURSIONS OFFERED BY LOCAL AGENCIES

Glass-Bottomed Boat Tours: The MV *Discovery* (© **800/262-0099** or 305/ 293-0099; www.discoveryunderseatours.com), a 78-foot motor craft, has 20 large viewing windows (angled at 45 degrees) set below the water line to allow passengers to view reef life in comfort from below deck. Two-hour tours depart daily at 10:30am, 1:30pm, and sunset from Land's End Village & Marina at the western end of Margaret Street, a 6-block walk from the cruise ship docks. The cost is $32.

ON YOUR OWN: WITHIN WALKING DISTANCE

The **Harry S Truman Little White House,** 111 Front St. (© **305/294-9911;** www.trumanlittlewhitehouse.com), is part of the 103-acre Truman Annex near the cruise ship docks. Originally the home of the Navy base commander, Truman commandeered it for use as a vacation home during his presidency. Today it remains just as he left it, decorated in perfect late-1940s style. By the time the guides get through their well-organized hour-long tour you'll feel as if you've gone back in time. Admission is $10 adults, $5 children.

The **Hemingway Home,** 907 Whitehead St. (© **305/294-1575;** www. hemingwayhome.com), provides a similar if less formal look back at the island's old days. "Papa" lived here with his second wife, Pauline, completing *For Whom the Bell Tolls* and *A Farewell to Arms* in the studio annex out back. Hemingway had some 60 polydactyl (many-toed) cats, whose descendants still live on the grounds. Admission is $10 adults, $6 children.

Audubon House and Tropical Garden, 205 Whitehead St., at Greene Street (© **877/281-2473** or 305/294-2116; www.audubonhouse.com), is dedicated to the 1832 Key West sojourn of the famous naturalist John James Audubon. The ornithologist didn't live in this three-story building, but it's filled with his engravings. The main reason to visit is to see how wealthy sailors lived in Key West in the 19th century, and the lush tropical gardens surrounding the house are worth the $9 price of admission.

Jessie Porter Newton, known as "Miss Jessie" to her friends, was the grande dame of Key West, inviting the celebrities of her day to her house, including Tennessee Williams and her girlhood friend Gloria Swanson, as well as family friend Robert Frost, who stayed in a cottage out back. Today, you can wander the grounds, look at the antique-filled rooms, and inspect her mementos and the exotic treasures collected by six generations of the Porter family at **The Heritage**

House Museum and Robert Frost Cottage, 410 Caroline St. ((C) **305/296-3573**).

On the waterfront at Mallory Square, the **Key West Aquarium,** 1 Whitehead St. ((C) **305/296-2051;** www.keywestaquarium.com), in operation since 1932, was the first tourist attraction built in the Florida Keys. The aquarium's special feature is a "touch tank" where you can feel a horseshoe crab, sea squirt, sea urchin, starfish, and, of course, conch, the town's mascot and symbol. It's worth taking a tour, as the guides are both knowledgeable and entertaining—and you'll get to pet a shark, if that's your idea of a good time. Admission is $9.

The late treasure hunter Mel Fisher used to wear heavy gold necklaces, which he liked to say were worth a king's ransom. He wasn't exaggerating. After long and risky dives, Fisher and his associates plucked more than $400 million in gold and silver from the shipwrecked Spanish galleons *Santa Margarita* and *Nuestra Señora de Atocha,* which were lost on hurricane-tossed seas some 350 years ago. Now this extraordinary long-lost Spanish treasure—jewelry, doubloons, and silver and gold bullion—is displayed at the **Mel Fisher Maritime Heritage Society Museum,** near the docks at 200 Greene St. ((C) **305/294-2633;** www.melfisher.com). Admission is $6.50.

Nancy Forrester's Secret Garden, 1 Free School Lane, off Simonton between Southard and Fleming streets ((C) **305/294-0015**), is the most lavish and verdant garden in town. Some 150 species of palms and thousands of species of other plants, including orchids, climbing vines, and ground covers, are planted here, creating a blanket of lush, tropical magic. It's a 20-minute walk from the docks, near Key West's highest point, Solares Hill. Pick up a sandwich at a deli and picnic at tables in the garden. Admission is $6.

If your ship leaves late enough, you can take in a unique local celebration: **viewing the sunset from Mallory Dock.** Sunset-watching is good fun all over the world, but in Key West it's been turned into a carnival-like, almost pagan celebration. People from all over begin to crowd Mallory Square even before the sun starts to fall, bringing the place alive with entertainment—everything from string bands to a unicyclist wriggling free of a straitjacket to a juggler tossing around machetes and flaming sticks. The main entertainment, however, is that massive fireball falling out of view, a sight that's always greeted with hysterical applause.

ON YOUR OWN: BEYOND THE PORT AREA

Nothin'. That's the beauty of Key West: Everything worthwhile is accessible by foot.

SHOPPING

Within a 12-block radius of Old Town, you'll find mostly tawdry and outrageously overpriced merchandise, but if you're in the market for some Key West kitsch, this is the neighborhood for you. Shopping by cruise ship passengers has become a joke among Key West locals, but that's their problem. We say be proud of your flamingo snow globe and floppy straw hat. What else says "vacation" better?

Among the less kitschy alternatives, a few standouts are located much farther along **Duval Street,** the main drag leading to the Atlantic, and on hidden back streets. You can reach all these stores from the cruise ship docks in a 15- to 20-minute stroll.

Haitian Art Company, 600 Frances St. ((C) **305/296-8932**), claims to inventory the largest collection of Haitian paintings in the United States. Prices range from $15 to $5,000. **Key West Aloe, Inc.,** 524 Front St. or 540 Greene St.

(℡ **305/294-5592**), is aloe, aloe, and more aloe; the shop's inventory includes shaving cream, aftershave lotion, sunburn ointments, and fragrances for men and women based on tropical essences such as hibiscus, frangipani, and white ginger. **Key West Hand Print Fashions and Fabrics,** 201 Simonton St. (℡ **305/292-8951**), sells bold, tropical prints—hand-printed scarves with coordinated handbags and rack after rack of busily patterned sundresses and cocktail dresses that will make you look jaunty on deck. **Key West Island Bookstore,** 513 Fleming St. (℡ **305/294-2904**), is well stocked with books on Key West and has Florida's largest collection of works by and about Hemingway. In the rear is a rare-book section where you may want to browse, if not buy.

BEACHES

Beaches are not too compelling here. Most are man-made, often with imported Bahamian or mainland Florida sand. Those mentioned below are free and open to the public daily from 7am to 11pm. There are few facilities, just locals hawking beach umbrellas, food, and drinks.

Fort Zachary Taylor State Beach (℡ **305/292-6883**) is the best and the closest to the cruise ship docks, a 12-minute walk away. This 51-acre man-made beach is adjacent to historic Fort Taylor, once known as Fort Forgotten because it was buried under tons of sand. The beach is fine for sunbathing and picnicking and is suitable for snorkeling. To get there, go through the gates leading into **Truman Annex** (℡ **305/292-6713**). Watering holes near one end of the beach include the raffish **Green Parrot Bar** (℡ **305/294-6133**) and **Meteore Smokehouse Barbecue** (℡ **305/294-5602**).

Higgs Memorial Beach lies a 25-minute walk from the harbor near the end of White Street, one of the main east-west arteries. You'll find lots of sand, picnic tables sheltered from the sun, and fewer of your fellow cruise ship passengers. Smathers Beach, named in honor of one of Florida's most colorful former senators, is the longest (about 1½ miles) in town. Unfortunately, it's about a $10 one-way taxi ride from the cruise docks. The beach borders South Roosevelt Boulevard. There's no shade here.

In the 1950s, **Southernmost Beach** drew Tennessee Williams, but today it's more likely to fill up with visitors from the motels nearby. Except for a nearby restaurant, facilities are nonexistent. The beach lies at the foot of Duval Street on the Atlantic side, across the island from the cruise ship docks. It takes about 20 minutes to walk there along Duval Street from the docks. The beach boasts some white sand but is not particularly good for swimming. Nevertheless, it's one of the island's most frequented.

SPORTS

FISHING   As Hemingway, an avid fisherman, would attest, the waters off the Florida Keys are some of the world's finest fishing grounds. You can follow in his wake aboard the 40-foot *Linda D III* and *Linda D IV* (℡ **800/299-9798** or 305/ 296-9798; www.charterboatlindad.com), which offer the best deep-sea fishing here. Full-day charters for up to six people are $675, half-day $450. Full-day shared charters are $165 per person, half-day $110. Make arrangements as far in advance as possible.

GOLF   Redesigned in 1982 by architect Rees Jones, the 18-hole, par-70 **Key West Resort Golf Club,** 6450 E. Junior College Rd. (℡ **305/294-5232;** www. keywestgolf.com), lies 2½ miles from the cruise docks, near the southern tip of neighboring Stock Island. It features a challenging terrain of coral rock, sand traps, mangrove swamp, and pines. Greens fees are $140, including cart. The course is a 10- to 15-minute, $10 taxi ride from the dock each way.

SCUBA DIVING   The largest dive outfitter is **Captain's Corner,** 125 Ann St., half a block from the dock (© **305/296-8865;** www.captainscorner.com). The five-star PADI operation has 11 instructors, a well-trained staff, and a 60-foot dive boat that was used by Timothy "James Bond" Dalton during the filming of *License to Kill.* To reach the departure point, walk to the end of Greene Street.

GREAT LOCAL RESTAURANTS & BARS

RESTAURANTS   All the restaurants listed below are within an easy 5- to 15-minute walk of the docks, except for Camille's and El Siboney, which are more than a mile away. Several "raw bars" near the dock area offer seafood, including oysters and clams, although the king here is conch—served grilled, ground into burgers, made into chowder, fried in batter as fritters, or served raw in a conch salad. Even if you don't have lunch, at least sample the local favorites: a slice of Key lime pie with a Cuban coffee. The pie's unique flavor comes from the juice and minced rind of the local, piquant Key lime.

Cruise ship passengers on a return visit to Key West often ask for The Rose Tattoo, a historic old restaurant named for the Tennessee Williams film partially shot on the island. The restaurant is now the **Bagatelle,** 115 Duval St., at Front Street (© **305/296-6609**), one of Key West's finest. Look for daily specials or stick to the chef's better dishes, such as conch seviche (thinly sliced raw conch marinated in lime juice and herbs). Lunch is about $13. **Blue Heaven,** 729 Thomas St. (© **305/296-8666**), is a dive that serves some of the best food in town, including fresh local fish, most often grouper or red snapper. Their hot and spicy jerk chicken is as fine as that served in Jamaica. Lunch is about $12. **Camille's,** 1202 Simonton St., at Catherine Street (© **305/296-4811**), is an unpretentious, hip cafe that serves the best breakfast in town and has the best lunch value. Try a sandwich made from the catch of the day, served on fresh bread, and finish off with some of their great Key lime pie. Lunch is about $10. **El Siboney,** 900 Catherine St. (© **305/296-4184**), is the place for time-tested Cuban favorites such as *ropa vieja* (shredded meat stew), roast pork with garlic and tart sour oranges, and paella Valenciana. Lunch is around $10.

Half Shell Raw Bar, Land's End Marina, at the foot of Margaret Street (© **305/294-7496**), is Key West's original raw bar, offering fresh fish, oysters, and shrimp direct from its own fish market. Lunch is about $15. To be honest, though, we prefer the food at **Turtle Kraals Wildlife Bar & Grill,** Land's End Village, at the foot of Margaret Street (© **305/294-2640**). Try the tender Florida lobster, spicy conch chowder, or perfectly cooked fresh fish (often dolphinfish with pineapple salsa or baked stuffed grouper with mango crabmeat stuffing). Lunch is around $14.

Pepe's Café & Steak House, 806 Caroline St., between William and Margaret streets (© **305/294-7192**), is the oldest eating house in the Florida Keys, established in 1909. Diners eat under slow-moving paddle fans at tables or dark pine booths with high backs. At lunch (served noon–4pm), choose from zesty homemade chili, perfectly baked oysters, fish sandwiches, and Pepe's deservedly famous steak sandwiches. Lunch is about $8.

If something cool would go down better than a full meal, check out the **Flamingo Crossing ice-cream shop,** 1105 Duval St., at Virginia Street (© **305/ 296-6124**).

BARS Key West is a bar town, and since many ships stay in town late, you'll likely have an opportunity to do some carousing. Most places recommended below offer fast food to go with their drinks. The food isn't the best on the island, but usually arrives shortly after you order it, which suits most rushed cruise ship passengers just fine. Try some of the favorite **local beer,** Hog's Breath, or some of the favorite **local rum,** Key West Gold (even though it's a cheat—it isn't actually made on the island).

Heavily patronized by cruise ship passengers, **Captain Tony's Saloon,** 428 Greene St. (© **305/294-1838**), is the oldest active bar in Florida, and is tacky as can be. The 1851 building was the original Sloppy Joe's, a rough-and-tumble fisherman's saloon. Hemingway drank here from 1933 to 1937, and Jimmy Buffett got his start here before opening his own bar and going on to musical glory. The name refers to Capt. Tony Tarracino, a former Key West mayor and rugged man of the sea who owned the place until 1988.

The current **Sloppy Joe's,** 201 Duval St. (© **305/294-5717**), is the most touristy bar in Key West, visited by almost all cruise ship passengers, even those who don't normally go to bars. It aggressively plays up its association with Hemingway, although the bar stood on Greene Street back then (see above). Marine flags decorate the ceiling, and its ambience and decor evoke a Havana bar from the 1930s.

Jimmy Buffett's Margaritaville, 500 Duval St. (© **305/296-3070**), is the third most popular Key West bar with cruise ship passengers. Buffett is the hometown boy done good, and his cafe, naturally, is decorated with pictures of himself. And, yes, it sells T-shirts and Margaritaville memorabilia in a shop off the dining room. His margaritas are without competition, but then they'd have to be, wouldn't they?

Open-air, very laid-back, and sometimes very loud, the **Hog's Breath Saloon,** 400 Front St. (© **305/296-HOGG**), near the cruise docks, has been a Key West tradition since 1976. Drinking is a sport here, especially among the fishermen who come in after a day chasing the big one, and the biker types who show up anytime. Live entertainment is offered from 1pm to 2am.

For a real local hangout within an easy walk of the cruise ship docks, head to **Schooner Wharf,** 202 William St., Key West Bight (© **305/292-9520**), the most robust and hard-drinking bar in Key West, drawing primarily a young crowd, many of whom work in the tourist industry or on the local fishing boats.

20 Les Saintes

You want charming? The eight islets of Les Saintes (pronounced *lay sant*) are irresistibly so: pastel-colored gingerbread houses with tropical gardens, sugarloaf hills that slope down to miniature beaches, and picturesque bays with pelicans, sailboats, and turquoise water. Only two of the islands in this French archipelago off the southern coast of Guadeloupe are inhabited: Terre-de-Bas and its more populous neighbor, Terre-de-Haut (more populous, in this case, meaning it has about 1,700 inhabitants). Terre-de-Haut (pronounced "t'air d'oh"), with only one village—the straightforwardly named Le Bourg ("town")—is the destination of most visitors. Some say it's what Saint-Tropez was like before Brigitte Bardot. For a U.S. point of reference, think Fire Island, Provincetown, Martha's Vineyard, or Sausalito with a French-Caribbean twist. Nautical and quaint are the watchwords.

But Les Saintes, also known as Iles des Saintes, isn't a fantasy park built to look enchanting. Although tourism is important to the island's economy, most

---

Fun Fact　Tormented by Love? Have a Pastry

As you leave your ship, you'll spot local women selling Les Saintes' signature sweet, tartlets known as *tourments d'amour* (love's torments). Legend has it that young maidens baked these flaky-crusted, coconut-filled treats to present to their betrotheds as they returned from lengthy fishing expeditions. From time to time, the cruel and heartless sea claimed the life of a beloved, leaving a teary-eyed damsel at the dock with nothing but her pain and pastry. Is it the suffering that makes the *tourments d'amour* so tasty?

---

people here still make their living from the sea. Les Saintois, as the locals are called, are widely regarded as the best fishermen in the Antilles, and it's this underlying saltiness that keeps the place from being cloyingly sweet.

COMING ASHORE　Cruise ships dock at **Le Bourg** in Terre-de-Haut. The village has two main streets, both parallel to the bay and lined with cafes, restaurants, and souvenir shops. **Telephones** at the dock require a telecarte, a prepaid phone card sold at the post office (a 10-min. walk from the dock; take a right) and other outlets marked TELECARTE EN VENTE ICI. Some phones now accept U.S. calling cards or major credit cards for long-distance calls.

LANGUAGE　The official language is **French,** but many islanders speak **Creole** with each other. Few locals feel comfortable with English, though, so take the opportunity to practice your high-school French. Most everyone is helpful and friendly, especially if you smile and make an effort.

CURRENCY　Les Saintes is part of the larger archipelago of Guadeloupe, an overseas region of France, so the **euro** (€) is now the official currency (exchange rate at press time: 1€ = US$1.22; $1 = .82€). Each euro is divisible by 100 cents. You can withdraw euros from the ATM next to the tourism office (see "Information," below). Unless otherwise specified, prices in this section are given in U.S. dollars.

INFORMATION　If you take a right on the main road after you leave the ship, you'll see signs for the **tourism office** (OFFICE DU TOURISME). It's less than a 5-minute walk. Most printed information available here is in French, but the maps are helpful even if you don't understand the lingo. For info before you go, contact the Tourism Board in the United States (© **410/286-8310;** www.french caribbean.com).

CALLING FROM THE U.S.　When calling Les Saintes from the U.S., dial the international access code (011) and 590 before the numbers listed here. Yes, the numbers listed here already begin with 590, but an effort by the French telephone authorities to standardize procedures requires that you dial those three digits twice. Really.

GETTING AROUND

If you're reasonably fit, there's no reason you can't walk wherever you want to go. If you're the type who runs 8km (5 miles) a day, you can hike up Le Chameau, traipse around Fort Napoléon, head over to Plage de Pompierre, and complete the Trace des Crêtes, with time for a meal or swim before returning to the ship.

BY TAXI　The island has a handful of minivans that serve as taxis. Each seats six to eight passengers, and most drivers offer 3-hour tours of the island for

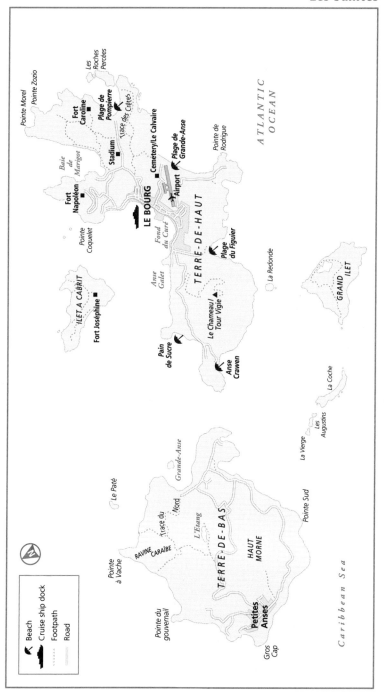

about $40 (be aware, though, that fluent English is not widely spoken). You'll find the cabs parked directly in front of the cruise ship dock.

BY SCOOTER   Terre-de-Haut is less than 6.4km (4 miles long) and less than 3.2km (2 miles) wide. Aside from tourist vans and the occasional private car, four-wheeled vehicles are rare (at last count, there were fewer than three dozen). Scooters rule the roads. Scores of them await you just off the dock along Le Bourg's main road. Expect to pay about $31 for a two-seater for the day. A $380 deposit (credit cards accepted) is required.

BY BICYCLE   You can rent bicycles for between $15 and $20 along Le Bourg's main road. The island is hilly, though. You'd do better to rent a scooter or walk.

BEST CRUISE LINE SHORE EXCURSIONS
Don't expect any. This is a wander-around-at-your-own-pace kind of place. See "Sports," below, for scuba, snorkeling, and fishing excursions you can arrange through local agencies.

ON YOUR OWN: WITHIN WALKING DISTANCE
Everything is within walking distance of the dock. **Fort Napoléon** looms over Le Bourg's picturesque bay. The French started building this stone bastion after they regained Les Saintes from the British in 1815 but didn't complete it until 1867. Today it houses engaging, detailed exhibits that cover the entire history of the islands, including life before Columbus, European expansion into the New World, early French settlements, the Battle of Les Saintes, and the development of the fishing industry. You can wander through barracks, dungeons, and the grounds, which feature an impressive array of cacti and succulents. Pick up the English-language brochure that describes the vegetation when you purchase your admission ticket; adult admission is about $2.80, children under 12 pay $1.40. For 80¢, you can rent a cassette that provides excellent English commentary as you walk through the museum. The fort is open a brief 3½ hours a day, from 9am to 12:30pm, so make it your first destination.

On the hill that leads to Fort Napoléon, visit **Jerome Hoff,** a fourth-generation Santois of Alsatian ancestry who paints religious icons in a heartfelt but slightly disturbing style. He has the wild-eyed air of a John the Baptist, but he's a gentle man, retired now, who loves to talk about his 50 years of singing in the church choir. You can't miss his modest home and studio—they're surrounded by numerous quirky signs that feature colorful saints and passionate prayers.

On the route to the tourism office and the ATM, you'll pass Le Bourg's **stone church.** It's humble, but worth the couple of minutes it takes to peek inside.

If you're up for some hiking, the **Trace des Crêtes trail** traces the spine of one of Terre-de-Haut's hills just north of the airport and offers remarkable views of beaches, cliffs, and neighboring islands. Although clearly marked, the path is rocky and challenging—you have an advantage if you're part goat. Wear sunscreen and bring water.

Be sure to stop for a few minutes at the **cemetery** next to the airport. You'll notice several graves adorned with conch shells, which signify a sea-related death. On Saturday nights, refrigerator-size speakers are brought in, makeshift food stands are set up, and the cemetery becomes a huge open-air disco. In the same vicinity, **Le Calvaire** is a giant Christ statue at the summit of a hill; numerous steps ascend to great panoramas.

Chameau means camel in French, and with a bit of imagination you can see that **Le Chameau,** the highest point on Terre-de-Haut, looks sort of like the hump of a dromedary. The concrete road to the 300m (984-ft.) summit is off-limits to all motorized vehicles, and, mercifully, it's shaded much of the way. After 30 to 60 minutes of arduous climbing, you're rewarded with spectacular views of the entire archipelago, Guadeloupe, and Dominica. **Tour Vigie,** a military lookout dating from the time of Napoleon, crowns the mountain; unfortunately, it's usually locked.

SHOPPING

Little boutiques that sell beachwear, T-shirts, jewelry, and knickknacks line the streets. Stop by Pascal Foy's **Kaz an Nou Gallery** behind the church. You can watch him make Cases Creoles, miniature carved wooden Creole houses in candy colors. They're becoming collector's items. **Galerie Martine Cotten,** at the foot of the dock, features the work of an artist originally from Brittany who celebrates the natural beauty and fishing traditions of Les Saintes. Beyond the town hall, **Ultramarine** is a tiny cottage where you can buy unusual dolls, clothes, T-shirts, and handcrafted items from France, Haiti, and Africa. **Galerie Marchande Seaside,** a group of shops situated around a patio, is just up the street after you turn right from the pier. Art, gifts, antiques, jewelry, lace, beachwear, and ice cream are available.

BEACHES

Beaches with golden sand are tucked away in almost all of the island's coves. Calm, crescent-shaped **Plage de Pompierre** (sometimes spelled Pont Pierre) is shaded by sea-grape bushes, as well as almond and palm trees. A 15-minute walk from the dock, it boasts soft white sand, shade from coconut palms, and quiet seclusion. The gentle water in the cliff-encircled cove is a stunning aquamarine. Because the bay is a nature preserve, fishing and anchoring are prohibited. It's the island's most popular sunbathing spot, so your best bet is to go early or late.

   Grande Anse, near the airfield, is large, but there's no shade, and the rough surf has a strong undertow. Although swimming is discouraged, the cliffs at

Frommer's Favorite Les Saintes Experiences

Meandering Around Fort Napoléon: The French built this impressive stone fortification after they regained Les Saintes in 1815, and today it houses engaging, detailed exhibits covering the entire history of the islands. (See "On Your Own: Within Walking Distance," above.)

Trekking to the Top of Le Chameau: The highest point on Terre-de-Haut, Le Chameau is located in the southern part of the island and offers a tough (though shaded) 30- to 60-minute climb, for which you're rewarded with spectacular views. (See "On Your Own: Within Walking Distance," above.)

Sunbathing on Picture-Perfect Plage de Pompierre: No beach on Terre-de-Haut is nicer than Plage de Pompierre, located only a 15-minute walk from the dock. (See "Beaches," below.)

Climbing Along the Trace des Crêtes: This trail across the center of Terre-de-Haut offers remarkable views of beaches, cliffs, the island's toylike airport, and neighboring islands. (See "On Your Own: Within Walking Distance," above.)

The Goats of Love

Don't leave anything unattended while swimming at Plage de Pompierre. Savvy goats hide out in the scrub behind the beach, patiently scoping out the action. Once you go into the water, they'll make a beeline for your unattended picnic basket and treat themselves to anything edible. They're especially fond of those *tourments d'amour* you just bought at the dock. Who's crying now?

---

either end of the beach and the powerful breakers make for a dramatic seascape. The usually deserted **Figuier,** on the southern coast, has excellent snorkeling.

SPORTS

FISHING   Going out to sea with a local fisherman is one way to experience Les Saintes' nautical heritage. Most of the local sailors will be delighted to take you out, if you can communicate well enough to negotiate a price. Most fishermen are stationed next to the cruise ship dock; just follow the waterfront to the fishing boats.

SCUBA, SNORKELING & OTHER WATERSPORTS   For scuba diving and snorkeling, go to **La Dive Bouteille Centre Nautique des Saintes** (© 590/ 99-54-25; www.dive-bouteille.com) at the Plage de la Colline west of town past the market, or **UCPA** (© 590/99-54-94), on the other side of Fort Napoléon hill in Marigot Bay. One-tank dives run about $65. Both also rent sea kayaks and windsurfing equipment.

GREAT LOCAL RESTAURANTS & BARS

Virtually every restaurant in Terre-de-Haut offers seafood that couldn't be fresher, and many feature Creole dishes. A local favorite is smoked kingfish *(thazard fumé).* **L'Auberge Les Petits Saints aux Anarcadiers** (© 590/99-50-99) is a hillside veranda restaurant overlooking the bay. On Route de Rodrigue, it boasts a tropical garden and countless antiques. Lunch is $33. Reservations are mandatory. The terrace restaurant at the **Hôtel Bois Joli** (© 590/99-50-38), on the island's western tip, offers a view of Pain de Sucre, Les Saintes' petite version of Rio de Janeiro's Sugarloaf Mountain, and is fringed with palm trees. For pasta, pizza, or salad, try **La Saladerie's** seaside terrace on the way to Fort Napoléon. **Café de la Marine** (© 590/99-53-78), on the bay and main street, serves thin-crusted pizzas and seafood. Lunch is $20. One of the island's best bakeries *(boulangeries),* **Le Fournil de Jimmy** (© 590/99-57-73), is on the same square as the town hall, across from the tourist office. If you stop in at the right time, you can get a crusty baguette hot from the oven. If you'd rather have something cold, try one of the Italian gelati at **Tropico Gelato** (© 590/99-88-12). Turn right off the dock; it's a couple of storefronts down on your right.

21 Martinique

Fairy-tale romance and horrific disaster: Who could resist such an enticing combination? As if being the birthplace and childhood home of Empress Joséphine, sweetheart and wife of Napoleon, weren't enough, Martinique mesmerizes with the epic tragedy that befell St. Pierre one fair day in 1902: bustling cosmopolitan capital one minute, devastated volcanic graveyard of 30,000 souls the next. Love and death make quite a one-two punch, but they're just the hook. Look a

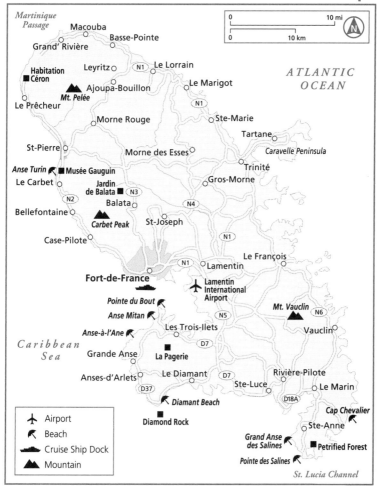

Martinique Passage

Macouba
Grand' Rivière
Basse-Pointe

0   10 mi
0   10 km

Habitation Céron
Leyritz
Le Lorrain
N1

ATLANTIC OCEAN

Ajoupa-Bouillon
Le Marigot

Mt. Pelée
N1

Le Prêcheur

Morne Rouge
Ste-Marie

Tartane

St-Pierre
Morne des Esses
Caravelle Peninsula

Anse Turin
Musée Gauguin
Trinité

Le Carbet
Jardin de Balata
N3
Gros-Morne

N2
Balata
N4

Bellefontaine

Carbet Peak
St-Joseph

Case-Pilote
N1

Le François

N1
Lamentin

Fort-de-France
Lamentin International Airport

Pointe du Bout
Mt. Vauclin
N6

Anse Mitan
N5

Anse-à-l'Ane
Les Trois-Ilets
Vauclin

Caribbean Sea
Grande Anse
La Pagerie
D7

Anses-d'Arlets
Le Diamant
D7
Rivière-Pilote

D37
Ste-Luce
Le Marin

Diamant Beach
D18A

Diamond Rock
Cap Chevalier
Ste-Anne

Grand Anse des Salines
Petrified Forest

Pointe des Salines
St. Lucia Channel

✈ Airport
🏖 Beach
🚢 Cruise Ship Dock
⛰ Mountain

bit deeper to appreciate Martinique's subtler attractions—quaint seaside villages, colonial ruins, and captivatingly beautiful rainforests and beaches.

Madiana, or "island of flowers," was the Carib name for the island, and hibiscus, bougainvillea, and bird of paradise grow in lush profusion alongside mango, pineapple, banana, and papaya. Like Guadeloupe and St. Barts, Martinique is as French as Bordeaux, and you'll find everything from baguettes to Balenciaga here. But with African and new-world roots forever entwined, Creole cuisine and traditions continue to flourish.

About 81km (50 miles) long and 35km (22 miles) wide, the island features a diverse topography. Rainforests drape the volcanic mountains of the north; small, rounded hills and enclosed valleys mark the central plain; and white-sand beaches ring the arid, flat south.

During the 18th and 19th centuries, France and England vied for the island. In 1946, Martinique became an overseas department of France, and in 1974, it achieved regional status—the French minister of the interior appoints a prefect, but the island's citizens elect representatives to the national legislature in Paris and the regional legislature in Fort-de-France.

Most of Martinique's 380,000 residents are descendants of African slaves, but others of European, Asian, and Middle Eastern ancestry add to the melting pot. Attesting to the generally amicable relations among the various peoples, every shade of skin color is represented.

COMING ASHORE   Most cruise ships dock in the heart of Fort-de-France, at the **Pointe Simon Cruise Dock,** which has quays for two large vessels. Because Martinique is a popular port of call, ships also dock at the **Passenger Terminal** at the main harbor, a cargo port on the north side of the bay, a $10 cab ride from the center of town.

If you want to check your e-mail, go to **Cyber Club Caraibes** (© **596/71-43-21**), an Internet cafe at 16 rue François Arago Fort-de-France. The cafe is open Monday from 8am to 8pm, Tuesday to Saturday from 8am to 10pm, and Sunday 2pm to 6pm. It costs $3 for 15 minutes—cheaper than aboard ship.

LANGUAGE   **French** is Martinique's official language, but you can get by with **English** at most restaurants and tourist sites. You'll also hear the island patois, **Creole,** on the street. Because many of the island's service employees work hard to improve their English, cruisers who speak no French find Martinique easier to navigate than Guadeloupe, the other big French Caribbean island. Ask for English-language brochures and commentaries when sightseeing; most sites have them.

CURRENCY   Martinique is an overseas region of France, so the **euro** (€) is now the official currency (exchange rate at press time: 1€ = US$1.22; $1 = .82€). Each euro is divisible by 100 cents. Unless otherwise specified, prices in this section are given in U.S. dollars. There are numerous ATMs *(distributeur de billets)* in downtown Fort-de-France, and you'll have no trouble using your credit cards and traveler's checks. You can change money at **Change Caraïbe** (© **596/60-28-40**), 4 rue Ernest Deproge, on the waterfront, or 1 block inland at **Change Point Change** (© **596/63-80-33**), 14 rue Victor Hugo.

INFORMATION   The **Tourism Office** of Fort de France (© **596/60-27-73**) opens an office at the pier when ships come in. For info before you go, contact the **Bureau** in the U.S. (© **410/286-8310;** www.martinique.org).

CALLING FROM THE U.S.   When calling Martinique from the U.S., dial the international access code (011) and 596 before the numbers listed here. The numbers listed here already begin with 596, but an effort by the French telephone authorities to standardize procedures requires that you dial those three digits twice.

GETTING AROUND
BY TAXI   Travel by taxi is convenient but expensive. Most cabs are metered, but they do offer flat rates for touring the island. Taxis wait for ships at the cruise pier, and several English-speaking drivers give tours of the island for roughly $50 an hour for up to four passengers. For a radio taxi, call © **596/63-63-62.**

BY BUS   For trips beyond Fort-de-France, collective taxi-minibuses are a cheap but iffy alternative. These privately owned minivans (look for the TC sign) generally seat eight and have flexible routes and unpredictable schedules. Often crowded and sometimes less than comfortable, they're widely used by adventurous tourists nonetheless, particularly those who speak some French. The reason?

Frommer's Favorite Martinique Experiences

Touring "Pompeii of the Caribbean": Mount Pelée erupted in 1902, killing all but one of St. Pierre's 30,000 residents. See the havoc this not-yet-dormant volcano wreaked on the town's church, theater, and other buildings, and view smaller relics at the volcano museum. (See "On Your Own: Beyond the Port Area," below.)

Traveling back to the 17th Century: The estate ruins at Habitation Céron, near the island's northern Caribbean coast, are enormously evocative of early colonial times, when sugar was king. The old stone plantation buildings are covered with moss, and the wild gardens abound with lush vegetation and singing birds. (See "On Your Own: Beyond the Port Area," below.)

Eavesdropping on Imperial Romance: Empress Joséphine, Napoleon Bonaparte's first wife, was born and reared at La Pagerie, her family's estate near the town of Trois Ilets. Part of the sugar plantation still stands, and the museum displays personal effects of the Martinican empress, including a passionate love letter from the Little Corporal to his Petite Creole. (See "On Your Own: Beyond the Port Area," below.)

Price: A one-way ride to Grande Anse des Salines beach is about $5. Vans leave from a parking lot at Pointe Simon, in the heart of Fort-de-France.

BY RENTAL CAR   Martinique's size and myriad attractions make renting a car especially worthwhile. You drive on the right on roads that are in excellent condition and almost always scenic. You need a valid driver's license and must be at least 21. **Avis, Budget,** and **Hertz** all have offices here.

BY FERRY   To reach La Pagerie (Empress Joséphine's birthplace), the island's golf course, horseback-riding stables, and the resort area of Pointe du Bout, take one of the blue ferries operated by **Somatour** (© **596/73-05-53**) from Quai d'Esnambuc, east of the cruise dock, in Fort-de-France. The trip across the bay takes 15 minutes, and round-trip tickets are $6 per person. Boats leave at least once an hour.

BEST CRUISE LINE SHORE EXCURSIONS

Rainforest & Plantations 4WD Safari ($84, 4 hr.): Take your off-road vehicle through tropical forests and sugar-cane plantations (stopping to sample the crop) to a banana plantation and a distillery where you'll do short tours.

Martinique Snorkeling ($52, 2½ hr.): Across the bay from Fort-de-France, the reef at Anse Dufour offers excellent snorkeling for experts and novices. The reef is filled with marine animals, including French grunts, blackbar soldierfish, and silversides. Snorkeling equipment is provided, as are professional instruction, supervision, and transportation.

EXCURSIONS OFFERED BY LOCAL AGENCIES

Adventure Excursions & Hiking: Martinique's lush, mountainous northern half provides myriad adventure opportunities. **Aventures Tropicales** (© **596/ 75-24-24**), based in Fort-de-France, is the island's premier adventure tour operator, offering jeep and hiking tours. Excursions require a minimum number of six participants. Make arrangements before arriving on the island.

Horseback Treks: Pros and novices are both accommodated on morning horseback rides offered by **Ranch Jack,** in Morne Habitué (*©* **596/68-37-69**), and Trois Ilets (*©* **596/68-37-80**). The daily promenades pass over hills, through fields, and onto beaches, as guides provide a running commentary on the history, fauna, and botany of the island. Transportation to and from the cruise dock can be arranged. The price of a half-day excursion with refreshments is about $68.

See "Sports," later in this section, for scuba diving and snorkeling.

ON YOUR OWN: WITHIN WALKING DISTANCE

Fort-de-France is a bustling, cosmopolitan town with 100,000 residents and an unmistakable French air. Part New Orleans, part French Riviera, it's full of ochre buildings, ornate wrought-iron balconies, cascading flowers, and tall palm trees. The town's narrow streets, cluttered with boutiques and cafes, climb from the bowl of the sea to the surrounding hills, forming a great urban amphitheater. There's plenty here to keep you busy.

At the eastern end of downtown, **La Savane** is a broad formal park with palms, mangoes, and manicured lawns, perfect for a promenade or rest in the shade. Its most famous feature is the **Statue of Empress Joséphine,** carved in 1858 by Vital Dubray. Like a variation on the Venus de Milo, this white marble empress is headless: Napoleon's Little Creole was unceremoniously decapitated and doused with red paint in 1995 by locals who remembered her role in reinstating slavery on the island in the early 1800s.

Across the street at 21 rue de la Liberté, the **Bibliothèque Schoelcher (Schoelcher Library;** *©* **596/70-26-67**) is one of Fort-de-France's great Belle Epoque buildings. Named in honor of Victor Schoelcher, one of France's most influential abolitionists, this elaborate structure, designed by French architect Henri Pick, was first displayed at the 1889 Paris Exposition. Four years later, the red-and-blue Romanesque portal, Egyptian lotus-petal columns, iron-and-glass cupola, and multicolored tiles were dismantled and then reassembled piece by piece at the present site. The interior light, mosaics, and tile floor are glorious. The proud repository of Schoelcher's 10,000-volume book collection, as well as an impressive archive of colonization, slavery, and emancipation documents, it's open Monday through Saturday. There's no admission charge.

Another Henri Pick masterpiece, **St. Louis Cathedral,** on rue Victor Schoelcher at rue Blénac, was built in 1895. A contemporary of Gustave Eiffel (of Eiffel Tower fame), Pick used massive iron beams to support the walls, ceiling, and spire. A grand example of Industrial Revolution architecture, it's been likened to a Catholic railway station. The organ, stained-glass windows, and ornamented interior walls are well worth a look and can be viewed every morning except Saturday.

Built in 1640, **Fort St. Louis,** Boulevard Alfassa, dominates the rocky promontory east of La Savane. A noteworthy example of 17th- and 18th-century military architecture, it first defended Fort-de-France in 1674 against Dutch invaders; beginning in 1762, it was the site of numerous battles between French and English forces. Today, the bastion remains the French navy's headquarters in the Caribbean. Guided tours leave daily every 30 minutes beginning at 9:30am. Bring a picture ID. The entrance fee, payable in dollars, is $5 for adults, $2.50 for students.

The best of Fort-de-France's many museums, the **Musée Départemental Archéologie Precolombienne Préhistoire,** 9 rue de la Liberté (© **596/71-57-05**), traces 2,000 years of Martinique's pre-Columbian past with more than a thousand relics from the Arawak and Carib cultures. Spread over three floors, the detailed exhibits document various pottery and tool styles, burial practices, agricultural methods, social and religious customs, and changes that occurred after the arrival of Europeans. Across the street from La Savane, it's open Monday from 1 to 5 pm, Tuesday through Friday from 8am to 5pm, and Saturday from 9am to noon. Admission is about $4 for adults, $3 for students, and $2 for children. The tiny gift stand sells pottery reproductions.

A less established museum, the **Musée du Carnaval** (© **596/73-49-07**), next to the cruise terminal on rue des Gabares, focuses on the history, costumes, and traditions of Martinique's unique version of Carnival—pajama parades, drag marriages, junkyard jump-ups, and decorated jalopies, to name a few. English-speaking guides help you navigate the tiny museum, which is open Tuesday through Friday from 9am to 4pm, and on Saturday from 9am to noon. Admission is about $4 for adults, $2.50 for students, and $1 for kids under 12.

ON YOUR OWN: BEYOND THE PORT AREA

Martinique is much too large to tackle in a single day. You'll have to make some tough choices about which of its many museums, plantations, floral parks, and natural wonders to visit. Here are three suggested itineraries for the day.

NORTH OF FORT-DE-FRANCE   Less than 8km (5 miles) north of Fort-de-France, on the scenic Route de la Trace (Rte. N3), **L'Eglise Sacré Coeur de Balata** overlooks the capital and its bay. This quiet village church is anything but typical: Built in 1924, it's a one-fifth-scale replica of the wedding-cake-pretty Sacré Coeur Basilica that crowns Montmartre in Paris. Rather than the white stone of the Paris original, this unintentionally whimsical copy uses gray freestone.

Martinique's Carib name, Madiana, means "island of flowers." To see what the Caribs were talking about, stroll through the **Jardin de Balata** (© **596/64-48-73**). Just minutes north of the Sacré Coeur church, this lush, Edenic garden showcases 200 species of plants, trees, and tropical flowers, including towering ferns, lotuses, alpinias, porcelain roses, anthuriums, and heliconias. The hillside oasis, which boasts resident hummingbirds, frogs, and lizards, is open daily from 9am to 5pm. Admission is about $6 for adults, $2.50 for kids under 12.

Yes, it's hot outside, but things could be worse. One of Martinique's must-see attractions, the village of **St. Pierre** on the northwest coast, was the cultural and economic capital of Martinique until 8am on May 8, 1902, when Mount Pelée, the hulking volcano that dominates the northern tip of the island, exploded in fire and lava. Three minutes later, all but 1 of St. Pierre's 30,000 inhabitants had been incinerated, buried in ash and lava, or asphyxiated by poisonous gas. The town once hailed as the "Paris of the Antilles" and the "Pearl of the West Indies" because of its beautiful buildings, imposing residences, and lively theaters suddenly became "the Pompeii of the Caribbean." It never regained its splendor, and today it's no more than a sleepy fishing village, home to fewer than 5,000 souls. Ruins of a church, theater, and other buildings punctuate the town, memorials to St. Pierre's former glory and the horrific fury of Pelée. In lieu of walking from one ruin to another, you can hop on the rubber-wheeled trolley known as the Cyparis Express, which departs from the Musée Volcanologique (see below). The 1-hour tours operate Monday to Friday and half-hour tours operate on the weekends. The fee is about $8 for adults, half that for kids. (The trolley is named in honor of Cyparis, a prisoner locked behind thick cell walls, who was the sole human to survive the eruption. Found in his dungeon 4 days after the disaster, he later toured with P. T. Barnum's circus, showing his burn scars to curious folks around North America.)

The town's touristic potential hasn't been grotesquely exploited: Aside from the ruins, the only other point of interest is the **Musée Volcanologique,** rue Victor Hugo (**© 596/78-15-16**). Founded by American vulcanologist Franck A. Perret, this one-room exhibit traces the story of the cataclysm through pictures and relics excavated from the debris, including petrified spaghetti, lava-encrusted teapots, twisted musical instruments, a human skull, and distorted clocks that stopped at the hour of destruction. Open daily from 9am to 5pm, it charges adults about $1.50; children under 8 enter free.

Part sugar-plantation ruins, part tropical paradise, **Habitation Céron** (**© 596/52-94-53**) is the most evocative of Martinique's historical agricultural sites. This sprawling 17th-century estate, 15 minutes north of St. Pierre, is almost as wild and tranquil as the surrounding rainforest, but its verdigris cisterns, moss-covered stone buildings, and archaic, still functioning water mill are all haunted with the ghosts of a time when sugar was king, slaves toiled in the heat, and French colonists lived in languid comfort. The site is open daily from 9:30am to 5pm. Self-guided tours of the estate cost $7.50. The on-site restaurant, housed in former slave quarters, serves crayfish, octopus, and other seafood.

A few miles south of St. Pierre, **Le Carbet** is where Columbus landed in 1502, the first French settlers arrived in 1635, and the French painter Paul Gauguin lived for 5 months in 1887. Too ill to return to France after a failed quest for "noble savages" in Panama, the artist wrote that "only in Martinique was I able to feel truly myself." An unassuming museum devoted to Gauguin and his Martinican works, the **Musée Paul Gauguin,** Anse Turin (**© 596/78-22-66**), sits not far from the hut the painter once occupied. It boasts no original paintings, but it does have reproductions of the dozen pictures he composed on the island, precursors of his later, more famous Tahitian works. Other items on display include biographical texts and whiny, self-pitying letters he wrote to his wife back in France. Other exhibits include Creole costumes and contemporary island art. The museum has extensive English commentary and is open daily from 9am to 5:30pm. Admission is about $5 for adults, $1 for children under 10, and free for those under 8.

SOUTH OF FORT-DE-FRANCE   Marie Josèphe Rose Tascher de la Pagerie was born in 1763 in the quaint little village of Trois Ilets, across the bay from Fort-de-France. As Joséphine, she became the wife of Napoleon Bonaparte in 1796 and Empress of France in 1804. Although reviled by some historians as ruthless and selfish, she's revered by some on Martinique as having been uncommonly gracious. Others, however, blame her for Napoleon's reintroduction of slavery. A small museum, the **Musée de la Pagerie** (**© 596/68-33-06**), sits in the former estate kitchen building, where Joséphine gossiped with her slaves. Displays include the bed that she slept in until she departed for France at age 16, portraits of her and of Napoleon, invitations to Parisian balls, bills attesting to her extravagance as the empress, and letters, the most notable being a passionate missive from lovelorn Napoleon. The plantation house itself was destroyed in a hurricane, but the kitchen and partially restored ruins of the sugar mill and church remain (the latter is in the village itself). The museum is open Tuesday through Sunday from 9am to 3pm, and an English-speaking guide is usually on hand. Admission is about $6 for adults, $2.50 for children under 16. The nearby **Parc**

des Floralies (© 596/68-34-50) displays more than a hundred species of flowers, trees, and greenery, as well as aviaries housing exotic birds. It's open from 8:30am to 5pm Monday through Friday, and from 9:30am to 5:30pm on weekends. Admission is just over $2 for adults, about 85¢ for kids.

Diamond Rock, a craggy, multifaceted protrusion in the bay south of Trois Ilets, not only resembles a diamond, but was once the jewel in the crown of the British Caribbean fleet. The British and French fought on so many fronts during the early 19th century that ships were sometimes in short supply. Only one ship was assigned to blockade the ports of Martinique, St. Pierre in the north and Fort-de-France in the south. Short of ships but not imagination, the British proclaimed Diamond Rock a man-of-war and proceeded to equip the islet with guns. No temporary gesture, it remained in service for 2 years. Birds have replaced Brits as the primary residents. On a misty day, the rock looks more like the Loch Ness Monster emerging from the depths than a diamond.

You'll have passed through a number of quaint coastal villages by this time but none sweeter than **Ste. Luce.** Absurdly picturesque with its blindingly white stucco walls, red-tile roofs, turquoise sea, and multicolored fishing boats, this town is pure sun-drenched maritime serenity. Swim or snorkel off the small, pleasant beach, meditate on horizon-dominating Diamond Rock, or check out the village boutiques and cafes. For an unhurried taste of French island life, this is as good a place as any to spend the day.

SHOPPING

Martinique offers a good selection of French luxury items—perfumes, fashionable clothing, luggage, crystal, and dinnerware—at prices that can be as much as 30% to 40% lower than those in the States. Unfortunately, because some luxury goods, including jewelry, are subject to a hefty value-added tax, the savings are ultimately less compelling. Paying in dollar-denominated traveler's checks or credit cards is sometimes good for a 20% discount. The main shopping district in Fort-de-France is bound by rue Ernest Deproge (on the waterfront), La Savane, rue Lamartine, and rue de la République, with rue Victor Hugo being the single most important stretch. Martinican goods, such as rum, Creole jewelry, madras fabric, folk paintings, and hand-woven baskets, are good buys and more representative of the island. The open-air market in **La Savane,** at rue de la Liberté and rue Ernest Deproge, has the best selection of these items. For sheer Caribbean color, stroll through the enclosed **vegetable and fruit market on rue Isambert near rue Blénac;** built in 1901, it's another work of architect Henri Pick. Stores generally open at 9am and close at 5pm; most close for lunch, usually between 1 and 3pm. On Saturdays, shops are open in the morning only; on Sundays virtually all are closed.

Duty-free divas invariably make **Roger Albert,** 7 rue Victor Hugo, their first stop. This well-known outlet frequently has the best buys on French perfume, china, and crystal. **Cadet-Daniel,** 72 rue Antoine Siger, is its chief competitor. Compare and save.

Centre des Métieres d'Art, rue Ernest Deproge, near the tourist office, is one of the best arts-and-crafts stores in Martinique. Pass over the junk and focus on the more accomplished handmade items, including ceramics, painted fabrics, and patchwork quilts.

The French consider libations an art, and aficionados consider Martinican rum among the world's finest. **La Case à Rhum,** in the Galerie Marchande, 5 rue de la Liberté, stocks all the local brands and allows sample nips to help you decide which bottle to buy.

If you find yourself across the bay in Pointe du Bout, stop by **La Belle Matadore,** Immeuble Vermeil Marina (midway between the La Pagerie Hôtel and the Méridien Hotel). This boutique takes the history and tradition of Creole jewelry seriously, and virtually every piece for sale replicates designs developed during slave days by matadores (prostitutes), midwives, and slaves.

BEACHES

Serious beach bunnies hop south of Fort-de-France to **Grand Anse des Salines,** widely regarded as Martinique's nicest strand. At the island's extreme southern tip, about an hour from the capital by car, it features coconut palm trees, views of Diamond Rock, and white sand that seems to go on for miles. During summer holidays and weekends, it's busy with families and children, but during the week, it's often quiet and uncrowded. Beachside stands offer refreshment. To get to the island's **main gay beach,** turn right at the entrance to Grand Anse des Salines and drive to the far end of the parking lot, near the sign for Petite Anse des Salines. Follow the path through the woods and then veer left till you find the quiet section with the good-looking guys.

Conveniently located across the bay from Fort-de-France, **Pointe du Bout** is Martinique's most lavish resort area. Aside from a marina and a variety of watersports, the area has some modest man-made, white-sand beaches. The sandy, natural beaches at nearby **Anse Mitan** and **Anses d'Arlet** are popular with both swimmers and snorkelers.

Beaches north of Fort-de-France have mostly gray (they like to call it silver) volcanic sand. The best of the bunch is **Anse Turin,** just to the side of the main Caribbean coastal road, between St. Pierre and Le Carbet. Extremely popular with locals and shaded by palms, it's where Gauguin swam when he called the island home.

Martinique has no legal nudist beaches, but toplessness is as common here as anywhere in France. As a rule, public beaches lack changing cabins or showers, but hotel lockers and changing cabanas can be used by nonguests for a charge.

SPORTS

GOLF   When Robert Trent Jones Sr. designed **Golf de la Martinique** (© 596/ 68-32-81) in 1976, he chose a picturesque, historic site: the seaside hills neighboring La Pagerie, the birthplace of Empress Joséphine. Thirty-two kilometers (20 miles) from Fort-de-France, this good, tough, 18-hole, 6,640-yard, par-71 course features emerald hills, swaying palms, constant vistas of the turquoise sea, and, thankfully, year-round trade winds that help keep things cool. The par-5 12th, with a dogleg to the right, is the most difficult hole. The fairway here is narrow, the green is long, and the wind, especially between December and April, is tricky. The 15th and 16th require shots over sea inlets. Facilities include a pro shop, a golf academy, a bar, a restaurant, and tennis courts. English-speaking pros are at your service. Greens fees and cart rental run about $116 for 18 holes, $78 for nine. A set of clubs is another $20.

SCUBA DIVING & SNORKELING   Favorite dives in the coastal waters off Martinique include the caves and walls of Diamond Rock and the dozen ships sunk by the 1902 volcanic eruption at St. Pierre (the most popular wreck, the metal-hulled *Roraima,* was made famous by Jacques Cousteau and rests on a slant in 45m/148 ft. of water). For cruisers, the most convenient dive operators are across the bay from Fort-de-France in Pointe du Bout. **Espace Plongée,** at the Kalenda Resort (formerly the Hôtel Méridien; © 596/66-01-79), and **Planète Bleue** (© 596/66-08-79), based at the Pointe du Bout marina, are among the island's best operators. If you want to dive around St. Pierre, try **UCPA** (© **596/78-21-03**). Single-tank dives with all equipment run about $40. The waters of Pointe du Bout and nearby Anse Mitan and Anse Dufour are popular with snorkelers, as are the small bays of Sainte Anne and Anses d'Arlet on the southwest coast. Snorkeling equipment from on-site vendors runs about $10.

GREAT LOCAL RESTAURANTS & BARS

Hey, it's France: Expect great food. More than any other island in the French West Indies, Martinique gives French and Creole cuisine equal billing. If you're on a mission to sample the booze of every port of call, Martinique's **local beer** is Lorraine; Clement, De Paz, and Saint James are among the island's **best rums.** Too early in the day for demon rum? Slake your thirst with Didier, the Caribbean's only naturally carbonated spring water.

IN FORT-DE-FRANCE   A small, elegant restaurant located in a beautiful 19th-century mansion in the hills above Fort-de-France, **La Belle Epoque,** Route de Didier (© **596/64-41-19**), serves exquisite classic French cuisine. The fixed-price lunch special, which includes an appetizer, a main course, and dessert, is a steal, costing about $25. Enjoy the languid, colonial atmosphere, and savor the seafood ravioli in wine and lobster sauce, and the rum shrimp flambé.

AT POINTE DU BOUT   Just minutes by car from the resorts of Pointe du Bout, **La Villa Créole,** Anse Mitan (© **596/66-05-53**), serves down-home Creole staples such as *accras de morue* (codfish beignets), *boudin Créole* (Creole blood sausage), and *féroces* (avocado, codfish, and manioc hushpuppies). Don't leave your garden table without indulging in the chocolate fondant with bittersweet chocolate and pear sauce. The nearby **Au Poisson d'Or,** Anse Mitan (© **596/66-01-80**), a rustic roadside eatery, offers more Creole choices such as grilled conch in coconut milk and stewed shrimp. Lunch is $15.

NEAR ST. PIERRE   Fifteen minutes north of St. Pierre, **Habitation Céron,** Anse Céron, Le Prêcheur (© **596/52-94-53**), a 17th-century sugar estate, offers Creole crayfish freshly harvested from the on-site farm. Vegetables straight from the garden, fish, and octopus, are also served at the open-air, riverside tables. Lunch is about $28.

22 Nevis

Off the beaten tourist track, south of St. Martin and north of Guadeloupe, Nevis is the junior partner in the combined Federation of St. Kitts and Nevis, which gained self-government from Britain in 1967 and became a totally independent nation in 1983. It's a stormy marriage, though: Nevis's 1998 referendum for separation from its larger partner failed by the slimmest of margins.

Though smaller than St. Kitts and lacking a major historical site like Brimstone Hill Fortress, Nevis is nevertheless the more appealing and upbeat of the two islands. When viewed from its sister island, about 3.2km (2 miles) away, Nevis appears to be a perfect cone, rising gradually to a height of 970m (3,182 ft.). Columbus first sighted the island in 1493, naming it Las Nieves, Spanish for "snows," because its peak reminded him of the Pyrenees. Settled by the British in 1628, the island became a prosperous sugar-growing island as well as the most popular spa island of the 18th century, when people flocked in from other West Indian islands to visit its hot mineral springs. Nevis's two most famous historical residents were **Admiral Horatio Nelson,** who married a local woman here in 1787, and **Alexander Hamilton,** who was born here and went on to find fame as a drafter of the American Federalist Papers, as George Washington's treasury secretary, and as Aaron Burr's unfortunate dueling partner. Today, the island's capital city, Charlestown, has a lovely mixture of port-town exuberance and small-town charm, and the popular Pinney's Beach is just a knockout.

COMING ASHORE   Only small ships call on Nevis, docking right in the center of Charlestown and/or dropping anchor off the coast of **Pinney's Beach.**

LANGUAGE   **English** is the language of both islands.

CURRENCY   The local currency is the **Eastern Caribbean dollar** (US$1 = EC$2.70; EC$1 = US37¢). Many shops and restaurants quote prices in U.S. dollars. Always determine which currency locals are talking about. We've used U.S.-dollar prices in this section.

INFORMATION   Nevis recently opened a **tourism authority office** in the historic Treasury Building on Main Street near the docks (© **869/469-7550;** www.nevisisland.com). Hours are 8am to 4pm Monday through Friday and 8am to noon on Saturday. For information before you go, call **866/55NEVIS.**

CALLING FROM THE U.S.   When calling St. Kitts or Nevis from the United States, you need dial only a "1" before the numbers listed here.

GETTING AROUND
BY TAXI   The entirety of Charlestown is accessible on foot, but if you want to visit Pinney's Beach or elsewhere on the island, you can hop a taxi in Charlestown. The cost to Pinney's is about US$5.50. Taxi drivers double as guides on Nevis, so if you want to take a general tour of the island, negotiate a price with your driver.

BY RENTAL CAR   Because driving is on the left side in Nevis and most of the worthwhile sites are within walking distance or easily reached by taxi, we don't recommend renting a car here.

BEST CRUISE LINE SHORE EXCURSIONS
Few organized excursions are offered on Nevis. Some of the small-ship lines offer a day at **Pinney's Beach** as part of their regular visit, and might also offer hiking and snorkeling options, but the island is so small and easy to negotiate on your own that excursions aren't really necessary. If you want some local commentary, you can hire a taxi driver to give you an island tour. (See "Getting Around," above.)

ON YOUR OWN: WITHIN WALKING DISTANCE
If your ship docks in Charlestown, you're dead center of a perfect walking-tour opportunity. Charlestown is a lovely little place, laid-back in somewhat the same manner as St. John, but with some of the really rural character of sister island St. Kitts.

   If you head left from the docks and walk a little ways (maybe .4km/¼-mile) along Main Street, you'll come to the **Alexander Hamilton Birthplace** (© **869/ 469-5786;** www.nevis-nhcs.org/nevishistory.html), where the road curves just before the turnoff to Island Road. It's a rustic little two-level house set right on the coastline. On the first floor is the Museum of Nevis History and gift shop (admission is US$5, US$2 children under 12), but in all honesty you'll do just as well to skip it and just appreciate the outside, taking a moment to read the historic plaque. Far be it from us to take a couple bucks out of the island's economy, though, so if you're feeling philanthropic, drop your five bucks and then head on for the rest of your walk.

Backtracking along Main Street, you'll pass several serviceable if unremarkable shops (see "Shopping," below). Keep walking through the center of town, saying "hi" to the occasional mama goat and kids you'll pass, and then turn left onto Government Road. One block up on the left, you'll find the **Jews' Burial Ground,** with graves from 1684 to 1768. Stones left atop the graves attest to the visitors who have been there before you to pay their respects. When we were there, the dead were being entertained with reggae music coming from the doorway of a shop across the street, while a breeze stirred the few trees on the property. All in all, not a bad resting spot.

Backtrack to Main Street, turn left, and continue on past the Grove Park Cricket Ground, bearing left when the road forks. Head up the hill (where you'll see first an abandoned hotel and then several buildings standing alone on the hill to your right), and then turn at the first right, which will bring you back behind those buildings, the first of which is the inaccessible Government House and the second of which is the **Nelson Museum** (✆ **869/469-5786;** www.nevis-nhcs. org/nelsonmuseum.html). A very small, very homemade kind of place, it's nevertheless an interesting and evocative spot, and well worth the US$5 admission (US$2 for children 12 and under). The museum traces the history of Admiral Horatio Nelson's career enforcing England's Navigation Acts in the Caribbean,

Frommer's Favorite Nevis Experiences

Wandering Around Charlestown: The capital city is a fine place to wander around on your own, visiting the birthplace of American statesman Alexander Hamilton, the small but appealing Nelson Museum, and the 17th-century Jewish cemetery; poking your head into some of the small shops; or greeting the goats and chickens that wander past, evidently taking their own walking tours. (See "On Your Own: Within Walking Distance," above.)

Taking Some Downtime on Pinney's Beach: Lounge back, have a beer, take a swim in the reef-protected waters, do a little snorkeling, or engage in some beachcombing. Talk about relaxation. (See "Beaches," below.)

and also houses artifacts from Nevis's Carib, Arawak, and Aceramic peoples; a small display on Nevis today; and a number of wonderful clay artworks, including a replica of the old "Coolie Man's Store," by local artist Gustage "Bush Tea" Williams. The timeline of Nelson's Caribbean career includes ship models, ceramic and bronze Nelson figures, paintings of his battles and other scenes, a scrap from the Union Jack under which the admiral was standing when he was shot, a miniature of his casket, and an actual ticket to his funeral, with wax seal. A tiny birdcage with wood enclosing box bears the inscription "In a number of letters written to Fanny Nisbet [Nelson's wife], Nelson mentioned his search for a traveling birdcage. This bird cage, though not the one Nelson finally procured, is from that period." Museum hours are 8am to 4pm Monday through Friday, Saturday 9am to noon.

Once back outside, amble slowly off in the same direction you were going (right from the gate). Keep bearing right and you'll eventually be back on Main Street, in plenty of time to do a little shopping or stop into one of the local bars or restaurants.

ON YOUR OWN: BEYOND THE PORT AREA

The 3.2-hectare (8-acre) **Botanical Garden of Nevis** (© 869/469-3509) is located 4.8km (3 miles) south of Charlestown on the Montpelier Estate. There are several gardens, including a tropical rainforest conservatory, a rose and vine garden, a cactus garden, a tropical fruit garden, and an orchid garden. Fountains, ponds, and re-creations of Mayan sculptures dot the grounds, which are open Monday through Saturday 10am to 4pm. Admission is US$9 adults, US$4 children. There's a restaurant and gift shop on-site.

SHOPPING

Nevis is not a shopping hub on the order of St. Thomas or even the much more laid-back St. John. In fact, it's no kind of shopping hub at all. Still, there are a few shops worth poking your head into, all of them along Main Street, right in the port area.

Island Hopper, on Main, 1 block north of Prince Charles Street (© 869/469-0893), is the best shop in town for visitors, stocking a huge selection of batik clothing. **Pemberton Gift Shop,** across Main Street from Island Hopper (© 869/469-5668), is also sparse, but has a selection of T-shirts, gift items, and a shelf of CSR (Cane Spirit Rothschild), the local cane-sugar liquor. **Jerveren's Fashions,** in the Cotton Ginnery complex right at the pier (© **869/469-0062**), has a decent selection of T-shirts and gifts.

For stamp collectors, the **Nevis Philatelic Bureau at the Head Post Office,** on Market Street next to the public market, 1 block south and 1 block east of the docks (© **869/469-5535**), has a range of Nevis stamps.

BEACHES

The name to know on Nevis is **Pinney's Beach,** located north of Charlestown. A lovely spot for swimming, snorkeling, beachcombing, or just sitting back and watching the pelicans divebomb into the surf, it's home to the Four Seasons resort, reopened in late 2000 after being obliterated by 1999's Hurricane Lenny. As a counterpoint to conspicuous luxury, the rickety **Sunshine's Bar and Grill** (© **869/469-5817**), "Home of the Killer Bee," sits right on the beach, offering beer and other refreshments along with the aforementioned Bee, a "killer" drink.

23 Panama

The Panama Canal is an awesome feat of engineering and human effort. Construction began in 1880 and wasn't completed until 1914, at the expense of thousands of lives, and the vast majority of the original structure and equipment is still in use. Transiting the canal, which links the Atlantic Ocean with the Pacific, is a thrill for anyone even vaguely interested in engineering or history.

Passing through the canal takes about 8 hours from start to finish, and is a fascinating procedure—the route is about 81km (50 miles) long and includes passage through three main locks, which, through gravity alone, raise ships over Central America and down again on the other side. Between the locks, ships pass through artificially created lakes such as the massive Gatun Lake, 26m (85 ft.) above sea level. It often costs ships about $100,000 to pass through, with fees based on each ship's weight. Your ship will line up in the morning, mostly with cargo ships, to await its turn through the canal. While transiting, there will be a running narration of history and facts about the canal by an expert who's brought on board for the day.

Cruises that include a canal crossing are generally 10 to 14 nights long, with popular routes between Florida and Acapulco, visiting a handful of Caribbean and Mexican ports and a few ports in Central America along the way, including Panama's San Blas Islands, Costa Rica's Puerto Caldera, and Guatemala's Puerto Quetzal.

COLON

In compliance with a treaty signed between the United States and Panama in 1977, canal operations passed from U.S. to Panamanian hands at the stroke of midnight on December 31, 1999. Not only did the transition go smoothly, but the canal changeover spurred government agencies and private developers in Panama to expand the canal zone's tourism infrastructure—not simply trying to attract as many ships as possible, but developing new attractions at the canal's Atlantic entrance to lure cruise passengers off their ships and into Panama's interior on shore excursions and for pre- and postcruise stays. Even ships not transiting the canal are being wooed, with a long-term goal of making the city of Colón a home port for cruise ships sailing to the southern Caribbean.

The linchpin project in the new canal-area developments is **Colón 2000,** a $45-million private port development that opened in October 2000 in Colón, near the canal's Caribbean entrance, and that is capable of handling any size cruise vessel—even the 100,000-ton-plus ships that are too large to pass through the canal. Colón 2000's developer, Corporación de Costas Tropicales, has created a tour company, **Adventuras 2000** (www.colon2000.com), which offers a series of shore excursions highlighting Panama's history, culture, and diverse natural attractions (see "Best Cruise Line Shore Excursions," below). The project has opened many new jobs to locals, who are being trained as bilingual tour guides, drivers, and so on.

Colón 2000's glass-and-marble terminal building has a large lounge, an Internet cafe, a huge duty-free shopping mall (part of the Colón Free Zone, the second largest tax-free zone in the world), restaurants, and craft shops. Unfortunately, the town surrounding the splashy new development remains depressed. So there's no question that passengers calling here should book an organized tour.

Princess, Holland America, Celebrity, and Carnival were some of the first lines to include Colón 2000 as a port of call on some Panama Canal itineraries. It doesn't hurt that they're getting incentives by the Panamanian government: Panama has hedged its bets by establishing a 5-year program that pays cruise ships $2.50 to $12 per passenger for calls at any Panamanian port. The incentives grow as the passenger count rises, and additional incentives are offered to lines that register their ships in Panama.

Another new development in Colón, the **Cristobal Cruise Terminal** (Pier 6), offers piers for two ships of any size and has a duty-free shopping area, restaurants, and telephones. A rail line here, connecting Colón and the capital of Panama City, is in the planning stages.

BEST CRUISE LINE SHORE EXCURSIONS

The following excursions represent a sampling of those offered from Colón:

Emberá Indian Village Tour ($89, 3½ hr.): Today, Panama's Emberá Indians live much as they did in the early 16th century, when their first tourist—Vasco Nunez de Balboa, who "discovered" the Pacific Ocean—came through. You'll travel by dugout canoe up the Chagres River, visit the Emberá village, witness a performance of traditional dance, and (surprise, surprise) have an opportunity to purchase handicrafts.

Kayaking the Canal ($75, 3¾ hr.): From Colón, you'll travel to Sol Melina, where you'll spend about 1 hour kayaking amid the plant life, mammals, and birds, then head by bus to the Gutun Locks for a look at the Canal's workings.

Panama City Tour ($75, 4½–6 hr.): Visit the ruins of Old Panama, founded in 1519 by Pedro Arias Davila and destroyed in 1671 by the pirate Sir Henry Morgan; head to colonial Panama, built to replace the original capital; and then visit the Miraflores Locks for a look at the Canal.

The Pirates Trail ($43, 4 hr.): Founded in 1597, Portobelo was a trading town through which passed the gold from Pizarro's plunder of Peru, which made it a frequent target of British pirates, including William Parker, Sir Henry Morgan, and Edward Vernon. On this tour, you'll visit Fort San Geronimo, Fort San Felipe, the Customs House, and the Black Christ Church; learn about the area's history; and then get a view of the Canal from the Gutun Locks.

PORTS ALONG THE CANAL ROUTE

The San Blas Islands are a beautiful archipelago and home to the Kuna Indians, whose women are well known for their colorful, hand-embroidered stitching. If you get a chance to go ashore, the tiny women, dressed in their traditional *molas* (bright, intricately appliquéd blouses), sell all manner of this textile art in square blocks and strips, all of which are known as *molas* and make great pillow covers or wall hangings. They cost about $5 to $10 each, but don't try to bargain too much—the women will only go so low before standing firm. When your ship anchors offshore at the islands, be prepared for throngs of Kunas to emerge from the far-off distance, paddling (or, in a few cases, motoring) their dugout canoes up to the ship, where they will spend the entire day calling for money or anything else ship passengers toss overboard. The Kuna seem to enjoy diving overboard to retrieve coins thrown to them, but, of course, it's a sad sight, too, watching entire families so needy. Makes you feel damn guilty for rolling in on that fancy cruise ship of yours.

In Costa Rica, many ships call at **Puerto Caldera** on the Pacific side or **Puerto Limón** on the Atlantic side. While there's nothing to see from either cargo port, both are great jumping-off points for tours that all visiting ships offer of the country's lush, beautiful rainforests, which are alive with some 850 species of birds, 200 species of mammals, 9,000 species of flowering plants, and about 35,000 species of insects. After a scenic bus ride, tours will take you on a nature walk through the jungle or a mild whitewater rafting trip.

In Guatemala, most Panama Canal–bound ships call at **Puerto Quetzal,** on the Pacific coast; a few may call at **Santo Tomas** on the Caribbean side. Both are used as gateways to Guatemala's spectacular Mayan ruins at **Tikal.** They're the country's most famous attractions and are considered the most spectacular, with more than 3,000 temples, pyramids, and other buildings of the ancient civilization—some of them dating as far back as A.D. 300—nestled in a thick, surreal jungle setting. Excursions here are neither cheap nor easy—a 10-hour tour involves buses, walking, and a 1-hour flight, and costs about $500—but the journey is well worth the effort. Excursions to the less-spectacular Mayan sites in Honduras are also offered from Puerto Quetzal, as are several overland tours of Guatemala's interior.

24 Puerto Rico

San Juan, the capital of Puerto Rico, has the busiest ocean terminal in the West Indies and is one of the cruise trade's most important ports. While cruise groups, by their sheer size, can overwhelm many ports of call, San Juan absorbs cruise passengers with ease. The San Juan metropolitan area, home to about a third of Puerto Rico's four million people, is one of the largest and most sophisticated urban centers in the Caribbean, offering all the amenities of a modern major city: great shopping, interesting neighborhoods, beautiful people, excellent restaurants, glamorous bars and nightclubs, and fine museums. It also offers some of the drawbacks: traffic, crowded sidewalks, and, in some areas, crime (avoid the La Perla neighborhood, along the north-central edge of Old San Juan).

Founded in 1521 by Spanish conquistador **Juan Ponce de León,** the city is one of the oldest in the New World. The cobblestone streets of the hilly old section of the city (**Old San Juan,** the ancient walled city on San Juan Island) are lined with brightly painted colonial town houses, ancient churches, intimate parks, and sun-drenched plazas. Like the pyramids of Egypt and the Great Wall of China, Old San Juan's Spanish colonial forts and city walls are United Nations World Heritage Sites. Another attraction is the people: Puerto Ricans are warm, quick to laugh, and proud of their multicultural heritage, a distinct blend of Amerindian, Spanish, African, and American influences that is present in the culture of the island, from salsa music to Puerto Rican cuisine.

San Juan's shopping ranks among the Caribbean's best, and the city's historic sites, beaches, gambling, and other diversions make it, overall, the number-one port of call in the region. You'll find some of the Caribbean's best restaurants here, as well as sprawling beaches with high-rise luxury hotels reminiscent of those in Miami.

Old San Juan is the prime tourist haunt, but there's much more to the metropolitan area. Other interesting neighborhoods include **Santurce,** linked with San Juan Island by a causeway; **Condado,** a strip of beachfront hotels, restaurants, casinos, and nightclubs on a peninsula stretching from San Juan Island to Santurce; **Hato Rey,** the business center; **Río Piedras,** site of the University of

---

Frommer's Favorite San Juan Experiences

Strolling Through Historic Old San Juan: Meander through block after block of narrow cobblestone streets lined with centuries-old Spanish colonial architecture. (See "Walking Tour: Old San Juan," below.)

Hiking Through El Yunque National Forest: One of Puerto Rico's most popular attractions, El Yunque covers 28,000 acres and receives up to 200 inches of rain per year. There are 240 different tropical trees, more than 50 orchid species, 150 varieties of ferns, 68 types of birds, and millions of tiny coquí tree frogs. You can hike, picnic, and swim in mountain streams. (See "Best Cruise Line Shore Excursions," below.)

Puerto Rico

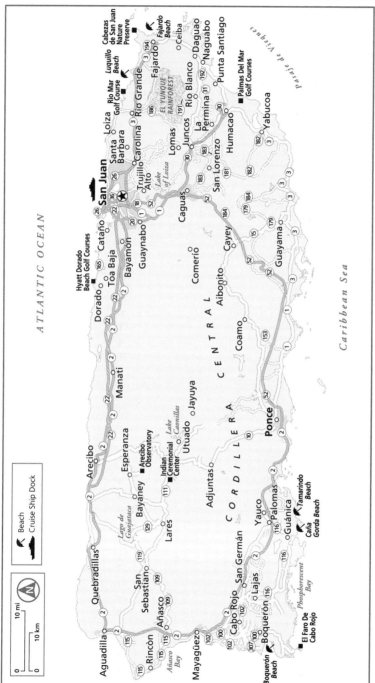

Puerto Rico; and **Bayamón,** an industrial and residential quarter. **Isla Verde,** another resort zone, is connected to the rest of San Juan by an isthmus.

Puerto Rico has been inhabited since about 3000 B.C., when the earliest people arrived from Florida or Central America. In 1493, Christopher Columbus landed on the island, and within 50 years, the native population had been decimated by forced labor, malnutrition, Western diseases, and warfare with the Spanish.

Puerto Rico remained part of Spain's empire for 4 centuries. Spanish rule ended in 1898, when the island was ceded to the United States in the wake of the Spanish-American War. In 1917, Puerto Ricans became U.S. citizens, and in 1952, the island became a semiautonomous commonwealth of the United States. In the last referendum on statehood, in 1998, slightly more Puerto Ricans voted for maintaining the status quo than for joining the union; a small fraction favored independence.

COMING ASHORE   Cruise ships dock on the historic Old San Juan, a short walk from the Plaza de la Darsena, Old San Juan's main bus station, and most of its historic treasures. A **small tourist information center** is located next to credit card phones on Plaza de la Darsena, just in front of Pier 1; the information center is open 8:30 am to 5:30pm Thursday and Friday, 9am to 8pm Saturday through Wednesday.

During periods of heavy volume—Saturday and Sunday in midwinter, when as many as eight cruise ships dock on the same day—additional, less convenient piers are used. Many of Old San Juan's shops and attractions are in walking distance from these docks. For information about the port, contact **the Port of San Juan,** P.O. Box 362829, San Juan, PR 00936-2829 (© **787/723-2260**).

LANGUAGE   **Spanish** is the native tongue, but most people on the island also speak **English** (both are the official languages here). The farther you venture from San Juan, the more likely it is you'll have to practice your Spanish.

CURRENCY   Puerto Rico is part of the United States, so the **U.S. dollar** is the coin of the realm. Canadian currency is accepted, albeit reluctantly, by some of San Juan's bigger hotels. Credit cards and traveler's checks are widely accepted.

INFORMATION   For advice and maps, drop by the **Tourist Information Center** at La Casita, near Pier 1 (© **787/722-1709**). For info before you go, contact the **Puerto Rico Tourism Company** (© **800/223-6530** or 800/866-7827; www.prtourism.com or www.GoToPuertoRico.com).

CALLING FROM THE U.S.   Calling Puerto Rico from the continental United States is as simple as dialing between U.S. states: Just dial "1" before the numbers listed here.

GETTING AROUND

Driving in congested San Juan is frustrating, and parking in some areas is impossible. You're better off walking around Old San Juan. Take buses or taxis to Condado, Ocean Park, and Isla Verde.

BY TAXI   Taxis operated by the Tourist Transportation Division are metered in San Juan, but the fare structure between major tourism zones is standardized. The set rates from the cruise ship piers are $6 to Old San Juan, $10 to Condado, and $16 to Isla Verde. You can also hire a taxi for an hour for $30. If a meter's used, the initial charge is $1, plus 10¢ for each additional ⅓th of a mile and 50¢ for each suitcase. The minimum fare is $3. After 10pm, there's a night charge (add $1 to the meter reading). For phone numbers of taxi companies, look in the Yellow Pages or call the **Tourist Transportation Division** (© **787/999-2100**).

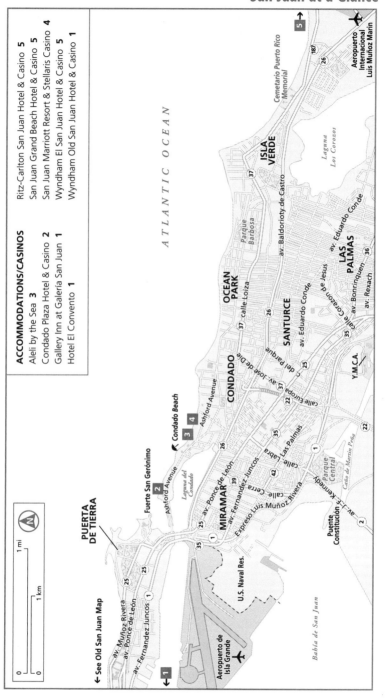

ACCOMMODATIONS/CASINOS

Aleli by the Sea **3**
Condado Plaza Hotel & Casino **2**
Gallery Inn at Galería San Juan **1**
Hotel El Convento **1**

Ritz-Carlton San Juan Hotel & Casino **5**
San Juan Grand Beach Hotel & Casino **5**
San Juan Marriott Resort & Stellaris Casino **4**
Wyndham El San Juan Hotel & Casino **5**
Wyndham Old San Juan Hotel & Casino **1**

San Juan as a Port of Embarkation

Puerto Rico is the number-one port of embarkation in the Caribbean, with more than 1.2 million visitors embarking on 700 cruises every year from here. Most cruise lines have packages that include hotel rooms on the island.

GETTING TO SAN JUAN & THE PORT   Luis Muñoz Marín International Airport (© 787/791-1014) is on the city's east side, about 7½ miles from the port. Taxi fares from the airport are fixed at $8 to Isla Verde, $12 to Condado and Ocean Park, and $16 to Old San Juan and the cruise ships. The ride to the port takes at least 30 minutes—longer if traffic is heavy, and it often is.

ACCOMMODATIONS

IN OLD SAN JUAN   The quietly elegant **Hotel El Convento,** 100 Calle del Cristo (© 800/468-2779 or 787/723-9020; www.elconvento.com), is Puerto Rico's most famous lodging. A former Carmelite convent, it offers large rooms, many with views of the Old Town. Rates: $325 to $385 winter; $160 to $250 summer. **Wyndham Old San Juan Hotel & Casino,** 100 Brumbaugh St. (© 877/999-3223 or 787/721-5100; www.wyndham.com), is on the waterfront across the street from the cruise ship docks. Rooms are comfortable, and Old San Juan is a step away. Rates: $165 to $365. On Old San Juan's highest hill, with a sweeping view of the sea, **Gallery Inn at Galería San Juan,** 204–206 Calle Norzagaray (© 787/722-1808; www.thegalleryinn.com), was the home of a Spanish aristocrat in the 1700s. Many of the rooms open to patios, fountains, and gardens. Art is everywhere, contributing to the hotel's cultured, contemplative, bohemian ambience. Rates: $165 to $370.

IN CONDADO   The original high-rise, high-glamour section of modern San Juan, Condado boasts numerous hotels, restaurants, and nightclubs. Among its best hotels are the **Wyndham Condado Plaza Hotel & Casino,** 999 Ashford Ave. (© 800/468-8588 or 787/721-1000; rates: $250 to $400; www.wyndham.com), and the **San Juan Marriott Resort & Stellaris Casino,** 1309 Ashford Ave. (© 800/981-8546 or 787/721-7000; www.marriottpr.com; rates: $230–$390). **Alelí by the Sea,** 1125 Sea View St., a block off Ashford Avenue (© 787/725-5313), is a small, charming option on the beach. Rooms are basic but clean; the big draws are the sound of the surf just outside your window and the rates—about $76 to $114.

BY TROLLEY   When you tire of walking around Old San Juan, board one of the free trolleys. They depart from Plaza de la Marina and Piers 2 and 4, but you can hop on anywhere along the route.

BY BUS   The **Metropolitan Bus Authority** operates extensive bus service in the greater San Juan area. Bus stops are marked by signs that read PARADA, and terminals are in front of Pier No. 4. For route and schedule information, call © 787/250-6064.

BY RENTAL CAR   Puerto Rico has expressways and thousands of miles of other paved roads, so travel by car is pretty effortless, except in metropolitan San

Motels in Condado include the **Holiday Inn Express,** 1 Mariano Ramirez Bages, off Ashford Avenue at Joffre Street, Condado (© 787/724-4160; www.ichotelsgroup.com/h/d/ex/1/en/home), and **San Juan Days Inn-Condado Lagoon Hotel,** 6 Clemenceau St. (© 787/721-0170; www.the.daysinn.com/sanjuan08830).

IN ISLA VERDE   Similar to Condado in atmosphere and abundance of hotels, but more recently developed, Isla Verde has a number of dazzlingly deluxe resort complexes, including the **Wyndham El San Juan Hotel & Casino,** 6063 Isla Verde Ave. (© 800/468-2818 or 787/791-1000; www.wyndham.com; rates: $162–$405), and the **Ritz-Carlton San Juan Hotel & Casino,** 6961 Rte. 187 (© 800/241-3333 or 787/253-1700; www.ritzcarlton.com; rates: $259–$569). At the other end of the spectrum, motels include the **Howard Johnson Carolina,** 4820 Isla Verde Ave. (© 787/728-1300; www.hojo.com).

SAN JUAN AFTER DARK

The San Juan club scene is hot. In general, people get pretty dressed up, so forget about T-shirts or shorts. **Babylon,** in the Wyndham El San Juan Hotel & Casino, 6063 Isla Verde Ave. (© 787/791-1000), attracts a rich and beautiful crowd, as well as hundreds of wannabes. On weekends, you may wait 2 hours to get in. For dance action in the Old Town, head for **Club Lazer,** 251 Calle del Cruz (© 787/725-7581), where you can dance the night away to the sounds of salsa and merengue. In Condado, **Club Millennium,** in the Condado Plaza Hotel, 999 Ashford Ave. (© 787/722-1900), draws disco devotees and features a cigar bar on the side. San Juan's exuberant gay scene is easily the Caribbean's best, and no club in town surpasses the energy of **Eros,** 1257 Avenida Ponce de León, in Santurce (© 787/722-1131). Also in Santurce, you'll find the enduringly popular lesbian bar **Cups,** 1708 Calle San Mateo (© 787/268-3570).

For a mellow experience and a sophisticated atmosphere, try **Carli Café Concierto,** in old San Juan on Plazoleta Rafael Carríon (© 787/725-4927), a bistro offering live piano and jazz music. Palm Court in the Wyndham El San Juan Hotel & Casino, 6063 Isla Verde Ave. (© 787/791-1000), has a giant chandelier and an intricate, wood-paneled ceiling, and is probably the island's most glamorous meeting place.

Juan, where traffic can be heavy and nightmarish—the 500-year-old streets in Old San Juan just weren't built with cars in mind. Driving is on the right side of the road, and all other U.S. rules apply. Signs are in Spanish, though, and the metric system is used for distance markers (kilometers rather than miles) and at gas stations (liters instead of gallons); confusingly enough, speed limits are posted in miles per hour. **Avis, Budget, Dollar,** and **Hertz** all have offices here.

BEST CRUISE LINE SHORE EXCURSIONS

Unless you want a guide to offer historical perspective ($33, 2½ hr.), don't bother with organized tours of Old San Juan—it's easy enough to get around on your own. On the other hand, if you explore somewhere farther afield, an organized tour is a good idea.

El Yunque Rainforest ($40, 4–5 hr.): Get acquainted with one of Puerto Rico's premier natural wonders. After arriving at Baño Grande, a natural swimming hole, hike half an hour along the Camimitillo trail and see parrot nests, giant ferns, orchids, and palms. Listen for the song of Puerto Rico's national symbol, the tiny coquí tree frog. After a short stop at an interpretive station, proceed to Yohaku observation tower and Coca waterfall.

Tropical Horseback Riding ($82, 3½ hr.): Meet your horse, briefly learn the ropes, and then ride down a beautiful beach. Take a quick swim during the refreshment stop.

Bioluminescence Bay Kayak Tour ($77, 4½ hr.): Ride to Las Cabezas de San Juan Natural Reserve, at Puerto Rico's northeasternmost point. Under the light of the stars, paddle down mangrove-lined channels and watch the water glow as billions of single-celled organisms light up as they sense the movement of your boat.

City Tour & Bacardi Rum Distillery ($28, 4 hr.): After a tour of the old city, with a stop at the San Christobal fort, you'll travel to the Bacardi distillery to learn about the Puerto Rican sugar and rum industries, watch giant fermenting tanks transform sugar cane into rum, learn how to pronounce the product's name (baa-carrrr-*di!*), then get a taste for yourself.

EXCURSIONS OFFERED BY LOCAL AGENCIES

If you're staying in a hotel before or after your cruise, book tours at the tour desk. Otherwise try **Rico Suntours,** 176 Calle San Jorge, San Juan (© **787/ 722-2080** or 787/727-2080), or **Castillo Tours & Travel Services,** 2413 Calle Laurel, Punta La Marias, Santurce (© **787/791-6195** or 787/726-5752). For serious adventure, rock climbing, rappelling, cave exploring, or canyoneering, your best bet is **Aventuras Tierra Adentro,** 268-A Avenida Piñero, Río Piedras (© **787/766-0470**). You can also check *Que Pasa Magazine* for more detailed information.

WALKING TOUR   **OLD SAN JUAN**

The streets are narrow and teeming with traffic, but strolling through Old San Juan is like walking through 5 centuries of history. More than 400 Spanish colonial buildings from the 16th and 17th centuries, many featuring intricate wrought-iron balconies with lush hanging plants, have been lovingly restored here. The streets' blue paving stones were used originally as ballast by ships crossing the ocean from Spain. Although Old San Juan is a National Historic Zone, it's as vibrant today as it ever has been. Block after block, you'll find shops, cafes, museums, plazas, people, and pigeons. The crowds thin out by late afternoon, so linger around to experience Old San Juan's more sedate charms.

Begin your adventure near the post office, amid the taxis, buses, and urban hubbub of:

❶ Plaza de la Marina

The Plaza is a small park that overlooks San Juan Bay, which was one of the New World's most important harbors for trading and for military protection.

Walking west from the plaza, you'll come to San Juan's showcase promenade, El Paseo de la Princesa. This renovated 19th-century walkway traces the ancient city walls past heroic statues, gurgling fountains, and landscaped gardens.

Old San Juan Walking Tour

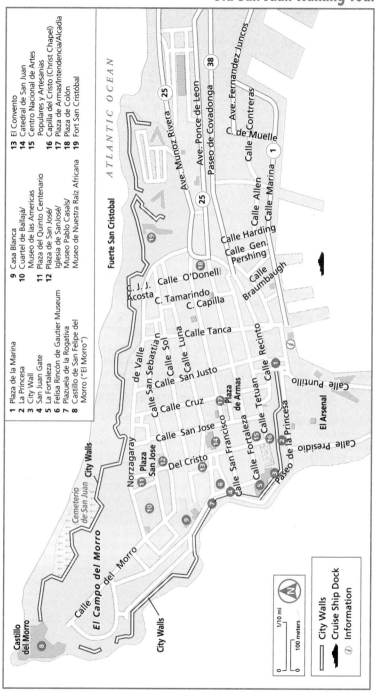

1 Plaza de la Marina
2 La Princesa
3 City Wall
4 San Juan Gate
5 La Fortaleza
6 Felisa Rincón de Gautier Museum
7 Plazuela de la Rogativa
8 Castillo de San Felipe del Morro ("El Morro")

9 Casa Blanca
10 Cuartel de Ballajá/ Museo de las Americas
11 Plaza del Quinto Centenario
12 Plaza de San José/ Iglesia de SanJosé/ Museo Pablo Casals/ Museo de Nuestra Raíz Africana

13 El Convento
14 Catedral de San Juan
15 Centro Nacional de Artes Populares y Artesanías
16 Capilla del Cristo (Christ Chapel)
17 Plaza de Armas/Intendencia/Alcaldía
18 Plaza de Colón
19 Fort San Cristóbal

ATLANTIC OCEAN

Fuerte San Cristobal

Castillo del Morro

Cementerio de San Juan City Walls

El Campo del Morro

Calle del Morro

City Walls

Norzagaray
de Valle
Plaza San Jose
Calle San Jose
Del Cristo
Calle San Sebastian
Calle Sol
Calle Luna
Calle San Justo
Calle Cruz
Calle Tanca
Calle San Francisco
Plaza de Armas
Calle Fortaleza
Calle Tetuan
Calle San Jose
Paseo de la Princesa
C. J. J. Acosta
C. Tamarindo
C. Capilla
Calle O'Donell
Calle Harding
Calle Gen. Pershing
Calle Braumbaugh
Calle Recinto
Calle Puntillo
Calle Presidio
El Arsenal

Ave. Muñoz Rivera
Ave. Ponce de Leon
Paseo de Covadonga
Ave. Fernandez Juncos
C. de Muelle
Calle Contreras
Calle Allen
Calle Marina

25
25
38
1
1

N

1/10 mi
100 meters
0

City Walls
Cruise Ship Dock
Information

243

Proceed along the Paseo to:

❷ La Princesa

This gray-and-white building on the right served as one of the Caribbean's most notorious prisons for centuries. Today it houses contemporary Puerto Rican art exhibits and the offices of the Puerto Rico Tourism Company.

Continue walking westward to the fountain near the sea's edge. Turn right and follow the promenade as it skirts the base of the:

❸ City Wall

The wall was completed in the 1700s and once formed part of the New World's most impregnable defenses against enemy invaders and pirates. Marvel at the immensity, antiquity, and engineering genius of the wall, which on average is 40 feet high and 20 feet thick.

Follow the promenade until you reach the:

❹ San Juan Gate

The Gate stands at Calle San Juan and Recinto del Oeste. Turn right through the portal. The gate was built in 1635 and served as the main entrance into San Juan. Today, it's the only remaining passage through the wall into the city.

Turn right at the first street and walk uphill along Calle Recinto del Oeste to the wrought-iron gates of:

❺ La Fortaleza

Also known as Santa Catalina Palace, La Fortaleza is the residence of Puerto Rico's governor. Although it initially served military purposes, it's the oldest executive mansion in continuous use in the Western Hemisphere (construction began in 1533). Over the past 4 centuries, numerous additions and alterations have been made, resulting in the current amalgam of marble, mahogany, and stained glass. The architectural pastiche includes medieval, baroque, gothic, neoclassical, and Moorish elements. English-language tours are given Monday through Friday (except holidays) every hour on the hour (except noon) from 9am to 3pm.

Now retrace your steps along Calle Recinto del Oeste, downhill to Caleta de San Juan. The colonial house at no. 51, on the northeast corner, is the:

❻ Felisa Rincón de Gautier Museum

This is the former home of one of San Juan's most popular mayors. An organizer of the city's women and other dispossessed, Fela, as her many admirers called her, swept into power in 1946 and led the city for 22 years. The first woman in the Western Hemisphere to be the chief executive of a major city, she was the brains behind Head Start, the preschool program for low-income children. Watch the short English-language documentary of her life, tour the modest rooms of her home, and view some of the hundreds of pictures of Madame Mayor with the world's celebrities (© **787/723-1897;** free admission; open weekdays, except holidays, 9am–4pm).

Walking back to Calle Recinto del Oeste, turn right and proceed 1 block to Caleta de las Monjas. Fork left to a panoramic view and a modern statue marking the center of:

❼ Plazuela de la Rogativa

According to local legend, the British, while besieging San Juan in 1797, misidentified the flaming torches of a *rogativa*, or religious procession, as Spanish reinforcements. Frightened by the display, the would-be invaders hastily retreated. Statues in this plaza memorialize the event.

Continue westward, parallel to the city wall, passing through a pair of urn-topped gateposts. The road will fork. Bear to the right and continue climbing the steep cobblestone-covered ramp to its top. Walk westward across the field toward the neoclassical gateway leading to the:

❽ Castillo de San Felipe del Morro ("El Morro")

This castle, whose treasury and strategic position were for centuries the envy of both Europe and the Caribbean, was where Spanish Puerto Rico defended itself against the navies of Great Britain, France, and Holland, as well as hundreds of pirate ships. First built in 1540, and substantially enhanced in 1787, the fortress was part of a comprehensive defense network. The six-level complex rises 140 feet above the sea on a rocky promontory. You can spend the better part of the morning exploring its labyrinth of dungeons, barracks, towers, ramps, and tunnels on your own. Check out the small, air-conditioned military museum and the gift shop. Both El Morro and San Cristóbal (see stop 19, below) are managed by the U.S. National Park Service, which provides continuous video presentations and scheduled guided tours in English (western end of Calle Norzagaray; © 787/729-6960; admission to El Morro and San Cristobal is $5 for adults, $2 for ages 13–17 and $4 for adults over 62; San Cristobal open daily 9 am–6pm, and El Morro 9am–5pm).

Retrace your steps through the treeless field to Calle del Morro, then walk uphill to the small plaza at the top of the street. On the right is:

⑨ Casa Blanca

Though it was his family home, Juan Ponce de León, the conquistador and Puerto Rico's first governor, never actually lived here: While the structure was being built, he was off looking for the Fountain of Youth, ironically dying (from battle wounds) along the way, in 1521. The city's oldest fort, Casa Blanca was San Juan's only defense against attacks until La Fortaleza was completed in 1533. Today, it features a small museum illustrating Indian life and 16th- and 17th-century colonial family life. The garden and fountains in back are a tranquil respite from the streets (1 Calle de San Sebastián; © 787/725-1454; $2 for adults, 50¢ for children and seniors; open daily Tues–Sat 9am–4pm, except for an hour at noon).

Exit through the front entrance and walk downhill, retracing your steps for a half block, then head toward the massive tangerine-colored building on your right, the:

⑩ Cuartel de Ballajá

These former military barracks once housed 1,000 Spanish soldiers and their families. Built between 1854 and 1864, the complex is the last and largest military building erected by Spain in the Western Hemisphere. The three-story quadrangular structure, constructed in a sober neoclassical style, has long arcades that enclose a large patio once used as a parade ground. Today, the building's second floor is home to the Museo de las Americas (Museum of the Americas), which showcases Caribbean as well as North, Central, and South American cultures. The popular art exhibits focus on housing and furniture styles, handicrafts, tools, musical instruments, toys, clothing, and religious objects. The carved wooden saints (santos) are especially interesting (Cuartel de Ballajá; © 787/724-5052; free admission; open Tues–Sun 10am–4pm).

Exit through the barracks' eastern door, where you'll immediately spot the dramatic and modern:

⑪ Plaza del Quinto Centenario (Quincentennial Plaza)

This plaza is dominated by a large, totem pole–like column that commemorates the 500th anniversary of Columbus's arrival.

Now, walk a short block southeast to the borders of:

⑫ Plaza de San José

This plaza features a statue of Juan Ponce de León cast from an English cannon captured during a 1797 naval battle. Three sites around this square are worth visiting. Built in 1532, the Iglesia de San José is where Ponce de León's descendants worshipped. Despite being looted over the years, the church, on the plaza's north side, still has several treasures, including a carved crucifix presented to Ponce de León, paintings by Puerto Rican 18th-century master José Campéche, and works by Francisco Oller, who painted in the late 1800s and early 1900s. A 15th-century Flemish work in the Chapel of Belém is venerated by many who believe it works miracles. The **Museo Pablo Casals** (✆ 787/723-9185; $1 for adults, 50¢ for children under 12; open Tues–Sat 9:30am–4:30pm) honors the Spanish-born cellist who adopted Puerto Rico as his home (his mother and wife were Puerto Rican). Original manuscripts of Casals's music, his cello, and his piano are displayed in the main hall. The video library upstairs archives many of his performances. Casals's legacy on the island includes the annual Casals Music Festival and the Puerto Rico Symphony Orchestra. The **Museo de Nuestra Raíz Africana** (Museum of Our African Roots) compactly and ingeniously chronicles the history of Africans in Puerto Rico. Various exhibits trace the slave experience and focus on African contributions to local music, dance, clothing, art, cuisine, religion, and language. Placards are in Spanish, but the exhibits are fascinating and often self-explanatory (✆ 787/724-4294; free admission; open Tues–Sat 9:30am–5pm, Sun 11am–5pm).

Exiting from the plaza's southwestern corner, walk downhill along one of the capital's oldest and best-known streets, Calle del Cristo. Two blocks down, on the north side of shady Plaza de las Monjas, look for:

⑬ El Convento

The New World's first Carmelite convent, El Convento opened in 1651 with 30-foot-thick walls designed to withstand hurricanes and enemy attacks. The building remained a convent for 250 years, but fell on hard times early in the 20th century and served as a dance hall and flophouse. Today, the beautifully restored building is the Hotel El Convento, possibly Puerto Rico's most elegant hotel.

Across the street from El Convento stands the island's most famous church, the:

⑭ Catedral de San Juan

The original thatch-roofed, wooden cathedral, built in the early 1520s, was destroyed by a hurricane in 1529. Reconstruction in 1540 added a circular staircase and vaulted Gothic ceilings, but most of the current church was built in the 1800s. Look for the tomb of Ponce de León and the wax-encased mummy of St. Pio, a Roman martyr (153 Calle del Cristo; ✆ 787/722-0861; free admission; open weekdays 8:30am–5pm).

Now walk 2 blocks south along Calle del Cristo, through one of the Caribbean's most attractive shopping districts. After passing Calle La Fortaleza, look on your left for the:

⑮ Centro Nacional de Artes Populares y Artesanias

Operated by the Institute of Puerto Rican Culture, this center displays a collection of the island's folk arts and crafts (253 Calle del Cristo; ✆ 787/722-0621; free admission; open Mon–Sat 9am–5pm).

Continue to the southernmost tip of Calle del Cristo (just a few steps away) to the wrought-iron gates that surround a chapel no bigger than a newspaper kiosk, the:

⑯ Capilla del Cristo (Christ Chapel)

Legend has it that in 1753 a young rider lost control of his horse in a race down Calle del Cristo during the feast of St. John the Baptist and plunged over the steep precipice at the street's end. A witness to the tragedy promised to build a chapel if the young man's life was saved. Records maintain that the horseman died, but lore contends otherwise. In another version of the story, the horseman, after himself praying to God while falling over the cliff, survived to build the chapel. The delicate silver altar here can be seen through glass doors (free admission; open Mon, Wed, and Fri 10:30am–3:30pm).

Retrace your steps about a block north along the Calle del Cristo, then turn right on Calle Fortaleza. One block later, take a left onto Calle San José, then proceed another block to the capital's liveliest square, the:

⑰ Plaza de Armas

This broad, open plaza has lots of pigeons, several old men playing dominos, office workers and shoppers basking in the sun, and a 19th-century statue representing the four seasons. Originally used for military drills, the plaza now hosts folk dances and concerts on weekends. The neoclassical Intendencia (which houses offices of the U.S. State Department) and the Alcadía (San Juan's City Hall) flank the square.

Walk eastward along the plaza's northern border, Calle San Francisco, for 4 blocks until you reach another square:

⑱ Plaza de Colón

This park is notable for its statue of Cristóbal Colón (Christopher Columbus). Bronze plaques at the monument's base commemorate episodes in the explorer's life.

Finally, walk to the plaza's northeast corner, where Calle San Francisco meets Boulevard del Valle. Turn left and follow the signs to:

⑲ Fort San Cristóbal

Built in 1634 (and expanded in the 1770s), this fortress rises more than 150 feet above the sea. A complex maze of tunnels and moats connects the central fort with wave after wave of outlying posts. Don't miss the Garita del Diablo (the Devil's Sentry Box), a lonely post at the edge of the sea where, legend has it, the devil himself snatched away solitary sentinels (uphill from Plaza de Colón on Calle Norzagaray; ℭ **787/729-6960;** $3 for adults, $1 for ages 13–17, adults over 62 and children under 13 are free; note that your ticket stub from El Morro is good for admission here; open daily 9am–5pm.)

CASINOS

Casinos are one of San Juan's biggest draws, and most large hotels have one. They're generally open daily from noon to 4am, but some never close. Dress, usually informal during the day, becomes impressive in the evenings. The **Casino at the Ritz-Carlton,** 6961 State Rd., Isla Verde (ℭ **787/253-1700**), is the largest in Puerto Rico. Combining elegant 1940s decor with tropical fabrics and patterns, it's one of the plushest entertainment complexes in the Caribbean. The **Inter-Continental San Juan,** 187 Isla Verde Ave. (ℭ **800/443-2009** or 787/791-6100), is another elegant place to rendezvous. One of its Murano glass chandeliers is "longer than a bowling alley." Most convenient for cruise ship passengers, the **Wyndham Old San Juan Hotel & Casino,** 100 Brumbaugh St. (ℭ **787/721-5100**), is directly across from Pier 3 and often bustling.

BEACHES

Puerto Rico is ringed by hundreds of miles of sandy beaches, and you won't have to leave San Juan to play in the surf. Perhaps the most famous beach in the Caribbean, **Condado Beach,** at the western end of Ashford Avenue, is the backyard playground of Condado's resort hotels. A favorite of families, it can get pretty crowded in winter. The beaches of **Isla Verde,** behind the hotels and condominiums along Isla Verde Avenue, are less rocky and are excellent for people-watching. If you're looking for a more picturesque, sedate scene, head to **Ocean Park,** north of McLeary Street. The waters here are sometimes choppy, but they're still swimmable. Popular with college students on weekends, the beach is also very gay-friendly. Condado Beach, Isla Verde, and Ocean Park all have white sand, palm trees, ocean breezes, beautiful bodies, and ample eating and drinking options. Snorkeling gear and other watersports equipment are available to rent.

If you're anxious to get out of the city, **Luquillo Beach,** about 30 miles east of San Juan, near the town of Luquillo, stretches along a vast coconut grove. Coral reefs protect the clear lagoon from the fierce Atlantic, and a "Sea Without Barriers" facility caters to people with physical disabilities. Be aware, however, that some sections of the beach aren't as well maintained as they once were.

All *balnearios*—government-run beaches with dressing rooms, showers, lifeguards, snack bars, and parking—are open to the public. They're closed on Mondays; however, if Monday is a holiday, the beaches will be open that day but closed the next. Hours are 9am to 5pm in winter, 9am to 6pm during the off-season. If you find a secluded spot, be vigilant about your surroundings: Solitude is nice, but there's safety in numbers.

SPORTS

DEEP-SEA FISHING   Many say that Captain Mike Benitez, who's chartered boats out of San Juan for more than 40 years, sets the standard by which other deep-sea-fishing captains are judged. Contact him at **Mike Benitez Marine Services,** P.O. Box 9066541, Puerto de Tierra, San Juan, PR 00906-6541 (© 787/723-2292; www.mikebenitezfishing.com). **Captain Bill Burleson,** P.O. Box 8270, Humacao, PR 00792 (© 787/850-7442), operates charters off the southeast coast. For both companies, expect to pay a little under $500 for a half-day excursion (up to six anglers).

GOLF   Puerto Rico is a golfer's dream, but you'll need to sign up for a ship excursion or rent a car to reach the major courses from San Juan. With 72 holes, **Hyatt Dorado Beach Resort & Country Club** (© 787/796-8916; www.hyatt.com) offers the greatest concentration of golf in the Caribbean. Greens fees are $115 for play before 1pm and $65 after 1 pm. Cost includes cart. Club rentals are $55. All four 18-hole courses at the **Hyatt's Regency Cerromar** and **Dorado Beach** properties here were designed by Robert Trent Jones Sr. Jack Nicklaus ranks the fourth hole at the Dorado Beach East course as one of the 10 best-designed holes in the world. Greens fees are $145 for 18 holes. **The Doral Resort at Palmas del Mar** (© 787/285-2256; www.palmasdelmar.com), 45 miles east of San Juan, has two courses: the par-72 Palm course designed by Gary Player and the newer 18-hole Flamboyan course designed by Rees Jones. Greens fees at the Palm are $150 for 18 holes and $170 at the Flamboyan course, including cart. **The Westin Rio Mar Country Club** (© 787/888-6000; www.westinriomar.com), 20 miles away from San Juan in Rio Grande, also has two 18-hole courses, one designed by Tom and George Fazio, the other by Greg Norman. Greens fees, including cart, are $190 and $130 for play after 2pm.

SCUBA DIVING & SNORKELING   Puerto Rico offers excellent diving and snorkeling, but the best sites aren't within easy reach of San Juan. **Caribe Aquatic Adventures,** P.O. Box 9024278, San Juan Station, San Juan 00902 (© 787/724-1882; www.caribeaquaticadventure.com), will take you to good diving and snorkeling sites around the capital or near Fajardo on the northeast coast. Caribe operates out of the Park Plaza Normandie (Av. Muñoz-Rivera, at the corner of Calle Los Rasales in Puerta de Tierra). A local reef dive is $50. Much more interesting trips to Fajardo (which include a picnic) require a minimum of four passengers (cost is $135 per person for certified divers, $115 for divers who've completed a resort course, and $85 for snorkelers). The Fajardo excursion must be booked a week in advance, the local reef dives a day in advance.

WINDSURFING, KITEBOARDING & JET-SKIING   The most popular windsurfing beach in the San Juan area is **Puntas las Marias,** between Isla Verde and Ocean Park. You can rent equipment and take lessons from nearby **Velauno,** 2430 Calle Loiza (© **866/778-3521** or 787/728-8716). Boards and a complete rig are $75 per day; 4-hour beginner lessons are $150. Velauno also offers kiteboarding—windsurfing powered by a large kite rather than sails. Kiteboarding lessons are $50 an hour, including equipment. A 1-hour introductory course is $49. Two-hour kite-control classes are $100. Another popular place for windsurfing is along the beachfront of the **Hyatt Resorts at Dorado,** about 30 miles west of San Juan. **Penfield Island Adventures** (© **787/796-1234,** ext. 3768, or 787/796-2188), at the Hyatt Regency Cerromar, rents windsurfing equipment, jet skis, kayaks, and sailboats.

SHOPPING

San Juan has some great bargains—prices are often even lower than those in St. Thomas—and U.S. citizens pay no duty on items bought in Puerto Rico. Every tourist zone offers ample shopping opportunities, but the streets of the **Old Town,** especially **Calle San Francisco** and **Calle del Cristo,** are the major venues. Generally, shopping hours are 8am to 6pm from Monday to Thursday and Saturday, 8am to 9pm Friday, and 11am to 5pm Sunday for some stores, though most are closed. Local handicrafts can be good buys, including *santos* (hand-carved wooden religious figures), needlework, straw work, hammocks, *guayabera* shirts (loose-fitting shirts), papier-mâché masks, and paintings and sculptures by local artists.

El Alcazar, 103 Calle San José, has the largest collection of antique furniture, silver, and art objects in the Caribbean. You'll need help to wade through the massive inventory, though—it fills several buildings. Smaller but still impressive, **Olé,** 105 Calle Fortaleza, has antique *santos,* coins, and silver. It's also the place to get a custom-fitted Panama hat. **Puerto Rican Arts & Crafts,** 204 Calle Fortaleza, has authentic handicrafts, including papier-mâché carnival masks from the town of Ponce. **José E. Alegria & Associates,** 152–154 Calle del Cristo, is half antiques shop, half gift arcade; while **Galería Botello,** 208 Calle del Cristo, once the home of late Puerto Rican artist Angel Botello, sells his paintings and sculptures, as well as antique *santos.*

Old San Juan's best book and music store, **Cronopios,** is at 255 Calle San José. Most books are in Spanish, but there are plenty in English too. Looking for Puerto Rican novels? Try *The House on the Lagoon,* by Rosario Ferré, or *The Renunciation,* by Edgardo Rodríguez Julia. And pick up some salsa CDs while you're browsing.

Designer outlet shops include London Fog, 156 Calle del Cristo; Polo Ralph Lauren, 201 Calle del Cristo; Coach, 158 Calle del Cristo; and Tommy Hilfiger, 206 Calle del Cristo.

GREAT LOCAL RESTAURANTS & BARS

San Juan has some of the best restaurants in the Caribbean and a variety of cuisines that only a major city can offer. A favorite **local beer** is Medalla. The most famous **local rum** is Bacardi, in all of its varieties; Don Q is also popular.

In Old San Juan, **Amadeus,** 106 Calle San Sebastián (© **787/722-8635**), offers nouvelle Caribbean dishes and features an intimate courtyard in back. Lunch is about $22. **El Patio de Sam,** practically next door at 102 Calle San Sebastián (© **787/723-1149**), is a popular gathering spot for expatriates, journalists, and shopkeepers. Lunch is around $13. The unpretentious **La Bombonera,** 259 Calle

San Francisco (© **787/722-0658**), famous for its homemade Puerto Rican meals and 1940s diner atmosphere, has attracted the island's literati and Old San Juan families for decades. San Juan's trailblazing nuevo Latino bistro, **Parrot Club,** 363 Calle Fortaleza (© **787/725-7370**), blends Spanish, Taíno, and African cuisines. Lunch is about $40.

In Condado, **Miró Marisquería Catalana,** 76 Condado Ave. (© **787/723-9593**), serves seafood and traditional Catalonian dishes. Lunch is around $20. Not far away, **Ajili Mójili,** 1052 Ashford Ave. (© **787/725-9195**), serves some of the island's best upmarket Puerto Rican cuisine. Lunch is about $20.

For stylish but relaxed beachfront dining and sublime Caribbean delicacies, no place beats **Pamela's,** 1 Calle Santa Ana (© **787/726-5010**), in Ocean Park. You'll savor every bite. Lunch is about $16.

25 St. Barts

Chic, sophisticated St. Barts (or, technically, St. Barthélemy, a name nobody ever uses) is internationally renowned as one of the ritziest refuges in the Caribbean, rivaled only by Mustique as the preferred island retreat of the rich and famous. From early fans Nureyev, Baryshnikov, and Buffett to later enthusiasts Mick Jagger, Princess Di, Calvin Klein, Madonna, and Naomi Campbell, the glitterati who've played here form a veritable who's who of fabulousness. Despite its transformation over the past couple of decades into a celebrity hot spot, St. Barts retains its charm, serenity, natural beauty, and Gallic flavor. Just 24km (15 miles) from St. Martin and politically part of Guadeloupe, the island's 21 sq. km (8 sq. miles) of dramatic hills and pristine white-sand beaches are decidedly French, like a peaceful slice of the Côte d'Azur transplanted in the Caribbean. The roller-coaster terrain, strict zoning and construction laws, and a local consensus that stratospheric pricing is the surest way to maintain exclusivity, protects the island from massive development that would certainly change its character.

First inhabited about 3,000 years ago by Ciboney Indians, then later by Arawaks (A.D. 200) and Caribs (A.D. 1000), St. Barts was first spotted by Europeans in 1496, when Christopher Columbus named the island after his baby brother, Bartolemeo. The French took possession of the island in the mid–17th century, then in 1784 traded it to the Swedes, who built forts, houses, and roads and declared St. Barts a free port. Sweden transferred it back to France in 1878 after its colony began to falter. It wasn't until the 1980s that St. Barts began to impress jet-setting tourists. Later, tax breaks for French nationals fueled investment in tourism.

In sharp contrast to most Caribbean islands, where descendants of African slaves form the majority, St. Barts's 7,000 year-round residents are primarily of French ancestry, mostly from Brittany and Normandy. Many affluent Americans and Europeans have villas on the island, some living in the Caribbean year-round, others making seasonal visits.

COMING ASHORE   Cruise ships anchor off **Gustavia,** the main town, and ferry passengers to the dollhouse-size harbor and town via tenders. Phones and ATMs are in the immediate vicinity of the harbor. The post office (or PTT), which also serves as a telecommunications center, is located at the back corner of the harbor opposite the dock. You can check your e-mail at the second-floor offices of **Centre @lizes** (© **590/29-89-89**), on rue de la République, a few blocks to the right of the dock. Access to the Internet is about $6 per 30 minutes.

Be sure to ask for an American keyboard: The position of letters on French keyboards is significantly different. The center is open Monday through Friday from 9am to 6:30pm; Saturday hours are 9am to 12:30pm and 2:30pm to 6pm.

LANGUAGE **French** is the official language, but virtually everyone speaks **English** as well.

CURRENCY St. Barts is part of the French overseas region of Guadeloupe, so the **euro** (€) is now the official currency (exchange rate at press time: 1€ = US$1.22; $1 = .82€). Each euro is divisible by 100 cents. Prices mentioned in this section are in U.S. dollars. You'll have no trouble using credit cards and traveler's checks.

INFORMATION The **Office Municipal du Tourisme** (© **590/27-87-27**), adjacent to the dock on Quai Général de Gaulle, is open Monday through Friday from 8:30am to 12:30pm, Friday from 2pm to 5pm, and Monday through Thursday from 2pm to 5:30pm. For information before you go, get on the horn to **Maison de la France** in the U.S. (© **212/838-7800;** www.st-barths.com).

CALLING FROM THE U.S. When calling St. Barts from the United States, dial the international access code (011) and 590 before the numbers listed here, which also begin with 590. That's right: If you want to make a connection, you have to dial 590 twice. It's just one of those oddities that makes the world go round.

Frommer's Favorite St. Barts Experiences

Making the Scene at Le Select: For more than 50 years this garden cafe has been the most popular gathering spot in Gustavia, and the best place to get a taste of local life. (See "Great Local Restaurants & Bars," below.)

Bronzing on the Beach: St. Barts has several gorgeous beaches, some social, some private. (See "Beaches," below.)

Zipping Around the Island in a Mini-Moke: Few experiences are as exhilarating as zooming along the island's roller-coaster roads in one of these open-air vehicles, half golf cart, half jeep. (See "Getting Around," above.)

GETTING AROUND

BY TAXI   Taxis meet cruise ships at Gustavia's harbor. Because the island is so small, no destination is too distant. Consequently, fares seem reasonable. Dial ℂ **590/27-66-31** for service if you don't spot a cab. The fare ranges from approximately $10 to $22, depending on your destination.

BY RENTAL CAR   If you love adventure, rent an open-sided **mini-moke** (a jeep–golf cart hybrid) or Suzuki Samurai: Zipping up and down St. Barts's jagged, picturesque hills is more thrilling than riding most amusement-park rides. Roads are in excellent condition, and local drivers are alert and competent, but tend to drive aggressively. Automatic transmissions are in short supply, so reserve in advance: If you're not already adept at using a stick shift, St. Barts is not the place to learn. **Budget, Avis, Hertz,** and **National** have offices here, as does **Europcar** (ℂ **590/27-74-34**). The island has only two gas stations: one near the airport, the other in Lorient. Both are closed on Sundays, but the airport station has a pump that accepts credit cards any time of day, any day of the week.

BY MOTOR SCOOTER   Terrified by winding roads and speeding drivers, mothers on St. Barts are loath to let their kids ride scooters. Few bikes have the power to make it up the steep hills anyway. If you have a death wish, go ahead and rent a motorbike or scooter from **Meca Moto** (ℂ **590/52-92-49**), rue du Général de Gaulle, or **Tropic'all Rent** (ℂ **590/27-64-76**), rue du Roi Oscar II, both in Gustavia. Expect to pay about $30 for the day, mandatory helmet included. A $200 deposit or credit card imprint is required.

BEST CRUISE LINE SHORE EXCURSIONS

Jet-Set Boat & Beach Excursion ($200, 4 hr.): Circumnavigate St. Barts in a 12m (40-ft.) cruiser, then tender ashore at St. Jean Beach for a swim, snorkel, and/or drinks from the open bar.

St. Barts on Horseback ($59, 2 hr.): Travel to northern St. Barts for a relaxed guided ride through the island's outback.

ON YOUR OWN: WITHIN WALKING DISTANCE

Aside from shopping, eating, and hanging out in sidewalk cafes, cruisers sticking close to port can visit Gustavia's modest points of interest. **St. Bartholomew's Church,** rue Samuel Fahlberg, dates from the 1850s and features limestone and volcanic stone walls, as well as imported pitch pine pews. Its tiny Anglican, English-speaking congregation is an anomaly on this overwhelmingly French Catholic island.

Evidence of St. Barts's faint but lingering Swedish presence, the **Wall House,** rue Duquesne, is a staid, stone building near the harbor's mouth, across from the dock. Once a Swedish home, the structure was rebuilt after fire devastated it (and much of Gustavia) in 1852. Since 1989, it has housed the **Municipal Museum** (℃ **590/29-71-55**), an unfocused but respectable introduction to the history, sociology, ethnology, economy, and ecology of the island. The most interesting items include Amerindian artifacts, rustic farm furnishings, clothing used by early French settlers, and photos documenting hurricane devastation. Admission for persons over 12 is $2; the exhibits are open Monday 2:30 to 6pm, Tuesday through Friday 8:30am to 12:30pm and 2:30 to 6pm, and Saturday 9am to noon.

ON YOUR OWN: BEYOND THE PORT AREA

Visiting the tiny fishing village of **Corossol** is a vibrant way to experience the St. Barts of the past. About 10 minutes by taxi from the dock, this quaint, totally un-chic hamlet is home to traditional folk who still live off the sea. It's your best bet for spotting women in traditional 17th-century bonnets and for watching roadside vendors weave items from palm fronds. On the town's waterfront, about 30m (98 ft.) to the left of the road from Gustavia, the **Inter Oceans Museum** (℃ **590/27-62-97**) catalogs thousands of shells, corals, sand dollars, sea horses, sea urchins, and fish from around the world. One (now very old) man's obsession, the museum's homemade, thorough displays are completely endearing and sure to enthrall the child in everyone. Don't miss the collection of sand from beaches around the world: A cocktail umbrella is planted in each specimen. Admission is $3. Doors to this extension of the owner's home are open from 9am to 1pm and 3pm to 5pm Tuesday through Saturday.

SHOPPING

A duty-free port, St. Barts is a good place to buy liquor, perfume, and other French luxury items. Good buys on apparel, crystal, porcelain, and watches can also be found, especially during April, the biggest sale month. Moisturizer mavens can stock up on the island's own cosmetic line, Ligne St. Barth. Shops are concentrated in Gustavia and St. Jean, where the quality-to-schlock ratio is as high as anywhere in the Caribbean. Most shops and offices close for a long lunch, usually from noon to 2pm.

In Gustavia, **Carat,** rue de la République; **Fabienne Miot,** rue de la République; and **Diamond Genesis,** rue du Général de Gaulle, offer an array of fine jewelry, some handcrafted on the premises. **Dovani,** rue de la République, and **Privilège,** rue du Roi Oscar II, are your best bets for perfumes and cosmetics. **St. Barth Style,** rue Lafayette, near the corner of rue du Port, stocks fashionable beachwear, while **Mandarine,** rue de la République, carries chic but casual women's clothing. Higher-style women's fashion is available at **Roberto Cavalli,** Le Carré d'Or; **Stéphane & Bernard,** rue de la République behind Carat; and **Sorélina,** rue du Général de Gaulle. Men in search of a new shirt or trousers should try **Images Boutique** or **L'Homme et la Mer,** both on rue du Général de Gaulle. Men's and women's shoes can be found at **Human Steps,** rue de la France. **Le Comptoir du Cigare,** rue du Général de Gaulle, sells cigars from Cuba and the Dominican Republic and connoisseur-quality rums, while **Nilaya,** rue du Roi Oscar II, stocks unique, handcrafted objets d'art from Asia and elsewhere around the world.

In St. Jean, **Kiwi Saint Tropez** stocks chic beachwear, **Bleu Marine** has French and Italian women's fashions, **Elysees Caraïbes** sells high-style handbags and luggage, and **Boutique Iléna** offers erotic lingerie.

BEACHES

The 22 beaches of St. Barts are first-rate. Few are ever crowded, even during the peak season, and all are public, free, and easily accessible by taxi from the cruise pier (make arrangements with your driver to be picked up at a specific time). As St. Barts is a French island, toplessness is common at all beaches. Full nudism is officially prohibited, but bathers at several sites—Saline and Gouverneur, to name a couple (see below)—willfully flout the rules. Defying a common stereotype, most nude bathers on the island actually have attractive bodies.

If you're looking for an active beach strand, with restaurants and watersports, **Grand Cul de Sac** fits the bill. The shallow, protected waters here are warm and relatively calm. Watersports are well represented, with windsurfing especially popular. An even busier and equally social beach, **St. Jean** is actually two beaches divided by a rock promontory. Protected by a coral reef, the calm waters here attract families and watersports enthusiasts, including windsurfers. When the winds gather greater force, surfer dudes appear. Near the end of the airport's incredibly short runway, St. Jean also provides numerous eating, drinking, shopping, and people-watching opportunities. **Gouverneur,** on the south central coast, is quiet and relatively remote. Its idyllic setting and unspoiled beauty make it number one with locals and discerning visitors who want privacy and serenity. Farther east, in a wild and rustic area that was once the site of salt ponds, **Saline** is reached by a 3-minute hike over a sand dune. Most famous for its adult environment and nude bathers, it also boasts great bodysurfing waves.

SPORTS

SAILING, SCUBA DIVING & SNORKELING   Marine Service, Quai du Yacht Club (✆ **590/27-70-34**), operates from the marina across the harbor from the busier side of Gustavia. Most dive sites served by this five-star PADI operator are a 10- to 20-minute boat ride from the harbor; depths vary from 3 to 30m (10–98 ft.). Reef dives are the rule, although one wreck dive for more experienced divers is a possibility. One-tank dives are about $55 to $60; two-tank dives are about $114, including beverages and all equipment. The operation also offers half-day snorkeling cruises (about $65, including snorkeling gear, a French snack buffet, and an open bar) and catamaran or sloop charters (starting at $540 for half a day during the low season; $650 during the winter, including cheese, fruit, beverages, and music). The cost is for a maximum of eight people and includes a crew. Prospective charterers should call Marine Service for Christmas and New Year's rates. Vendors at both St. Jean and Grand Cul de Sac rent snorkel gear and other watersports equipment—jet skis, Sunfish sailboats, and so on.

WINDSURFING   Try St. Barth Wind School (✆ **590/27-71-22**) near the Tom Beach Hotel at St. Jean or **Windwave Power** (✆ **590/27-82-57**) at Grand Cul de Sac. Expect to pay about $32 an hour for a full rig.

GREAT LOCAL RESTAURANTS & BARS

Mix lots of rich, discerning diners with the French tradition of culinary expertise, and it's no wonder that so many of St. Barts's restaurants consistently receive high accolades. It's a pity that some of the best open only for dinner, well after your ship has gone out to sea. Luckily, enough serve lunch to assure you one of the best meals of your cruise.

IN GUSTAVIA   More interested in seeing and being seen than in satisfying your taste buds? Make a beeline to **Le Select,** rue de la France at rue du Général de Gaulle (© **590/27-86-87**), the epicenter of Gustavia's social life for more than 50 years. This cafe's tables rest in a tree-shaded garden a block from the harbor. A full bar is available to complement burgers, salads, and other simple fare. Salty locals, celebrities, and chic tourists are among the clientele. The classic, funky ambience inspired Jimmy Buffet's "Cheeseburger in Paradise." Lunch costs around US$15. At the foot of Gustavia harbor, **La Route des Boucaniers** (© **590/27-73-00**) looks like any seaside restaurant around Chesapeake Bay or on the Jersey shore, but its traditional and nouvelle Creole cuisine is anything but run-of-the-mill. Try the octopus gratin served in a potato shell or the braised scallops with passion fruit. Lunch is about $20. **L'Iguane,** Quai de la République (© **590/27-88-46**), offers an international menu that includes sushi and light sandwiches and salads. Lunch is about $10.

AT ST. JEAN   Eden Rock (© **590/29-79-99**) has three restaurants at St. Jean beach: one on the rock promontory that bisects the strand, one next to the ocean, and one in the sand, aptly dubbed the Sand Bar, which serves lunch at a cost of about $42. Traditional French cuisine, seafood, and tropical drinks are the trio's strong suits. For great pizza and friendly ambience, try **The Hideaway** (© **590/27-63-62**). Lunch will be around $20. Relax on the open-air terrace or get your order to go. If you're more in the mood for a sandwich and want to get back to the sun, head to **KiKi-e Mo** (© **590/27-90-65**), an Italian gourmet shop that whips up divine light fare to go. Lunch is about $7.

AT GRANDE SALINE   A handful of restaurants are within walking distance of Saline beach. **Grain de Sel** (© **590/52-46-05**) looks no-frills, but the seafood and Creole specialties are deluxe. Lunch is about $22. Prettier and more upscale, but just as relaxing, **Le Tamarin** (© **590/27-72-12**) specializes in beef, salmon, and tuna carpaccios; fresh grilled lobster; and inventive Creole dishes. Lunch is around $55.

26 St. Kitts

Somewhat off the beaten tourist track, south of St. Martin and north of Guadeloupe, St. Kitts forms the larger half of the combined Federation of St. Kitts and Nevis, which gained self-government from Britain in 1967 and became a totally independent nation in 1983. The two islands are separated by only about 3.2km (2 miles) of ocean, but the emotional distance is a little wider, with Nevis's citizens often expressing a strong urge for independence from St. Kitts.

St. Kitts—or St. Christopher, a name hardly anyone uses—is by far the more populous of the two islands, with some 35,000 people. It was the first English settlement in the Leeward Islands, and during the plantation age its 176 sq. km (69 sq. miles) enjoyed one of the richest sugar cane–economies in the Caribbean. Of course, the plantation age depended on slave labor for cultivation, and today, though the bulk of the island's revenue still comes from the nationalized sugar industry, the back-breaking and low-paying work of sugar harvesting is shunned by most of St. Kitts's citizens—in their place, Guayanese workers come in for the harvesting season. Cane fields climb the slopes of a volcanic mountain range, and you'll see ruins of old mills and plantation houses as you drive around the island.

St. Kitts is lush and fertile, dotted with rainforests and waterfalls and boasting some lovely beaches along its southeast coastline, but it's also extremely poor and has suffered catastrophically in recent years, being hit with several successive hurricanes in the late 1990s. Despite efforts at wooing tourists to bring in badly needed cash, the country lags behind in amenities and infrastructure.

The island is crowned by the 1,138m (3,733-ft.) **Mount Liamuiga,** a crater that, thankfully, remains dormant. The island's most impressive landmark is the **Brimstone Hill fortress,** one of the Caribbean's most impressive forts. **Basseterre,** the capital city, is rife with old-time Caribbean architecture, and has a few worthwhile landmarks, but overall the city has little to hold the interest of visitors.

COMING ASHORE **Port Zante,** which was hit hard by successive hurricanes, has undergone a rebuilding and expansion that was completed in late 2002. The new port, which stretches from the center of town into the deep waters offshore, offers 4,050 sq. m (43,594 sq. ft.) of shopping and office space, restaurants, and a welcome center.

LANGUAGE **English** is the language of both islands.

CURRENCY The local currency is the **Eastern Caribbean dollar** (US$1 = EC$2.70; EC$1 = US73¢). Many shops and restaurants quote prices in U.S. dollars. Always determine which currency locals are talking about. We've used U.S.-dollar prices in this section.

INFORMATION You can get local tourist information at the **St. Kitts Tourism Authority,** Pelican Mall, Bay Road, in Basseterre (© 869/465-4040), open Monday to Friday from 7:30am to 5pm. For info before you go, contact the **tourism board office in the U.S.** (© 800/582-6208; www.stkitts-tourism.com).

CALLING FROM THE U.S. When calling St. Kitts or Nevis from the United States, you just need to dial a "1" before the numbers listed here.

GETTING AROUND
BY TAXI Taxis wait at the docks in Basseterre and in the Circus, a public square near the docks at the intersection of Bank and Fort streets. Since most taxi drivers are also guides, this is the best means of getting around the island. Taxis aren't metered, so you must agree on the price before heading out. Always ask if the rates quoted are in U.S. dollars or Eastern Caribbean dollars.

Frommer's Favorite St. Kitts Experiences

Visiting Brimstone Hill Fortress: Begun by the British in 1690, the fort subsequently changed hands from British to French and back to British again. This is one of the most impressive forts in the Caribbean, with battlement after battlement leading up to a spectacular view of the sea. (See "Best Cruise Line Shore Excursions," below.)

Hiking Mount Liamuiga: The hike up this dormant volcano will take you through a rainforest and along deep ravines up to the rim of the crater at a cool 788m (2,585 ft.). (See "Best Cruise Line Shore Excursions," below.)

Rainforest Adventure Hike: Departing from Romney Gardens, about 8km (5 miles) from Basseterre, you'll hike along a loop of trail through rainforest, and get a feel for the island's lush interior. (See "Best Cruise Line Shore Excursions," below.)

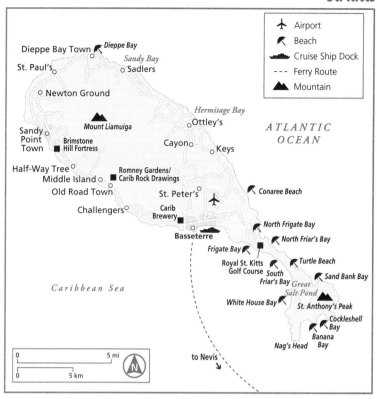

Legend:
- ✈ Airport
- ⚑ Beach
- ⛴ Cruise Ship Dock
- --- Ferry Route
- ▲ Mountain

Dieppe Bay Town *Dieppe Bay*
St. Paul's *Sandy Bay* Sadlers
Newton Ground
Hermitage Bay
Ottley's
ATLANTIC OCEAN
Sandy Point Town *Mount Liamuiga* Cayon Keys
Brimstone Hill Fortress
Half-Way Tree Romney Gardens/ Carib Rock Drawings Conaree Beach
Middle Island
Old Road Town St. Peter's
Challengers Carib Brewery
Basseterre North Frigate Bay
Frigate Bay North Friar's Bay
Royal St. Kitts Golf Course South Friar's Bay Turtle Beach
Caribbean Sea Sand Bank Bay
White House Bay *Great Salt Pond*
St. Anthony's Peak
Cockleshell Bay
Banana Bay
Nag's Head
to Nevis

0   5 mi
0   5 km
N

BY RENTAL CAR   We don't recommend renting a car here.

BEST CRUISE LINE SHORE EXCURSIONS

Brimstone Hill Fortress (US$39, 3 hr.): The price is right for this tour, making it a good way to visit the island's premier attraction. Among the largest and best preserved of all the forts in the Caribbean, Brimstone Hill (www.brimstone hillfortress.org) dates from 1690, when the British fortified the hill to help recapture Fort Charles, located below, from the French. In 1782, an invading force of 8,000 French troops bombarded the fortress for a month before its small British garrison, supplemented by local militia, surrendered. When the British took the island back the next year, they proceeded to enlarge the fort into "The Gibraltar of the West Indies." In all, the structure took 104 years to complete. Today it's the centerpiece of a national park crisscrossed by nature trails, with a population of green vervet monkeys to keep things lively. Perched on the upper slopes of a tall, steep hill, it's a photographer's paradise, with views of mountains, fields, and the Caribbean Sea—on a clear day you can see six neighboring islands. From below, the fort presents a dramatic picture, poised among diabolical-looking spires and outcroppings of lava rock. Its name comes from the odor of sulfur released by nearby undersea vents. Tours typically include a visit to the beautiful **Romney Gardens,** located amidst the ruins of a sugar estate between Basseterre and the fort. You can check out the lush hillside gardens (featuring giant ferns, orchids, poinsettias, and "The Tree," a 350-year-old Saman tree), say

hi to the cows that graze just across the hill, or shop at **Caribelle Batik** (© 869/
465-6253), one of the island's most popular boutiques, where you'll find rack
after rack of Indonesian-style, hand-printed, brightly colored clothes. (If you're
coming here on your own, look for signs indicating a turnoff along the coast
road, about 8km/5 miles north of Basseterre in the town of Old Road.)

Mount Liamuiga Volcano Hike (US$102, 7 hr.): This dormant volcano, in the
northwest area of the island, has long been known as "Mount Misery." It sput-
tered its last gasp around 1692, and today its summit is a major goal for hikers.
On this excursion you'll hike about 1,140m (3,800 ft.) to the summit, traveling
along narrow trails and through the island's cloud forest. It takes about 2½ hours
to reach the top. Two lookout points offer views of the crater below. Refreshments
are offered before the hike back down. This is a great trip if you're in shape.

Mountain Biking & Beach Tour (US$71, 4 hr.): From the pier, you'll ride
through Basseterre then out through sugar-cane fields and up 450m (1,500-ft.)
Olivees Mountain for views and refreshments. After the ride down, you'll stop
at Friar's Bay for a swim and snack. It's a nice way to see this lush island.

Rainforest Adventure Hike (US$58, 4 hr.): Departing from Romney Gardens,
you'll hike along a loop of trail through lush rainforest. With luck, you'll catch
sight of some of the island's resident monkeys.

Sail & Snorkel Catamaran Trip (US$68, 3–4 hr.): A sailing catamaran takes you
to secluded Smitten's Bay for snorkeling among diverse reef fish and coral formations. Complimentary rum punch is served aboard the boat on your return trip.

EXCURSIONS OFFERED BY LOCAL AGENCIES

Rainforest Tours: For a great rainforest walk in the thickets around Romney Gardens, contact Addy of **Addy's Rainforest Safaris** (© 869/465-8069). He knows
the flora and fauna of St. Kitts like the back of his hand and delivers a satisfying,
personal rainforest experience, ending his tour by sharing a plate of his wife's tasty
homemade banana bread and some fresh guava and passion fruit juices.

Taxi Tours: You'll find a fleet of taxis waiting in the dock as you disembark from
the ship. Taxi drivers will take you on a 3-hour tour of the island for about
US$60. Lunch can be arranged at one of the local inns. Good inn choices are
Golden Lemon at Dieppe Bay (© 869/465-7260) or **Rawlins Plantation,**
Mount Pleasant (© 869/465-6221).

ON YOUR OWN: WITHIN WALKING DISTANCE

The capital city of Basseterre, where the docks are located, has typical British
colonial architecture and some quaint buildings, a few shops, and a market
where locals display fruits and flowers—but even this description might be giving you the wrong idea about this place. The truth is, it's a very poor town, with
few attractions aimed at visitors. When we were last there, there were chickens
walking around in front of the government buildings. **St. George's Anglican
Church,** on Cayon Street (walk straight up Church St. or Fort St. from the
dock), is the oldest church in town and is worth a look. **Independence Square,**
a stone's throw from the docks along Bank Street, is pretty, with its central fountain and old church, but there's no good reason to linger unless it's to sit in the
shade and toss back a bottle of Ting, the local grapefruit-based soda.

ON YOUR OWN: BEYOND THE PORT AREA

All of the good out-of-town sites here are covered under "Shore Excursions,"
above.

SHOPPING

Basseterre is not a shopping town, despite handout maps that show a listing of shops that would put St. Thomas to shame. Look closer and you'll see entries such as "R. Gumbs Electrical," "TDC/Finco Finance Co.," and "Horsford Furniture Store." Turns out they just listed every business on every street in town, no matter whether it's of interest to visitors or not. Strength in numbers, we suppose. The port complex offers a number of shopping options.

At Romney Gardens, you'll find **Caribelle Batik** (*©* **869/465-6253**), one of the island's most popular boutiques. Inside, you'll find Indonesian-style handprinted, brightly colored clothes. Brimstone Hill and rainforest-hike shore excursions typically include a stop here. If you're coming on your own, look for signs indicating a turnoff along the coast road, about 8km (5 miles) north of Basseterre in the town of Old Road.

BEACHES

The narrow peninsula in the southeast contains the island's salt ponds and also boasts the best white-sand beaches (approach via the windy, hilly road for a dramatic and gorgeous view). You'll find the best swimming at **Conaree Beach,** 4.8km (3 miles) from Basseterre; **Frigate Bay,** with its talcum-powder-fine sand; the twin beaches of **Banana Bay** and **Cockleshell Bay,** at the southeast corner of the island; and **Friar's Bay,** a peninsula beach opening onto both the Atlantic and the Caribbean. All beaches, even those that border hotels, are free and open to the public. However, you must usually pay a fee to use a hotel's beach facilities.

SPORTS

GOLF   The **Golden Rock Golf Course,** Frigate Bay (*©* **869/465-7512**), is a 5-minute drive from the cruise port. Greens fees at the nine-hole, par-34 course are $30. Cart rental is $15 per person and club rentals $15 per person.

SCUBA DIVING & SNORKELING   One of the best diving spots is **Nagshead,** at the southern tip of St. Kitts. This is an excellent shallow-water dive for certified divers, starting at 3m (10 ft.) and extending to 21m (69 ft.). You'll see a variety of tropical fish, eagle rays, and lobster here. Another good site is **Booby Shoals,** between Cow 'n' Calf Rocks and Booby Island. Booby Shoals has abundant sea life, including nurse sharks, lobster, and stingrays. Dives here are up to 9m (30 ft.) in depth, and are good for both certified and beginning divers.

GREAT LOCAL RESTAURANTS & BARS

The favorite **local beer** is Carib, brewed right on the northern edge of Basseterre. There's a **local cane-sugar drink** called CSR (Cane Spirit Rothschild) that tastes a bit like Brazilian *cachaça,* but with a slight licorice flavor.

Ballahoo Restaurant (*©* **869/465-4197**), located in Basseterre's most picturesque intersection (the Circus, right by the cruise dock), serves some of the best baby back ribs in town. Seafood platters, such as garlic shrimp, curried conch, or fresh lobster, are served with salad and rice. Lunch is $15.

27 St. Lucia

With a turbulent history shared by many of its Caribbean neighbors, St. Lucia (pronounced *Loo*-sha), second largest of the Windward Islands at about 622 sq. km (243 sq. miles), changed hands often during the colonial period, being British seven times and French seven times. Today, though, it's an independent state that's become one of the most popular destinations in the Caribbean, with some of the finest resorts. The heaviest development is concentrated in the northwest, between the capital of Castries and the northern end of the island, where there's a string of white-sand beaches. The interior boasts relatively unspoiled green-mantled mountains and gentle valleys, as well as the volcanic **Mount Soufrière.** Two dramatic peaks **(the Pitons)** rise along the southwest coast.

Castries, the capital, has grown up around an extinct volcanic crater that's now a large harbor surrounded by hills. Because of fires that devastated many of its older structures, the town today has touches of modernity, with glass-and-concrete buildings, although there's still an old-fashioned Saturday-morning market on Jeremie Street. The country women dress in traditional cotton head-dress to sell their luscious fruits and vegetables, while weather-beaten men sit close by playing warrie (a fast game played with pebbles on a carved board) or fleet games of dominoes using tiles the color of cherries.

COMING ASHORE   Most cruise ships arrive at a fairly new pier at **Pointe Seraphine,** within walking distance of the center of Castries. Unlike piers on other islands, this one boasts St. Lucia's best shopping. You'll also find a visitor information bureau. Phone cards are sold for use at specially labeled phones.

If Pointe Seraphine is too crowded (not too likely, as two megaships can pull alongside at once), your ship might dock at **Port Castries** on the other side of the colorful harbor. There's a shopping terminal here called La Place Carenage. At press time, the port was in the process of adding to La Place Carenage a cen-ter depicting St. Lucia's history. If you still want to shop in Pointe Seraphine, a water taxi (US$1) runs between the two locations all day. A land taxi will cost you around US$4, or you can also walk between the two areas. Some smaller vessels, such as Star Clippers', Seabourn's, and Clipper's, anchor off **Rodney Bay** to the north or **Soufrière** to the south and carry you ashore by tender.

There are telephones inside La Place Carnage's duty-free shopping mall and at the Pointe Seraphine pier.

LANGUAGE   **English** is the official language.

CURRENCY   The official monetary unit is the **Eastern Caribbean dollar** (EC$). The exchange rate is US$1 = EC$2.70; EC$1 = US73¢. Prices quoted in this section are in U.S. dollars, which are accepted by nearly all hotels, restau-rants, and shops.

INFORMATION   The **St. Lucia Tourist Board** is located at Vide Bouteille outside the town of Castries (© **758/452-4094**). The board runs a visitor infor-mation bureau at Pointe Seraphine, which is open Monday to Friday from 9am to 5pm. For info before you go, contact the tourism board office in the U.S. (© **800/456-3984** or 212/867-2950; www.stlucia.org).

CALLING FROM THE U.S.   When calling St. Lucia from the United States, you just need to dial a "1" before the numbers listed here.

GETTING AROUND

BY TAXI   Most taxi drivers have been trained to serve as guides. Their cars are unmetered, but the government fixes tariffs for all standard trips. Be sure to determine if the driver is quoting a rate in U.S. or EC dollars. There is an offi-cial taxi association servicing both Pointe Seraphine and La Place Carenage. The taxi association will have standard fares posted. You can hire a taxi to go to Soufrière on your own, too. A taxi for four will cost about $120 for a 3- to 4-hour tour, including a beach stop, photo ops, shopping, and sightseeing.

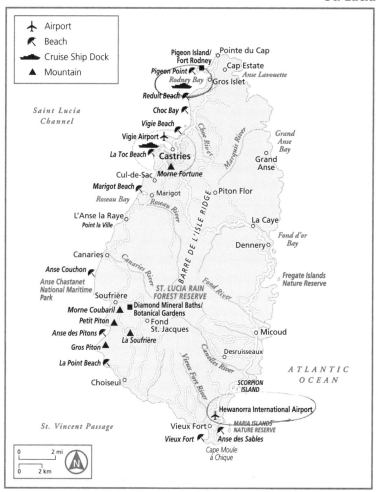

Map legend:
- ✈ Airport
- 🏖 Beach
- 🚢 Cruise Ship Dock
- ▲ Mountain

Pointe du Cap
Pigeon Island/ Fort Rodney
Cap Estate
Pigeon Point
Anse Lavouette
Rodney Bay
Gros Islet
Reduit Beach
Choc Bay

Saint Lucia Channel

Vigie Beach
Vigie Airport
Grand Anse Bay
La Toc Beach
Castries
Grand Anse
Cul-de-Sac
Morne Fortune
Marigot Beach
Marigot
Piton Flor
Roseau Bay
Roseau River
L'Anse la Raye
Point la Ville
La Caye
Fond d'or Bay
Canaries
Canaries River
Dennery
Anse Couchon
Anse Chastanet National Maritime Park
Soufrière
ST. LUCIA RAIN FOREST RESERVE
Fregate Islands Nature Reserve
Morne Coubaril
Diamond Mineral Baths/ Botanical Gardens
Petit Piton
Fond St. Jacques
Micoud
Anse des Pitons
La Soufrière
Gros Piton
Desruisseaux
La Point Beach
Vieux Fort River
ATLANTIC OCEAN
Choiseul
SCORPION ISLAND
St. Vincent Passage
Hewanorra International Airport
Vieux Fort
MARIA ISLANDS NATURE RESERVE
Vieux Fort
Anse des Sables
Cape Moule à Chique

BARRE DE L'ISLE RIDGE
Choc River
Marquis River
Fond River
Canelles River

0 2 mi
0 2 km
N

BY RENTAL CAR   Driving is on the left, and roads are decent (but not great). The roads are not always clearly marked and are narrow. We wouldn't recommend renting a car, but if you're set on it, **Avis, Budget,** and **Hertz** all have offices here, as does **Courtesy Rent-A-Car** (© 758/452-8140).

BEST CRUISE LINE SHORE EXCURSIONS

Because of the difficult terrain, shore excursions are the best means of seeing this beautiful island in a day or less. In addition to the sampling below, most ships typically offer bus tours (many visiting the island's banana plantations), and snorkeling cruises.

Pigeon Island Sea Kayaking (US$65–US$70, 3 hr.): After transferring to Rodney Bay, you'll make the approximately 30-minute paddle out to the island, where you'll have time to swim, kayak some more, or make the steep climb up to Fort Rodney. From the summit of Fort Rodney, you'll have great views of the Pitons, and sometimes you'll even be able to see Martinique. (See below for more info.)

Frommer's Favorite St. Lucia Experiences

Coastal Cruise: The best way to really see the lush coast of St. Lucia and the mighty Pitons is from the water. This tour allows you to explore the coast via catamaran or boat, with a chance for a quick swim in crystal clear waters of Anse Cochon. Then via minibus, visit the Sulphur Springs, where you can drive right into a volcanic crater to see pools of bubbling mud, and drive through the Roseau banana plantations and the fishing villages of Anse-La-Raye and Canaries, before heading back to the ship (this tour is also offered in reverse).

Exploring a Banana Plantation: See how St. Lucia's leading export is grown and harvested. (See "On Your Own: Beyond the Port Area," below.)

Hiking up to Fort Rodney in Rodney Bay: The beautiful Pigeon Island on Rodney Bay offers the chance to hike up to Fort Rodney, an 18th-century English base that was used as an American signal station during World War II. From the top you can catch sight of Martinique. (See "Best Cruise Line Shore Excursions," below.)

Rainforest Bicycle Tour (US$69, 4½ hr.): After being dropped off by bus in the middle of the forest, you'll ride past banana plantations and the Errard Falls waterfall, stopping to sample various fruits that grow along the roadside. Some time for swimming is usually included at the falls. A different tour called **Jungle Mountain Biking** takes you by boat to the Jungle Biking facility, located on an 18th-century sugar plantation. There, you can explore 3km (10 miles) of trails at your own pace. Beach time is included at the end (US$99, 4½ hr.).

Soody Nature Hike & Mineral Waterfall (US$55, 7 hr.): Drive along the west coast through fishing villages, banana plantations, and the edge of the rainforest before arriving at Soufrière, location of the Pitons and the Diamond Botanical Gardens. A guided hour-long hike through the volcanic forest introduces you to the island's flora and fauna, and ends up at a therapeutic sulphuric waterfall where you can take a dip to cure what ails ya. Lunch at a Creole restaurant is included.

Beach Snorkel (US$64, 3½ hr.): Snorkeling is spectacular around St. Lucia. This trip departs Castries harbor by boat, traveling an hour en route to the island's marine reserve, which has an area set aside especially for snorkeling. There's also a supersized 7-hour (US$93) version of this trip that includes a buffet lunch.

EXCURSIONS OFFERED BY LOCAL AGENCIES

Horseback Treks: Trim's National Riding Stables, north of Castries, offers picnic trips to the Atlantic side of the island, with a barbecue lunch and drinks included. Departure is at 10am. The fee is US$70 for a 2-hour ride. Nonriders can also join the excursion; they are transported to the site in a van and pay half price. To make arrangements, contact René Trim at © 758/450-8273.

ON YOUR OWN: WITHIN WALKING DISTANCE

First, a tip: The last time we were at the duty-free marketplaces right at Castries' dock, a guy was doling out 5-minute massages for $5. If he's still there, this could save you a bundle on those expensive Steiner massages aboard the ship!

The principal streets of Castries are William Peter Boulevard and Bridge Street. Don't miss a walk through town: People are very friendly, and **Jeremie Street** is chockablock with variety stores of the most authentic local kind, selling everything from spices to housewares. A Roman Catholic cathedral stands on **Columbus Square,** which has a few restored buildings. Take a gander at the enormous 400-year-old "rain" tree, also called a "no-name" tree, which grows in the square. The nearby Government House is a late Victorian structure.

Beyond Government House lies **Morne Fortune,** which means "Hill of Good Luck." Actually, no one's had much luck here, certainly not the French and British soldiers who battled for Fort Charlotte. The fort switched nationalities (from French to English, and vice versa) many times. You can visit the 18th-century barracks, complete with a military cemetery, a small museum, the Old Powder Magazine, and the Four Apostles Battery—four grim muzzle-loading cannons. The view of the harbor of Castries is panoramic from this point. You can also see north to Pigeon Island or south to the Pitons. To reach Morne Fortune, head east on Bridge Street. Castries has a very colorful **Central Market,** right near the dock, which is also worth a visit. The airplane-hangar-size emporium sells local food, trinkets, and produce. Buy some banana ketchup or local cinnamon sticks to take home.

ON YOUR OWN: BEYOND THE PORT AREA

Bananas are St. Lucia's leading export, so if you're being taken around the island by a taxi driver, ask him to take you to one of the huge plantations. (Most island tours include a drive through one of the plantations as a matter of course.) We suggest a look at one of the three biggest: the **Cul-de-Sac,** just north of Marigot Bay; **La Caya,** on the east coast in Dennery; or the **Roseau Estate,** south of Marigot Bay.

St. Lucia's first national park, **Pigeon Island National Landmark,** was originally an island but is now joined to the northwest shore of the mainland by a very environmentally unfriendly causeway that has disrupted offshore currents, thereby upsetting the local fishing industry. The 18-hectare (44-acre) island got its name from the red-neck pigeon, or ramier, which once made this island home. It's ideal for picnics and nature walks, and is covered with lemon grass, which spread from original plantings made by British light opera singer Josset, who leased the island for 30 years and grew the grass to provide thatch for her cottage's roof. Every few years the grass, which is full of volatile oils, catches fire and immolates much of the island before it can be put out (© **758/450-0603**). Hours are 9am to 5pm daily; admission is US$5 for adults, US$1 for children 6 to 12.

The island's **Interpretation Centre** contains artifacts and a multimedia display of local history, covering everything from the Amerindian settlers of A.D. 1000 to 1782's Battle of Saints, when Admiral Rodney's fleet set out from Pigeon Island and defeated the French admiral De Grasse. Right below the interpretation center is the cozy **Captain's Cellar pub** (© **758/450-0253**), located in what was formerly a soldier's mess. From the tables outside you get wonderful views of the crashing surf on the Atlantic coast, just a few steps away.

From the center, you can walk up the winding and moderately steep path to a lookout from which you can see Martinique. In 1780, Admiral Rodney said of this spot, "This is the post the Governor of Martinique has set his eye on and if possessed by the enemy would deprive us of the best anchorage place in these islands, from which Martinique is always attackable." Remember that when planning your own assault. From the pinnacle you get a wonderful view, and the cannons that ring the space are a nice place to pose for "I was there" pictures.

On Pigeon Island's west coast are two white-sand beaches. There's also a restaurant, Jambe de Bois ("Leg of Wood;" ℂ 758/452-0321), named after a peg-legged pirate who once used the island as a hideout.

The best way to get to Pigeon Island National Landmark is to take a taxi and arrange to be picked up in time to return to your ship (the trip is 30 min., at most, back to the docks). Some small ships anchor here and bring passengers ashore by tender.

La Soufrière, a fishing port and St. Lucia's second largest settlement, is dominated by the dramatic Pitons, Petit Piton and Gros Piton, two pointed peaks that rise right from the sea to 738m and 786m (2,421 ft. and 2,578 ft.), respectively. Formed by lava and once actively volcanic, these mountains are now cloaked in green vegetation, with waves crashing around their bases. Their sheer rise from the water makes them such visible landmarks that they've become the very symbol of St. Lucia.

Near the town of Soufrière lies the famous "drive-in" volcano, **La Soufrière,** a rocky lunar landscape of bubbling mud and craters seething with fuming sulfur. You can literally drive into an old crater and walk between the sulfur springs and pools of hissing steam. The fumes are said to have medicinal properties. A local guide is usually waiting nearby; if you do hire a guide, agree—then doubly agree—on what the fee will be.

Nearby are the **Diamond Mineral Baths** (ℂ 758/452-4759), surrounded by a tropical arboretum. They were constructed in 1784 by order of Louis XVI, whose doctors told him that these waters were similar in mineral content to the waters at Aix-les-Bains. The baths were built to help French soldiers who had been fighting in the West Indies recuperate from wounds and disease. Later destroyed, they were rebuilt after World War II. The water's average temperature is 106°F (41°C). You'll also find another fine attraction here: a waterfall that changes colors (from yellow to black to green to gray) several times a day. For about US$3.75 you can bathe and benefit from the recuperative effects of the baths yourself.

SHOPPING

Many stores sell duty-free goods, and will deliver tobacco products and liquor to the cruise dock. Keep in mind, you are allowed to purchase only one bottle of liquor here (in St. Thomas, you can buy five). You'll find some good, but not remarkable, buys in bone china, jewelry, perfume, watches, liquor, and crystal. Souvenir items include designer bags and mats, local pottery, and straw hats—again, nothing remarkable. *A tip:* If your cruise is also calling in St. Thomas, let the local vendors know; it may make them more amenable to bargaining.

Built for cruise ship passengers, **Pointe Seraphine** has the best collection of shops on the island. You must present your cruise pass when making purchases here. Liquor and tobacco will be delivered to the ship.

Gablewoods Mall, on Gros Islet Highway, 3.2km (2 miles) north of Castries, has three restaurants and one of the densest concentrations of stores on St. Lucia. Since this mall is near some lovely beaches (and near the Sandals St. Lucia resort), it's possible to plan a day that combines shopping and sunbathing.

At **Caribelle Batik,** Howelton House, Old Victoria Road, The Morne (ℂ 758/452-3785), just a 5-minute taxi ride from Castries, you can watch St. Lucian artists creating intricate patterns and colors through the ancient art of batik, which involves application of removable wax before dyes are applied, so that the waxed area repels the dye. **Eudovic Art Studio,** Goodlands, Morne Fortune (© 758/452-2747), sells woodcarvings by St. Lucia native Vincent Joseph Eudovic and some of his pupils. Take a taxi from the cruise pier. Southwest of Soufrière, just past the small village of Choiseul, **Choiseul Craft Centre,** La Fargue (© 758/459-3226), is a government-funded retail outlet and training school that perpetuates the tradition of handmade Amerindian pottery and basketware. Some of the best basket weaving on the island is done here, using techniques practiced only in St. Lucia, St. Vincent, and Dominica. Look for place mats, handbags, woodcarvings (including bas-reliefs crafted from screw pine), and pottery. The craft center is open Monday to Friday 8:30am to 4:30pm.

BEACHES

If you don't take a shore excursion, you might want to spend your time on one of St. Lucia's famous beaches, all of which are open to the public, even those at hotel properties (but you must pay to use a hotel's beach equipment). Taxis can take you to any of the island's beaches, but we recommend that you stick to the calmer shores along the western coast, since the rough surf on the windward Atlantic side makes swimming potentially dangerous.

Leading beaches include **Pigeon Island,** off the northern shore, with white sand and picnic facilities; **Vigie Beach,** north of Castries Harbour, with fine sand; **Marigot Beach,** south of Castries Harbour, framed on three sides by steep emerald hills and skirted by palm trees; and **Reduit Beach,** between Choc Bay and Pigeon Point, with fine brown sand. For sheer novelty, you might want to visit the black-volcanic-sand beach at **Soufrière.**

Just north of Soufrière is a beach connoisseur's delight, **Anse Chastanet** (© 758/459-7000), boasting an expanse of white sand at the foothills of lush, green mountains. This is a fantastic spot for snorkeling.

SPORTS

SCUBA DIVING In Soufrière, **Scuba St. Lucia** (© 758/459-7755; www.scubastlucia.com) in the **Anse Chastanet Hotel** (© 758/459-7000), is a five-star PADI dive center offering great diving and comprehensive facilities. The hotel is at the southern end of Anse Chastanet's .4km (¼-mile) secluded beach. Some of St. Lucia's most spectacular coral reefs—many only 3m to 6m (10 ft.–20 ft.) below the surface—provide shelter for sea creatures just a short distance offshore.

WATERSPORTS **St. Lucian Watersports,** on Reduit Beach at the Rex St. Lucian Hotel (© 758/452-8351), is the best place to rent watersports equipment and arrange water-skiing.

GREAT LOCAL RESTAURANTS & BARS

A really, really great **local beer** is Piton—very refreshing on a hot day, like Corona but better. A favorite **local rum** is Bounty.

IN CASTRIES At the **Green Parrot,** Red Tape Lane, Morne Fortune, about 2.4km (1½ miles) east of the town center (© 758/452-3399), there's an emphasis on St. Lucian specialties and homegrown produce (the restaurant has trained cruise ship chefs in the use of local products). Try the *christophine au gratin* (a Caribbean squash with cheese) or the Creole soup made with callaloo (a leafy green) and pumpkin. Lunch is about $10. **Jimmie's,** Vigie Cove Marina (© 758/452-5142), is known for its fresh-fish menu and tasty Creole cookery.

AT MARIGOT BAY **Doolittle's,** at the Marigot Beach Club (© 758/451-4974; www.marigotdiveresort.com/dining.htm), showcases Caribbean and international dishes. To reach the place, you'll have to take a ferryboat across Marigot Bay. The ferry runs to and from the Moorings Marigot Bay Resort about every 10 minutes throughout the day and evening. Lunch is about $20.

IN THE SOUFRIERE AREA **Chez Camilla Guest House & Restaurant,** 7 Bridge St., 1 block inland from the waterfront (© 758/459-5379), is the only really good place to eat in the village of Soufrière itself. It serves sandwiches, cold salads, omelets, and burgers at lunch. Lunch is about $6. **Dasheene Restaurant & Bar,** in the Ladera Resort, between Gros and Petit Piton (© 758/459-7323), serves the most refined and certainly the most creative cuisine in St. Lucia. The chef is particularly adept in the creation of seafood pasta and marinated sirloin steak. Your best bet is the catch of the day, likely to be kingfish or red snapper, grilled to perfection. Other standouts are the dumpling-and-callaloo soup, the fresh pumpkin risotto with red-pepper coulis, and the banana-stuffed pork with ginger-and-coconut sauce. The restaurant is perched atop a 300m (984-ft.) ridge and is framed by the rising twin peaks of the Pitons. Everything is locally produced, including the furniture. Lunch is about $15.

IN RODNEY BAY **The Lime,** north of Reduit Beach (© 758/452-0761), is a casual local place specializing in stuffed crab backs and Creole-seasoned fish steaks. It also serves shrimp, steaks, lamb, pork chops, and *rotis* (Caribbean burritos). Lunch will be around $9. **The Mortar & Pestle,** in the Harmony Marina Suites, Rodney Bay Lagoon (© 758/452-8711), offers indoor-outdoor dining with a view of the boats moored at the nearby marina. For something truly regional, try the Barbados souse, full of marinated pieces of lean cooked pork, or the frogs' legs from Dominica. Lunch is $13.

28 St. Martin/Sint Maarten

Who can resist a two-for-one sale? On the island of St. Martin, you get two cultures, two nationalities, and two different experiences for the price of one. Occupying the bend where the Lesser and Greater Antilles meet, about 242km (150 miles) southeast of Puerto Rico, this is the smallest territory in the world that is shared by two sovereign states: France, with 52 sq. km (20 sq. miles), and the Netherlands, with 44 sq. km (17 sq. miles). The two nations have shared the island in a spirit of neighborly cooperation and mutual friendship for more than 350 years. Although the border between the two sides is virtually imperceptible— a monument along the road marks the change in administration—each side retains elements of its own heritage. The French side, with some of the best beaches and restaurants in the Caribbean, emphasizes quiet elegance. French fashions and luxury items fill the shops, and the fragrance of croissants mixes with the spicy aromas of West Indian cooking. The Dutch side, officially known as Sint Maarten, reflects Holland's anything-goes philosophy: Development is much more widespread, flashy casinos pepper the landscape, and strip malls make the larger towns look as much like Anaheim as Amsterdam. The 100% duty-free shopping has turned both sides of the island into a bargain-hunter's paradise.

St. Martin's first inhabitants, the Stone Age hunter-gatherer Ciboneys, arrived as early as 1800 B.C. The first Dutch and French colonists arrived in the early 17th century, and exchanged some martial rumblings before deciding, in March 1648, to just get along, splitting the island roughly in two. Coffee, sugar, rum, and salt brought relative prosperity to the island, but not to the slaves brought

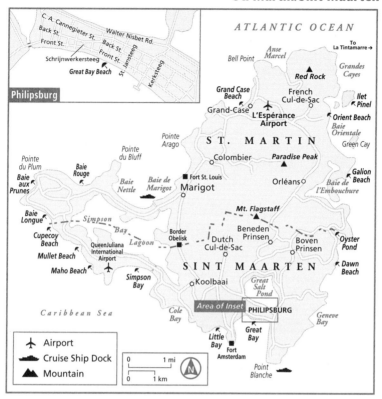

Philipsburg

C. A. Cannegieter St.
Back St.
Front St.
Walter Nisbet Rd.
Back St.
Front St.
St. Jansteeg
Kerksteeg
Schrijnwerkersteeg
Great Bay Beach

ATLANTIC OCEAN

Bell Point
Anse Marcel
To La Tintamarre →
Red Rock
Grandes Cayes
Grand Case Beach
French Cul-de-Sac
Ilet Pinel
Grand-Case
L'Espérance Airport
Orient Beach
Baie Orientale
Pointe Arago
S T.   M A R T I N
Green Cay
Pointe du Bluff
Colombier
Paradise Peak
Pointe du Plum
Baie Rouge
Baie Nettle
Baie de Marigot
Fort St. Louis
Galion Beach
Baie aux Prunes
Marigot
Orléans
Baie de l'Embouchure
Baie Longue
Simpson
Mt. Flagstaff
Cupecoy Beach
Bay
Border Obelisk
Beneden Prinsen
Boven Prinsen
Oyster Pond
Mullet Beach
QueenJuliana International Airport
Lagoon
Dutch Cul-de-Sac
Maho Beach
S I N T   M A A R T E N
Dawn Beach
Simpson Bay
Koolbaai
Great Salt Pond
Caribbean Sea
Cole Bay
Area of Inset
PHILIPSBURG
Geneve Bay
✈ Airport
🚢 Cruise Ship Dock
▲ Mountain
Little Bay
Fort Amsterdam
Great Bay
Point Blanche
0   1 mi
0   1 km
N

over from Africa. Tourism supplanted agriculture as the major industry in the last half of the 20th century.

Today, the Dutch side holds a slight population edge: 41,000 people to the French side's 36,000. Most locals are descendants of African slaves, but residents born in France, Holland, and the U.S. occupy many of the villas and condominiums around the island.

COMING ASHORE Most cruise ships dock on the Dutch side, at **A. C. Wathey Pier,** about 1.6km (1 mile) southeast of Philipsburg. The majority of passengers are then tendered to the smaller **Captain Hodge Pier** at the center of town, but others choose to walk the distance on a newly developed boardwalk or take taxis. The Wathey pier has credit card phones, cafes and bars, and a shopping area. For its part, Hodge Pier offers access to phones, tourist information, and taxis.

Smaller vessels sometimes dock on the French side of the island, at **Marina Port la Royale,** adjacent to the heart of Marigot. The waterfront here features restaurants, shopping arcades, and a tourist office. The pier accommodates only one ship at a time, so passengers on subsequently arriving vessels are tendered ashore.

LANGUAGE Surprise, surprise: The official language on the Dutch side is **Dutch,** and the official language on the French side is **French.** Most people on both sides also speak **English.** Among locals on the street, patois is often spoken: **Papiamento** on the Dutch side, **Creole** on the French.

CURRENCY   The legal tender in Dutch Sint Maarten is the Netherlands Antilles guilder, or NAf (NAf1.9 = US$1; NAf1 = US55¢), and the official currency on the French side is the euro (exchange rate at press time: 1€ = US$1.22; $1 = .82€). Each euro is divisible by 100 cents. U.S. dollars are widely accepted on both sides, though, so there's no need to change money. Most prices are quoted in U.S. dollars, too, so you're spared the work of calculating exchange rates. Credit cards and travelers checks are readily accepted, as well. Prices in this chapter are given in U.S. dollars. ATMs abound in both Philipsburg and Marigot.

INFORMATION   On the Dutch side, the Tourist Information Bureau headquarters, in the Vineyard Office Park at 23 W. G. Buncamper Rd. in Philipsburg (© **599/542-2337**), is open Monday to Friday from 8am to 5pm. There's a smaller but more conveniently located satellite office at the town pier. For information before you go, call the tourist board office in the U.S. (© **800/786-2278;** www.st-maarten.com).

The **Tourist Information office on the French side** is adjacent to the pier at Marina Royale in Marigot (© **590/87-57-21**). It's open Monday to Friday from 8:30am to 1pm and 2:30 to 5:30pm. For info before you go, contact the French St. Martin Tourism Board in the U.S. (© **212/475-8970;** www.st-martin.org).

CALLING FROM THE U.S.   When calling **Dutch** Sint Maarten from the United States, simply dial the international access number (011) before the numbers listed here. Calling **French** Saint Martin requires more of an effort: Dial 011, then 590 before the numbers listed. Yes, 590 appears in our listed numbers, but those three digits must be dialed twice to make a connection.

GETTING AROUND

BY TAXI   Taxis on both sides of the island are unmetered. Agree on a rate and currency before getting in. Dutch law requires that drivers list government-regulated fares, which assume two passengers (each additional passenger is another $4). Shorter rides, including the route between Marigot and Philipsburg, average around $12; longer trips can climb to $20-plus. Drivers, who greet cruisers in both Philipsburg and Marigot, expect at least a $1 tip for short runs, more for extended 2-hour sightseeing trips around the island. To call a taxi on the **Dutch** side, dial © **599/545-4317.** On the **French** side, dial © **590/87-56-54.**

BY MINIVAN   Privately owned and operated minivans are a reasonable way to get around, if you don't mind frequent stops, potential overcrowding, and the local *zouk* and soca music that's usually playing (a plus or a minus, depending on your tastes). These jitneys run daily from 7am to midnight and serve much of the island. The most popular run, between Philipsburg and Marigot, has almost constant service. Fares range from about $1 to $2. The vans, which have signs to indicate their destination, can be hailed anywhere on the street.

BY RENTAL CAR   Rental cars are a great way to make the most of your day and see both sides of the island. Driving is on the right side, roads are generally in decent shape, and signage is in either international symbols or English. Parking can be a headache in both Philipsburg and Marigot, and road construction and drawbridges sometimes exacerbate congestion. Away from the two main towns, however, zipping along is a breeze. **Avis, Budget,** and **Hertz** all have offices here.

BEST CRUISE LINE SHORE EXCURSIONS

America's Cup Sailing Regatta ($89, 3 hr.): Get a taste of nautical exhilaration by competing in a race aboard an America's Cup–winning sailboat. This hands-on, extremely popular excursion lets you grind winches, trim sails, and duck under booms—after professionals have trained you, of course. Alternatively, sit back and watch others do all the work.

Ilet Pinel Snorkeling Tour ($37, 3½ hr.): After a scenic bus ride to the French town of Cul de Sac, along the northeast coast, hop on a tender to the small off-shore island of Ilet Pinel for some of St. Martin's best snorkeling.

Amphibious Duck Adventure ($49, 1½ hr.): A little goofy, but how can you not enjoy a drive around Phillipsburg in a 12m (39-ft.) amphibious vehicle that's got calypso music playing and passengers armed with rum punch and their own duck quackers? From Phillipsburg, the duck heads to the island's Great Salt Pond and up into the hills for a view, then drives right into Simpson Bay for a tour by water.

Hidden Forest Hike ($85, 4 hr.): You'll take a 45-minute drive to Loterie Farm, where you'll do a 2-hour hike through the tropical forest, eventually emerging at Pic Paradise, the island's highest point. Along the way, your guide will point out a secret freshwater spring and the island's famous guavaberry trees. Return to the farm for a complimentary rum or fruit punch and a typical Caribbean farmhouse lunch.

Butterfly Farm & Marigot ($39, 3½ hr.): After a scenic drive through both the French and Dutch sides of the island, walk through a surrealistic enclosed garden that features pools, waterfalls, and hundreds of exquisitely beautiful and exotic butterflies from around the world. Amusing guides identify species, describe courtship and mating rituals, and give tips on attracting butterflies to your garden at home. Afterward, absorb the Creole charm and French atmosphere of Marigot.

EXCURSIONS OFFERED BY LOCAL AGENCIES

Horseback Treks: Bayside Riding Club, Coconut Grove, next to the Butterfly Farm (© **590/87-36-64**), offers 2-hour riding expeditions ($60 per person) that conclude on an isolated beach, where horses and riders enjoy a cool post-ride romp in the water. Half-hour pony rides with a handler, for the little ones, are $25. Riders of all experience levels are welcome.

Frommer's Favorite St. Martin Experiences

Sizzling in the Sun: On the French side, colorful open-air restaurants and bars line Orient Beach, a social, very European strand humming with motorized water toys. (See "Beaches," below.)

Dejeuner Chez Madame Claude's Mini Club: Savor the rich flavors of Creole and French cuisine on the cozy, colorfully painted upstairs terrace of Marigot's oldest restaurant. (See "Great Local Restaurants & Bars," below.)

Competing for the America's Cup: Race on and against 12m (39-ft.) yachts that once competed in the famed America's Cup race. (See "Best Cruise Line Shore Excursions," above.)

Trekking up to the Ramparts of Fort St. Louis: A 10- or 15-minute walk from the heart of Marigot will take you to the top of the fort, where you're treated to panoramic views of Marigot and beyond. (See "On Your Own: Within Walking Distance," below.)

Mountain Biking Tours: Frog Legs (© 590/87-05-11), based in Marigot, offers three tours, which vary in difficulty (5%–30% climb), time (from a little under 2 hr. to more than 4 hr.), and price ($40–$45). Some stay along the coast, others move to inland hills.

Scuba Diving: Of the island's 40 dive sites, the 1801 British man-of-war HMS *Proselyte,* which sank to a watery grave on a reef 1.6km (1 mile) off the coast, is the most popular. Other favorites include Ilet Pinel, for shallow diving; the Green Key barrier reef; and Flat Island, for its sheltered coves and geologic faults. On the Dutch side, **Pelican Watersports,** Simpson Bay (© 599/544-2640), employs some the most knowledgeable guides on the island. Dives are $45 to $90. One of the French side's premier dive operators, **Marine Time,** is in Quartier d'Orléans, not far from Coconut Grove Beach (© 590/87-20-28). Single-tank dives with all equipment run about $45; two-tank dives are around $90.

ON YOUR OWN: WITHIN WALKING DISTANCE

Shopping, sunbathing, and gambling are the pastimes that interest most cruisers who hit this island, but folks with a taste for culture and history can make a day of it here as well.

ON THE DUTCH SIDE   Directly in front of the Philipsburg town pier, on Wathey Square, the **Courthouse** combines northern European sobriety with Caribbean brightness. Originally built in 1793 of freestone and wood, this venerable old building has suffered numerous hurricanes, but has been restored after each tempest and continues to house government offices. East of the Courthouse, at 7 Front St. (down a little shopping alley), the tiny **Sint Maarten Museum** (© 599/542-4917) features modest, cluttered exhibits that focus on the island's history and geology. The second-floor gallery is open every day but Sunday. There's no admission fee, but donations are appreciated. The museum is open Monday through Friday 10am to 4pm, and Saturday 10am to 2pm. The street-level gift shop stocks handicrafts, postcards, and books.

Historically, **Fort Amsterdam** is the Dutch side's most important colonial site. Since 1631, the fort has looked out over Great Bay from the hill west of Philipsburg. The fort was the Netherlands' first military outpost in the Caribbean. The Spanish captured it 2 years later, making it their most significant bastion east of Puerto Rico. Peter Stuyvesant, who later became governor of New Amsterdam (now New York), lost his leg to a cannonball while trying to reclaim the fort for Holland. The site provides grand views of the bay, but ruins of the walls and a couple of rusty cannons are all that remain of the original fort.

ON THE FRENCH SIDE   **Fort St. Louis** is Marigot's answer to Fort Amsterdam. Built in 1767 to protect the waterfront warehouses that stored the French colony's agricultural riches, the cannons of this bastion frequently fired on hostile British raiders from Anguilla. After restorations and modification in the 19th century, the fort was eventually abandoned. You'll find cannons, crumbling walls, and a French *tricouleur* (tricolor) flag flapping in the breeze. The short climb up the hill flanking Marigot Bay's north end affords splendid vistas. As a respite from the sun, duck into **Marigot's Museum of Saint Martin** (© 590/29-22-84), next to the Tourism Office and adjacent to the marina. Much more thorough and scholarly than its Philipsburg counterpart, this institution boasts a first-rate collection of Ciboney, Arawak, and Carib artifacts excavated from the island's Amerindian sites, plus a reproduction of a 1,500-year-old burial mound. Another display details the history of the plantation and slavery era, and early-20th-century photographs trace the island's modern development. It's open Monday through Friday 9am to 4pm, Saturday 9am to 1pm. Admission is $5 for adults, $2 for children.

GAMBLING

Slot machines and game tables can be found in the Dutch side's dozen casinos. Most of the heavy betting takes place after dark, but a handful of casinos open before noon. In the heart of Philipsburg on Front Street, **Coliseum Casino** (© 599/543-2101), **Diamond Casino** (© 599/543-2565), **Paradise Plaza Slots World** (© 599/54-4721), and **Rouge et Noir** (© 599/542-2952) all open at 11am, early enough to snag cruisers. West of Philipsburg, **Hollywood Casino,** at the Pelican Resort on Simpson Bay (© 599/544-2503), features a panoramic view of the water and offers craps, roulette, blackjack, stud poker, and slots after 1pm. Farther west, at Maho Bay, **Casino Royale** (© 599/545-2590) has roulette, Caribbean stud poker, craps, blackjack, baccarat, minibaccarat, and slots, also after 1pm.

SHOPPING

St. Martin is a true free port—no duties are paid on any item coming in or going out—and neither side of the island has a sales tax.

ON THE DUTCH SIDE   Shops in the much busier Dutch side are concentrated in **Philipsburg,** along Front Street and the numerous alleys radiating from it. The district is largely nondescript, but you'll find all the usual suspects—the omnipresent jewelry and luxury-item shop **Little Switzerland** and a host of other jewelry/gift/luxury-item shops—as well as some quirky local boutiques. In general, prices in the major stores are nonnegotiable, but at small, family-run shops, you can try your luck with a little polite bargaining. The T-shirt and souvenir epicenter is in the open-air market behind the Courthouse in front of the town pier.

    Guavaberry Emporium, 8–10 Front St., sells Guavaberry "island folk liqueur," an aged rum with a distinctive fruity, woody, almost bittersweet flavor; it's available only on St. Martin. Parrot heads in search of all things Jimmy Buffett should cross the street to **Last Mango in Paradise,** 17 Front St., for CDs, T-shirts, and more—you name it, they got it. Walking west, **Old Street,** off Front Street, features a couple dozen boutiques, including **Colombian Emeralds** and **The Belgian Chocolate Shop.** For cigars, **La Casa del Habano,** 24 Front St., has Cohibas, Montecristos, and the like; while **Lipstick,** 31 Front St., is your best bet for perfumes and cosmetics. Next door, **Dutch Delft Blue,** 29 Front St., stocks the distinctive blue-and-white porcelain.

ON THE FRENCH SIDE   Marigot features a much calmer, more charming, and sophisticated ambience, with waterfront cafes where you can rest your weary overshopped feet. Many shops here close their doors for a 2-hour lunch break starting at noon.

    The wide selection of European merchandise is skewed toward an upscale audience, but French crystal, perfume, liqueur, jewelry, and fashion can be up to 50% less expensive than in the States. At Marina Port la Royale, **Havane** offers casual and high-fashion French clothing for men; while **L'Epicerie** stocks caviar, foie gras, and a host of French wines. For chic women's clothing, especially Italian styles, start your search at **La Romana,** 12 rue de la République. **Oro de Sol Jewelers,** rue de la République, is one of many purveyors of bracelets, necklaces, and watches; while **Beauty & Scents,** rue du Général de Gaulle, has your favorite perfumes and cosmetics.

An inviting open-air craft market sprawls along the waterfront next to Boulevard de France every day, while on Wednesdays and Saturdays, another open-air market stretches from the base of Fort St. Louis to the wharves below, offering a colorful array of homegrown produce, tropical fruits and spices, and fresh fish. **Gingerbread & Mahogany Gallery,** Marina Port la Royale (in a narrow alleyway at the marina), deals in Haitian art by both old masters and talented amateurs.

BEACHES
Beach lovers rejoice: St. Martin has more than 30 beautiful white-sand beaches, some social, some serene. The busier ones boast bars, restaurants, watersports, and hotels, where changing facilities are usually available for a small fee. Toplessness is ubiquitous, and nudism is common on the French side, and increasingly found on the Dutch side as well.

ON THE DUTCH SIDE   **Great Bay Beach** is your best bet if you want to stay in Philipsburg. This 1.6km-long (1-mile) stretch is convenient, but because it borders the busy capital, it lacks the tranquility and cleanliness of the more remote beaches. The water is calm, though, and all the amenities of Philipsburg are a step away.

Just west of the airport, on the west side of the island, **Maho Beach** boasts a casino, shade palms, and a popular beachside bar and grill. It's biggest attraction, however, seems to be its views of takeoffs and landings (keep your belongings outside the flight path; jumbo jets sometimes blow items into the surf). Farther west, **Mullet Beach** borders the island's golf course. Shaded by palm trees and crowded on weekends, it's popular with swimmers and snorkelers. On-site vendors rent an array of watersports equipment. Just around the corner to the west (just below the Dutch-French border), but miles away mentally, lies perfectly serene **Cupecoy Beach.** Set against a stunningly beautiful backdrop of mysterious caves and sandstone cliffs that provide morning shade, this beach has no facilities, but a vendor at the parking lot rents beach chairs and shade umbrellas. The clientele is adult, primarily in the buff, quiet, and, not infrequently, gay. The surf can be strong, and aficionados claim that the sun here is more intense than anywhere else on the island.

ON THE FRENCH SIDE   Far and away the island's most visited strand, **Orient Beach,** on the northeast coast, fancies itself "the Saint Tropez of the Caribbean." Hedonism is the name of the game here: plenty of food, drink, music, and flesh (a naturist resort occupies the beach's southern tip, but nudism isn't confined to any one area). Watersports abound. South of Orient Beach, the waveless waters of **Coconut Grove** or **Galion Beach** are shallow 30m (98 ft.) out. Protected by a coral reef, this area is number one with kids and popular with windsurfers.

On the island's west coast, just north of the Dutch border, **Long Bay** is the island's longest beach and another refuge for adults seeking peace and quiet. There are no facilities here, but this wild beach bordering some of the island's grandest mansions is popular with the rich and (sometimes) famous. The water and sand here are silky.

SPORTS
GOLF   The **Mullet Bay Golf Course** (© 599/545-2850), on the Dutch side, has an 18-hole course designed by Joseph Lee that's considered one of the more challenging in the Caribbean, especially the back nine. Mullet Pond and Simpson Bay lagoon provide both beauty and hazards. Greens fees and cart rental for

18 holes is $88 with shared cart and $98 when using a cart alone; for nine holes it's $55 and $65; club rental is an additional $26 for 18 holes and $21 for nine. The course opens at 7am, 7 days a week.

SNORKELING   Tiny coves and calm offshore waters make St. Martin a snorkeler's paradise. **Dawn Beach,** on the Dutch east coast, is the best snorkeling site on the island (rent equipment from **Busby's Beach Bar,** which is right on the beach), followed by **Maho** (Dutch side) and the French side's **Baie Rouge** and **Ilet Pinel,** the latter of which can be reached by ferry from Cul de Sac (about $5 per person, round-trip). Most hotels and restaurants at these sites rent equipment for about $10.

WATERSPORTS   Most of the large hotels on Orient Beach offer an array of watersports adventures, often from makeshift kiosks on the beach. Two independent operators function from side-by-side positions near the Esmeralda Hotel: **Kon Tiki Watersports** (© 590/87-46-89) and **Bikini Watersports** (© 590/87-43-25). From these operators, jet skis and WaveRunners go for about $40 for 30 minutes, $70 for an hour; and parasailing $50 to $80.

GREAT LOCAL RESTAURANTS & BARS

A favorite **local beer** (on both the Dutch and French sides) is Red White and Blue, while the indigenous **rum liqueur** is the fruity and slightly bitter Guavaberry.

ON THE DUTCH SIDE   As might be expected, food is usually better on the French side, but Dutch St. Maarten has a number of appealing restaurants, too. In Philipsburg, **Da Livio Ristorante,** 159 Front St. (© 599/542-2690), serves delicious seafood, veal, and pasta, including the house specialty, homemade manicotti. Dine alfresco with views of Great Bay, and check out the photos of celebrities who've sated their hunger here. Lunch is about $29. Next to the historic courthouse, just off Front Street at 6 Hendrikstraat, **Kangaroo Court** (© 599/542-7557) is Philipsburg's coziest coffeehouse. Stop in for a quick latte and muffin or grab a table in back for a salad, burger, or sandwich. The rich, gooey desserts can satisfy the most insatiable sweet tooth. Lunch is around $10. Indonesian *rijstafel* is yours for the asking at **Wajang Doll,** 167 Front St. (© 599/542-2687). Order the 14-dish sampling of this Javanese, Balinese, and Sumatran cuisine, or opt for something lighter, such as red snapper with ginger, chile, and lemon grass. Lunch is about $20.

ON THE FRENCH SIDE   In Marigot, Madame Claude runs the show at **Mini Club** (© 590/87-50-69), one of the oldest restaurants in town, on the waterfront street rue des Pêcheurs. Savor the rich flavors of spicy conch stew, Creole-style fresh fish, or other West Indian and French dishes on the cozy, bright-yellow upstairs terrace. **La Brasserie de Marigot,** 11 rue du Général-de-Gaulle (© 590/87-94-43), is another great choice for good food at modest prices. Dishes include pot-au-feu, duck breast with peaches, and steak tartare. For light salads, sandwiches, and ice-cream concoctions, claim a harborside table at **La Vie en Rose,** at the corner of rue de la République and Boulevard de France (© 590/87-54-42). Lunch is $15.

29 Trinidad & Tobago

The southernmost islands in the Caribbean chain, Trinidad and tiny Tobago (which together form a single nation), manage to encompass nearly every facet of Caribbean life. Located less than 16km (10 miles) east of Venezuela's coast, Trinidad is large (the biggest and most heavily populated Caribbean island) and diverse, with an industrial, cosmopolitan capital city, Port of Spain, and an outgoing, vibrant culture that combines African, East Indian, European, Chinese, and Syrian influences. Little-sister Tobago is the more natural of the two, with rainforested mountains and spectacular secluded beaches.

Trinidad and Tobago won independence from Britain in 1962 and became a republic in 1976, but some British influences, including the residents' love of cricket, remain. Trinidad grew rich from oil, and the islands are still the Western Hemisphere's largest oil exporters.

Trinidad's music is another local treasure. The calypso, steel-pan, and soca styles that originated here have influenced musical trends worldwide. Trinidad's rhythmic, soulful music is a main feature of Carnaval, the Caribbean-wide bacchanalian celebration held each year on the Monday and Tuesday before Lent. Among all the Carnaval celebrations in the Caribbean, Trinidad's is king.

Trinidad's residents are charming, are friendly, and love to talk. With a literacy rate of 97%, the populace is full of well-informed conversationalists. You'll find Trinis (as residents call themselves) happy to socialize with visitors and discuss just about anything.

LANGUAGE   The official language is **English,** but like many of their Caribbean neighbors, Trinis speak English with a distinct patois. Hindi, Creole, and Spanish are also spoken among various ethnic groups.

CURRENCY   The unit of currency is the Trinidad & Tobago dollar, sometimes designated by the same symbol as the U.S. dollar ($) and sometimes just by "TT." The exchange rate is US$1 = TT$6.22; TT$1 = US16¢. Vacationers can pay in U.S. dollars, but be sure you know what currency prices are being quoted in, and try to get change in U.S. dollars. Unless otherwise specified, prices in this section are given in U.S. dollars. Local ATMs mainly dispense TT notes.

CALLING FROM THE U.S.   When calling Trinidad and Tobago from the United States, you just need to dial "1" before the numbers listed here.

TRINIDAD

Trinidad is one of the most industrialized countries in the Caribbean, and it shows—if you're looking for a sleepy, quiet Caribbean retreat, go to Tobago instead. Trinidad's capital and commercial center, **Port of Spain,** is an energetic, bustling metropolis of 300,000. There are few distinct attractions—Port of Spain isn't necessarily a tourist city—but the central shopping area at the south end of Frederick Street is a colorfully crowded mix of outdoor shopping arcades and air-conditioned mini-malls.

Independence Square, in the heart of Port of Spain, is the place to get a taxi, find a bank, and get good, cheap food. There are mosques, shrines, and temples here, and locals gather at Woodford Square to hear public speakers or attend outdoor meetings.

While Port of Spain is interesting and not threatening by day, it's unsafe at night, and strolling around is not recommended if your ship happens to be in port late.

COMING ASHORE   Cruise ships visiting Trinidad dock at **Port of Spain**'s 1.6-hectare (4-acre) cruise terminal, built in the early 1990s to accommodate the island's growing cruise traffic. The complex includes a shopping mall and car-rental agencies, and is easy walking distance to the center of town. Steel-pan musicians and colorfully dressed dancers usually greet arriving passengers. Outside the terminal, there's a craft market with T-shirts, straw items, and other souvenirs.

Trinidad

INFORMATION The **Tourism and Industrial Development Corporation of Trinidad and Tobago (TIDCO)** is located at 10–14 Phillips St., at the terminal in Port of Spain (© **868/623-6022**). It's open Monday to Friday from 8am to 4:30pm. For info before you go, contact the tourism board office in the U.S. (© **212/682-7272;** www.visittnt.com).

GETTING AROUND

BY TAXI Taxis are available at the cruise terminal. The registered taxi association at the Port-of-Spain is the **Trinidad and Tobago Tourist Transport Association.** These drivers are trained tour guides who are identified by dark pants and shirts with printed taxi association monograms. Another identifier is that these drivers' car license plates begin with the letter "H" (for "hiring car"). The Port Authority posts cab fares on a board by the main entrance (the cars don't have meters). Always establish a fare before loading into the taxi and shoving off. Private cabs can be relatively expensive.

BY VAN **Maxitaxis** (minivans operating regular routes within specific zones) have a yellow stripe and are lower priced than taxis. There are also route taxis, which are shared cabs that travel along a prescribed route and charge about US$1–US$1.50) to drop you at any spot along the route.

BY RENTAL CAR Driving is on the left. Trinidad has a fairly wide network of roads, and roads in town are generally well marked, but traffic is frequently heavy. None of the major rental companies have offices here.

Frommer's Favorite Trinidad Experiences

Visiting the Asa Wright Nature Center: This 80-hectare (198-acre) preserve, located in Trinidad's rainforest in the northern hills, features intertwined hiking trails, a bird sanctuary, and a conservation center. (See "Best Cruise Line Shore Excursions," below.)

Touring the Caroni Bird Sanctuary: This ecological wonder features dense mangroves, remote canals, and shallow lagoons that are the breeding grounds for spectacular scarlet ibis. Visitors tour the sanctuary in guided boats. (See "Best Cruise Line Shore Excursions," below.)

Trying a Drink with Angostura Bitters: This local specialty contains citrus-tree bark and is made from a secret recipe.

BEST CRUISE LINE SHORE EXCURSIONS

Caroni Bird Sanctuary (US$54, 3 hr.): This sanctuary is a pristine network of lush mangroves, quiet canals, and shallow lagoons, and is considered a world-class bird-watching preserve. Following a 30-minute drive from the cruise pier, passengers embark for the tour in flat-bottomed boats, which glide through calm canals and lagoons. Guides will point out unique flora and fauna during the ride. Heron, osprey, and scarlet ibis are among the bird species native to this area.

Sportfishing (US$150, 5 hr.): Head off to Trinidad's northern coast for a day of fishing for wahoo, tuna, marlin, sailfish, tarpon, and mahimahi. Tour includes all tackle and other equipment, as well as a snack lunch and open beer bar.

Asa Wright Nature Center (US$72, 6 hr.): Set within 80 hectares (198 acres) about 360m (1,200 ft.) up into Trinidad's rainforested mountains, the Asa Wright center is known to bird-watchers throughout the world. You can see hummingbirds, toucans, bellbirds, manakins, several varieties of tanagers, and the rare oilbird. Hiking trails line the grounds. A Creole-style buffet lunch is served at the center's Old Plantation House.

ON YOUR OWN: WITHIN WALKING DISTANCE

Among Port of Spain's chief centers of activity, **Independence Square,** a stone's throw from the cruise complex, isn't really a square at all but parallel streets running east and west and connected at one end by a pedestrian mall. The scene here resembles a Middle Eastern bazaar, with a dense thicket of pushcarts, honking cabs, produce hawkers, and inquisitive shoppers moving to the irresistible beat of soca, reggae, and calypso music blaring from nearby stores and sidewalk stands. Some parts of the square have become run-down, and some locals consider the area less than safe. Visitors should keep an eye out for pickpockets and petty thieves.

   Woodford Square, laid out by Ralph Woodford, Trinidad's early-19th-century British governor, is among the most attractive areas in town, full of large, leafy trees surrounding a rich lawn with landscaped walkways. This area has traditionally served as a center for political debates, discussions, and rallies. The **Cathedral of the Holy Trinity,** built in 1818 by Woodford, lies on the square's south side. The church's carved roof is designed as a replica of Westminster Hall in London. Inside the church is a memorial statue of Woodford himself. To reach the square, take Independence Square North and then go left on Abercromby Street, or Wrightson Road to Sackville Street.

On the square's western border is **Red House,** an imposing (and, yes, red) Renaissance-style edifice built in 1906. Today, it houses Trinidad's parliament. The building was badly damaged in 1990 when militants took the prime minister and parliament members hostage. A little farther north of the city center is **Queen's Park Savannah,** originally part of a 80-hectare (198-acre) sugar plantation, and now a public park with 32 hectares (79 acres) of open land and walkways, with great shade trees. A depression at the park's northwest section, known as the Hollows, has flower beds, rock gardens, and small ponds. The area has become a popular picnic spot. Most streets heading north from the cruise complex end at the park.

There are a number of notable sights along the park's outer, western edge, including the **Magnificent Seven,** a row of seven colonial buildings constructed in the late 19th and early 20th centuries. The buildings include Queen's Royal College, White Hall (the prime minister's office), and Stollmeyer's Castle, which was designed to resemble a Scottish castle—complete with turrets.

Beyond the northern edge of Queen's Park Savannah lies the **Emperor Valley Zoo** (© **868/622-3530**), featuring local animals including tropical toucans and macaws, porcupines, monkeys, and various snakes. The zoo emphasizes colorful tropical plants, which are in evidence all over the grounds. It's open 9:30am to 6pm daily; admission is US$4 adults, US$2 for children.

The 28-hectare (69-acre) botanical gardens are east of the zoo. Laid out in 1820, the gardens are landscaped with attractive walkways and great flowering trees, among them the wild poinsettia, whose bright red blossom is the national flower. **The President's House,** built in 1875 as the governor's residence, is adjacent to the gardens.

All out-of-town attractions are covered in "Shore Excursions," above.

SHOPPING

Shopping in the Port of Spain area means crafts, fabrics, and fashions made by local artists, a range of spices, and colorful artwork. Most of the shopping opportunities lie in the area around Independence Square, particularly near Frederick and Queen streets. Art lovers will find a handful of galleries and studios featuring the work of local and regional artists. **Art Creators,** at Seventh Street and St. Ann's Road in the Aldegonda Park section (© **868/624-4369**), is a serious gallery offering year-around exhibits of both newly emerging and established artists. **Aquarela Galleries,** at 1A Dere St., exhibits the work of recognized and up-and-coming Trini artists and also publishes high-end art books. If you're in the mood for distinctive gift and apparel shopping, hire a cab to the Hotel Normandie, 10 Nook Ave. in the St. Ann's section (© **868/624-1181**), where the **Village Market** shops feature clothing and jewelry by some of the country's top designers.

For craft creations outside of the cruise terminal area, try the **Trinidad and Tobago Blind Welfare Association,** at 118 Duke St., with accessories and gifts of rattan and other natural materials, all made by blind craftsmen. **Art Potters Ltd.,** located at the cruise terminal, is a pottery specialist.

Music is another of Trinidad's signature products, and the latest soca and reggae can be purchased at **Rhyner's Record Shop** at 54 Prince St., Port of Spain (© **868/625-2476**). There's also **Crosby Records** (© **868/622-7622**), located in the St. James area.

BEACHES

Unlike its tiny sister Tobago, Trinidad was not blessed with many beautiful beaches. The most popular of the beaches is **Maracas Bay,** a scenic, 40-minute drive from Port of Spain. The drive takes vacationers over mountains and through a lush rainforest. As you near the beach, the coastal road descends from a cliffside. The beach itself is wide and sandy, with a small fishing village on one side and the richly dense mountains in the background. There are lifeguards, changing rooms and showers, and areas for picnics. There are also many stands selling "shark and bake" sandwiches (a local favorite made with fresh slabs of shark and fried bread).

SPORTS

GOLF[em[The oldest and best-known golf course on the island is the 18-hole, par-72 **St. Andrews Golf Club** in the suburb of Maraval (✆ **868/629-2314**). Also known as Moka Golf Course, it was established in the late 19th century. Greens fees are US$64.

GREAT LOCAL RESTAURANTS & BARS

A favorite **local beer** is Stag; a favorite **local rum** is Vat 19 Old Oak.

Trinidad is home to some of the most diverse culinary styles in the Caribbean, a result of its African, Chinese, English, French, Indian, Portuguese, Spanish, and Syrian influences. **Rafters,** at 6A Warner St. (✆ **868/628-9258**), is an old rum house with brick walls and hand-finished ceilings, which offers sandwiches, chili, and chicken in its bar. There's also an elegant dining room for more formal meals. Lunch is about US$9. **Plantation House,** at 38 Ariapita Ave. (✆ **868/628-5551**), is a quality restaurant housed in a charming colonial house. Lunch is around US$14. **Solimar,** at 6 Nook Ave. near the **Normandie Hotel** (✆ **868/624-6267**), features a changing menu of international dishes engineered by owner Joe Brown, a peripatetic Englishman who was once a chef for the Hilton hotel chain. Lunch is about US$30.

Cricket Wicket, 149 Tragarete Rd., is a pub with various bands performing on weekends.

TOBAGO

Tobago is the antithesis of its larger cousin, as peaceful, calm, and easygoing as Trinidad is loud, crowded, and frenetic. The island is filled with magical white-sand beaches, languid palm trees, and clear blue waters, and you'll find lots of spots for diving and snorkeling. There are also magnificent rainforests and hundreds of tiny streams and waterways carved into a steep crest of mountains that rise 600m (1,968 ft.) and snake down the island's center. The bird life and nature trails here are impressive.

COMING ASHORE   Most cruise passengers arrive at a small but orderly cruise terminal in central **Scarborough,** the island's main town. There's usually a fleet of taxis ready to go just outside of the cruise terminal, and detailed cab rates are posted inside the terminal at the main entrance. Larger ships must anchor offshore and transfer passengers to the terminal via tenders.

There are a number of phones inside the terminal, although last time we were here they weren't taking our AT&T phone card and we had to buy a local phone card.

INFORMATION   There is a small information booth at the terminal in **Scarborough,** open from 9am to 3pm Monday through Friday. For info before you

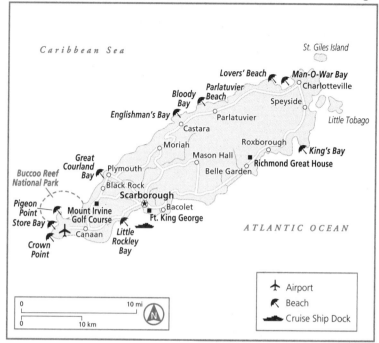

Caribbean Sea

St. Giles Island

Lovers' Beach
Man-O-War Bay
Parlatuvier Beach
Charlotteville
Bloody Bay
Englishman's Bay
Speyside
Parlatuvier
Little Tobago
Castara
Moriah
Roxborough
Mason Hall
King's Bay
Great Courland Bay
Plymouth
Richmond Great House
Belle Garden
Buccoo Reef National Park
Black Rock
Scarborough
Pigeon Point
Bacolet
Store Bay
Mount Irvine Golf Course
Ft. King George
ATLANTIC OCEAN
Canaan
Crown Point
Little Rockley Bay

✈ Airport
🗡 Beach
⛴ Cruise Ship Dock

0   10 mi
0   10 km

go, contact the tourism board office in the U.S. (℗ **212/682-7272;** www.visit tnt.com).

GETTING AROUND

BY TAXI   Taxi is the preferred mode of transportation for visitors here; the island is small enough that any location worth visiting can be reached this way. Distances can be deceiving, though, because some of the roads are in very bad shape and others wind along the coast and twist through the mountains. There is no road that completely circles the island. Like Trinidad, visitors should use registered drivers who are part of the **Trinidad and Tobago Tourist Transport Association** network. See the Trinidad taxi section for more information.

BY RENTAL CAR   There's really no need for a cruise passenger to rent a car on Tobago.

BEST CRUISE LINE SHORE EXCURSIONS

Pigeon Point Beach Trip (US$49, 5½ hr., including lunch): By taxi, you'll head toward Tobago's most popular beach, where you'll find a restaurant, a bar, restrooms, and small cabanas lining the beach. You have your pick of watersports, including snorkeling and banana-boat rides (for a fee, of course).

Argyle Waterfalls (US$57, 4 hr.): Drive along Tobago's windward coast to Roxborough, then hike 20 minutes though a forest preserve to the three-tiered waterfall for a swim.

Bucco Reef Snorkeling (US$45, 3 hr.): From Pigeon Point, board a glass-bottom boat for the ride out to Bucco Reef for your snorkeling dip. From there, you'll head off to the Nylon Pool, a sand bank named for its crystal-clear water.

ON YOUR OWN: WITHIN WALKING DISTANCE

The well-restored, British-built **Fort King George,** dating from 1777, overlooks Scarborough's east side. There's no admission charge to enter the grounds. The fort offers a great view of Tobago's Atlantic coast. Other historic buildings here include **St. Andrew's church** (built in 1819) and the **Courthouse** (built in 1825). The small **Tobago Museum** (© **868/639-3970**) is located in the fort's old barracks guardhouse. **Scarborough's botanical gardens** (© **868/639-3421**) are situated between the main highway and the town center, less than .4km (¼ mile) from the cruise dock, but they are not much more than a glorified public park with a few marked trees.

Other than this, there aren't many attractions within walking distance of the cruise terminal, and even the terminal shops are small and limited.

SHOPPING

There simply isn't much here beyond the shops inside the cruise terminal and sporadic craft merchants at the popular beaches at Fort King George. It's best to put aside the shopping excursions for another port and enjoy Tobago's relaxed atmosphere and fine beaches.

BEACHES

Pigeon Point, near the southern tip of Tobago on the Caribbean side, is the best beach on an island filled with great beaches. **Store Bay,** south of Pigeon Point, has white sands and good year-round swimming (there's a lifeguard, too). Here you'll find vendors hawking local wares and glass-bottom-boat tours departing to Buccoo Reef. Despite their names, **Parlatuvier** and **Bloody Bay,** on Tobago's Caribbean (west) coast, are tranquil, secluded, and beautiful.

SPORTS

GOLF   About 8km (5 miles) from Pigeon Point, the championship 18-hole, par-72 **Mount Irvine Golf Course,** at the Mount Irvine Hotel (© **868/639-8871**), is among the most scenic courses in the Caribbean, overlooking the sea from gently rolling hills. The clubhouse sits on a promontory and offers great views. Greens fees are US$55, club rentals US$15, and cart rentals US$42.

SCUBA DIVING   Tobago is virtually surrounded by shallow-water reefs filled with colorful marine life, easily visible through the clear water. All kinds of diving experiences, from beginner-level dives at Buccoo Reef to drift diving for

---

Frommer's Favorite Tobago Experiences

Visiting Pigeon Point Beach: One of the most beautiful and distinctive spots in the Caribbean, Pigeon Point is an oasis of white sand, aqua water, and tall palm trees. (See "Best Cruise Line Shore Excursions," above.)

Snorkeling at Buccoo Reef: The spot is a must-visit for its exotic fish and impressive underwater coral, which can also be observed by glass-bottom boat. (See "Best Cruise Line Shore Excursions," above.)

Checking Out Nylon Pool: Named for its crystal-clear water, this small lagoon is located near Buccoo Reef and is filled with tropical fish. It's great for wading and swimming.

experienced divers at Grouper Ground, are offered. **Dive Tobago,** at Pigeon Point (© **868/639-0202**), is the island's oldest dive operation, offering resort courses and rentals, and catering to both beginners and experienced divers.

GREAT LOCAL RESTAURANTS & BARS

There are several moderately priced restaurants in Tobago, including **The Old Donkey Cart House,** on Bacolet Street in Scarborough (© **868/639-3551**), which occupies a restored colonial home that once served as Tobago's first guesthouse. Today it's a bistro serving French wines, light snacks, salads, and specialties such as armadillo and opossum (called *manicou*). Lunch is about US$8.

The beach at Store Bay is lined with a row of cheap-food stands offering *rotis* (chicken or beef wrapped in Indian turnovers and flavored with curry), shark and bake, crab with dumplings, and fish lunches. **Chrystal's** (© **868/639-7648**), on the corner of Store Bay and Milford Road, is a local favorite for flying fish, shark and bake, and fruit juices. Lunch is US$5.

30 U.S. Virgin Islands: St. Thomas, St. John & St. Croix

Ever since Columbus discovered the Virgin Islands during his second voyage to the New World in 1493, they have proven irresistible to foreign powers seeking territory, at one time or another being governed by Denmark, Spain, France, England, Holland, and, since 1917, by the United States. Vacationers discovered **St. Thomas,** the largest of the islands, right after World War II and have been flocking here in increasing numbers ever since to enjoy its fine dining, elegant resorts, and, in recent years, its shopping. Tourism and U.S. government programs have raised the standard of living to one of the highest in the Caribbean, and today the island is one of the busiest and most developed cruise ports in the Caribbean, often hosting more than six ships a day during the peak winter season. **Charlotte Amalie** (pronounced Ah-*mahl*-yah), named in 1691 in honor of the wife of Denmark's King Christian V, is the island's capital and has become the Caribbean's major shopping center.

St. Croix, the largest of the USVIs, gets nowhere near as many visitors as St. Thomas, making for a more tranquil port experience. The island's major attraction is Buck Island Reef National Monument, an offshore park full of gorgeous coral reefs.

By far the most tranquil and unspoiled of the islands, however, is **St. John,** the smallest of the lot, more than half of which is preserved as the gorgeous Virgin Islands National Park. A rocky coastline, forming crescent-shaped bays and white-sand beaches, rings the whole island, whose miles of serpentine hiking trails lead past the ruins of 18th-century Danish plantations and let onto panoramic ocean views.

By far, the largest number of cruise ships dock in St. Thomas's Charlotte Amalie, but a few anchor directly off St. John or tie up at the Anne Abramson Pier in Fredericksburg, St. Croix. Those that dock in St. Thomas usually offer excursions to St. John, but if yours doesn't, it's quite easy to get there on your own via water taxi or shuttle.

LANGUAGE   **English** is spoken on all three islands.

CURRENCY   The U.S. dollar is the local currency.

INFORMATION   For information before you go, contact the **U.S. Virgin Islands Department of Tourism** (© **800/372-USVI;** www.usvitourism.vi).

Frommer's Favorite St. Thomas Experiences

Biking Around the Island: You'll get great views and a great workout, too. Biking on Water Island is a great experience, too. (See "Best Cruise Line Shore Excursions," below.)

Kayaking Among the Island's Mangroves: You'll learn about the local lagoon ecosystem and get some exercise to boot. (See "Best Cruise Line Shore Excursions," below.)

Visiting the Colorful Village of Frenchtown: Have lunch in a village settled by French-speaking citizenry who were uprooted after the Swedes invaded the island of St. Barts. (See "On Your Own: Beyond the Port Area," below.)

Taking a Nature Walk: The lush St. Peter Greathouse Estate and Gardens has 200 varieties of plants and trees, plus a rainforest, an orchid jungle, and more. (See "On Your Own: Beyond the Port Area," below.)

CALLING FROM THE U.S.   When calling the Virgin Islands from the 50 states, you just need to dial a "1" before the numbers listed in this section.

ST. THOMAS

With a population of about 50,000 and a large number of American expatriates and temporary sun-seekers in residence, tiny St. Thomas isn't exactly a tranquil tropical retreat. You won't have any beaches to yourself. Shops, bars, and restaurants (including a lot of fast-food joints) abound here, and most of the locals make their living off the tourist trade. Most native Virgin Islanders are the descendants of slaves brought from Africa. In fact, Charlotte Amalie was one of the major slave-trading centers in the Caribbean.

COMING ASHORE   Most cruise ships anchor at **Havensight Mall,** at the eastern end of Charlotte Amalie Harbor, 1½ miles from the town center. The mall has a tourist information office, restaurants, a bookstore, a bank, a U.S. postal van, phones that accept long-distance credit cards, and a generous number of duty-free shops. Many people make the long, hot walk to the center of Charlotte Amalie, but it's not a scenic route in any way—you may want to opt for one of the open-air taxis for about $3 per person.

If Havensight Mall is clogged with cruise ships, your ship will dock at the **Crown Bay Marina,** to the west of Charlotte Amalie. A taxi is your best bet—the 30-minute walk into Charlotte Amalie feels longer on a hot day, and isn't terribly picturesque. A taxi ride into town from here costs about $4.

INFORMATION   The **U.S. Virgin Islands Department of Tourism** has offices at Tolbod Gade in Charlotte Amalie (© **340/774-8784**), open Monday to Friday from 8am to 5pm and Saturday from 9am to 1pm. Stop by and pick up *St. Thomas This Week,* which includes maps of St. Thomas and St. John. There's also an office at the Havensight Mall.

GETTING AROUND

BY TAXI   Taxis are the chief means of transport here. They're unmetered, but a guide of point-to-point fares around the island is included in most of the

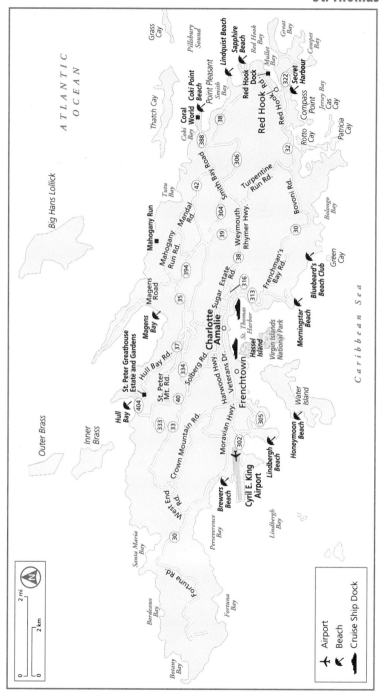

Airport

Beach

Cruise Ship Dock

tourist magazines. The official fare for sightseeing is about $50 for two passengers for 1½ hours. For radio-dispatch service, call ℰ **340/774-7457.**

BY BUS Comfortable and often air-conditioned, government-run **Vitran buses** serve Charlotte Amalie and the countryside as far away as Red Hook, a jumping-off point for St. John. You rarely have to wait more than 30 minutes during the day. A one-way ride costs about 75¢ within Charlotte Amalie, $1 to outer neighborhoods, and $3 for rides as far as Red Hook. For routes, stops, and schedules, call ℰ **340/774-5678.**

BY TAXI VAN Less structured and more erratic are "taxi vans," privately owned vans, minibuses, or open-sided trucks operated by local entrepreneurs. They make unscheduled stops along major traffic arteries and charge the same fares as the Vitran buses. If you look like you want to go somewhere, one will likely stop for you. They may or may not have their final destinations written on a cardboard sign displayed on the windshield.

BY RENTAL CAR No need to rent a car here.

BY FERRY Ferries run every 2 hours from Charlotte Amalie until 5:30pm. and all day hourly from Red Hook to St. John. The ride from Charlotte Amalie takes about 45 minutes and costs $7 one-way; from Red Hook the ride is 20 minutes and costs $1. For information, call ℰ **340/776-6282.**

BEST CRUISE LINE SHORE EXCURSIONS

In addition to the excursions below, a bajillion booze cruises, island tours, and beach/snorkeling tours are offered here. The waters off these islands are rated among the most beautiful in the world.

Coral World & Island Tour ($39, 3 hr.): Coral World Underwater Observatory and Marine Park is St. Thomas's number-one attraction. The 3½-acre complex features a three-story underwater observation tower 100 feet offshore, plunging into the depths to provide views of tropical fish, coral formations, sharks, and other sea beasts. In the Marine Gardens Aquarium, saltwater tanks display everything from sea horses to sea urchins, and a touch pool lets you fondle some of them. Another tank is devoted to sea predators, including circling sharks. From here, the tour zips around the island for a brief tour, visiting Cassie Hill for great views of St. John and the British Virgin Islands.

Kayaking the Marine Sanctuary ($72, 3½ hr.): Kayak from the mouth of the marine sanctuary at Holmberg's Marina and spend nearly an hour paddling among the mangroves while a naturalist explains the mangrove and lagoon ecosystem. Includes a free half-hour to snorkel or walk along the coral beach at Bovoni Point.

Golfing at Mahogany Run ($166, 5 hr.) Designed by Tom and George Fazio, Mahogany Run is one of the most beautiful courses in the West Indies. This 18-hole, par-70 course rises and drops like a roller coaster on its journey to the sea. Cliffs and crashing sea waves are the ultimate hazards at the 13th and 14th holes. It's located on the north shore, and you can also make arrangements for play on your own (ℰ **800/253-7103** or 340/777-6006). Greens fees are $130, including cart, and the taxi there will cost you about $10 each way.

St. John Eco-Hike ($55, 4½ hr.): Take the ferry to St. John for a walkabout through the Virgin Islands National Park. The Lind Point Trail ascends about 250 feet to the Lind Point Overlook for views of St. John, St. Thomas, and the surrounding islands. An expert guide discusses the park's ecosystem and St. John's cultural history while you walk to Honeymoon Beach for a little swimming.

St. John Catamaran Cruise ($119, 6 hr.): A sailing catamaran takes you to the pristine beaches of St. John. Snorkeling equipment, lunch, and champagne are provided. Shorter, cheaper versions of this tour are also available.

Kon-Tiki Party Cruise ($36, 3 hr.): One of the liveliest party boats in the Caribbean sails over a coral reef where you can watch coral, sponges, and other marine life through glass panels—assuming you can see through those beer goggles you may be wearing by then. Steel-band music plays throughout. At Palm Fringed Bay, you'll have time to swim before heading back to the pier.

Atlantis Submarine Odyssey ($89, 2 hr.): Descend about 100 feet into the ocean in this air-conditioned submarine for views of exotic fish and sea life.

Water Island Bike Trip ($74, 3½ hr.): After a ferry ride to Water Island, a 5-minute bus ride brings you to the island's highest point, from which you get a nice downhill ride. Your guide will point out various historic sites and wildlife en route to Honeymoon Beach, where you can swim and enjoy a drink.

EXCURSIONS OFFERED BY LOCAL AGENCIES
St. John Yachting/Snorkeling Excursion: Many yachts and catamarans are available for snorkel and scuba excursions and champagne sails. You can join a full-day or half-day sail aboard Top Tours' 49-passenger catamaran *Dancing Dolphin* (© 340/775-7245 or 340/998-6789; www.thedancingdolphin.com), visiting local beaches, coves, wrecks, and reefs. The owner, Captain Sharee Winslow, makes special accommodations for handicapped passengers and runs special sails for children as well.

For a more personal experience, the six-passenger *Fantasy* (© 340/775-5652; www.daysailfantasy.com) departs from the American Yacht Harbor at Red Hook (on the west coast of St. Thomas) at 9:30am daily, sailing to St. John and nearby islands for swimming, snorkeling, beachcombing, or trolling. The normal full-day trip departs at 9:30am and returns at 3:30pm, but shorter sailings can be arranged. The cost is $120 per person, including continental breakfast, open bar, a hot lunch served on board, and snorkel gear. Only six people can be accommodated per trip.

ON YOUR OWN: WITHIN WALKING DISTANCE
Depending on your level of energy, you can either walk from the port into **Charlotte Amalie** (about 1½ miles) or take a taxi. In days of yore, seafarers from all over the globe flocked to this old-world Danish town, including pirates and, during the Civil War, Confederate sailors. The old warehouses that once held pirates' loot still stand and, for the most part, house shops. The main streets (called "Gades" here in honor of their Danish heritage) are a veritable shopping mall, usually packed with visitors. Sandwiched among the shops are a few historic buildings, most of which can be covered on foot in about 2 hours.

Before starting your tour, stop off at the so-called **Grand Hotel,** near Emancipation Park. No longer a hotel, it has a restaurant, a bar, shops, and a visitor center. There are views of the harbor below from the wood-paneled pub/restaurant at **Hotel 1829,** one street farther up Government Hill. It's a great place for a drink or some lunch.

Stray behind the seafront shopping strip (Main St.) of Charlotte Amalie and you'll find pockets of 19th-century houses and the truly charming, cozy, brick-and-stone **St. Thomas Synagogue,** built in 1833 by Sephardic Jews. There's a great view from here as well. It's located high on the steep sloping Crystal Gade.

Dating from 1672, **Fort Christian,** 32 Raadets Gade, rises from the harbor to dominate the center of town. Named after the Danish king Christian V, the structure has been everything from a governor's residence to a jail. Many pirates were hanged in its courtyard. Some of the cells have been turned into the rather minor American-Caribbean Historical Museum, displaying Indian artifacts of only the most passing interest. The fort is open Monday to Friday from 8am to 3pm. Admission is $8 for adults and $4 for children.

Seven Arches Museum, Government Hill (© **340/774-9295**), is a 2-century-old Danish house completely restored to its original condition and furnished with antiques. You can walk through the yellow ballast arches and visit the great room with its view of the busy harbor.

The **Paradise Point Tramway** (© **340/774-9809**) affords visitors a dramatic view of Charlotte Amalie Harbor at a peak height of 697 feet. The tramways transport customers from the Havensight area to Paradise Point, where riders disembark to visit shops and a popular restaurant and bar.

ON YOUR OWN: BEYOND THE PORT AREA
Coral World Marine Park & Underwater Observatory, 6450 Coki Point, off Route 38, 20 minutes from downtown Charlotte Amalie (© **340/775-1555;** www.coralworldvi.com), is the number-one attraction in St. Thomas. The 3½-acre complex features a three-story underwater observation tower 100 feet offshore—you'll see sponges, fish, coral, and other underwater life in their natural state through the windows. In the Marine Gardens Aquarium, saltwater tanks display everything from sea horses to sea urchins. An 80,000-gallon reef tank features exotic Caribbean marine life. Another tank is devoted to sea predators, including circling sharks. The entrance is hidden behind a waterfall. Coral World is open daily from 9am to 5pm. Admission is $18 for adults and $9 children 3 to 12.

West of Charlotte Amalie, **Frenchtown** was settled by a French-speaking citizenry who were uprooted when the Swedes invaded and took over their home of St. Barts. These settlers were known for wearing cha-chas, or straw hats. Many of the people who live here today are the direct descendants of those long-ago residents. This colorful fishing village contains several interesting restaurants and taverns. To get there, take a taxi down Veterans Drive (Rte. 30) west and turn left at the sign to the Admirals Inn.

The lush **St. Peter Greathouse Estate and Gardens,** at the corner of St. Peter Mountain Road (Rte. 40) and Barrett Hill Road (© **340/774-4999**), ornaments 11 acres on the volcanic peaks of the island's northern rim. It's the creation of Howard Lawson DeWolfe, a Mayflower descendant who, with his wife, Sylvie, bought the estate in 1987 and set about transforming it into a tropical paradise. It's filled with some 200 varieties of plants and trees, including an umbrella plant from Madagascar. There's also a rainforest, an orchid jungle, waterfalls, and reflecting ponds. From a panoramic deck you can see some 20 of the Virgin Islands. The house itself is worth a visit, its interior filled with local art. Admission is $10 for adults, $5 children. The estate and gardens are open daily 9am to 5pm.

SHOPPING
St. Thomas is famous for its shopping opportunities. As in St. Croix and St. John, American shoppers can bring home $1,200 worth of merchandise without paying duty—twice the amount of other Caribbean islands. You'll sometimes find well-known brand names at savings of up to 40% off stateside prices,

but you'll often have to plow through a lot of junk to find the bargains. The main goodies are jewelry, watches, cameras, china, and leather.

Many cruise ship passengers shop at the **Havensight Mall,** where the ships dock, but the major shopping goes on along the harbor of **Charlotte Amalie. Main Street** (or Dronningens Gade, its old Danish name) is the main shopping area. Just north of Main Street is merchandise-loaded **Back Street,** or Vimmel-skaft. Many shops are also spread along the Waterfront Highway (also called Kyst Vejen). Running between these major streets is a series of side streets, walkways, and alleys, all filled with shops. All the usual Caribbean megatourist shops sell all the usual jewelry, watches, perfume, gift items, and so on; but there are a number of other interesting, and more unique, shops. Just do a little comparison shopping from place to place and be a little cautious of people trying to lure you into their shop and offering you a special rate if you bring in others from your group.

Upstairs at 14 Dronningens Gade, the **Camille Pissarro Building Art Gallery** is in the house where the impressionist painter Pissarro was born on July 10, 1830. In three high-ceilinged and airy rooms, you'll see all the available Pissarro paintings relating to the islands. Many prints and note cards by local artists are available, too, as well as original batiks.

Huddled under oversize parasols, hundreds of street vendors ply their trades in a designated area called **Vendors Plaza,** at the corner of Veterans Drive and Tolbod Gade. It's open Monday to Saturday from 7:30am to 5:30pm, and on Sunday if a cruise ship is expected. Food vendors set up on sidewalks outside.

MAPes MONDe (© **340/776-2886;** www.mapesmonde.com) has two locations in St. Thomas—one in Riise Alley and the other at The Grand Hotel—and another at Mongoose Junction on St. John. Its elegant books, reproductions, historic maps, and archival photos of the Caribbean are a nice break from jewelry and tourist knickknacks. It also carries lovely prints, silk screens, and greeting cards featuring indigenous birds and vegetation.

BEACHES

St. Thomas has some good beaches, all of which are easily reached by taxi. Arrange for your driver to return and pick you up at a designated time. All the beaches in the U.S. Virgin Islands are public, but some still charge a fee. Mind your belongings, as St. Thomas has pickpockets and thieves who target visitors. If you're going to St. John, you may want to do your beaching there (see "Beaches," under "St. John," below).

THE NORTH SIDE   Located across the mountains, 3 miles north of the capital, **Magens Bay Beach** was once hailed as one of the world's 10 most beautiful beaches, but its reputation has faded. Though still beautiful, it isn't as well maintained as it should be and is often overcrowded, especially when many cruise ships are in port. It's less than a mile long and lies between two mountains. Admission is $3 for adults and 25¢ for children under 12. Changing facilities, bathrooms, a snack bar, snorkel gear, and float rentals are available. Magens Bay also has picnic tables and benches. There's no public transportation here, so take a taxi. The gates are open daily from 6am to 6pm (you'll need insect repellent after 4pm).

Located in the northeast near Coral World, **Coki Beach** is good, but it, too, becomes overcrowded when cruise ships are in port. Snorkelers come here often, as do pickpockets—protect your valuables. Lockers can be rented at Coral World, next door. An East End bus runs to Smith Bay and lets you off at the gate to Coral World and Coki.

Also on the north side is **Renaissance Grand Beach Resort,** one of the island's most beautiful beaches. It opens onto Smith Bay, right off Route 38, near Coral World. Many watersports are available here.

THE SOUTH SIDE On the south side, **Morningstar** lies about 2 miles east of Charlotte Amalie at Marriott's Frenchman's Reef Beach Resort. You can wear your most daring swimwear here, and you can also rent sailboats, snorkeling equipment, and lounge chairs. The beach can be easily reached via a cliff-front elevator at the Marriott.

The **Bolongo Bay Beach Club** lures those who love a serene spread of sand. You can feed hibiscus blossoms to iguanas and rent snorkeling gear and lounge chairs. They also offer a variety of watersports, including parasailing. There's no public transportation, but it's a $9 ride by taxi from Charlotte Amalie. Unlike Magens Bay Beach (see above), where there's only a snack bar, Iggy's Restaurant is right on Bolongo's beach. **Bluebeard's Beach Club** (formerly known as Limetree Beach) offers a secluded setting and is a quick ride from the cruise ship pier.

Brewer's Beach, one of the island's most popular, lies in the southwest near the University of the Virgin Islands, also along the Fortuna bus route.

THE EAST END Small and special, **Secret Harbor** sits near a collection of condos. With its white sand and coconut palms, it's a veritable cliché of Caribbean charm. No public transportation stops here, but it's an easy taxi ride east of Charlotte Amalie heading toward Red Hook.

Sapphire Beach is one of the finest on St. Thomas, set against the backdrop of the Doubletree Sapphire Beach Resort & Marina complex, where you can lunch or order drinks. Windsurfers like this beach a lot. You can rent snorkeling gear and lounge chairs here. A large reef lies close to the shore, and there are great views of offshore cays and St. John. To get here, take the East End bus from Charlotte Amalie, going via Red Hook. Ask to be let off at the entrance to Sapphire Bay; it's a short walk to the water.

SPORTS

GOLF Designed by Tom and George Fazio, **Mahogany Run** on the north shore, Mahogany Run Road (© **800/253-7103** or 340/777-6006), is one of the most beautiful courses in the West Indies. This 18-hole, par-70 course rises and drops like a roller coaster on its journey to the sea. Cliffs and crashing sea waves are the ultimate hazards at the 13th and 14th holes. The golf course is an $8 to $10 taxi ride from the cruise dock. Greens fees are $130, including cart.

SCUBA DIVING & SNORKELING The waters off the U.S. Virgin Islands are rated as one of the "most beautiful areas in the world" by *Skin Diver* magazine. Thirty spectacular reefs lie just off St. Thomas alone. **Dive In!,** in the Doubletree Sapphire Beach Resort & Marina, Smith Bay Road, Route 36 (© **800/ 524-2090;** www.diveinusvi.com), offers professional instruction, daily beach and boat dives, custom dive packages, underwater photography and videotapes, and snorkeling trips.

GREAT LOCAL RESTAURANTS & BARS

IN CHARLOTTE AMALIE **Beni Iguana's Sushi Bar,** in the Grand Hotel Court, just behind Emancipation Park in downtown (© 340/777-8744), is the only Japanese restaurant on St. Thomas. Lunch is around $20. **Greenhouse,** Veterans Drive (© **340/774-7998**), attracts cruise ship passengers with daily specials, including American fare and some Jamaican-inspired dishes. Lunch is about $10. **The Hard Rock Cafe,** 5144 International Plaza (on the second floor

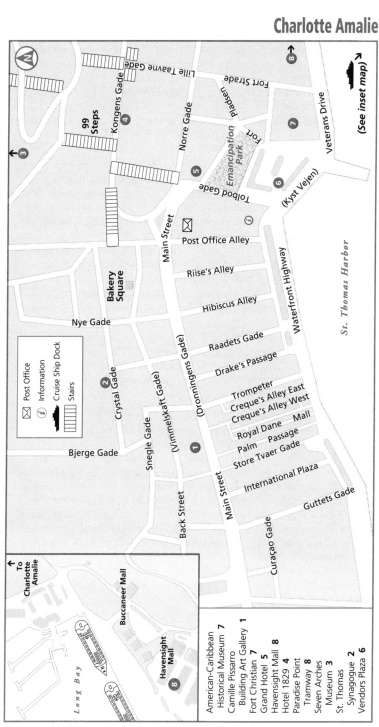

Charlotte Amalie

N

Lille Taavne Gade

Kongens Gade

99 Steps

Kongens Gade

3

Norre Gade

4

5

Tolbod Gade

Emancipation Park

Fort

Fort Strade

Pladsen

8

7

Veterans Drive

6

(Kyst Vejen)

(See inset map)

Main Street

Post Office Alley

1

Riise's Alley

Hibiscus Alley

Bakery Square

Nye Gade

Raadets Gade

Drake's Passage

Waterfront Highway

St. Thomas Harbor

Crystal Gade

2

(Dronningens Gade)

Trompeter

Creque's Alley East

Creque's Alley West

Royal Dane   Mall

Palm   Passage

Store Tvaer Gade

Snegle Gade

(Vimmelskaft Gade)

1

International Plaza

Bjerge Gade

Main Street

Guttets Gade

Back Street

Curaçao Gade

Legend
- ⊠ Post Office
- ⓘ Information
- ▨ Cruise Ship Dock
- ▥ Stairs

← To Charlotte Amalie

Buccaneer Mall

Long Bay

Havensight Mall

8

American-Caribbean Historical Museum **7**
Camille Pissarro Building Art Gallery **1**
Fort Christian **7**
Grand Hotel **5**
Havensight Mall **8**
Hotel 1829 **4**
Paradise Point Tramway **8**
Seven Arches Museum **3**
St. Thomas Synagogue **2**
Vendors Plaza **6**

289

of a pink-sided mall), on the Waterfront (© **340/777-5555**), has the best burgers in town, but people mainly come for the good times and the T-shirts. Lunch is about $9. **Virgilio's,** 18 Dronningens Gade, entrance on a narrow alleyway running between Main and Back streets (© **340/776-4920**), is a good northern Italian restaurant that serves excellent lobster ravioli. Lunch is about $18. **Lillian's Caribbean Grill,** 43–46 Norre Gade, in the Grand Galleria Courtyard directly across from Emancipation Park (© **340/774-7900**), serves authentic Caribbean dishes. Conveniently located near the Vendor's Plaza shopping area, it makes for a nice lunch stop. Lunch is about $10.

IN FRENCHTOWN At **Alexander's,** rue de St. Barthélemy, west of town (© **340/774-4349**), there's a heavy emphasis on seafood—the menu even includes conch schnitzel on occasion. Other dishes include a mouthwatering Wiener schnitzel and homemade pâté. Lunch is about $18. **Craig & Sally's,** 22 Honduras (© **340/777-9949**), serves dishes that, according to the owner, are not "for the faint of heart, but for the adventurous soul"—roast pork with clams, filet mignon with macadamia-nut sauce, and grilled swordfish with a sauce of fresh herbs and tomatoes. Lunch is about $15.

ON THE NORTH COAST **Glenda's Caribbean Spot,** 66–67 Smith Bay, Route 38, just east of the Coral World turnoff (© **340/775-2699**), is one of the island's best-known West Indian restaurants. It oozes local color. The place made news around the world on January 5, 1997, when Bill and Hillary Clinton showed up unexpectedly for lunch. Surrounded by secret service men, they shared a conch appetizer, and then Mrs. Clinton went for the vegetable plate while the president opted for the catch of the day, which he reportedly loved.

ST. JOHN

A tiny gem of an island, lush St. John lies about 3 miles east of St. Thomas across Pillsbury Sound. It's the smallest and least populated of the U.S. Virgins, only about 7 miles long and 3 miles wide, with a total land area of some 19 square miles. The island was slated for big development under Danish control, but a slave rebellion and the decline of the sugar-cane plantations ended that idea. Since 1956, more than half of St. John's land mass, as well as its shoreline waters, have been set aside as the **Virgin Islands National Park,** and today the island leads the Caribbean in eco- (or "sustainable") tourism. Miles of winding hiking trails lead to panoramic views and the ruins of 18th-century Danish plantations. Mysterious geometric petroglyphs incised into boulders and cliffs can be seen all over the island (ask a guide to point them out if you can't find them). These figures, of unknown age and origin, have never been deciphered. Since St. John is easy to reach from St. Thomas and the beaches are spectacular, many cruise ship passengers spend their entire day here.

COMING ASHORE Cruise ships cannot dock at either of the piers in St. John. Instead, they moor off the coast at **Cruz Bay,** sending in tenders to the National Park Service Dock, the larger of the two piers. Most cruise ships docking at St. Thomas offer shore excursions to St. John's pristine interior and beaches.

If your ship docks on St. Thomas and you don't take an organized shore excursion to St. John, you can get here from Charlotte Amalie by ferry. Ferries leave the Charlotte Amalie waterfront for Cruz Bay at 1- to 2-hour intervals, from 9am until around 5:30pm. The last boat leaves Cruz Bay for Charlotte Amalie at 3:45pm. The ride takes about 45 minutes and costs $7 each way. Call © **340/776-6282** for more information. Another ferry leaves from the Red

St. John

> ## Frommer's Favorite St. John Experiences
>
> **Touring the Island in an Open-Air Safari Bus:** The views are spectacular from the island's coastal road, and you'll visit the ruins of a plantation and one of St. John's excellent beaches. (See "Best Cruise Line Shore Excursions," below.)
>
> **Beaching Yourself in Trunk Bay:** Although it can get somewhat crowded, it's a gorgeous beach and there's some decent snorkeling, too. (See "Beaches," below.)

Hook pier on St. Thomas's eastern tip more or less every half-hour, starting at 6:30am. It's a 30-minute drive from Charlotte Amalie's port to the pier at Red Hook; the ferry trip takes another 20 minutes each way. The one-way fare is $3 for adults, $1 for children under 11. Schedules can change without notice, so call in advance (© **340/776-6282**). You can take a Vitran bus from a point near Market Square (located near the west end of Main St. in Charlotte Amalie) directly to Red Hook for $1 per person each way, or negotiate a price with a taxi driver.

GETTING AROUND
BY TAXI　The most popular way to get around is by surrey-style taxi. Typical fares from Cruz Bay are $5.50 to Trunk Bay, $7.50 to Cinnamon Bay, and $11 to Maho Bay. Taxis wait at the pier. In the very unlikely event you don't see a taxi at the pier, you can call **St. John Taxi Service** at © **340/693-7530.** Almost any taxi at Cruz Bay can take you on a 2-hour taxi tour of the island. Tours cost from $45 for one or two passengers, or about $16 per person for three or more riders.

BY RENTAL CAR　The extensive Virgin Islands National Park has kept the island's roads undeveloped and uncluttered, opening onto some of the most panoramic vistas anywhere. Renting a vehicle is the best way to see these views, especially if you like to linger at particularly beautiful spots. Open-sided Jeep-like vehicles are the most fun of the limited rentals here. There's sometimes a shortage of cars during the busy midwinter season, so try to reserve early. Remember to drive on the left (even though steering wheels are on the left, too—go figure). **Avis** and **Hertz** both have offices here. Your car is likely to come with just enough fuel to get you to one of the island's two gas stations, so fill 'er up: Due to the distance between stations, it's never a good idea to drive around St. John with less than half a tank of gas.

BEST CRUISE LINE SHORE EXCURSIONS
Island Tour ($39, 4–5 hr.): Since most ships tie up in St. Thomas, tours of St. John first require a ferry or tender ride to Cruz Bay in St. John. Then you board open-air safari buses for a tour that includes a stop at the ruins of a working plantation (the Annaberg Ruins), as well as a pause at Trunk Bay or one of the other beaches. The island and sea views from the coastal road are spectacular.

ON YOUR OWN: WITHIN WALKING DISTANCE
Most cruise ship passengers dart through **Cruz Bay,** a cute little West Indian village with interesting bars, restaurants, boutiques, and pastel-painted houses.

Wharfside Village, near the dock, is a complex of courtyards, alleys, and shady patios with a mishmash of boutiques, restaurants, fast-food joints, and bars. Down the road from the dock is Mongoose Junction (see "Shopping," below).

Located at the public library, the **Elaine Ione Sprauve Museum** (© **340/ 776-6359**) isn't big, but it does have some local artifacts, and will teach you about some of the history of the island. It's open Monday to Friday from 9am to 5pm. Admission is free.

ON YOUR OWN: BEYOND THE PORT AREA

In November 1954, the wealthy Rockefeller family began acquiring large tracts of land on St. John. They then donated more than 5,000 acres to the Department of the Interior for the creation of the **Virgin Islands National Park,** which Congress voted into existence on August 2, l956. Over the years, the size of the park has grown steadily; it now totals 12,624 acres, including over two-thirds of St. John's landmass plus submerged land and water adjacent to the island. Stop off first at the **visitor center** (© **340/776-6201**) right on the dock at St. Cruz, where you'll find some exhibits and learn more about what you can see and do in the park. You can explore the park on the more than 20 miles of biking trails; rent your own car, Jeep, or mini-moke; or hike. If you decide to hike, stop at the visitor center first to watch an 18-minute video about the park and to pick up maps and instructions. The starting points of some trails are within walking distance while others can be reached by taxi for about $5 to $20. Trails can also be reached by Vitran bus service for $1. All trails are well marked.

Within the park, try to see the **Annaberg Ruins,** Leinster Bay Road, where the Danes founded thriving plantations and a sugar mill in 1718. You'll find tidal pools, forest, hilltops, wild scenery, and the ruins of several Danish plantations. It's located off North Shore Road, east of Trunk Bay on the north shore. On certain days of the week (dates vary), guided walks of the area are given by park rangers. Check at the visitor center.

SHOPPING

Compared to St. Thomas, St. John is a minor shopping destination, but the boutiques and shops at **Cruz Bay** are generally more interesting than those on St. Thomas. Most of them are clustered at **Mongoose Junction** (www.usvi.net/ shopping/mongoose), in a woodsy area beside the roadway, about a 5-minute walk from the ferry dock. **Bamboula** (© 340/693-8699) has an unusual and appealing collection of gifts from the Caribbean, Haiti, India, Indonesia, and Central Africa. **The Canvas Factory** (© 340/776-6196) produces its own rugged, colorful handmade canvas bags. **Donald Schnell Studio** (© 800/253-7107 or 340/776-6420) deals in handmade pottery, sculpture, and blown glass. **The Fabric Mill** (© 340/776-6194) features silk-screened and batik fabrics from around the world. **R and I Patton Goldsmithing** (© 800/626-3445 or 340/776-6548) has a large selection of locally designed jewelry, made with sterling silver, gold, and precious stones. In case you forgot your Tevas or need a new bathing suit, check out **Big Planet Adventure Outfitters** (© 340/776-6638), which stocks lots of outdoor-gear brands.

BEACHES

For a true beach lover, missing the great white sweep of **Trunk Bay** would be like touring Europe and skipping Paris. Trouble is, the word is a little more than out. This gorgeous beach is usually overcrowded, and there are sometimes pickpockets lurking about. The beach has lifeguards and rents snorkeling gear to those wanting to explore the underwater trail near the shore. Both taxis and "safari buses" to Trunk Bay meet the ferry as it docks at Cruz Bay.

Caneel Bay, the stamping ground of the rich and famous, has seven perfect beaches on its 170 acres, but only one—**Honeymoon Beach**—that's open to the public. Since it's the closest beach to Cruz Bay (and is very beautiful, if a bit narrow and windy), it's often overcrowded. Safari buses and taxis from Cruz Bay will take you along North Shore Road.

The campgrounds of **Cinnamon Bay** and **Maho Bay** have their own beaches. Snorkelers find good reefs here, and it's a great place to spot turtles and schools of parrotfish. Changing rooms and showers are available. There's also **Hawksnest Beach,** on the island's north shore. It's known as the beach locals frequent during peak tourist season.

SPORTS

HIKING　The network of trails in Virgin Islands National Park is the big thing here. The visitor center at Cruz Bay hands out free trail maps of the park. Since you don't have time to get lost—you don't want the ship to leave without you—it's best to set out with someone who knows his or her way around. Both **Maho Bay Camps** (© 340/776-6226) and **Cinnamon Bay Campground** (© 340/776-6201) conduct nature walks.

KAYAKING & WINDSURFING　The **Cinnamon Bay Watersports Center** on Cinnamon Bay Beach (© 340/776-6330) rents kayaks and 12- or 14-foot Hobie monohull sailboats, and the windsurfing here is some of the best anywhere, for both beginners and experts.

SCUBA DIVING & SNORKELING　**Low Key Watersports,** Wharfside Village (© 800/835-7718 or 340/693-8999; www.divelowkey.com), offers two-tank, two-location wreck dives on its own custom-built dive boats. They also arrange day-sailing charters, kayaking tours, deep-sea sportfishing, and snorkel tours, and rent watersports gear, including masks, fins, snorkels, and dive skins. **Cruz Bay Watersports,** at Palm Plaza (© 340/776-6234; www.divestjohn.com), is a PADI and NAUI five-star diving center. Snorkel tours are available daily.

GREAT LOCAL RESTAURANTS & BARS

In Wharfside Village, at Cruz Bay, the upscale **Cafe Wahoo** (© 340/776-6600) offers a lovely view of Cruz Bay Harbor. Lunch is about $11. For a more casual meal and drinks, try **The Beach Bar,** downstairs (© 340/777-4220), with the same view to go with your burgers and bar food. Lunch is about $9.

ST. CROIX

More tranquil and less congested than St. Thomas, St. Croix is rocky and arid on its eastern end (which, incidentally, is the easternmost possession of the U.S.) but more lush in the west, with a rainforest of mango and mahogany, tree ferns, and dangling lianas. Rolling hills and upland pastures make up much of the area between the two extremes, and the vivid African tulips are just one of the many tropical flowers that add a splash of color to the landscape, which is dotted with the ruins of sugar-cane plantations. The major St. Croix attraction are the coral reefs of **Buck Island Reef National Monument,** located offshore. There are some fine beaches here as well, including **Sandy Point, Sprat Hall,** and **Rainbow Beach.**

Although large cruise ships moor at **Frederiksted,** most of the action is really in **Christiansted,** located on a coral-bound bay about midway along the north shore and featuring more sights and better restaurants and shopping. Showing

St. Croix

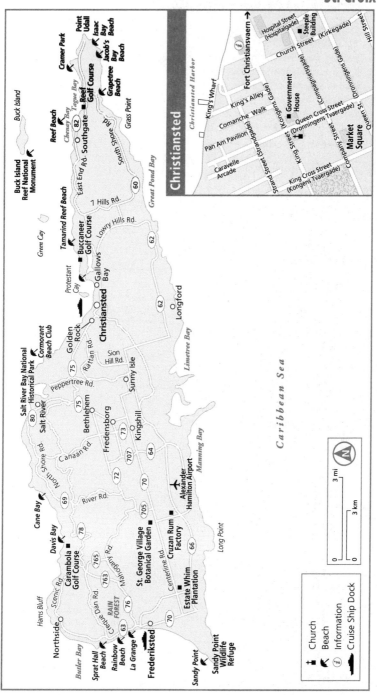

Christiansted (inset map)

- Hospital Street (Hospitalgade)
- Steeple Building
- Church Street (Kirkegade)
- Fort Christiansvaern
- King's Wharf
- King's Alley
- Comanche Walk
- Government House
- Pan Am Pavilion
- Queen Cross Street (Dronningens Tvaergade)
- King Street (Kongens Gade)
- King Cross Street (Kongens Tvaergade)
- Caravelle Arcade
- Market Square
- Strand Street (Strandgade)
- Compagniesgade
- Company Street
- Queen St. (Dronningens Gade)
- Queen Street
- Hill Street
- Christiansted Harbor

Point Udall
Isaac Bay Beach
Jacob's Bay Beach
Cramer Park
Grapetree Beach
Reef Golf Course
Southgate
Reef Beach
Chenay Bay
Tague Bay
East End Rd.
South Shore Rd.
Grass Point
Great Pond Bay
60
Buck Island
Buck Island Reef National Monument
Tamarind Reef Beach
1 Hills Rd.
Buccaneer Golf Course
Lowry Hills Rd.
62
Green Cay
Gallows Bay
Protestant Cay
Christiansted
62
Longford
Golden Rock
Cormorant Beach Club
Salt River Bay National Historical Park
75
Rattan Rd.
Sion Hill Rd.
Limetree Bay
80
Salt River
Peppertree Rd.
Bethlehem
Sunny Isle
North Shore Rd.
Canaan Rd.
Fredensborg
75
Kingshill
707
73
64
72
70
Alexander Hamilton Airport
Manning Bay
River Rd.
69
705
St. George Village Botanical Garden
Cruzan Rum Factory
66
Long Point
Cane Bay
Davis Bay
78
Carambola Golf Course
765
763
Mahogany Rd.
Centerline Rd.
Estate Whim Plantation
Scenic Rd.
Creque Dan Rd.
RAIN FOREST
76
Hams Bluff
Northside
63
La Grange
70
Butler Bay
Sprat Hall Beach
Rainbow Beach
Frederiksted
Sandy Point
Sandy Point Wildlife Refuge

Caribbean Sea

Legend:
- ✝ Church
- ⚓ Beach
- ⓘ Information
- ⚓ Cruise Ship Dock

3 mi
3 km

Frommer's Favorite St. Croix Experiences

Visiting Buck Island Reef National Monument: Within this 800-acre preserve (the only underwater national monument in the United States), you can snorkel over a series of unique marked underwater trails and experience some of the best-preserved coral reefs in the Caribbean. A snorkeling instructor guides the excursion. (See "Best Cruise Line Shore Excursions," below.)

Strolling Through Christiansted: Because of its well-preserved 18th- and 19th-century Danish architecture (particularly evident at Fort Christiansvaern), Christiansted has been designated a National Historic Site. In the late 1700s, it was a crown colony of Denmark and one of the Caribbean's major ports. Today, many street signs are still in Danish.

2½ centuries of Danish influence in its architecture, the town is being handsomely restored and the entire harborfront area is a national historic site. St. Croix's population is descended from both Africa and Europe, and some families have been here for 10 generations, with roots dating back to colonial times.

COMING ASHORE   Only cruise ships no longer than 350 feet can land directly at the dock at **Christiansted.** Others moor at newly renovated **Anne Abramson Pier at Frederiksted,** a sleepy town that springs to life only when the ships arrive. There's space for two megaships, and both piers have information centers and telephones. We suggest you spend as little time as possible in Frederiksted and head immediately for Christiansted, some 17 miles away. It's easy to explore either town on foot (it's the only way, really). You might want to consider one of the shore excursions outlined below to see more of the island, especially its underwater treasures.

Although St. Croix is relatively safe, it's wise to stay on the beaten path and watch your belongings on the beaches (as you should on any island); in late 2001, four incidences of muggings and robberies were reported involving Carnival Cruise Lines passengers and crew.

GETTING AROUND
BY TAXI   Taxis are unmetered, and rates are set from point to point. The **St. Croix Taxicab Association** (✆ **340/778-1088**) offers door-to-door service. Taxi tours are a great way to explore the island. The cost is $100 for one to four people for 3 hours. All tours are a minimum of the hours. It costs from $25 to $30 to take a taxi from Christiansted to Frederiksted.

BY BUS   Air-conditioned buses run between Christiansted and Frederiksted about every half hour between 5:30am and 9pm. The main stop in Christiansted is on Hospital Street, near the National Park office; the main stop in Frederiksted is on Budhoe Park, near Fort Frederick and King Street. The fare is $1 for adults, 75¢ for children, and 55¢ for seniors. For more information, call ✆ **340/778-0898.**

BY SEAPLANE   Daily seaplane shuttles between St. Croix and St. Thomas are available for $135 round-trip. It is strongly recommended to book in advance. Flights depart every 15 to 45 minutes in both directions, and flight time is a mere 18 minutes, but figure 30 minutes from dock to dock. For more information, contact **Seaborne Airlines,** 34 Strand St., Christiansted (© **340/773-6442;** www. seaborneairlines.com).

BY RENTAL CAR   We don't recommend renting a car here.

BEST CRUISE LINE SHORE EXCURSIONS

Buck Island Tour/Snorkeling ($80; 6½ hr.): The most popular tour in St. Croix takes you to a tropical underwater wonderland of blue water, a dazzling rainbow of sea life, and colorful coral reefs, sailing aboard either a glass-bottom catamaran or a speedboat. An experienced guide provides snorkel lessons. A shorter version of this tour is available for $60 (4½ hr.).

Salt River Kayak Tour ($53, 4 hr.): The Salt River Bay National Historical Park and Ecological Preserve, on the island's northern shore, is the only site that Columbus is known to have landed on in what is now U.S. territory. The park today is in a natural state, with the largest mangrove forest in the Virgin Islands, sheltering many endangered animals and plants. You'll kayak for about 2 hours through secluded estuaries, birding areas, and mangroves as well as visiting the site of the original Carib village Columbus and his men explored.

St. Croix Heritage Tour ($55, 6 hr.): Visit St. George Village Botanical Garden, the Cruzan Rum Factory; the Whim Plantation Museum, and a patch of rainforest in the company of a local guide, stopping for lunch along the way.

Golf at Carambola ($155, self-timed): Your cruise line will probably offer an excursion to Carambola, one of the Caribbean's most famous golf courses. If not, you can do it on your own (see "Sports," below).

EXCURSIONS OFFERED BY LOCAL OPERATORS

Horseback Tour: On this 1½-hour tour, run by Paul and Jill's **Equestrian Stables,** Sprat Hall Plantation, Route 58 (© **340/772-2880;** http://pws.prserv.net/paul-and-jills), you'll pass ruins of abandoned 18th-century plantations and sugar mills, and climb the hills of St. Croix's western end. Tour guides give running commentaries on island fauna and history and on riding techniques. The stables, owned by Paul Wojcie and his wife, Jill Hurd (a daughter of the establishment's original founders), are set on the sprawling grounds of the island's oldest plantation, and are known throughout the Caribbean for the quality of the horses and the exceptionally scenic forest trails. The grounds also boast an exquisite tropical fruit orchard. Both beginner and experienced riders are welcome. Make reservations in advance.

ON YOUR OWN: WITHIN WALKING DISTANCE

IN FREDERIKSTED   Frederiksted is nothing great, but if you decide to hang around, you should begin your tour at russet-colored **Fort Frederik** (© **340/772-2021**), next to the cruise ship pier. Some historians claim it was the first fort to sound a foreign salute to the U.S. flag, in 1776. The structure, at the northern end of Frederiksted, has been restored to its 1840 look. You can explore the courtyard and stables, visit the police museum, peruse exhibits of antique cannons and clothing, and see photographs of life on St. Croix in the days of yore. Admission is free. The fort is open Monday to Friday from 8am to 5pm.

IN CHRISTIANSTED   You can begin your visit at the **visitor bureau** (© **340/ 773-0495**), a yellow building with a cedar roof near the harbor front. It was built as the Old Scalehouse in 1856 to replace a similar, older structure that burned down. In its heyday, all taxable goods leaving and entering the harbor were weighed here. The scales could once accurately weigh barrels of sugar and molasses weighing up to 1,600 pounds.

The **Steeple Building** (© 340/773-1460), or Church of Lord God of Sabaoth, was completed in 1753 as St. Croix's first Lutheran church. It, too, stands near the harbor front, and contains an exhibit on island heritage in general and the church in particular, with photos and artifacts. Get there via Hospital Street. The building was deconsecrated in 1831 and has served at various times as a bakery, a hospital, and a school. Admission is $3, which also includes admission to **Fort Christiansvaern** (© 340/773-1460), the best-preserved colonial fortification in the Virgin Islands. The National Park Service maintains the fort as a historic monument, overlooking the harbor. Its original star-shaped design was at the vanguard of the most advanced military planning of its era. Hours are 8am to 5pm Monday to Friday and 9am to 4:45pm Saturday and Sunday.

ON YOUR OWN: BEYOND THE PORT AREA

Salt River, on the island's northern shore, is the only site that Columbus is known to have landed on in what is now U.S. territory. To mark the 500th anniversary of the arrival of Columbus, former President George Bush signed a bill creating the 912-acre **Salt River Bay National Historical Park and Ecological Preserve.** The landmass includes the site of the original Carib village explored by Columbus and his men, along with the only Taíno ceremonial ball court (used for ceremonial sporting events) ever discovered in the Lesser Antilles. At the Carib settlement, Columbus's men liberated several Taíno women and children held as slaves. On the way back to their vessels, the Spaniards faced a canoe filled with hostile Caribs, armed with poison arrows. One Spanish soldier was killed, and perhaps six Caribs were either slain or captured. This is the first documented case of hostility between invading Europeans and Native Americans. Sailing away, Columbus named this part of St. Croix "Cape of the Arrows."

The park today is in a natural state. It has the largest mangrove forest in the Virgin Islands, sheltering many endangered animals and plants, plus an underwater canyon attracting scuba divers from around the world. The **St. Croix Environmental Association,** 3 Arawak Building, Gallows Bay (© 340/773-1989; www. seastx.org), conducts tours of the area. Hours are 9am to 5 pm Monday to Friday.

The **Cruzan Rum Factory,** West Airport Road, Route 64 (© 340/692-2280), distills the famous Virgin Islands rum. Guided tours depart from the visitor pavilion.

Restored by the St. Croix Landmarks Society, the **Estate Whim Plantation Museum,** Centerline Road, about 2 miles east of Frederiksted (© 340/772-0598), is composed of only three rooms and is unique among the many old sugar plantations dotting the island, with 3-foot-thick walls made of stone, coral, and molasses. Also on the museum's premises are a woodworking shop, the estate's original kitchen, a museum store, servant's quarters, and tools from the 18th century. The ruins include remains of the plantation's sugar-processing plant, complete with a restored windmill.

The **St. George Village Botanical Garden of St. Croix** (© 340/692-2874) is a much-loved, popular Eden of tropical trees, shrubs, vines, and flowers, located 4 miles east of Frederiksted.

SHOPPING

Americans get a break here, since they can bring home $1,200 worth of merchandise from the U.S. Virgin Islands without paying duty, as opposed to a paltry $400 from most other Caribbean ports. And liquor here is duty-free.

The **King's Alley Complex,** a pink-sided compound created right on the Christiansted waterfront following the hurricanes of 1995, is filled with the densest concentration of shopping options on St. Croix. There are a number of worthwhile specialty shops in Christiansted as well. **Skirt Tails,** Pam Am Pavilion, is one of the most colorful and popular boutiques on the island, specializing in hand-painted batiks for both men and women. **The White House/Black Market,** King's Alley Walk, stocks women's clothing, ranging from dressy to casual and breezy—with all apparel in black and white. **Elegant Illusions Copy Jewelry,** 55 King St., sells credible copies of the baroque and antique jewelry your great-grandmother might have worn, priced from $10 to $1,000. **Larimar,** on The Boardwalk/King's Walk, specializes in its namesake, a pale-blue pectolyte stone prized for its sky-blue color, in various gold settings. **Sonya Ltd.,** 1 Company St., specializes in traditional Caribbean hook bracelets.

Folk Art Traders, 1B Queen Cross St., deals in Caribbean art and folk-art treasures, such as carnival masks, pottery, ceramics, original paintings, and hand-wrought jewelry. **Many Hands,** in the Pan Am Pavilion, Strand Street, sells Virgin Islands handicrafts, spices and teas, handmade jewelry, and more.

GAMBLING

St. Croix's first casino opened in early 2000 at the new **Divi Carina Bay Hotel,** 25 Estate Turner Hole, in Christiansted, on the east side of the island (© **340/ 773-9700;** www.divicarina.com). By taxi, it takes approximately 45 minutes and costs about $30 per person to get to the casino from Frederiksted. The casino opens at noon.

BEACHES

Beaches are the biggest attraction on St. Croix. The drawback is that getting to them from Christiansted or Frederiksted isn't always easy. Taxis will take you, but they can be expensive. From Christiansted, you can take a ferry to the **Hotel on the Cay,** a palm-shaded island in the harbor.

NEAR FREDERIKSTED   Most convenient for passengers arriving at Frederiksted is **Sandy Point,** the largest beach in all of the U.S. Virgin Islands. Its waters are shallow and calm, perfect for swimming. You may remember this beach from the last scene of the movie *The Shawshank Redemption.* Sandy Point is also the nesting ground for endangered leatherback, hawksbill and green sea turtles, who lay their eggs every year between early April and early June. Parts of the beach are roped off during this time, but you can watch these fascinating creatures from outside of the protected areas.

On Route 63, a short ride north of Frederiksted, **Rainbow Beach** is inviting, with its white sand and ideal snorkeling conditions. **Sprat Hall** is another good beach in the vicinity, also on Route 63, about 5 minutes north of Frederiksted. You can rent lounge chairs here, and there's a bar nearby.

We highly recommend **Cane Bay** and **Davis Bay.** They're both the type of beaches you'd expect to find on a Caribbean island—palms, white sand, and good swimming and snorkeling. Cane Bay attracts snorkelers and divers with its rolling waves, coral gardens, and drop-off wall. It's near Route 80 on the north shore. **Davis Beach,** also off Route 80 on the north shore in the vicinity of the Carambola Beach Resort, draws bodysurfers. There are no changing facilities.

NEAR CHRISTIANSTED   At the **Cormorant Beach Club,** about 5 miles west of Christiansted, palm trees shade some 1,200 feet of white sand. A living reef lies just off the shore, making snorkeling ideal.

SPORTS

GOLF   St. Croix has the best golfing in the U.S. Virgin Islands, hands down. In fact, guests staying on St. John and St. Thomas often fly over to St. Croix for a day, just to play. The 18-hole, par-72 **Carambola Golf Course,** on the northeast side of St. Croix (© **340/778-5638**), was designed by Robert Trent Jones Sr., who called it "the loveliest course I ever designed." Golfing authorities consider its collection of par-3 holes to be the best in the Tropics. Greens fees are $110, including cart. The 18-hole, par-70 **Buccaneer,** 2 miles east of Christiansted (© **340/773-2100**, ext. 738), is a challenging 5,810-yard course with panoramic vistas. Players can knock the ball over rolling hills right to the edge of the ocean. Greens fees are $70 and car rentals $16. The 3,100-yard, nine-hole, par-35 **Reef Golf Course** is located at Teague Bay on the east end of the island (© **340/773-8844**). Greens fees are $12 (yes, that's correct), plus $10 for those wishing to rent a cart

SCUBA DIVING   Divers love St. Croix's sponge life, beautiful black-coral trees, and steep drop-offs near the shoreline. This island is home to the largest living reef in the Caribbean. Its fabled north-shore wall begins in 25 to 30 feet of water and drops—sometimes almost straight down—to 13,200 feet. There are 22 moored diving sites. Favorites include **Salt River Canyon,** the coral gardens of **Scotch Banks,** and **Eagle Ray,** filled with cruising eagle rays. **Pavilions** is another good dive site, boasting a pristine coral reef. The best site of all, however, is **Buck Island,** an underwater wonderland with a visibility of more than 100 feet and an underwater nature trail. All minor and major agencies offer scuba and snorkeling tours to Buck Island. **Dive St. Croix,** 59 King's Wharf (© **340/773-2628**; fax 340/773-7400), operates the 38-foot diver boat *Reliance.*

GREAT LOCAL RESTAURANTS & BARS

A couple of **favorite local beers** are Carib and Blackbeard's (made on St. Thomas); the **favorite local rum** is Cruzan.

IN CHRISTIANSTED   **Harvey's,** 11B Company St. (© **340/773-3433**), features the thoroughly zesty cooking of island matriarch Sarah Harvey. Main dishes are the type of food Sarah was raised on: barbecue chicken, barbecue spareribs (barbecue is big here), broiled filet of snapper, and lobster when she can get it. Lunch is about $7.

   Paradise Cafe, Queen Cross St. at 53B Company St., across from Government House (© **340/773-2985**), serves burgers and New York deli-style sandwiches throughout the day—everything from a Reuben to a tuna melt. Lunch is about $8. **Fort Christian Brew Pub,** King's Alley Walk (© **340/713-9820**), has one of the best harbor views in Christiansted and serves beer, plus burgers, sandwiches, and Cajun cuisine. It's the only restaurant/microbrewery in the Virgin Islands. Lunch is around $9.

IN FREDERIKSTED   **Le St. Tropez,** Limetree Court, 67 King St. (© **340/772-3000**), is the most popular bistro in Frederiksted, offering crepes, quiches, soups, and salads for lunch in its sunlit courtyard. Lunch is about $15. **Pier 69,** 69 King St. (© **340/772-0069**), looks like a combination of a 1950s living room and a nautical bar. It's a hangout for Christiansted's counterculture and a top spot for sandwiches and salads. Lunch is about $10.

Index

FROMMER'S® COMPLETE TRAVEL GUIDES

Alaska
Alaska Cruises & Ports of Call
American Southwest
Amsterdam
Argentina & Chile
Arizona
Atlanta
Australia
Austria
Bahamas
Barcelona, Madrid & Seville
Beijing
Belgium, Holland & Luxembourg
Bermuda
Boston
Brazil
British Columbia & the Canadian
  Rockies
Brussels & Bruges
Budapest & the Best of Hungary
Calgary
California
Canada
Cancún, Cozumel & the Yucatán
Cape Cod, Nantucket & Martha's
  Vineyard
Caribbean
Caribbean Cruises & Ports of Call
Caribbean Ports of Call
Carolinas & Georgia
Chicago
China
Colorado
Costa Rica
Cuba
Denmark
Denver, Boulder & Colorado
  Springs
England
Europe
Europe by Rail
European Cruises & Ports of Call

Florence, Tuscany & Umbria
Florida
France
Germany
Great Britain
Greece
Greek Islands
Halifax
Hawaii
Hong Kong
Honolulu, Waikiki & Oahu
India
Ireland
Israel
Italy
Jamaica
Japan
Kauai
Las Vegas
London
Los Angeles
Maryland & Delaware
Maui
Mexico
Montana & Wyoming
Montréal & Québec City
Munich & the Bavarian Alps
Nashville & Memphis
Newfoundland & Labrador
New England
New Mexico
New Orleans
New York City
New York State
New Zealand
Northern Italy
Norway
Nova Scotia, New Brunswick &
  Prince Edward Island
Oregon
Ottawa
Paris

Peru
Philadelphia & the Amish
  Country
Portugal
Prague & the Best of the Czech
  Republic
Provence & the Riviera
Puerto Rico
Rome
San Antonio & Austin
San Diego
San Francisco
Santa Fe, Taos & Albuquerque
Scandinavia
Scotland
Seattle
Shanghai
Sicily
Singapore & Malaysia
South Africa
South America
South Florida
South Pacific
Southeast Asia
Spain
Sweden
Switzerland
Texas
Thailand
Tokyo
Toronto
USA
Utah
Vancouver & Victoria
Vermont, New Hampshire &
  Maine
Vienna & the Danube Valley
Virgin Islands
Virginia
Walt Disney World® & Orlando
Washington, D.C.
Washington State

FROMMER'S® DOLLAR-A-DAY GUIDES

Australia from $50 a Day
California from $70 a Day
England from $75 a Day
Europe from $70 a Day
Florida from $70 a Day
Hawaii from $80 a Day

Ireland from $80 a Day
Italy from $70 a Day
London from $90 a Day
New York from $90 a Day
Paris from $90 a Day
San Francisco from $70 a Day

Washington, D.C. from $80 a
  Day
Portable London from $90 a Day
Portable New York City from $90
  a Day
Portable Paris from $90 a Day

FROMMER'S® PORTABLE GUIDES

Acapulco, Ixtapa & Zihuatanejo
Amsterdam
Aruba
Australia's Great Barrier Reef
Bahamas
Berlin
Big Island of Hawaii
Boston
California Wine Country
Cancún
Cayman Islands
Charleston
Chicago
Disneyland®
Dominican Republic
Dublin

Florence
Frankfurt
Hong Kong
Las Vegas
Las Vegas for Non-Gamblers
London
Los Angeles
Los Cabos & Baja
Maine Coast
Maui
Miami
Nantucket & Martha's Vineyard
New Orleans
New York City
Paris

Phoenix & Scottsdale
Portland
Puerto Rico
Puerto Vallarta, Manzanillo &
  Guadalajara
Rio de Janeiro
San Diego
San Francisco
Savannah
Vancouver
Vancouver Island
Venice
Virgin Islands
Washington, D.C.
Whistler

FROMMER'S® NATIONAL PARK GUIDES

Algonquin Provincial Park	Grand Canyon	Yellowstone & Grand Teton
Banff & Jasper	National Parks of the American	Yosemite & Sequoia/Kings
Family Vacations in the National	West	Canyon
Parks	Rocky Mountain	Zion & Bryce Canyon

FROMMER'S® MEMORABLE WALKS

Chicago	New York	San Francisco
London	Paris	

FROMMER'S® WITH KIDS GUIDES

Chicago	Ottawa	Vancouver
Las Vegas	San Francisco	Walt Disney World® & Orlando
New York City	Toronto	Washington, D.C.

SUZY GERSHMAN'S BORN TO SHOP GUIDES

Born to Shop: France	Born to Shop: Italy	Born to Shop: New York
Born to Shop: Hong Kong,	Born to Shop: London	Born to Shop: Paris
Shanghai & Beijing		

FROMMER'S® IRREVERENT GUIDES

Amsterdam	Los Angeles	San Francisco
Boston	Manhattan	Seattle & Portland
Chicago	New Orleans	Vancouver
Las Vegas	Paris	Walt Disney World®
London	Rome	Washington, D.C.

FROMMER'S® BEST-LOVED DRIVING TOURS

Austria	Germany	Northern Italy
Britain	Ireland	Scotland
California	Italy	Spain
France	New England	Tuscany & Umbria

THE UNOFFICIAL GUIDES®

Beyond Disney	Hawaii	Paris
Central Italy	Las Vegas	San Francisco
Chicago	London	Skiing & Snowboarding in the
Cruises	Maui	West
Disneyland®	Mexico's Best Beach Resorts	Walt Disney World®
England	Mini Las Vegas	Walt Disney World® for
Florida	Mini-Mickey	Grown-ups
Florida with Kids	New Orleans	Walt Disney World® with Kids
Inside Disney	New York City	Washington, D.C.

SPECIAL-INTEREST TITLES

Athens Past & Present	Frommer's Road Atlas Europe
Cities Ranked & Rated	Frommer's Road Atlas France
Frommer's Best Day Trips from London	Frommer's Road Atlas Ireland
Frommer's Caribbean Hideaways	Frommer's Wonderful Weekends from
Frommer's China: The 50 Most Memorable Trips	New York City
Frommer's Exploring America by RV	The New York Times' Guide to Unforgettable
Frommer's Gay & Lesbian Europe	Weekends
Frommer's Best RV and Tent Campgrounds	Retirement Places Rated
in the U.S.A.	Rome Past & Present

Travel Tip: He who finds the best hotel deal has more to spend on facials involving knobbly vegetables.

Hello, the Roaming Gnome here. I've been nabbed from the garden and taken round the world. The people who took me are so terribly clever. They find the best offerings on Travelocity. For very little cha-ching. And that means I get to be pampered and exfoliated till I'm pink as a bunny's doodah.

travelocity

Travel Tip: Make sure there's customer service
for any change of plans — involving
friendly natives, for example.

One can plan and plan, but if you don't book with the
right people you can't seize le moment and canoodle
with the poodle named Pansy. I, for one, am all for
fraternizing with the locals. Better yet, if I need to
extend my stay and my gnome nappers are willing, it
can all be arranged through the 800 number at, oh look,
how convenient, the lovely company coat of arms.

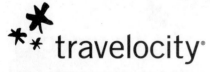

travelocity®

1-888-TRAVELOCITY / travelocity.com / America Online Keyword: Travel